Through the darkness of future past

The magician longs to see

*One chants out **BETWEEN TWO WORLDS**:*

'Fire Walk With Me'

BETWEEN TWO WORLDS:

Perspectives on TWIN PEAKS

by H. Perry Horton

TABLE OF CONTENTS

APPENDICES

BETWEEN TWO WORLDS

How TWIN PEAKS Changed Television By Being Like Nothing on Television

If you're reading a book about TWIN PEAKS, I'm going to wager you don't need an introduction to said book recounting the series' cultural or creative impact. You're obviously a part of that impact; why tell you what you already know? So instead I'm going to open this episode guide/essay collection with a brief look at the series' historical and industrial consequences, which in my opinion boil down to this:

TWIN PEAKS is the origin point of modern auteur television and thus directly responsible for the drastic shift in dramatic programming that over the last quarter-century has led to our current, so-called Golden Age of Television.

Let's take this step by step. First step: what do I mean by the Golden Age of Television? I'm just reporting the term, I didn't coin it, but I do happen to agree with it. Television shows, at least in terms of dramas, used to break down into pretty much one of four categories: cop shows, lawyer shows, doctor shows, and family shows. Think about every great drama of the 1980's and you'll see what I mean: HILL STREET BLUES, CAGNEY & LACEY, L.A. LAW, ST. ELSEWHERE, THIRTYSOMETHING, DALLAS, MIAMI VICE, MAGNUM P.I., DYNASTY, MATLOCK, 21 JUMP STREET, QUINCY and so on and so forth down the line.

Whereas we still have shows like that on the air today – CHICAGO P.D., CHICAGO MED, CHICAGO LAW – they aren't the ones racking up the highest critical acclaim and winning all the top awards. Those shows, by and large, are creator-driven content about non-traditional and even non-likeable main characters that air not on broadcast networks but on cable or pay cable. They're shows about mobsters with consciences, high school teachers with a meth-making problem, zombie hunters, good-hearted serial killers, drunk and debaucherous advertising executives et cetera, and even when they do fall into the Big Four categories, the cops are crooked, the lawyers are disillusioned, the medical professionals are popping pills, and the family is fractured and running a funeral home.

This shift didn't just happen on its own. Molds don't break until someone tries to stuff something into them that won't fit, until someone comes along with something that's bigger, broader, and at the same time more appealing than the existing parameters. Someone has to force this shift, and that someone, or rather some*ones*, were David Lynch and Mark Frost.

Everything about TWIN PEAKS as a broadcast television program was different, from the way it sought to tell its story, to the elements it infused into the traditional crime procedural, to the way it was approached technically. At this particular point in his career, fresh off his biggest cultural and critical hit yet, BLUE VELVET, Lynch was the most unique American director in decades, possibly ever. He was an auteur the way we hadn't seen since Orson Welles, and at the same time in a way that didn't resemble Welles at all. Lynch was uncompromising in his vision and uninterested in box office returns or fame, which meant he could be hired but he couldn't be bought, there was nothing you could give him that was greater than a chance to accurately realize his vision. If you hired David Lynch, you didn't hire him as some journeyman director there to pick up a paycheck, you hired him for his specific aesthetic; you were, for lack of a better way of stating it, paying for "Lynchian" as much as you were Lynch.

1

Mark Frost, on the other hand, was the alternate side of the coin. He had a history in television, most notably as a writer on HILL STREET BLUES, which was innovative in its own way – each episode took place in one day, for example – but was also still rooted in tradition. Where Frost leaned towards a more Lynchian realm was in the structure of his plotting: the man can weave multiple characters and their multiple storylines with a grace that is flat out enviable.

It was thought that by pairing the industry experience of Frost with the unfettered artistry of Lynch, a show might be created that could satisfy both the outsider ambitions of its creators as well as the financial goals of the network; in the end, this idea only half-succeeded because the latter inevitably interfered with the former. The story, the characters, the atmosphere, the approach – these were the elements that made the show marketable to viewers, because they all boiled down to one, single, distilled thing: intrigue. TWIN PEAKS knew how to hook you, how to reel you in, and how to keep your imagination in Pete's percolator until it was bubbling with ideas. When this intrigue started translating into ad revenue, the network began insisting on a fast and traditionally-satisfying solution to the Laura Palmer murder. The ensuing compromises and conflicts caused Lynch to all but abandon the series for a return to feature filmmaking, which left the evolving narrative of TWIN PEAKS in the hands of Frost and a host of other writers, most notably Harley Peyton and FIRE WALK WITH ME co-screenwriter Robert Engels. This team was of course more than capable of continuing the storyline, but the absence of Lynch did effect the auteur aspect of the series that he and Frost as a creative unit comprised. When the show failed to mimic its prior success under these new conditions, ABC jostled it around the line-up from week to week, pre-empted it seemingly more times than not, and ultimately buried the most significant series finale (or so we thought at the time) in television history on a late Saturday night at the beginning of summer after May Sweeps were a memory. By forcing the auteur-effect out of TWIN PEAKS, the network forced the show into a territory where it had never intended to dwell, and thus it went "off course" from a mainstream perspective, alienating all but the die-hard viewers, and eventually suffering a premature and frustrating death.

But TWIN PEAKS surprised everyone by surviving. It lived in the memories and imaginations of those die-hard fans who started magazines like WRAPPED IN PLASTIC, or websites like WelcomeToTwinPeaks.com, or countless blogs and video series and podcasts and columns that helped reinvigorate interest in the show and attract new viewers, enough so that a quarter-century after it was cancelled, a new season is both popularly and commercially viable. No one's trying to get L.A. LAW off the ground again, and no one's hankering for a ST. ELSEWHERE reunion. That's because TWIN PEAKS' fandom was small but steadfast, they … we are not fly by night, we're not fair-weather, and we didn't get here on a bandwagon. To like TWIN PEAKS is to love TWIN PEAKS is to dedicate a bit of your life, however big or small, to understanding it. This is the rarest and most powerful form of success because it breeds not just appreciation but devotion, and not one iota of this success is owed to the network that aired TWIN PEAKS, ABC, or to how they marketed or promoted the series. TWIN PEAKS wasn't anyone's success but the series' own.

And a generation of writers took note. Those on the verge of making it when TWIN PEAKS left the airwaves, the ones in school or just out toying with their own projects, hoping to break into the big time, these men and women weren't influenced by THIRTYSOMETHING anymore, DALLAS had no appeal because suddenly everything about these shows was so predictable. Lynch and company had drawn attention to the clichés of the medium by not adhering to them and by in fact subverting them to use against the medium. Once seen, these trite commonalities couldn't be unseen. In this way TWIN PEAKS created a new culture in television in which to go back to these old clichés would be just that: a step back. TWIN PEAKS pushed the starting point to a different level, and there was nowhere to go but up.

Even the network that wasted TWIN PEAKS immediately changed their game. Within a year of the series' cancellation, ABC aired WILD PALMS, a miniseries from another film figure, writer/director Oliver Stone, that was a blatant rip off of the style and ambiance of TWIN PEAKS, and the Alphabet's next big cop show, NYPD BLUE, was a rule-breaker in terms of language, violence, and sexual situations, something absolutely proven to be within the range of public interest thanks to TWIN PEAKS. But there was only so far broadcast networks could go, and nobody in the business recognized this more than HBO.

HBO is where the golden ball really started rolling. David Chase – who will be first to tell you TWIN PEAKS paved the way for his own series – perfected auteur television with THE SOPRANOS in that he made his program intriguing, marketable, palatable to executives, and able to spread out to other writers and directors without compromising his singular vision. From the launchpad of THE SOPRANOS' massive success, the channel once only known for first-run movies became the most powerful force in dramatic programming for a solid dozen or so years on the backs of series like SIX FEET UNDER, THE WIRE, DEADWOOD, OZ, BIG LOVE, CARNIVALE, ROME, TRUE BLOOD, TREME, THE NEWSROOM, BOARDWALK EMPIRE, GAME OF THRONES, and TRUE DETECTIVE. Not only are all of these on the list of the best televised dramas produced in the last 25 years, they're also all largely driven by singular voices like Alan Ball, David Milch, David Simon, Aaron Sorkin, Terrence Winter, and Nic Pizzolatto.

Other non-broadcast networks took note: Showtime gave us DEAD LIKE ME, HUFF, THE L WORD, QUEER AS FOLK, BROTHERHOOD, SLEEPER CELL, NURSE JACKIE, DEXTER and other series that at the time (the early 2000s in most cases) wouldn't have been allowed on broadcast networks, let alone greenlit by them. Cinemax got in the game, then later the idea trickled down from pay cable to basic cable networks like USA, TNT, FX, and AMC, and eventually back down to the broadcast level with shows like LOST, DOLLHOUSE, and HEROES that struggled against censors to try and compete in a new, no-holds-barred, anything-goes narrative environment.

Now we find ourselves here, in an age where one person can write and direct an entire series on their own, something that only a generation ago would have seemed next to impossible from both a creative and commercial standpoint. TV seasons todays are shorter, more distilled, and the traditional fall-launch has been done away with for year-round programming, which allows writers to infuse their narratives with seasonal ambiance. These changes and more have opened the market to so many individual and distinct voices that television the medium has branched beyond television the appliance into streaming services like Netflix, Hulu, Amazon Prime, and Playstation, where the limits are even less defined and the possibilities even more bountiful. And the tipping point to all this, the moment in time on which the medium pivoted and turned the direction that led to now, when it is widely considered to be the best it has ever been, is undeniably TWIN PEAKS. I'm not saying we wouldn't have gotten to this point without the series, but I am saying we wouldn't be right here, right now, the way we are, if TWIN PEAKS hadn't come along when and how it did.

The nice thing about the impending third season of TWIN PEAKS is that even if it's a disaster – which we all know it won't be – it can't damage or take away from what the original two seasons were, nor what they accomplished or contributed to the medium overall. Enough time has passed that this new cycle is its own entity the way that the new STAR WARS trilogy is connected to but separate from the episodes that came before it. And should we expect TWIN PEAKS season three to have the same sort of impact as the earlier seasons? Absolutely not, even if it does that's the worst way to approach the new episodes. All we should expect, based on the pedigree of those involved, is an innovative and unique trip back to a world that so captivated audiences in the past that news of a resurgence is met with a fan fervor that surpasses that original buzz.

That's why I'm here, because the promise of new TWIN PEAKS so inflamed my imagination and curiosity that it caused me to dive headfirst into an old obsession and re-view it with aged eyes and ideas. This collection is the result of that new exploration, as well as a new appreciation for what I have always considered to be the most significant television program ever made. I won't claim to be a scholar or (god forbid) a critic, I'm just a guy who's watched the series in it's entirely at least half a dozen times, who's read pretty much everything I could find on it, and who has a handful of ideas about the things I've seen. I'm also a guy who likes to write. Put all this together and here we are, at the crux between two worlds – the world of TWIN PEAKS and our own – looking to see how and where they intersect.

Cast List

Kyle MacLachlan ...... *Special Agent Dale Cooper*

Michael Ontkean ..... *Sheriff Harry S. Truman*

Madchen Amick ..... *Shelly Johnson*

Dana Ashbrook ..... *Bobby Brooks*

Richard Beymer ..... *Benjamin Horne*

Lara Flynn Boyle ..... *Donna Hayward*

Sherilyn Fenn ..... *Audrey Horne*

Warren Frost ..... *Dr. Will Hayward*

Peggy Lipton ...... *Norma Jennings*

James Marshall ..... *James Hurley*

Everett McGill ..... *Big Ed Hurley*

Jack Nance ..... *Pete Martell*

Joan Chen ..... *Josie Packard*

Kimmy Robertson ..... *Lucy Moran*

Michael Horse ..... *Deputy Tommy "Hawk" Hill*

Piper Laurie ..... *Catherine Martell*

Harry Goaz ..... *Deputy Andy Brennan*

Eric DaRae ..... *Leo Johnson*

Wendy Robie ..... *Nadine Hurley*

Ray Wise ..... *Leland Palmer*

Sheryl Lee ..... *Laura Palmer/Maddy Ferguson*

Russ Tamblyn ..... *Dr. Lawrence Jacoby*

Don S. Davis ..... *Major Garland Briggs*

Chris Mulkey ..... *Hank Jennings*

Gary Hershberger ..... *Mike Nelson*

Grace Zabriskie ..... *Sarah Palmer*

Catherine E. Coulson ..... *Margaret Lanterman The Log Loday*

Ian Buchanan ..... *Dick Tremayne*

Mary Jo Deschanel ..... *Eileen Hayward*

Frank Silva ..... *BOB*

Kenneth Welsh ..... *Windom Earle*

Al Strobel ..... *Phillip Michael Gerard/MIKE*

David Patrick Kelly ..... Jerry *Horne*

Miguel Ferrer ..... *FBI Agent Albert Rosenfield*

John Boylan ..... *Mayor Dwayne Milford*

Victoria Catlin ..... *Blackie O'Reilly*

Charlotte Stewart ..... *Betty Briggs*

Jill Engels ..... *Trudy*

David Lynch ..... *FBI Reigonal Bureau Chief Gordon Cole*

Heather Graham ..... *Annie Blackburn*

Robyn Lively ..... *Lana Budding Milford*

Dan O'Herlihy ..... *Andrew Packard*

Billy Zane ..... *John Justice Wheeler*

James Booth ..... *Ernie Niles*

Don Amendolia ..... *Emory Battis*

Annette McCarthy ..... *Evelyn Marsh*

Michael Parks ..... *Jean Renault*

Ron Blair ..... *Randy St. Croix*

Carel Struycken ..... *Giant*

Mak Takano ..... *Asian Man*

Lance Davis ..... *Chet in INVITATION TO LOVE*

Phoebe Augustine ..... *Ronette Pulaski*

Michael J. Anderson ..... *Man From Another Place*

Lenny von Dohlen ..... *Harold Smith*

Brenda Strong ..... *Jones*

Robert Bauer ..... *Johnny Horne*

6

Hank Worden ….. *Room Service Waiter*

Jan D'Arcy ….. *Sylvia Horne*

Rick Giolito ….. *Montana in INVITATION TO LOVE*

David Duchovny ….. *DEA Agent Dennis/Denise Bryson*

Walter Olkewicz ….. *Jacques Renault*

David Lander ….. *Tim Pinkle*

Jane Greer ….. *Vivian Smythe Niles*

David Warner ….. *Thomas Eckhardt*

Tony Jay ….. *Dougie Milford*

Nicholas Love ….. *Malcolm Sloan*

Galyn Gorg ….. *Nancy*

Brian Straub ….. *Einar Thorson*

Erika Anderson ….. *Emerald/Jade in INVITATION TO LOVE*

Brett Vadset ….. *Joey Paulson*

Peter Michael Goetz ….. *Jared in INVITATION TO LOVE*

Royal Dano ….. *Judge Clinton Sternwood*

Clarence Williams III ….. *FBI Agent Roger Hardy*

Jed Mills ….. *Wilson Mooney*

Gavan O'Herlihy ….. *RCMP Officer Preston King*

Ritch Brinkley ….. *D.A. Daryl Lodwick*

Royce D. Applegate ….. *Rev. Clarence Brocklehurst*

Ron Kirk ….. *Cappy*

Claire Stansfield ….. *Sid*

Ron Taylor ….. *Coach Wingate*

Mary Stevin ….. *Heba*

John Apicella ….. *Jeffrey Marsh*

Ted Raimi ….. *Heavy Metal Youth*

Craig MacLachlan ….. *The Dead Man*

Jessica Wallenfels ….. *Harriet Hayward*

Joshua Harris ….. *Little Nicky*

Julee Cruise ….. *Road House Singer*

Andrea Hays ..... *Heidi*

Clay Wilcox ..... *Bernard Renault*

Brenda E. Mathers ..... *Caroline Earle*

Frances Bay ..... *Mrs. Tremond*

Austin Jack Lynch ..... *Grandson*

Emily Fincher ..... *Louise Dombrowski*

Molly Shannon ..... *Judy Swain*

Alicia Witt ..... *Gersten Hayward*

Mark Frost ..... *TV Newscaster*

Lesli Linka Glatter ..... *One Eyed Jacks' Servant*

SEASON ONE

"To introduce this story, let me just say it encompasses the All,
it is beyond the 'Fire,' though few would know that meaning.
It is a story of many but begins with one, and I knew her.
The one leading to the many is Laura Palmer. Laura is the one."

Margaret Lanterman, The Log Lady

"NORTHWEST PASSAGE"

Written by Mark Frost & David Lynch, Directed by David Lynch

Original Airdate April 8th, 1990

When the murdered body of 17 year-old homecoming queen Laura Palmer is found washed ashore a rocky beach on the morning of February 24th, 1989, naked and wrapped in plastic, it send ripples all throughout the citizenry of Twin Peaks, a small logging town in Washington State just shy of the Canadian border to the north and the Idaho border to the east. It's not only Laura's parents Leland and Sarah who bear the weight of this tragedy, but also folks like Pete Martell, who found Laura while going out to fish, his sister Catherine and sister-in-law Josie who run the town's saw mill; Sheriff Harry S. Truman and Deputies Andy Brennan and Tommy "Hawk" Hill who are the investigating officers; Bobby Briggs, Laura's boyfriend, and Shelly Johnson, the diner waitress he's cheating with who's married to Leo, an abusive trucker; Donna Hayward, Laura's best friend, and her lughead boyfriend and Bobby-BFF Mike Nelson; James Hurley, Laura's secret lover and his uncle Big Ed, who's carrying on an affair with diner owner Norma Jennings; Ben Horne, owner of The Great Northern Hotel, all-around magnate and client of Leland, as well as father to Audrey and Johnny, Laura's classmate and tutee, respectively; and more, so many, many more.

Of particular note in these opening scenes when the word of Laura's death is spreading around town is the way her parents, Leland and Sarah, are informed. That morning, Sarah is already aware Laura is missing, and calls Leland out of a meeting with Ben and potential investors for the Ghostwood Estates development to share her concerns. It is at this moment that Sheriff Truman arrives with a dour expression, and Leland knows without being told – Truman simply says "I'm sorry" – that his worst fears have come true: his daughter is dead. He reacts by dropping the phone, which tells Sarah on the other end all she needs to know. Her screams of grief are as unnerving as they are heartbreaking, and the way Lynch lingers on them is downright uncomfortable. In the indispensable REFLECTIONS: AN ORAL HISTORY OF TWIN PEAKS by Brad Dukes, actress Grace Zabriskie, who played Sarah, reveals she thought Lynch was leading her in an over-the-top direction with the reaction, especially as she had never worked with him before. But the end result convinced her he was a trustworthy leader, allowing her to give of herself more fully.

Back to the narrative: Bobby, being Laura's boyfriend and the last known person to see her, has his cocky ass dragged in by Truman and his deputies and deposited in a holding cell while they go to the Palmer house and make a cursory search of the place. In Laura's bedroom, Hawk discovers the girl's diary and a videotape that might be of interest. Downstairs the case intensifies when Andy informs Truman that another local high school girl, Ronette Pulaski, is also missing. At that very moment Ronette is wandering across the Idaho border disoriented, dressed only in a dirty, blood-stained slip, and with ropes dangling from her wrists. She's discovered by a railworker. This crossing of state lines requires Truman to call in the FBI, who sends Special Agent Dale Cooper, a man of simple pleasures and particular investigative insight who arrives in town knowing exactly what he's looking for. He asks to see Ronette first, and though she's in a coma from the shock and can't help them verbally, Cooper is more interested in her fingernails, which he examines, finds nothing, then asks to see the body of Laura Palmer. There he finds what he was trepidatiously seeking: a typed letter 'R' inserted under the fingernail of her left ring finger – the wedding finger, if you will – which connects her to the murder of another girl, Teresa Banks, one year earlier in nearby Deer Meadow, Washington. That victim was discovered with a 'T' under her fingernail. This connection makes these murders the work of a serial killer.

Later than afternoon Andy discovers the crime scene, an abandoned train car deep in the woods. Meanwhile, at the station Coop and Truman examine Laura's diary – finding among other things her final entry which reads in part "Nervous about meeting J," and a small key in a baggie that has traces of cocaine – then sit down with Bobby and afterwards Donna, but neither can offer any insight as to who might have killed Laura or who she might have been with late last night. Cooper introduces the videotape found in Laura's room of her and Donna dancing at a mountainside picnic shot by a mysterious third to try and jog their memories, but neither teenager reveals anything, though they both know the video was shot by James Hurley. Bobby keeps this information to himself for purposes of revenge – seems it's okay if he steps out on his girlfriend as long as she doesn't step out on him in return – while Donna does it to protect James, who she secretly loves. Cooper doesn't really need their help, however, and proves himself more than merely adept at detection when he points out to Truman afterwards that whoever shot the picnic video is a biker, because there's a motorcycle reflected in the close-up of Laura's eye. Truman knows that means James, who is instantly catapulted to the top of the suspect list.

In between these interviews, at The Great Northern Audrey has started to display her willfully disobedient side by intentionally revealing to her father's foreign investors the circumstances of Laura's death, namely murder, which Ben was explicitly trying to keep from them. As he feared, the news gives the investors cold feet and they high-tail it out of town. Gorgeous and manipulative: that Audrey Horne is a potent cocktail. And while we're here, though I don't usually disparage anything TP-related, the music that plays in this scene is horribly out of place, like the kind of march a calliope might play to accompany the parading of elephants. It's also worth noting that unlike most of the other musical themes in the pilot, this piece will never be heard again.

Later that afternoon, the crime scene is explored. Cooper and Truman discover in the train car two potentially valuable pieces of evidence – half a heart necklace on a mound of dirt, and a scrap of paper at the base of this mound that reads "Fire Walk With Me" in blood. Cooper makes the assumption that if they find the other half of the necklace, they'll find the killer. After this, they take the key found in the cocaine baggie taped into Laura's diary and use it to open her safe deposit box, in which they find 10k in cold hard cash and a copy of Flesh World magazine, a trashy skin rag in which there's a picture of Ronette Pulaski (and also, unbeknownst to them just now, Leo Johnson's truck). The plot just thickened like hour-old oatmeal.

That night while trying to unearth James, Cooper and Truman stake out The Road House, Twin Peaks' local watering hole/art house music venue. Norma and Ed are inside, discussing how their separate marriages are shams – Norma's married to some Hank character who's presently in priosn for manslaughter – and it's time for them to enter the "Tammy Wynette" phase of things, namely "D-I-V-O-R-C-E." Donna shows up, having snuck out of her house for a pre-arranged meet with James, but runs into Bobby and Mike, both of whom are drunk, and Mike's anger at her unavailability to him that day leads to a bar-wide brawl during which Donna escapes with another biker, Joey, who's been sent to deliver her to James. Cooper and Truman see them fleeing and try to follow, but along the dark and winding backroads by the mill they lose sight of their prey.

When James and Donna reunite, he tells her he's been hiding out all day because he's worried, he has no alibi for last night: he was with Laura, but she was manic and addled and scared, she jumped off his bike and ran off into the forest while he was stopped at a red light. Donna reveals the problem is even bigger than that, she overheard her dad – the town doctor – telling her mom about Laura's half-heart necklace found at the crime scene. She knows James is the one who gave Laura the necklace and has the other half, so they bury it out in the woods to save James further culpability, which is fortunate, because only minutes later he's apprehended by Cooper and Truman, taken into custody, and given a nice holding cell across the way from Bobby and Mike, who are verrrry happy to see the guy making time with both their ladies.

The pilot's final sequence happens back in the woods where James and Donna buried his half of Laura's necklace. A flashlight beam finds the spot then a gloved hand reaches into the soil and plucks the necklace free. Across town at the same exact moment, Sarah Palmer wakes screaming from a troubled sleep of prophetic visions. If you look in the upper right hand corner, you can see one of those visions reflected in the mirror above her: that's our first glimpse of BOB, ladies and gentlemen. Dum. Dum. Dummmmmmmmm.

Fun Fact: BOB in the mirror is a totally unplanned, happy accident. The character wasn't even created until shooting on the pilot was underway, and the man who portrayed him, Frank Silva, was hired as a set dresser on the project, not an actor. After Silva inadvertently trapped himself behind a dresser in Laura's room while a scene was being filmed, Lynch liked his look and decided to craft the character for him and re-shoot the scene intentionally (it shows up as another Sarah vision in Episode 1, "Traces to Nowhere," also directed by Lynch). Later that same day, after shooting the final scene with Zabriskie, a crew member pointed out the shot was ruined because another crew member had inadvertently been reflected in the mirror behind her. When Lynch saw the footage and who it was, he loved it, tied it into the narrative, and the rest is terrifying history.

While all of the above addresses the story of TWIN PEAKS, the emotional atmosphere of the show – which is really its selling point – comes from the actors and the unique ways they have of expressing their characters and interacting with each other. Idiosyncrasies and eccentricities abound, from Cooper's cassette recorder, which allows for lines like "Diane, I'm holding in my hand a small box of chocolate bunnies," to the lady walking around town carrying a log, or as Truman explains, "We call her the Log Lady." There's also a tremendous amount of visual elements reflecting this atmosphere, from the eerie natural environment and settings to more forced and deliberately off-putting gags like the kid breakdancing away from his locker at Twin Peaks High School. The narrative combines the best of both its creators – Mark Frost, who gained renown as a procedural ace for his work on HILL STREET BLUES, and David Lynch, the weird mastermind behind BLUE VELVET, THE ELEPHANT MAN, DUNE, and ERASERHEAD – while the visual aesthetic of the show – it's other calling card – is all Lynch.

In addition to his moody cinematography, dimly-lit interiors, pitch-black exteriors, and Douglas-Sirk-meets-Dali production design, there are a few technical highlights of the pilot that help establish the world of TWIN PEAKS and bear mentioning. I've already noted how Lynch allowed his camera to linger for an uncomfortable amount of time on Sarah's reaction to the news of her daughter's death, but she wasn't the only character to whom this was limited. In fact, as various characters learn of Laura's death the camera stays with them longer than we think it should, which draws we the audience into their pain, which in turn informs us of the kind of person Laura was, though at this point we know little about her: she was the kind of person for whom an entire community mourns, she was beloved, emblematic, even, of the pristine purity and until-now-unwavering innocence of their idyllic locale. Lynch even applies this lingering to all three shots of Laura in the pilot – as a corpse, in her homecoming photo, and frozen in the picnic video.

Then there's the scene with Ronette Pulaski crossing the bridge. Her slip is soiled and fluttering in the light morning breeze. The ropes with their frayed, dangling ends are drawn so tight about both her wrists that you can intuit the numbness in her fingers. Her lip is busted and her eyes aren't focused on anything in this world, she looks like a lost zombie, a dead thing sleepwalking through existence. Until this moment, we knew only that Laura had been murdered. But seeing Ronette, and learning that she was somehow involved, Lynch shows us secondhand the savagery Laura's murder must have entailed, the premeditation of it, and the twisted sanity of her killer. This isn't going to be a regular murder case Lynch is showing us, it's going to be something far more insidious. By removing us from the murder scene itself for the initial revelation of its brutality, we once again are drawn into the pain of our own imaginations: if this is how bad it was for the girl who survived, what must it have been like for the girl who did not?

And the shot Lynch closes with, that of the stoplight at dusk shifting from green to a cautious yellow then into the full-on halt of red. Its lights are eyes on the night, all-seeing, all-knowing, and seemingly warning us about continuing through this place. But red lights turn green eventually, and as such Lynch knows he's done enough to cause us to throw that caution to the wind and come with him into the darkest of TV territories.

Pilot episodes have a lot of responsibility not just in terms of establishing their world and the people who inhabit it, but also in regards to the narrative thread and the hooks sewn into it meant to snare an audience. TWIN PEAKS does an exceptionally good job of establishing its characters – which is especially difficult because there are so many of them, and all fleshed out with intricate and interweaving backstories – as well as their secrets and indeed their motivations, taken or not taken, for killing Laura, or at least wanting her dead. That's the best part about this episode, I think: not only does it do what it's supposed to narratively, its characterization is so well done and well-paced that by the end of the episode, anyone could be a suspect, which means everyone is a suspect. That's the world ultimately established by the pilot: one like ours but not ours, a perversion of it, of our ideals and social fabric, and a world in which enough people are lying that nothing can seem true. The only thing we know for certain at the end of the pilot is that for all we've just learned, ultimately we know nothing, and that's an intriguing damn spot to start.

EPISODE 1: "TRACES TO NOWHERE"

Written by Mark Frost & David Lynch, Directed by Duwayne Dunham

Airdate April 12th, 1990

The series pick-up for TWIN PEAKS by ABC stipulated that they would get seven episodes, not including the two-hour pilot, to constitute their first season. After the resounding success of the pilot, both critically and commercially, fans and the network alike were eager to see where the narrative would go. So four nights after the pilot premiered – not even a full week – ABC added TWIN PEAKS to the regular schedule and the series was off and running.

This first official episode opens in The Great Northern, where Special Agent Dale Cooper has taken residence and is conversing with his assistant, Diane, via his microcassette recorder about the details thus far known in the Laura Palmer case. He ends this conversation with a musing sidebar on Marilyn Monroe's connection to the Kennedys. That the lead investigator of Laura's death ruminates in these terms opens the show to an air of conspiracy and outside thinking that will become customary for the series. Furthermore, that Coop gets to Ms. Monroe from Laura is no massive leap: both are tragic blondes and in fact the character of Laura Palmer was based in part on Marilyn.

Cooper has breakfast – including one damn fine cup of coffee – and his first meeting with Audrey, at her initiation. He can't tell her much about the investigation but that's not the point of this scene, their chemistry is. It's powerful like potential energy, sultry and somehow simultaneously innocent, some connection more than a schoolgirl crush or an older man's wandering fancy. There is something real between them, as characters or actors one, and it shows from this first meeting.

Later that morning Doc Hayward reveals the results of Laura's autopsy to Cooper and Sheriff Truman, and it paints a tawdry, tortuous picture. Her official cause of death is blood loss from several shallow wounds. Bite marks were found on her tongue and shoulder, and there are lesions on her wrists and upper arms from where she was bound. A toxicology screen is pending, but it was determined that Laura had three different sexual partners in the last 24 hours of her life. The girl is suddenly as mysterious and full of secrets as are the circumstances surrounding her death. And Ronette Pulaski is still in a coma, so still no help, but her wounds match Laura's, so wherever they were that night, the two girls were together.

Shelley's truckin' husband Leo is home from the road and gives her some clothes to wash like the sexist, misogynistic asshole he is. Among them, Shelley finds a shirt with waaaaay too much blood in it. Leo being Leo, she decides to hide it instead of washing it.

Finally James is taken from his cell to be interrogated by Cooper and Truman. He admits to shooting the video of Laura and Donna at the mountainside picnic, as well as to being Laura's secret boyfriend. He also concedes that he knew about her drug use, and worries it has something to do with her death. Lately, he says, she'd been afraid of someone, but he didn't know who. He tells them about the last time he saw her, around midnight the night she died. He was taking her home after they had rendezvoused. He describes her as emotional and erratic, says she got off the back of his motorcycle when they were stopped at a red light and ran into the woods. Cooper shows James the half-a-heart necklace found at the crime scene and asks if he knows who has the other half. Knowing it will only incriminate him further, James lies and says he does not know. He, of course, gave her the necklace and buried his half at the end of the pilot when Donna told him the authorities were looking for it. In reality, though, it isn't in the woods at all, but was stolen and now is in the possession of an unknown other. Whether or not Cooper believes him on this point, he does believe James isn't Laura's killer, so releases him.

Meanwhile, Leo is looking for his bloody shirt in the cab of his truck and can't find it. He worries he might have accidentally given it to Shelley to wash. But when he checks the laundry, the shirt isn't there. Leo is not happy about this.

Maybe his ears are burning because at that moment Bobby and Mike Nelson – still in jail for the bar fight they incited the night before at The Road House – are discussing Leo and some deal with him that involves a boatload of cash for teenagers: 20k. Half they've already given him, that's where Bobby was the night Laura died, but the other half is still owed, and it's in Laura's safety deposit box. Ruh-roh.

Donna – Laura's best friend – is having conflicting feelings and shares them with her mother, Eileen. On the one hand, she's super sad her bestie was murdered, but on the other, she's totes in love with James and now he's in love with her, too. She's afraid this makes her a bitch. Eileen lies and tells her it doesn't, because that's what moms are for. Speaking of moms, Eileen is a pretty famous one in real life. Her name is Mary Jo Deschanel, and in addition to being married to Caleb Deschanel, who will direct three TWIN PEAKS' episodes, she's also the mom of NEW GIRL's Zooey Deschanel and BONES' Emily Deschanel. If you haven't seen TWIN PEAKS since those shows catapulted the sisters Deschanel to stardom, the family resemblance might startle you a little, in a super cute way.

Big Ed the gas station owner is having an off-the-record conversation with his buddy Truman about the bar fight last night, in which he was a participant on the side of good. He's got a bump on his noggin, but says it didn't come from a punch, rather from his head hitting the floor when he passed out: he thinks his drink was spiked. One of the reasons he thinks this is because of the guy tending bar, a one Jacques Renault. The frown on Truman's face tells us all we need to know about the sort of fellow this Renault is: the unsavory sort.

At the craft store in town, Norma, Ed's mistress, runs into Nadine, Ed's one-eyed wife. Nadine is recently obsessed with creating completely silent drape runners and has come for supplies. You can't reason with Nadine, only deflect her politely, so that's what Norma does.

When at last they're brought up from the holding cells, Bobby and Mike Nelson think they're going to be questioned but instead they are released with a stern warning from Cooper that should any harm befall James Hurley, they'll be the first people he comes for.

Next on Coop and Truman's list of people to question is Josie Packard, the lovely widow of mill owner Andrew Packard, which makes her the mill owner now. She and Catherine (Andrew's sister) and Pete (Catherine's husband) all live under the same spacious roof. Josie is from Hong Kong, and Laura was tutoring her in English. The girl had come by the night she died, but only for an hour or so and was gone by evening. When Josie is called away to take a phone call, Coop correctly infers from body language that she and Truman are bumping uglies. Then Pete steals the scene by rushing in hoping to prevent the men from drinking the coffee he served them. Seems there was a fish in the percolator. Unfortunately, Pete was a sip too late with this news.

As all this is going on, Catherine is at an out of the way motel with Ben Horne, who is not only her secret lover, he's also her co-conspirator in a plan to steal the mill land from her sister-in-law Josie. By this point of the episode, you're starting to figure out the town of Twin Peaks didn't need a murder to get mysterious.

Donna pays a visit to Sarah and Leland, Laura's parents, for the first time since Laura's death. While Leland seems to be holding it together best as can be expected under the circumstances, Sarah is an emotional and psychological wreck. She weeps and hallucinates Laura's face over Donna's own (shades of Robert Blake in LOST HIGHWAY here), clings to the girl like a drowning person, and then she has a full-on vision of a wiry man with long gray hair and beady eyes, clad in a denim jacket. He is hiding behind the couch, peering out at her. This is BOB, though he is not

16

yet named, and this is his first official appearance, not counting blurred in the mirror at the end of the pilot. From the looks of him, and from the way he instantly shreds whatever's left of Sarah's sanity and reduces her to a shrieking mess, you can tell he's important.

Deputy Hawk is at the hospital interviewing the parents of Ronette Pulaski. He learns from them that Ronette had a job after school working the perfume counter at Horne's Department Store. That's Horne as in Ben Horne. Hawk gets distracted when he sees a one-armed man exit the elevator and walk down the corridor. Hawk follows him at a distance, but loses him somewhere near the morgue.

Audrey is dancing with herself in her father's office when he returns from his tryst with Catherine, and he isn't happy to find her there. He knows she used Laura's murder to scare off the Norwegians he was hoping would invest in his Ghostwood Estates development. This is his stake in the collusion with Catherine: she gets Josie's mill, he gets Josie's land, and Audrey's attention-seeking tattle-telling has set him back significantly. Seems Ben Horne is a far better businessman than he is a father, or indeed even a person. Across town another strained parent-child relationship is explored at the Briggs', where rebellious Bobby tries to light a cigarette at the dinner table only to have it slapped out his mouth and into his mother's slice of meatloaf by his father, a strict, by-the-book Major in the United States Air Force.

Truman takes Coop to the Double R for some coffee and pie and to meet Shelley and Norma, the latter of whom sponsors the Meals On Wheels program which Laura created. Coop loves the cherry pie and needs a list of the clients on Laura's route. While Norma gets that, Margaret the Log Lady comes over and tells Cooper that, "One day my log will have something to say" about the death of Laura Palmer, because it saw something that night. Coop is invited to ask the log exactly what it saw, but it's a log, and it's his first time talking to Margaret, so he hesitates long enough to offend her and off she goes, log in tow.

When Shelley gets home from work, Leo is waiting for her. He thinks she lost his bloody shirt, and now he has to teach her a lesson about respecting his things by beating her with a bar of soap in a sock. So then not only is Leo a misogynistic asshole, he's also a sadistic piece of shit.

Elsewhere, Donna has invited James to have dinner with her parents. To be clear, Laura hasn't been dead 48 hours at this point, and Donna's already pilfered her man, not to mention he's already allowed himself pilfered. Inside it's all fruit punch and pleasantries, but outside Bobby and Mike Nelson cruise by, see James' motorcycle there, and know it's official, this dude took *both* their girls. Cooper's warning be damned, they'll have their revenge.

The episode draws to a close in the tropical-themed office of Dr. Jacoby, Laura's secret psychiatrist. He's listening to an audio tape she made for him in which she's crying about how dumb and sweet James is. She says she just knows she's "going to get lost in those woods tonight," then adds, "remember how I told you about that mystery man? Well…" and that's when Jacoby plugs in his headphones and we lose the audio. As he continues to listen, he opens a coconut and inside is the other half of Laura's heart necklace, James' half, the half buried by him and Donna at the end of the pilot. Which makes Jacoby's the gloved hand that dug it up. Is he another suspect?

On a technical note, this episode was directed by Duwayne Dunham, the first of three he would helm over the course of the series. Dunham started his career as an editor, working on RETURN OF THE JEDI as well as two films for David Lynch, BLUE VELVET and WILD AT HEART. In the 2000's he would shift into a director of TV movies, but his first experience working for the small screen was with TWIN PEAKS. Dunham does a good job of maintaining the aesthetic Lynch devised in the pilot, but there are obviously some differences in terms of tone and atmosphere. Most notably, this looks like what it is, a television show. Nothing too daring is done, stylistically, a reversal of the pilot which stands on its own as a movie, and a David Lynch movie at that. But this was to be the new norm, and it was encouraged by the producers. They wanted the basic atmosphere intact, but at the same time they also wanted the individual directors they hired to put their own stamp on things, which is why some episodes are Peakier than others; some directors came at it from an artistic standpoint, some from a narrative. Truth be told, this tug of war between stylistic consistency and inconsistency only adds to the other worldliness of the show, how it feels simultaneously separate from and a part of our reality, thus heightening its intrigue and allure.

Overall, then, this first episode was the first time TWIN PEAKS was working with room to grow. The show being picked up meant Frost, Lynch, and the other writers had the time and space to unfurl and broaden their tale. As a result, this episode has a slower pace than the pilot, but it needs to. Now that the basic set-up is out there, the story needs to simmer if it's going to cook all the way through. This is a dense narrative, and this episode sets in motion a lot of subplots that were hinted at or absent from the pilot, but Lynch and Frost did an excellent job sewing everything together with the thread of Laura; even the stuff separate from the murder has ties to the girl. This is how you start a show, with dozens of questions begging for answers.

EPISODE 2 – "ZEN, OR THE SKILLS TO CATCH A KILLER"

Written by Mark Frost & David Lynch, Directed by David Lynch

Airdate April 19th, 1990

Lynch returns to both write and direct the series' second episode, but fans shouldn't get too used to the idea. This will be the last time he directs in season 1, and the last time he's credited on a script for the entire series. He next returns behind the camera for the first episode of season2, which is also the only other time he's credited as a writer, but in that instance he only contributed to the story, while it was Frost who wrote the actual script. All that said, it's this episode where TWIN PEAKS really becomes TWIN PEAKS, setting the tone and trail the rest of the series would follow.

We start episode 2 at the dysfunctional Horne family dinner as it's interrupted by the arrival of Ben's globetrotting younger brother Jerry who's home from France and bearing brie-and-butter baguettes that are so delectable Ben excuses himself mid-meal with a sarcastic "Always a pleasure" to the fam. As the Brothers Horne gorge themselves, Ben brings Jerry (yes, yes, like the ice cream) up to speed on the murder of Laura Palmer and the retreat of the Norwegians before he could convince them to invest in the Ghostwood Estates development project. This completely bums Jerry out until Ben promises to cheer him up with a trip across the Canadian border to One Eyed Jacks, where there's a new girl "freshly scented from the perfume counter." This, besides being super-gross, is an allusion to the perfume counter at Horne's department store, which we learned about last episode because it's where Ronette Pulaski had an afterschool job. This would seem to insinuate that this One Eyed Jacks place has a connection to Ben.

Meanwhile across town at the Hayward house, Donna and James are finishing up that first dinner with the 'rents. At long last the old folks head up to bed, leaving the two new lovebirds all alone on the couch.

It might be love brewing at the Haywards', but when Ben and Jerry arrive at One Eyed Jacks, it's a similar but distinctly different emotion on their minds. The place is very obviously a brothel. They meet with Blackie, who manages the place and dresses like she's a backup dancer for Prince circa-PURPLE RAIN. She presents them with the new girl, a pretty young thing on her very first night of work. Ben wins *prima nocta* privileges over his brother and adjourns with the girl to the boudoir, further cementing his general scuzziness.

Upon returning to his room at The Great Northern at the end of the day, Special Agent Dale Cooper gets a call from Deputy Hawk updating him on the interview with Ronette's parents. Hawk also mentions the one-armed man he saw, and this in particular piques Coop's interest. The call is followed by a knock on his door. When he opens it there's no one to be seen, but a perfume-scented note has been left for him. All it says, in sensual script, is "Jack with One Eye." A hint of music suggests the sender is Audrey. And I get that she's trying to be cryptic, but, I mean, seems to me if you're going to go that far, you just go all the way, but what do I know?

Bobby and Mike Nelson are walking through the woods with a bag and a switchblade. They find a deflated football, cut it open, and there's cocaine inside. They're expecting this, but they're expecting more of it. Cue Leo Johnson, who steps from the shadows to inform them they're only getting half the promised product because they still owe him half the promised money. Bobby sees someone in the woods behind Leo but Leo is insistent on wanting his cash so won't be distracted. Bobby explains they have the cash, that's not the problem, the problem is that the cash is in Laura's safety deposit box, and, well, she'd dead. This is another thing that Leo doesn't care about, all he cares about is how "Leo needs a new pair of shoes." He goes on to insinuate he knows his wife Shelley has been stepping out on him, which makes Bobby especially nervous as he's the one she's been stepping out with. Leo chases them off then tosses the deflated football an amazing distance with amazing accuracy at their car.

Coming home with greasy hands, Big Ed accidentally destroys the prototype of Nadine's completely silent drape runners. This displeases her, to say the least. The fractures in their marriage are revealed, as are the fractures in Nadine's psyche. She also appears to possess above-average strength – for a gorilla – as demonstrated by the destruction of a rowing machine.

Bobby pops by Shelley's the next day when Leo is out and sees the bruises she has from the soap-assault. She's scared, she wants to slow things down between them, but Bobby's not having it, it seems he truly loves Shelley, and he vows to protect her. They seal it with a kiss. As my wife, a first-time viewer, noted, Bobby must be one hell of a kisser because he's gripping Shelley by one of the bruises on her face and she's not even wincing. I hadn't noticed this, but now I've noticed my wife seems to have a thing for Bobby Briggs.

In the woods by the Sheriff's station, Coop has gathered Truman, Deputies Hawk and Andy, as well as receptionist Lucy for a demonstration of a Tibetan "deductive technique involving mind-body coordination operating hand-in-hand with the deepest levels of intuition" and which Coop says he acquired in a dream some years ago. He then takes up a stone from a bucket of them Hawk holds with oven mitts – or "kitchen mittens" as Coop calls them – and has Truman read aloud one at a time the name of everyone in town whose name starts with a J, as referenced in Laura's final diary entry: "Nervous about meeting J tonight." After Truman reads each name, Coop repeats it and throws a rock at a glass bottle some distance away by which Andy is standing. The stone misses on James and Josie, knocks but doesn't break the bottle on Dr. Jacoby, misses again on both Johnny Horne (Audrey's brother) and Norma Jennings, and ricochets off a tree to hit Andy square in the forehead upon mention of Shelley Johnson. The next name on the list is Jack with One Eye, which Truman describes as a casino up north, so it's taken off the list with an assertion from Coop that they need to pay this place a visit soon. That leaves the last name on the list, Leo Johnson. The stone shatters the bottle.

Audrey stops in at the Double R for some coffee after church. The Haywards are there having some pie and Donna excuses herself to go say hello. Naturally the girls talk about Laura and how sad all that is, then about how kinda dreamy that FBI fella is, then Audrey asks if Donna ever heard Laura talk about her father, Ben Horne. Donna can't recall anything. So then Audrey stands up and slow dances with herself to the music on the jukebox like she's three hours into a mushroom trip.

Agent Albert Rosenfeld descends upon the Sheriff's station like a grumpy force of nature. He's the best forensics expert Coop has ever known, but he's also a bit rough around the edges and lacking in the social niceties. Albert quickly proves both these things to be egregiously true, and while the former is helpful, Truman tries to nip the latter in the bud with some good, old-fashioned, tried-and-true teeth threatening.

When Ed at last returns home after giving Nadine some space, she's an emotional 180 degrees from where he left her. Seems that in the process of destroying her prototype, he dripped some grease on it as well. This was just the innovation she needed. Her drape runners are now 100% completely silent, and she is now 100% completely nuts.

The Martells are readying themselves for bed. When Catherine goes into the powder room, Pete sneaks a key to Josie, who's waiting outside the door. Catherine doesn't see him, but perhaps senses the deceit. The key, it turns out, opens Catherine's hidden safe behind a bookcase in which there are two ledgers for the mill, one real, and one fudged to hide illegalities and paint a picture of a thriving business.

Leland Palmer is at home playing some records, crying, screaming, and dancing like a lunatic with a picture of his daughter for a partner. When Sarah tries to stop him, the picture breaks and Leland drops to his knees, sobbing uncontrollably, and all Sarah can do is demand of no one to know "what is going on in this house?" That's a *real* good question.

As he retires for the evening, Agent Cooper has a dream. He's an older man in a curiously decorated room. The floors are a chevron design and every wall is a thick, rich red curtain. The dream starts as a series of images. A little man in a red suit with his back to Coop. Sarah Palmer running down the stairs of her house. Laura on the morgue slab, blue-lipped. The one-armed man from the hospital manifests to read a poem: "Through the darkness future past/the magician longs to see/One chance out between two worlds/Fire walk with me." One-y then describes living with someone in an apartment above a convenience store, and being touched by the devil via a tattoo he got rid of by hacking off his own arm. He says his name is Mike. He says the other's name, the one he lived with, is BOB. Cooper sees this BOB, and it's the same figure Sarah saw lurking by her couch in the last episode. BOB can sense Coop, and promises not only to catch him with his "death bag," but that he will kill again. There's a ring of 12 candles around a mound of dirt like the one discovered in the train car with the half of Laura's heart necklace atop it, then Old Coop is back in the room and Laura is there as well. The little man, the Man From Another Place, is talking oddly. Laura touches her nose in a coke-snorting gesture. The Man From Another Place takes a seat and tells Coop "That gum you like is going to come back in style," then refers to the woman next to him as his cousin, "But doesn't she look almost exactly like Laura Palmer?" Not-Laura offers that sometimes her arms bend back. The Man From Another Place says she's full of secrets, and where they're from the birds sing a pretty song and there's always music in the air. Then, as if to prove it, music manifests and the Man From Another Place dances for them. Not-Laura crosses to Coop, kisses him, and whispers something in his ear. The dream ends. Coop wakes, immediately calls Truman, and tells him he knows who killed Laura Palmer.

On the technical side of things, Lynch really puts a seal on the visual style he's going for in episode 2, and despite being only four-hours old, TWIN PEAKS now has a definitive aesthetic personality. The real *coup de grace* of episode 2, though, is the last eight minutes, our first trip into the red-curtained waiting room, and our first real introduction – along with the Tibetan Rock Throw – to the mystical side of TWIN PEAKS.

From a narrative standpoint, the red room wasn't originally written into the series, it was an add-on to the European version of the pilot which was presented as a standalone film and therefore needed some closure. But Lynch so loved the look of the set and the implications it opened the narrative to, that he incorporated it starting here. One possible way to note this distinction – that the red room wasn't intended to be in the series – is the fact that the floor this time around and this time around only is dirty to the point of being shades of brown, not the iconic black-and-white design we all remember. It's funny that the first visual most people think of when they think of TWIN PEAKS, the scenes that really set it apart from conventional television, were never written in to the original story. Just goes to show you a script is never finished until the scene is in the can.

Overall, the sequence plays like a hallucinogenic nightmare and is pure Lynchian in every aspect: the fades, the strobing lights, the production design and characterization – its intentional misguidedness is meant to pique our curiosity while confounding our imaginations and thus demanding explanation, which means we're likely to stick around until we get it.

From a production standpoint, this was some pretty complicated stuff to shoot. The characters' movements and speech are presumed to have been shot normally then reversed, but this isn't the case. Actors were required to move backwards and had *that* footage reversed, and as for the speech, the dialogue was recorded and reversed, then presented to the actors to phonetically learn that way. The lines they speak in the scene are as they said them, the only added effect is a slight reverb. Michael J. Anderson, the Man From Another Place – who incidentally is the only TWIN PEAKS character to speak in this fashion throughout the entire season – has said the easiest way for him to learn this was to disregard the words' meanings and simply mimic their phonemes, or units of sound, which wound up creating that off-kilter inflection.

As I said at the beginning, episode 2 is really where TWIN PEAKS becomes TWIN PEAKS. What was already an unconventional, dark and quirky murder mystery here now broadens – again, as mentioned – into the metaphysical with the introduction of Cooper's interest and indeed reliance upon Eastern mysticism in his deductive skillset, and then blows up completely with the last act in the red room. By the end of episode 2, the gloves were off, the window was open, and the rules had been thrown out it. Whatever audiences thought they were getting, they now realized they were getting something totally beyond that, and in fact totally beyond anything network television had ever even dreamed of doing with a straight face. Audiences understood now that there was more than one mystery in Twin Peaks, and there were going be to layers and levels, dimensions, even, to all of them that were going to cause the overarching narrative of TWIN PEAKS to deviate from anything we could expect or anticipate, thus placing us completely in the hands of its creators.

I assume television writing is a college-level course at this point, and if so I hope they're teaching the first four hours of TWIN PEAKS as a perfect example of how to expertly unleash 20+ characters and their secrets on an audience at the same time, because this pacing and unfurling is masterful, and unparalleled until you get to something like LOST, which still took longer to establish itself. With only two episodes behind it, TWIN PEAKS was firmly established, if on uncertain ground, and for the moment at least, no one in the country could look away.

EPISODE 3 – "REST IN PAIN"

Written by Harley Peyton, Directed by Tina Rathbone

Airdate April 26th, 1990

We open on Audrey at The Great Northern. She's spying on Coop for the purpose of surreptitiously arranging a flirty morning meet with the Special Agent. Coop humors her because a) she's Audrey, and b) he wants to test her handwriting against that on the note he found slipped under his door the previous day which alerted him to look into One Eyed Jacks. It's a match, and not just the handwriting but the perfume that scented the envelope, as well. She tells him she did it because she wants to help him solve Laura's murder. She says One Eyed Jacks is more than a casino, she insinuates it's a brothel, and when Coop asks if Laura worked there, Audrey doesn't know but she does know Laura worked afterschool at her dad's department store, specifically at the perfume counter. This sets off an alarm in Coop because that's the same place Ronette Pulaski worked. Furthermore, if you remember Ben Horne's gross comment to his brother Jerry about a new girl working at OEJ "freshly-scented from the perfume counter," you'll realize there is indeed a connection between one job and the other. This interlude is interrupted when Truman and Lucy show up, there to hear who Cooper thinks killed Laura, which he called Truman about in the middle of the night after his dream at the end of the last episode. Coop explains his dream to them, how two men, Mike and BOB – not Mike Nelson and Bobby Briggs – were a pair of killers living above a convenience store; Mike wanted to stop killing so chopped off his arm with a FIRE WALK WITH ME tattoo on it – the same phrase found written in blood on a scrap of paper at Laura's murder scene – while BOB wanted to keep killing. To settle this dispute, Mike shot BOB*. Coop explains the Man From Another Place, the Laura-who's-not-Laura-and-might-be-her-cousin, and all the other cryptic clues from the red room, and reveals the thing that Laura whispered in the ear of his older self was the name of her killer. Unfortunately, he doesn't remember it. This is why I keep a notepad by the bed, Coop. Regardless, his ultimate point is that the dream is a code that if broken will solve the crime.

(* the "Mike shot BOB" thing is a matter of some confusion because it doesn't really explain itself and it never comes up in the rest of the series. That's because it's a reference to the ending of the European pilot, which was a part of the initial deal with ABC: in case the pilot hadn't been picked up, the network wanted an alternate ending that would close the narrative circle so they could sell it as a movie in Europe. In this alternate ending – and this is spoiler free for the actual series, don't worry – BOB is shot and killed by Mike. This is also the reason Coop says Truman and Lucy were in his dream, which we didn't see – another reference to the European pilot.)(This alternate ending is also proof that the Black and White Lodges hadn't been conceived yet when the series began, but that's a note for another time.)

Coop and Truman get called to the morgue by an irate Doc Hayward, who's pissed at forensics specialist Agent Albert Rosenfield on account of some invasive tests he wants to run; the girl is set to be buried today. Oddly enough, it's an inexplicably-present Ben Horne who brokers order and intercedes on behalf of the absent Palmers. Albert in his Albert fashion tells them all to screw off and starts to proceed anyway, which leads to a minor physical altercation in which Truman ends up slugging Albert. Coop sides with the others and orders Albert to release the body for the funeral and produce his results toot suite.

23

At the Palmer's house, Leland is being administered intravenous sedatives, which he needs when Laura's brunette doppelganger walks in. This is Madeline Ferguson, and like the not-Laura in Coop's dream, she is a cousin (Sarah's sister's kid) who looks exactly like Laura Palmer but for the darker locks (curled for now) and a pair of big-ass Sally Jessie Raphael glasses. She's come to town from Missoula, Montana (where David Lynch was born) for Laura's funeral. Leland, sobbing, embraces her, which makes her sob as well, but really all you're paying attention to is the fact that this girl looks exactly like Laura Palmer. It's creepy times 10.

Maddy was another afterthought by Lynch after working with Sheryl Lee and discovering she had tons more to offer the series than just portraying a beautiful corpse. After the pilot had been shot and before the series had started to air Lynch convinced Sheryl Lee to take a leap of faith and move to Los Angeles. At that point Maddy hadn't even been created, only the spark of her existed, but it was enough for Lee to feel like she could trust her instincts and go for it. Thank god she did, because Maddy provides a lot of the heart Laura was supposed to have, and fills an emotional void.

Meanwhile at the Double R diner, Norma is meeting with a parole officer, but not hers. Her heretofore unseen husband Hank is an inmate whose latest hearing is tomorrow and if all goes well, he could be released shortly thereafter. The officer wants to know if Norma can help Hank find gainful employment if that becomes the case, which of course she can because she owns the diner. The officer also hits on her pretty blatantly, but she shuts him down with that trademark Norma-coolness.

Coop and Truman go pay a visit to Leo Johnson, who was "identified" by Coop's Tibetan deductive stone-throwing last episode. The three men discuss Leo's knowledge or claimed lack thereof regarding Laura, his minor but steadily-escalating criminal record, and his whereabouts the night of Laura's murder: according to him he was on the road and called home from Montana, which he's very, very certain his wife Shelly can verify, because he's an abusive asshole.

As they ready themselves for the funeral, Major Briggs attempts to have a heart-to-heart with his son Bobby. As usual, the Major's practical, analytical nature conflicts with Bobby's hyper-rebellion to jarringly-melodramatic effects. Their relationship is one of the best on the show and gets more dynamic with each interaction.

Albert meets with Coop and Truman to present his results. The baggie found taped in Laura's diary holding the safety deposit key did indeed have cocaine inside, and her toxicology exam was positive for the drug as well. There were two types of twine found in the ligature marks pressed into her wrists and upper arms; one type matches that found in the traincar, one matches that used to bind Ronette Pulaski. Albert concludes from all this that Laura was tied up twice the night she died, in two different places – once at the wrists, and once at the bicep with her arms pulled back. This recalls what not-Laura said in Coop's dream: "sometimes my arms bend back." Albert continues: there were traces of some kind of soap outside the traincar that matched traces found on the back of Laura's neck. This soap is not the brand she used at home, which causes Albert to draw the super-creepy conclusion that the killer killed Laura, washed their hands, took her by the neck as they leaned in for a kiss, then vamoosed. Furthermore – yeah, there's more, the grisly details of that night are starting to become appallingly clear – there are distinctive wounds on Laura's neck and shoulders that Albert has determined are claw marks, animal in nature. Finally, there was a small piece of plastic found in Laura's stomach which Albert will have to take elsewhere to analyze, owing to something-something-backwoods-dimwits, but in the meantime he points out a mark on the plastic that looks like the letter J. More answers that ask questions. At the scene's conclusion, Albert tries to get Coop to sign his complaint against Truman for the sucker punch earlier that day. Coop refuses and stands up for the good people of Twin Peaks, which it is obvious he has developed a deep affinity for. After Albert leaves, perturbed, Coop makes a mention to Diane that he's thinking of looking into property in Twin Peaks, property for himself, he means. This is the first solid evidence that the Special Agent is taking more than a passing fancy to the town, and is thinking about laying down roots. This is both very charming, and very, very dangerous.

In an ickily-amorous bit of exposition as they too are preparing for Laura's funeral, Naomi reveals that she, Ed and Norma all went to high school together, and Ed and Norma were the quarterback-head cheerleader It couple. What she doesn't reveal is how the tables turned so drastically for Big Ed, although this does explain the origins of the affair between Ed and Norma. Nephew James comes home amidst this and refuses to go with them to the funeral. He can't do it. He just can't.

Audrey has a secret passage between the walls of The Great Northern that allows her to spy in on her father's office. Today she uses it to eavesdrop on an argument between her parents about whether or not they will be taking mentally-disabled brother Johnny to the funeral wearing his authentic Native American headdress. Mrs. Horne wants to let the boy alone, but Ben angrily thinks it's inappropriate. It's the first time he's been on the right side. Fortunately, Dr. Jacoby is there to mediate, and the headdress comes off.

It's time for Laura's funeral. Pretty much everyone in town is there, even James, though he hangs back moodily from the graveside. During the service, Bobby flips the fuck out and starts blaming everyone, saying they all knew Laura was in trouble but no one did anything to help her. He calls them hypocrites, he says *they* killed Laura, every single one of them. Then he spies James. They lock eyes, separate loves for the same woman burning bright and hatefully in each. They charge at each other but get separated by the crowd before they can clash. Bobby publically vows to kill James, which in itself would be a pretty lousy way to end a funeral if not for what happens next: Leland, overwrought with grief, belly-flops onto Laura's casket as it's being lowered into the grave. The impact messes with the hydraulics, which raises the coffin then lowers it again, the raises it, lowers it, over and over again. I dare you not to laugh. Sarah however is not amused, and chides her husband not to "ruin this too."

This is the only instance in the entire series in which all of the regular cast was on set the same day, and despite how it looks, the scene wasn't shot in Washington State, but rather in a cemetery in Southern California where potted pines had to block out the palm trees in the background. According to recollections in Bradley Dukes' most-excellent REFLECTIONS: AN ORAL HISTORY OF TWIN PEAKS, there was a lot of flexibility to the scene in terms of improvisation. Dana Ashbrook (Bobby) stole the scene with his bombastic tantrum, and Ray Wise (Leland) suggested the tragically-hilarious coda. Just another example of TWIN PEAKS as a living, breathing collaboration.

Back in the narrative, in a rare moment of non-sweetness, Shelly entertains diner patrons with her napkin-dispenser rendition of Leland's funeral freak out. Admittedly it's pretty funny, but too soon Shell, too soon. In the background, Truman, Hawk and Ed are meeting. Ed's afraid "someone" won't be able to figure out "something" on his own, and warns Truman to be careful who he trusts. Truman isn't worried, though, because the "someone" in question is Coop. The Special Agent shows up and they let him in on a town secret: someone's been bringing in drugs from Canada. They've been working six months on a bust that targets everyone in the operation from top to bottom, including Road House bartender Jacques Renault. Coop notes that this is a police matter and Ed's not police, which leads to Truman explaining how Twin Peaks' idyllic isolation isn't always as serene as it seems; there is an evil here, a darkness in the woods that takes many forms and has existed as long as recorded history, but so have the men of Twin Peaks who have sworn to fight off this evil, men like those seated with Coop at the table, known in respected whispers as the Bookhouse Boys. They swipe the outside of their right eye, their secret signal, and take Coop to this Bookhouse they're named for where James and another biker Joey Paulson – the same kid who took Donna from The Road House to rendezvous with James at the end of episode one – have Bernard Renault, Jacques' brother, bound and gagged. Bernard was caught that morning crossing the Canadian border with an ounce of cocaine, and they want to ask him a couple questions, Bookhouse-style. Bernie-boy claims the coke is for personal use, and dispels the theory that Jacques is on the run, saying he'll be at work that very night. Seems a little too easy to Coop, and turns out it is.

As he's walking to The Road House, Jacques notices a small red light flashing on top of the building, which causes him to turn tail and skedaddle. He calls Leo and tells him he's got to give him a lift northward. Leo obliges. Shelly meanwhile, takes a pistol from her purse and hides it away with Leo's bloody shirt.

25

At her place, Josie and Truman are sharing a bottle of red and some do-me eyes, but she's troubled, convinced something horrible is going to happen to her via Catherine and Ben Horne. She insinuates her husband Andrew's accidental death maybe wasn't an accident at all, and tells Truman about the two mill ledgers she found in Catherine's safe, one legit, one not so much. Josie doesn't think Catherine knows she knows, but oh she knows, cuz she's listening over the intercom. C'mon, Josie! This awareness is punctuated when Josie takes Truman to the safe to show him the two ledgers but can't because there's only one ledger in there now. Guess which one? Catherine herself is clutching the fakie, which she re-hides.

Staking out Laura's gravesite that night, Coop observes Dr. Jacoby saying the solemn and solitary goodbye he hadn't been able to say at the funeral because he hadn't been in attendance. Coop approaches him. Jacoby tells how Laura was more than a patient to him, her trauma reached him emotionally, it forged a connection that constitutes a feeling like love for the girl. It's creepy in a sad way, but doesn't seem predatory.

Back at the Packard place, a nervous Josie now knows what Catherine and Ben want – the mill and the land, respectively – and worries they'll try to kill her to get it. Not while Sheriff Harry S. Truman is around they won't. Smooching ensues.

And finally, at The Great Northern Coop and Hawk have a soulful discussion, literally, and Leland makes the dance floor a real uncomfortable place when "Transylvania 6-5000" comes on and he starts crying and begging women to dance with him. Coop and Hawk take him home, and the last thing we see is a red, wind-swung stoplight perhaps warning them against it.

This episode was the first written by Harley Peyton, who would go on to become one of the series' main scripters along with Frost and Robert Engels (who gets his solo shot next episode). Peyton was Emmy nominated for this episode, and over the course of the series would write or contribute to a dozen others. No one, not even Frost, had his name on more scripts than Peyton. At the time his only credit was the screenplay for LESS THAN ZERO (which kicks ass and is the first on-screen pairing of Iron Man and Ultron, if you want to get weirdly technical), but since then he's gone on to write a slew of features including the Bruce Willis-Cate Blanchett vehicle BANDITS and the biopic THE BRONX IS BURNING about 1977 New York City and its beloved Yankees.

At the helm of the episode was Tina Rathborne, who was hot off the acclaim of her 1988 feature ZELLY AND ME, which starred Isabella Rossellini and featured David Lynch in an acting role. At the time, Rossellini and Lynch were in a romantic relationship that sprang out of their work on BLUE VELVET and would last until roughly around the time TWIN PEAKS started to air. ZELLY AND ME remains Rathborne's only feature, and the episodes of TWIN PEAKS she directed (she returns in season 2) were the last time she's listed as being behind the camera.

All in all, after a couple episodes of secrets and cryptic clues, the investigation into the death of Laura Palmer finally starts to get some traction this episode, and the meticulous progress through the case showcases Mark Frost's police procedural background from his days as a writer and story editor on HILL STREET BLUES. Coop and co. are chasing down leads and looking for evidence the old fashioned way, with interrogations and observation-based deduction. This is more linear storytelling, like the crime dramas audiences of the time were used to, and it's a stroke of genius to balance this against the previous episode and its eight-minute trip into the red room, because this is the TWIN PEAKS narrative aesthetic: give them something weird then give them something they recognize, balance the offbeat with the conventional, using the former to subvert the latter. This reminds the more skeptical audience members that though the way TWIN PEAKS arrives at a solution is going to be unpredictable, there is indeed a solution, and it will be unearthed.

EPISODE 4 – "THE ONE-ARMED MAN"

Written by Robert Engels, Directed by Tim Hunter

Airdate May 3rd, 1990

We rejoin the town of Twin Peaks at the home of Leland and Sarah Palmer, where Sheriff Truman has Sarah sitting down with Deputy Andy, who's apparently a sketch artist as well, and describing the man she saw when Donna came to visit in episode two – even though it was just a vision – who we know as the man Coop saw in his dream and who was named by the One-Armed Man as BOB. Donna's there, as is Cousin Maddy. Leland somewhat sardonically mentions that Sarah had another vision the night after Laura died, this one about a necklace. Sarah describes essentially what is the last scene of episode one when Dr. Jacoby took James' half of the heart necklace from where James and Donna buried it in Ghostwood Forest. Donna of course recognizes this tableau as more than a mere vision, but keeps this information to herself, for James' sake.

When he returns to the station, Truman grabs Coop and they go to have a conversation with Dr. Jacoby, while in the lobby Andy and Lucy reveal they're in a romantic relationship, albeit one that at present is best described as "rocky." Coop has questions for the good psychiatrist, but Jacoby has that pesky confidentiality clause standing in the way. He'll concede nothing but that Laura was a troubled young lady, so much so she was beyond the scope of his professional help. The only real new nugget of info he drops is that the night after Laura died he followed a man she had spoken to him about, a man who drove a red Corvette, but lost track of him out on a mill road. This interview ends when Lucy breaks in on the intercom with a call for Coop from a one Gordon Cole. After dismissing Jacoby and before taking the call, Coop confirms with Truman that Leo Johnson drives a red Corvette like the one mentioned. Truman also informs Coop that an APB has gone out for Jacques Renault. As for the call, Coop says only that Cole is his supervisor, then picks up the line. Cole (performed by David Lynch himself) is calling for two reasons: the first is to discuss further forensic findings – the fibers of twine in Laura's arms were from a common brand, the fibers in her wrists were not; also, the marks on her shoulder Albert called scratches are actually bite marks, as from a bird. The second reason Cole is calling is to discuss the physical altercation between Albert and Truman, a.k.a. when Harry slugged him last episode for being an asshole. Coop goes to bat for Harry though, and asserts Albert got what was coming to him, and that puts a plug in the matter for now. Andy brings in the sketch Sarah provided, and Coop confirms it's the same man he saw in his dream, BOB, and further confirms he's not surprised her vision and his dream are linked. Then, as if all this wasn't enough, Deputy Hawk calls in and says he's found the One-Armed Man. Busy morning in Twin Peaks.

Meanwhile at their seedy Love Inn on the outskirts of town, Catherine is regaling Ben with the story of Josie's foiled ledger exposure, while unbeknownst to her Josie is outside staking the place out with a camera. Catherine and Ben in post-coital conversation reveal their ultimate plan is to burn down the mill, frame Josie for it, collect a boatload of insurance money, and open the Ghostwood Forest land Josie owns to Ben's development plans. As nothing in Twin Peaks is ever really a coincidence, this is the same motel to which Hawk has followed the One-Armed Man, whose last name he learned from the desk agent is Gerard. The authorities raid Gerard's room and find him indeed one-armed, indeed the man Coop saw in his dream, and fresh out of the shower. Ben and Catherine hear this commotion but don't fret, at least Ben doesn't. He heads into the bathroom to "wash his little Elvis," not noticing the poker chip from One Eyed Jacks that's fallen from his pocket. Catherine, on the other hand, notices it with ire.

Gerard is interrogated and says he doesn't know the man in the sketch but he does have a friend named Bob, a veterinarian who was assaulted outside a bar and is currently in a coma at the same hospital where Ronette Pulaski is, which is why Hawk would have seen him there. Truman confirms the assault is real and Gerard's telling the truth. Furthermore, Gerard, whose first name is Phillip but whose middle name is Michael, has no criminal record or warrants out for his arrest. He claims he lost his arm in a car accident, not by cutting it off himself, as Mike told Coop in Coop's dream. Coop has but one last question: did the lost arm have a tattoo? It did, but Gerard is hesitant to elaborate. Coop pushes. Gerard breaks into tears: the tattoo said MOM. Nothing gained from this jaunt to the motel then, except that Truman learns from Hawk that Josie had been on a stakeout of some sort when Hawk arrived.

In the little girls' room at Twin Peaks High School, Donna's checking her look in the mirror while Audrey's puffing a quick butt and scheming. She admits to her crush on Coop and figures the best way to his heart is through solving Laura's murder, and for that she wants Donna's help. She knows Laura and James were seeing each other behind Bobby's back, and she knows about Laura's problem with the nose candy. Furthermore, she shares how she learned from eavesdropping on her folks and Dr. Jacoby before the funeral that Laura was a patient of the good doctor's. This is the first thing Donna didn't know. Donna also didn't know that Laura worked at One Eyed Jacks, which Audrey can't prove as of yet, but if she can, if *they* can that is, it's bound to lead somewhere big. Audrey says they can start with the fact that Laura and Ronette both worked at the same place: the perfume counter at her dad's store.

Norma goes to prison to meet with her husband Hank before his parole hearing. Theirs is a chilly encounter. He gives the usual "I've changed" spiel to try and win her help with the board. It works. Norma tells the board she can give Hank a job if he's released, as well as a place to live; he is her husband, after all.

On the way back from the motel, Coop and Truman stop at the vet clinic run by Gerard's friend Bob. It's next to a convenience store (which reminds Coop of another part of his dream, where Mike said he and BOB lived, "above a convenience store") and Coop sends Andy inside for twine while he and Truman stop in the clinic, meet a llama, and get the receptionist to verify that the BOB of the sketch isn't the Bob of the clinic. When Andy returns with the twine, it's the same common brand that was used to bind Laura's arms. Because of this, Coop deduces that the bird who bit the girl must be a client of this clinic.

Shelly and Booby are making out at Shelly's place. This is risky, but she says Leo's out hanging with his buddy Jacques Renault and isn't due back anytime soon. The news of this particular duo freaks Bobby out. He lies and tells Shelly he "found out" Leo is running coke across the Canadian border and selling it at the high school. He adds how he thinks Laura might have been involved. All these sketchy revelations cause Shelly to show Bobby the bloody shirt she stole from Leo's laundry; she knows it's his shirt because it has his initials sewn into the collar. This pleases Bobby greatly. He takes the shirt and makes Shelly swear she never saw it. Leo won't be a problem for them anymore, he says.

Truman and Coop return to the station with the veterinarian's files and start Lucy going through them looking for bird owners. The guys go down to the gun range to get more comfortable with their pieces, inspired in part by Andy mishandling his weapon back at the motel. After the group discusses Andy's Lucy troubles, Coop reveals that he once knew a women who taught him the responsibility and bliss of commitment, and who also taught him what a broken heart was. He then unloads six kill shots into a paper target. Some hard feelings there, seems like.

Shelly's late to work and in a mood thanks to her shitty husband. She confides in Norma about Leo's abusive behavior because she knows a) Norma's been in a similar situation in the past with Hank, and b) she too has a side-piece she loves more than her husband, namely Big Ed. James shows up to ring Donna on the payphone. For our younger readers, those are phones strategically placed around public places that you had to put coins into before they would work, and you could only call on them, not post to Facebook or catch Pokemon. I know. Lame. James concludes his call and nearly shits himself when he runs into Maddy for the first time. She's the spitting image of

Laura, you'll recall. They chit-chat, which consists mostly of her talking and him staring really obviously, then she splits. Meanwhile Norma gets the call: Hank's been paroled. He's coming home.

Ben's in his office on the phone with brother Jerry in Iceland, where the latter has found possible new investors for the Ghostwood Estates development, when Audrey appears. She wants to know if her father is ashamed of her. He's not, he just wants to be able to depend on her. She says he can, and expresses an interest in the family business, suggests she start working in it, says she's even willing to start at the bottom, like, say, at the department store? Maybe at, I don't know, wild stab here, the perfume counter? She's a crafty girl, that Audrey. Despite the fact that he's funneling hookers through that particular position, Ben agrees. He's a sick, sick man underneath it all. A phone call interrupts this ~~Tinder~~ tender father/daughter moment, and whoever it is, Ben wants to meet them down by the river in half an hour. That's never good.

Coop, Truman and Andy are discovering that the veterinarian files are endless, even with the birds separated. There are just too many breeds of the feathered friends. Serendipitously, Cole calls back to say he's faxing over info on the plastic fragment found in Laura's stomach during her autopsy, and oh yeah, the bird that clawed her was either a parrot or a mynah bird, if that helps. Hawk brings in the fax from Cole: the plastic fragment is a piece of poker chip from One Eyed Jacks. Right on the heels of this, Andy finds the file on Waldo. Waldo is a mynah bird. Owned by Jacques Renault.

Authorities descend upon Renault's apartment. They knock, announce themselves, but Jacques isn't in there. Bobby Briggs, however is, and he scoots out the window before the door gets kicked in, but not before planting Leo's bloody shirt for Coop to find, monogramed collar and all.

As for Leo, he's down by the river as Ben requested. Ben is hiring him to burn down the mill, on Hank's recommendation, but he's concerned and condescending about Leo's drug business, he wonders if arson is out of the man's league. Leo updates his resume by revealing he's expanded his empire by killing the younger Renault, Bernard, banishing Jacques to Canada, and running their operation himself. Ben accepts these augmentations to Leo's criminal prowess and grants him the job: he wants the arson to go down in three days.

Elsewhere in the woods, Donna and James return to where they buried his half of Laura's heart necklace, prompted by Sarah's vision of it being stolen. Sure enough, it's gone. An owl hoots. Donna and James make out. Pick your moment, kids.

The episode closes with Josie getting a call from Truman. He can't rendezvous with her tonight, but he wants to know why she was at the motel that afternoon, who she was staking out. She evades his questions. After making Pete a sandwich, she goes through the day's mail and finds an envelope containing a very nice drawing of a domino. Then the phone rings again. It's the artist. Hank Jennings. He says he'll catch her later. Whaaaaa?

Continuing the trend of working with great independent directors of the day, this episode was handed over to Tim Hunter, who at the time was famous for co-writing OVER THE EDGE, Matt Dillon's film debut, and directing RIVER'S EDGE with Keanu Reeves, Crispin Glover, and Dennis Hopper, which won Best Picture at the 1986 Independent Spirit Awards. If you've seen either of these excellent films, you know that Hunter is no stranger to the dark narratives that can be spun from teenagers in small towns. If you haven't seen either of these excellent films, you should fix that as soon as possible. Since TWIN PEAKS, of which he directed three episodes, Hunter has gone on to become one of the most sought-after and prolific television directors in the business, with credits on nearly every major drama since the early 90's including (deep breath) HOMICIDE: LIFE ON THE STREET, CHICAGO HOPE, CSI:NY, CARNIVALE, HOUSE M.D., DEADWOOD, BREAKING BAD, MAD MEN, SONS OF ANARCHY, DEXTER, NIP/TUCK, GLEE, AMERICAN HORROR STORY, PRETTY LITTLE LIARS, HANNIBAL, GOTHAM, and THE BLACKLIST. But he honed his chops right here in TWIN PEAKS, where this episode he pays visual homage to two films very influential to show co-creator David Lynch: Hitchcock's VERTIGO and Bergman's PERSONA, the former with quick zooms and the latter with an alignment of character's faces. Worth noting that the character name "Madeleine Ferguson" comes from VERTIGO – "Madeline" is the first character played by Kim Novak, and "Ferguson" is the last name of Jimmy Stewart's character.

The episode's writer is Robert Engels, who I mentioned briefly last week. Along with Mark Frost and Harley Peyton, Engels would contribute to more TWIN PEAKS scripts than anyone, and he and Peyton served as the translators, so to speak, of the overarching narrative Frost and Lynch had designed. It was Engels who co-wrote FIRE WALK WITH ME with Lynch, as well as a trio of episodes for ON THE AIR, the other, even shorter-lived TV series from Frost and Lynch.

This episode, to me, is all about expanding the other, more minor relationships of the show: Norma and Hank, Lucy and Andy, Bobby and Shelly, Leo and Jacques. This is also where the series first starts to shine a light onto the other (natural) mysteries of Twin Peaks: the drug game, the land grab, the prostitution funneling, and whatever Hank's up to. The story was branching out from the trunk of Laura's murder and sowing the seeds that would outlast the solution to that crime, telling us quite plainly, whether we chose to listen or not, that the show was about the town, not the murder, and there's was more than one thing worth watching in Twin Peaks.

Written by Mark Frost, Directed by Lesli Linka Glatter

Airdate May 10th, 1990

At The Great Northern, Cooper is being kept awake by Icelanders who have descended upon the town to hopefully invest in Ben Horne's Ghostwood Estates development project. Their revelry lasts throughout the night. The next morning at breakfast, Audrey drops by Coop's table and tells him she got a job. She's about to tell him where – the perfume counter at her father's department store, same as Laura and Ronette Pulaski – hoping he'll let her help with the case, but he's in a hurry and cuts her off. Their conversation ends with him asking how old she is. A perfectly-legal 18 is her reply. Mmm-hmm. "We'll see you later, Audrey," he says, which could be Coop's version of "All right, all right, all right."

The Horne brothers reunite. Jerry says any noise complaints from the other guests are worth the trouble, because the Icelanders are nuts for the Ghostwood idea, and furthermore he's fallen head-over-heels in love with a snow queen named Heppa. She gave him an entire leg of lamb, so obviously she feels the same. They discuss a gala planned for that evening in which they hope to cinch the deal with the Icelanders, but if that doesn't do it, Ben's thinking a trip to One Eyed Jacks for some drinking, gambling, and whoring will. Then a disheveled and disoriented Leland arrives. He's heard there's a new investment group in town and as Ben's lawyer he thinks he should be there to help them finalize things. Absolutely no one else agrees with him. Leland collapses, crying.

When Coop shows up at the apartment of Jacques Renault, Truman gets him up to speed on the man. Jacques is Canadian and used to work in lumber before he blimped up and said adios to manual labor, started bartending at The Road House. He's been missing going on two days now, as has his younger brother Bernie. Doc Hayward's there as well and on the phone with the medical examiner: the blood on Leo's shirt doesn't belong to Laura or even Leo – it belongs to Jacques. There's already an APB out on Leo but it hasn't yielded anything as of yet. Coop notices something about the apartment ceiling and gets Truman to give him a leg up. Behind the panels there he finds an issue of Flesh World (for "Swingers Coast to Coast"), the same magazine found in the train car where Laura was murdered. Coop mentions the magazine ad featuring Ronette Pulaski also found at the train car; he thinks it came out of Flesh World. Confirmation follows shortly when they find an envelope in the magazine addressed to Ronette care of a PO Box Coop is willing to wager is registered to Jacques. They read the correspondence and study a photo of a bearded man in lingerie. As their stupefaction expands, Coop casually wonders aloud if Truman noticed the picture of Leo's truck on the open page of Flesh World?

At Leo and Shelly's, she's making breakfast for Bobby. Bobby acts out a hypothetical encounter with Leo if the man were to happen upon them, using Shelly's pistol for added effect. The act is interrupted by Deputy Andy coming to call. Bobby tells Shelly to remember what he told her then disappears in the back. Andy's looking for Leo. Shelly wants to know why, and if it's about Laura. Andy wonders why she wonders that, and that's when she feeds him the rehearsed line about seeing Leo with this guy named Jacques Renault and they were arguing about Laura before driving off together. Andy buys it hook, line, and sinker, and splits. Bobby and Shelly celebrate their duplicitous victory with some grade-A making out that gets interrupted when Leo calls. His ears must be burning, because he's wondering if anyone's come by looking for him. Shelly says no, the coast is clear and it's safe for him to come home. The pistol she stares at longingly would seem to suggest otherwise.

31

Norma drops by Big Ed's Gas Barn cuz she knows Nadine's out of town for the afternoon. She tells her secret lover that Hank's been released from prison and will be returning to town. She hasn't told Hank about her and Ed, just like Ed hasn't said anything to Nadine about him and Norma, mostly because Nadine is fucking nuts. Their love is still star-crossed and Norma's starting to think it's going to stay that way. She wants her distance to think things over. Ed, ever the gentleman, consents to her wishes.

At Horne's Department Store, manager Emory Battis tries to stick Audrey in the gift-wrapping department, but she uses her ample wiles to bump herself up to the perfume counter. She's so persuasive, in fact, she even convinces Battis to keep her relocation a secret from her father. I'm pretty sure with those eyes she could've convinced him to go skinny-dipping in Pearl Lakes on New Year's Day.

James and Donna meet at gazebo in the park. James, as usual, is emoting: he says he lied about his dad being dead, the dude's a bum musician who abandoned him and his mom a long time ago. Mom is a poet and an alcoholic (as if those two professions are separate). She's out of town like he tells folks, but she isn't travelling, she's off on a binder of booze and boys, it's a regular thing for her. He's telling Donna all this out of the clear blue because secrets destroy happiness, he says, and he wants nothing but happiness for them. That includes figuring out what happened to Laura so it doesn't haunt them.

Back at Jacques' apartment, Coop finds a picture of a cabin with red drapes, like the room in his dream. Hawk returns with letters from Ronette's PO Box, which was indeed registered to Jacques as Coop suspected. Looking through the letters, Coop realizes there are two ads being responded too, both using the same address. Ronette's ad is one of them and the other he looks up in the issue of Flesh World. When he finds it, though the picture of the girl doesn't include her face, Coop knows it's Laura because of the red drapes in the background. He also finds among Jacques' papers a bill for heating oil, something an apartment dweller wouldn't need, but a guy who owned a cabin – like the one in the photo – would. Truman offers that during interrogation Bernie Renault mentioned just such a cabin out in the woods by the Canadian border.

Laura's cousin Maddy meets James and Donna at the Double R. Donna has her swear to secrecy, because they want her in on the hunt for the truth. Donna knows Laura had a secret hiding place somewhere in her bedroom, and they need Maddy to find it and see what's hidden there. Maddy agrees. Little do they realize that recently-paroled Hank is sitting in the booth right behind them, and he seems quite intrigued by their discussion. Just then Norma and Shelly return from the salon. This is the first time in a long time that Norma has seen her husband out of prison, in person, and without supervision. She marks the occasion by putting him to work washing dishes.

Major and Mrs. Briggs are worried about Bobby's recent behavior in the wake of his girlfriend's murder and so have taken him to Dr. Jacoby for family counseling. Jacoby, however wants to see Bobby alone. He wants to talk about Laura, specifically the first time they made love. He's wondering if Bobby cried. He's wondering if Laura laughed when Bobby cried. Jacoby knows these things from sessions he had with Laura in which she discussed them. With nowhere else to go, Bobby aims for the truth and tells the doctor Laura told him she wanted to die because everything in the world was rotten and terrible. Jacoby wonders if Laura wanted to die because of a horrible secret she held, the same secret that made her mean and manipulative and controlling. Bobby can testify she was all those things, and confesses it was Laura who made him sell Leo's cocaine.

Coop, Truman, Hawk and Doc take a hike through the woods looking for Jacques Renault's cabin. They find a cabin, but not the one they're looking for. This one belongs to Margaret the Log Lady, and she's been waiting for them. She invites them inside for tea and cookies, but no cake. Better to talk inside, she explains, because the owls can't see them there. Coop is hesitant but the others convince him to play along. They're two days late, she says once all are settled, and her log has been waiting because as mentioned in the pilot, it saw something significant the night Laura died. Margaret touches briefly on her own backstory, how her husband "met the Devil" and died in a fire the day after their wedding, and how the log might possibly hold his spirit. Then, with the introductions out of the way, she tells Coop he may address her log now. He asks the log what it saw that night Laura. Margaret translates in staccato images and riddles: dark, laughing, the owls were flying, many things were blocked, two men, two girls, flashlights pass by…the dark was pressing in on her…later footsteps, one man passes by, then screams from far away, female. It dawns on Coop and the others that Margaret aurally witnessed the murder. They continue through the woods the way she indicates. They know who the two girls she heard are – Laura and Ronette, obviously – and speculate that the first two men are Leo and Jacques. But when it comes to the third man, the later-footsteps man, they have no idea who it could be. A sonic trail of eerie music playing on repeat leads them to the right cabin, the one from the photograph with red curtains in the windows. Inside the music is revealed to be coming from a skipping record player. Coop remembers the line, "And there's always music in the air," from his increasingly-prophetic dream. The cabin walls are covered in red curtains, like the room from Coop's dream. But there's no one here. No one human, that is. There is a mynah bird, presumably the famed Waldo owned by Jacques and suspected of being responsible for the bite and claw marks on Laura's shoulder. Hawk discovers a camera with film in it, and Coop locates the common brand of twine use to bind Laura. Truman finds a cuckoo clock full of One Eyed Jacks poker chips, and one of them is missing a sliver just the size of the one recovered from Laura's stomach.

Josie is alone in a room at The Great Northern, having a smoke. Elsewhere the gala welcoming the Icelanders has begun. Pete and Catherine are there, as are the Briggs. Jerry and his snow queen Heppa are canoodling. Everyone's having a swell time eating, drinking, and making merry. Then Leland shows up. Before he can go off the rails, Catherine takes an opportunity to mess with Ben and facilitates an immediate secret meeting in his office. Audrey sees this going down and slips into her hidden corridor between the walls to spy on them. Catherine's pissed about the poker chip that fell from Ben's pants at the hotel during their last tryst. He offers a non-gross excuse, but she doesn't buy it. He's unconcerned, and they kiss anyway then talk of their plans to burn the mill. Audrey hears it all. Back at the gala, some idiot plays "Transylvania 6-5000," which you might recall is Leland's trigger song, and he starts cry-dancing with himself again in the middle of everyone. Ben, desperate not to let Leland's lunacy ruin another deal, coerces Catherine into dancing with Leland. It diffuses the situation and even starts a new dance craze I'm calling the Bullwinkle. In her room, Josie continues to smoke.

Maddy sneaks to the telephone after Sarah's gone to sleep to call Donna and tell her she found a cassette tape hidden in a bedpost and will share it with them tomorrow.

Ben goes to where Josie is waiting for him. Turns out they're colluding, too, and might have had romantic relations in the past. That Ben Horne, he gets around. He learned from Catherine where she hid the real mill ledger then alerted Josie as to where she could find it; in return, she's brought it to him. Furthermore, it would seem she's in on the plan to burn down the mill.

Leo returns home. Before going inside he gets two gas canisters from under the house and starts to load them in his truck but is ambushed by Hank, who's pissed because Leo was supposed to look after Hank's drug business, not steal it. He threatens to kill Leo and Shelly, then leaves. Leo goes inside and starts to take it out on Shelly but she pulls the gun on him, she won't be hurt again. He doesn't think she has the guts, but she does and shoots him. We don't see where the bullet hits him, but from the sounds he makes, nowhere good.

The episode ends where it began, at The Great Northern. Coop is returning to his room after a long day. When he gets there, though, the door is already ajar. Coop draws his weapon and enters. The room is dark. He senses a presence. He tells the presence to reach over and turn on the light. The presence obeys. It's Audrey. In Coop's bed. Naked.

This episode was the first of four directed by Lesli Linka Glatter, who at the time was known for directing an Academy-Award-nominated live action short and some work on AMAZING STORIES. Since TWIN PEAKS she's worked on tons of A-list primetime programs like NYPD BLUE, LAW & ORDER SVU, FREAKS AND GEEKS, GILMORE GIRLS, THE O.C., THE WEST WING, GREY'S ANATOMY, HEROES, ER, WEEDS, MAD MEN, PRETTY LITTLE LIARS, TRUE

BLOOD, THE NEWSROOM, and HOMELAND, among others. Fun fact: in the season 1 finale, Glatter earned her only-ever acting credit as "One Eyed Jacks Servant." Blink and you'll miss her.

Co-creator Mark Frost wrote the episode, which deals with the merging of the two worlds of TWIN PEAKS – the physical realm and the metaphysical realm – via the nexus of Cooper's dreams. Everything about Jacques Renault's cabin in particular, with the music, the dark floor, the red drapes is an appropriately cheap recreation of the red room Coop dreamt of, down to the shadow of a bird manifesting as Waldo in reality. These real-world clues discovered by (or more likely, delivered to) Coop's subconscious are the only things advancing the case at this point, which opens the weird factor even wider, because it's one thing for a place to produce these kinds of visions, but it's another for them to be true when the visions end. Makes one wonder who or what, consciously-speaking, is communicating these things to Cooper, and Sarah, and why. Laura's murder, it turns out, isn't the bigger mystery, it's merely a symptom of the bigger mystery, of which we're only at the outskirts.

EPISODE 6: "REALIZATION TIME"

Directed by Caleb Deschanel, Written by Harley Peyton

Airdate May 26th, 1990

A half-moon over The Great Northern is looking down on the same scene that closed the last episode, the one with a naked Audrey in Coop's bed, much to Coop's surprise. He gently rebukes her bold advance, while not altogether denying his desire for her: "What I want and what I need are two different things," he concedes. He recognizes however that what she needs most is a good friend, not a lover, and they agree to leave it at that.

The next morning at the sheriff's station, Andy and Lucy are still on icy terms, and Lucy gets a mysterious phone call that depresses her. Coop meanwhile joins Doc Hayward and Truman, who are busy studying up on the habits and behaviors of mynah birds in the presence of Waldo, Jacques Renault's pet and a possible witness to Laura's murder. It was Waldo, you'll remember, who was responsible for the bite marks on Laura's shoulder. The bird isn't speaking yet because he's malnourished. Deputy Hawk arrives with forensics results that place Laura, Ronette and Leo all in Jacques's cabin the night of the murder. Coop leaves his trusty micro-cassette recorder on voice-activation mode next to Waldo's cage in case the bird decides to start talking while they go check out One Eyed Jacks, where forensics reveals the fragment of poker chip found in Laura's stomach came from, and where Jacques Renault is known to be employed dealing cards. The thing is, One Eyed Jacks is over the Canadian border and thus out of Coop's federal jurisdiction, which is why he's thinking they ought to go as Bookhouse Boys.

Leo, having been chased off by Shelly in a hail of gunfire at the end of last episode, is somehow unharmed and spying on the house. He sees Bobby arrive, sees Bobby and Shelly embrace, then he grabs his rifle. Inside, Shelly tearfully recounts the previous evening, and knows now that Leo will stop at nothing to kill her. Bobby once again swears to protect her. Outside, Leo hears Lucy gabbing about Waldo on his police scanner and reckoning that the more pressing matter, he takes off before he can kill Bobby.

At the Palmer's, Maddy plays the cassette she found hidden in Laura's bedpost for Donna and James. It was made for Dr. Jacoby, and on it Laura talks about her sex appeal like it's something to be ashamed of. Maddy found an empty cassette case as well, and they figure Jacoby must have the actual cassette that goes with it. But based on what Laura says about Dr. J "liking" her, they suspect he might not be too willing to give it up. So James devises a break in, using a manipulation of Laura's voice from the tape to lure Jacoby away from his office, then using Maddy in disguise as her cousin as a visual deterrent to keep him away.

At the perfume counter of Horne's Department Store, Audrey is bored by the work but intrigued by the environment. She sneaks into store manager Emory Battis' office for a smoke and a snoop, and ends up hiding in the closet overhearing a conversation between Battis and her coworker from the counter, Jenny. They're talking about a "club" and how the people there like her and want her to continue. She can do so as a hostess, a waitress, or if she's *really* lucky, a "hospitality girl," a.k.a. prostitute. Battis gives Jenny a phone number and tells her to ask for Black Rose. After they're gone but before Audrey leaves, she finds a notebook filled with girls' names and hearts beside them. Ronette's name is one on the list.

Hank and Shelly are working the morning shift together at the diner. Hank's thanking her for being around for Norma while he was inside, says she wrote him how helpful they were, Shelly and Pete. Shelly's confused: Pete? Hank starts reeling her in: Is that not his name, the fella who's always around? Shelly falls for it: You mean Ed? Ed, yeah that's it. See what he did there? Then, as if blatant manipulation wasn't shady enough, Hank reinforces his criminal past by stealing a customer's lighter while clearing plates from the counter. Coop and Truman show up as second after this so the Sheriff can fill Hank in on his parole requirements.

Back at the department store talking to Jenny, Audrey uses what she overheard to play like she's in on the "club" deal, but gosh she lost the number for Black Rose. Jenny, gullible as Shelly, gives it to her and Audrey makes the call.

Pete's showing off a taxidermied fish to Truman while the Sheriff is waiting to talk with Josie. He wants to know what she was doing at the motel where they busted the one-armed man. She denies being there but he knows Hawk saw her. She's scared but he convinces her to talk. She tells him Ben and Catherine were at the motel, and shows him the pictures she took, says they're proof these two are colluding against her. He wants to know how, and all she knows is she heard them talking about a fire at the mill. This is bullshit of course, because we know from the last episode that Josie is conspiring with Ben against Catherine, and knows fully about the plans for the mill fire. To her conniving credit though, Josie feigns ignorance well, all doe-eyed and pouty-lipped.

Coop donned now in a different kind of black suit, a dapper tux, meets with Truman and Ed at The Great Northern. He's brought along 10k of bureau money for gambling purposes. Before they go, though, Truman needs a word alone with Coop. He shares Josie's concerns with the Special Agent. Hawk shows up and the gang's all there. Their cover will be that they're oral surgeons from the Tri-Cities on vacation. Meanwhile Audrey is trying to reach Coop to relay the info she learned from the Department Store that day, but he's already gone.

Catherine gets a housecall from a lawyer. It turns out her life insurance policy – which takes effect at midnight, hence his showing up – still needs her signature. As she peruses the document, she notices Josie is listed as her beneficiary to the tune of a cool million smackeroos. Obviously Catherine didn't do this, but she doesn't let on to this degree, merely notes how odd it is she and this particular lawyer have never met. He says that's because the policy was arranged and filed by Josie and Ben Horne, who had said they were going to collect her signature, but gosh they must have forgotten. Catherine declines to sign the policy and dismisses the lawyer. She's been double-crossed and knows it, so she checks for the real ledger and of course, it's gone.

Still desperately seeking Cooper, Audrey sees an Asian man checking into the hotel. This is more important than it seems in this moment.

Meanwhile, at the station Coop and Ed are getting wired up and costumed in preparation for heading to One Eyed Jacks. In the conference room, though, unbeknownst to them, Waldo starts to talk. He repeats Laura's name, the tape recorder clicks on to capture some of it, then he's shot from outside the station by Leo. Coop and co. race into the conference room, but it's too late, Waldo's dead. Leo flees unseen. Coop tries his recorder and it caught everything Waldo was saying, including a very chilling partial transcript of the night Laura was killed: "don't do that," "hurting me," "stop it," and "Leo no."

Later at One Eyed Jacks, Ed and Coop enter unmolested and are approached by Blackie, who buys their cover and directs them towards the casino. They radio the scene to Hawk and Truman, who are observing out in the truck since Jacques Renault knows them both on sight.

Maddy is sneaking out of the Palmer house, she thinks undetected, but Leland is awake in the dark of the living room and watches her go. As she's going to meet James and Donna in the park to hoodwink Dr. J, she's wearing a blond wig and has lost her glasses, both of which conspire to make her the spitting image of Laura. This seems to pique Leland's interest.

The Icelanders are partying down at The Great Northern. Ben and Jerry have an aside: Ben is impatient, he wants the Icelanders to sign the investment contracts for Ghostwood Estates immediately. Jerry says they're close but they want a big signing party ... complete with gambling and sex workers at One Eyed Jacks, which they might have

36

found out about through Jerry. Ben agrees, but wants to nip this in the bud tonight. All of it. He calls Josie to find out where Catherine is, she needs to be in the mill when it catches fire. Josie says she'll get her there and hangs up, revealing Hank at her side. What a tangled web she weaves.

Now Audrey's at One Eyed Jacks – hopping place – meeting with Blackie and pretending to be the new girl Gattis sent from the perfume counter. She's going by the name Hester Prynne. How well-read our Miss Horne is. She tries to talk her way through a fake resume but Blackie calls her out on it, as well as the name. Seems she's read Hawthorne as well. Audrey convinces her to let her stay anyway by tying a cherry stem into a knot using only the strength and contorting powers of her tongue. She didn't invent this gag, but you'd think she did. Naturally, she gets the damn job.

In the casino, Coop's racking up the chips playing blackjack. Then Jacques Renault takes over the dealing.

Jacoby is watching the latest installment of INVITATION TO LOVE when he gets the call from "Laura." Naturally, he doesn't believe it, thinks it's a sick gag, but she directs him to the door where there's a package containing a videotape. On the videotape is "Laura" holding up the day's newspaper. She says she wants to meet him and tells him where, a red-herring location. The call complete, James and Donna leave her by the gazebo in the park to go break in to Jacoby's office. Bobby is on the scene too, following James. He creeps up and sees Maddy as Laura. But someone's watching him, too, or also watching her. Bobby flees but this second, unseen person remains, focused on Maddy. Or Laura. Dr. J can tell from the background of the video that "Laura" isn't where she told him to go, the gazebo gives her away. He takes off for the park instead and Donna and James break in to his office. Bobby sees them, and while they're inside he plants a big ol' bag of cocaine in James' gas tank, then hits bricks.

The episode draws to a close with Maddy still being watched by an unknown man, his gender given away by his breathing, hard and fast, either scared or agitated.

This episode was the first of three to be directed by Caleb Deschanel – husband to Mary Jo, who plays Eileen Hayward, Donna's mom, and father to Zooey NEW GIRL and Emily BONES – who was already quite accomplished as a cinematographer when he came to TWIN PEAKS, having been nominated for a pair of Oscars by that time, once for THE RIGHT STUFF and once for THE NATURAL. To date, he has three additional nominations in the same category, for FLY AWAY HOME, THE PATRIOT, and THE PASSION OF THE CHRIST. Deschanel is another storied graduate of the equally storied University of Southern California School of Cinematic Arts, and he was there at the really cool time in the late 60's/early70's when everybody was there, including Francis Ford Coppola and George Lucas, with whom Deschanel was a founding member of the famed American Zoetrope production team, for whom he shot THE BLACK STALLION and MORE AMERICAN GRAFFITTI. Deschanel has only directed two features, THE ESCAPE ARTIST from 1981 about a young would-be Houdini, and CRUSOE, a take on Daniel Defoe's stranded hero starring Aiden Quinn, which came out just before TWIN PEAKS began to air. The episode was written yet again by Harley Peyton, the show's top writer after Frost.

In summary, for everything that goes down this episode in regards to the investigation – Jacques Renault, Leo, Waldo, and One Eyed Jacks – the real action happens at the very end and is focused on Maddy, because whoever this unseen figure is who's having this reaction to seeing "Laura" obviously means her harm. It could be Leo, who is unaccounted for after killing Waldo, but also we remember what the Log Lady said about a third man, alone, passing through the forest after Jacques, Leo, Laura, and Ronette the night Laura died, and we know this could be that person. This is the first really tantalizing clue that the mystery is close to being solved: the killer has come out of hiding. And with just one episode to go in the first season, anticipation is running high. But this is TWIN PEAKS, so if you're expecting a straight-forward resolution … wait, hang on, I'm laughing too hard to type …

EPISODE 7: "THE LAST EVENING"

Written and Directed by Mark Frost

Airdate May 23rd, 1990

Rarely has so much anticipation been directed at a season finale. Everyone in the world assumed we were going to learn the identity of Laura Palmer's killer. What we got instead was so much more interesting, and opened so many new doors, one of them perhaps fatally. But I'm getting way ahead of myself. The finale beings in Dr. Jacoby's office, right where we left off. Donna and James have broken in and are trying to find other audio tapes made by Laura. Among the doctor's more interesting possessions is a collection of cocktail umbrellas tagged with dates and such vague identifiers as "I first laid eyes on whimsy." Eventually they find the missing tape in a coconut along with the half a heart necklace that they buried way back in the pilot. They flee, but not undetected; Bobby is hiding in the shadows, looking on.

Meanwhile at the park by the gazebo, Jacoby is lurking about and feeling double-crossed because "Laura" tried to send him to the wrong address. When he catches full sight of her, though, this anger melts into overwhelmed emotion, so much so he doesn't even notice the dark, masked figure with a rock who sneaks up behind him and starts beating him. Jacoby, however seems more concerned with getting to "Laura," but neither he nor the masked figure can, because Donna and James return to the park then all three of them leave. So instead, Jacoby has a heart attack in the grass.

The Bookhouse Boys' undercover operation at One Eyed Jacks continues. Coop is playing blackjack at Jacques Renault's table – and winning. He tips Jacques the chip with the missing fragment (which was discover in Laura's stomach during her autopsy) and explains he's a friend of Leo's. Jacques plays dumb at first, but not so dumb he doesn't accept the chip and Coop's invitation for a drink. Elsewhere in the club, Audrey, a.k.a Hester Prynne, is all dolled up in skimpy lingerie for her first night undercover as a hooker. While Blackie looks her over approvingly, Audrey notices Coop on the security monitor. Blackie distracts her by saying it's a good night to "break her in" because the owner is coming by and he likes to "spend some time" with the new girls. Everything in quotes in that last sentence means banging. Audrey asks who the owner is, but no-names is a house rule. Back having that drink, Coop is trying to pass himself off as a superior of Leo's in the drug trade, his financier. He says he knows about the night with Laura. Jacques admits to being with the girls in so many words, and Coop flashes a wad of cash meant to entice Jacques to return to the States for a job (and a pair of handcuffs). Jacques takes the bait and Coop sets up a meet for a couple of hours later. Before they part, Coop amends his earlier statement, says he knows all about that night with Laura but for one thing, how the chip got broken: Jacques says that bird – Waldo – was always saying Laura's name, like he loved her, and that night when they were all high and participating in group bondage sexual activities, the bird got loose and landed on Laura's shoulder, started pecking her, love pecks, Jacques says, and this inspired Leo to take the chip and stick it in Laura's mouth as he's fornicating with her and telling her to, and this is a quote, "bite the bullet, baby, bite the bullet." It's comical to Jacques but not to Coop, who does his best to maintain his cover. Especially because this is all being recorded through the wire he's wearing by Hawk and Ed outside in a van. This confession explains almost everything about Laura's forensic state – the bite marks, the ligature marks, the plastic fragment in her stomach – and places her with Leo, Jacques and Ronette the night she died. The only thing it doesn't explain how she died, and at whose specific hand.

Shelly's home alone washing her hair in the sink. At her right hand is her pistol, just in case. Predictably, the shampoo runs down her forehead and stings her eyes. As she reaches for the towel, she can't see it's being slowly pulled out of her reach. She realizes too late what's happening and reaches for her pistol, but Leo slaps it away first. He offers the typical abusive-douchebag epithet of "You made me do this!" then absconds with her.

Truman and Andy are at the meet-spot Coop set up and awaiting word Jacques is headed their way. They get it. He shows. They flip on the lights and roll on him. They manage to arrest him without incident for the attempted murder of Ronette and the murder of Laura, and it seems like it's going to be a clean nab but as he's being cuffed, Jacques gets and officer's gun and aims it at Truman. Before he can shoot, however, Andy calmly and accurately disarms and drops him with a bullet to the shoulder. Badass.

Donna, James and Maddy listen to the tape found in Jacoby's coconut. It's the same one Dr. J listened to at the end of episode one where Laura talks about how sweet but dumb James is, how she was getting tired of him, and about the mystery man she's been mentioning in their sessions. She says if she told Jacoby the man's name the good doctor could get hurt. She thinks this man has tried to kill her a few times and remarks oddly that she gets off on it. Sex is weird she further elaborates, but this mystery man lights her fire. The only possible clue she reveals as to this guy's identity is a red corvette. Like Leo's. That's all there is, but it's enough to convince the trio that Jacoby didn't kill Laura, though they still don't how he got his hands on the necklace they buried.

Leo has taken Shelly to the mill, which he's been contracted by Ben Horne to burn down. Leo's thinking is, couple birds, same stone, so he binds his wife to a post inside and gags her for good measure. Leo loves him some bondage, I tell you what. He then reveals an incendiary device and sets its timer for an hour from now in order to give Shelly time to think about what she's done, and to live with the knowledge of Bobby's impending murder at Leo's hands.

Nadine is wearing a prom dress and sealing a letter in an envelope. She has a bottle of water and a pretty dish full of two types of pills. The intimation is, depressed over the rejection of her silent drape runner patent, she's decided to send herself to that big cotton ball in the sky.

At the Packard place, Hank is accepting money from Josie, money she's owed him since before he went to prison. There's an agreement in place between them but he wants to renegotiate the deal. The (kinda confusing) gist is, Josie paid Hank $90,000 to kill her husband Andrew, then commit vehicular manslaughter on a vagrant and go away for the lesser crime to avoid being implicated in the greater one, which was staged to look like a boat accident. Like I said, confusing. Hank killed Andrew because Josie paid him to, basically. Now, seeing as he's the one who went to jail, and he's the one who knows her secret, he's thinking his compensation should be greater. Josie stands firm, though, and Hank doesn't push it, but he does pronounce them partners for life and seals this with a creepy blood oath. He leaves and she, trance-like, smears their comingled blood across her lips, either completely unaware or unconcerned that she's living during the apex of the AIDS epidemic.

Catherine is in her office at the mill trying in vain to find the real account ledger. She confronts Pete, but he says he knows nothing about it. She pleads, plays up the love they once shared, that though soured was still real. A summer's indiscretion, she calls their romantic origin, and decades later there they are. It's a touching glimpse into their relationship, if fraudulent on Catherine's part. She tells him she's in trouble and he's the only hope she has. It works because Pete is the ultimate softie and willing to believe in the good in people even when there isn't any.

At the station Andy's being championed in retellings of his heroic feat at the arrest of Jacques Renault. Everyone's impressed, including Lucy. He takes advantage of this break in the clouds to try and repair the coldness between them. It works like gangbusters and they smooch like only Lucy and Andy can. While pausing to come up for air, Lucy reveals her frigidity was caused by the fact that she's presently pregnant. Andy reacts by saying nothing and leaving, which causes Lucy's coldness to returns chillier than ever. The scene ends with a call supposedly from Bobby posing as Leo leaving a message for the Sheriff to check out James Hurley because "he's a real easy rider."

Jacques, in the hospital now on account of his gunshot wound, is being questioned by Coop and Truman. They want to know, on the record, if he took the Laura and Ronette to his cabin the night in question. He admits he did, and that it wasn't the first time; the cabin is where the Flesh World photos were taken. He says that night he and Leo ended up fighting over drunken nothings that ended when Jacuqes got hit in the head by a whisky bottle, which caused him to bleed profusely. He says he used Leo's shirt to soak up the blood, then staggered outside and passed out. When he woke up, Leo and the girls were gone. He claims he doesn't know anything about the train car, says he ended the night by coming down the hill to find Leo's car gone, so he walked home. Weighing all this, Coop and Truman figure Leo is Laura's sole killer, and he's on the lam. Turns out Jacoby is alive, and Doc Hayward describes to Coop everything the other doctor said about seeing Laura at the park before his assault.

Pete and Catherine are tearing up their house searching for the ledger. In the midst of this, Catheirne takes a call telling her the ledger is at a specific spot inside the mill, then hangs up. It's Hank making the call on behalf of Ben and Josie. Catherine goes, but not without a gun.

Off the phone, Hank tries to charm Norma with jokes about prison beds. He's laying on the reformed- and penitent-husband shtick pretty thick, but she's letting him. He's thinking about their future, the many ways he can make up his many transgressions. He seals this promise with a kiss that leaves her unsettled.

Big Ed comes home to find Nadine overdosed in her prom dress. He calls 911.

Coop, Truman and Doc Hayward return to the station to start the hunt for Leo when Lucy gives them the message presumably left for them by Leo about James. Lucy dabbles in a little sleuthing of her own when she adds she could hear a clock tolling in the background of the call, like the one at Easter Park. Coop moves surveillance from Leo and Shelly's house to the park. James shows up with news to share and Coop – who's read the message from "Leo" – steers him into a conference room while handing off the message to Truman. Truman reads it and starts for the parking lot but can't get out of the building before Leland Palmer is in his face asking to know if it's true what he's heard, that they have Laura's killer in custody. Truman will only say that they have a suspect, and splits. Doc Hayward tells Leland he should go home, be with Sarah, and Leland agrees but asks slyly if Doc is going *back* to the hospital, correctly intuiting his presence at the station. Doc says no, but that's all Leland needs to know: his daughter's killer is at the hospital.

James gives Coop the coconut tape. He says the killer is all but named on it: they're looking for a guy with a red corvette. Coop breaks the news of Dr. Jacoby's health scare and wants to know what kind of dangerous game James has been playing? That's when Truman comes in and drops on the table the bag of cocaine Bobby planted in James' motorcycle's gas tank. Nice EASY RIDER reference, Bobby. James has some explaining to do.

Back at One Eyed Jacks, Ben Horne finally gets the Icelanders to sign the investment papers for the Ghostwood Estates development project. Ben gets a brief call from Hank updating him on the hunt for Leo. Ben advises him to proceed.

Bobby meanwhile is lurking around Leo and Shelly's place looking for her but comes across the man of the house instead. Leo goes after him with an axe and knocks the boy into a corner but gets shot through the window – as he shot Waldo – before he can deliver a fatal blow. Bobby raises up enough to see it was Hank who shot Leo, but not enough that Hank can see him. Leo isn't dead, but he isn't in good shape. Bobby leaves him like this as the latest episode of INVITATION TO LOVE plays in the background.

The clock is ticking down on the bomb at the mill and Shelly's still tied up. Catherine shows up looking for her ledger and finds the girl just as the timer goes off and the fire is ignited. Catherine cuts Shelly loose and the two of them run for it as the mill is engulfed in flames.

At the hospital, Leland sneaks around and sets off the fire alarm to give himself some privacy with Jacques Renault, the man he believes killed Laura. He uses this precious time to smother the man to death with a pillow.

The mill is burning to the ground and people have arrived on the scene. Pete notices Catherine's car is in the parking lot but there's no sign of her among the crowd so he runs inside the conflagration to try and save her.

Ben and the Icelanders decide to celebrate their new deal by banging some high class escorts. Ben himself is especially eager to visit with the new girl. Blackie has her all ready for him. Audrey's getting a playing card she selected from Blackie's deck earlier, the queen of diamonds, stitched onto her lingerie. That's when the knock comes and Ben lets himself in. He can't see her, but she recognizes the voice of her father. **Worst. Case. Scenario.** On, like, half a dozen fronts. This begs the question: what was her best-case scenario?

Coop is returning to his room after a long night, updating Diane about the one suspect in custody and the one still at large. He notes with glee the lack of noise connoting the Icelanders' absence; he's anticipating a good night's sleep. In his room there's another note from Audrey under his door, telling him about the perfume counter connection to One Eyed Jacques and her intention to investigate, but before he can read it, the phone rings. The call is garbled, Coop can't understand it. There's a knock at the door. Coop sets the phone down to answer it, as he's expecting room service with a glass of warm milk. The call clears up, it's Andy saying that Leo's been found shot. And it isn't room service at the door, but an unseen gunman who shoots Coop in three times in the chest. There's your cliffhanger.

This was the first and only episode of the series directed by co-creator Mark Frost, and it turns out he's somewhat playful behind the camera. There are a few sight gags – like Hank positioning himself so it appears antler mounted on the wall are coming out of his head – and some daring visuals – like Doc Jacoby's eye transitioning to a spinning roulette wheel – that make the episode distinct, as well as some shots like the one above that tingle with noir. Frost directed only two other times, once before TWIN PEAKS, an episode of HILL STREET BLUES, and once immediately after, the 1992 political drama STORYVILLE with James Spader. Frost also wrote the episode, which is why it's so good at being not exactly what people were hoping for – a hard and fast resolution – but rather the intimation of that plus a whole lot of new, equally intriguing stuff to chew on. Is Coop dead? Who shot him? Is it the same person who killed Laura? Is it the same person who assaulted Dr. Jacoby? Or someone entirely different? In terms of cliffhangers, it's a pretty stellar one – up there with Who Shot JR?, which influenced this, and Who Shot Mr. Burns, which was influenced *by* this – but that's just one of the many ledges Frost leaves us on. There's the burning mill with Catherine, Shelly, and Pete inside. There's the shooting of Leo – which mean he couldn't have shot Coop – by Hank. And of course there's the unwitting incest brewing at One Eyed Jacks between Ben and Audrey. And these are just the subplots.

In terms of the Laura Palmer case, it seems like it's been narrowed down to Leo Johnson as the sole killer, because as Coop notes, Jacques Renault is too dumb to lie. Leland gets a little (mistaken) vindication, and from that we get an indication as to the depths of his mental deterioration. His killing Jacques might have been emotion-based and fueled by madness, but the method by which he gained access to Jacques and his sudden emotional shift when that access became threatened by returning personnel indicates more than mere madness, it indicates an awareness of deed, intent, purpose, which makes Leland not a blindly-grieving father, but a murderous avenging angel.

It would be another four months before TWIN PEAKS returned, a thing the cast and crew learned only a few days before the season one finale aired, and in that intervening time the hype and interest surrounding the show would only blossom thanks in very large part to the release of the book THE SECRET DIARY OF LAURA PALMER ("as seen by" Jennifer Lynch, David's daughter and the director of BOXING HELENA, SURVEILLANCE, and CHAINED), and in small part to the increased visibility of its stars, namely Kyle MacLachlan, who hosted the series premiere of SATURDAY NIGHT LIVE the night before the second season of TWIN PEAKS premiered. The world was waiting to see what happened next, not realizing they were on the precipice of the oddest arc television had (has?) ever seen, one that would provide a resolution, yes, but in the process of doing so would also open another door on a place both wonderful and strange.

SEASON TWO

"Harry, I have no idea where this will leave us, but I have a definite feeling it will be a place both wonderful and strange."

FBI Special Agent Dale Cooper

EPISODE 8: "MAY THE GIANT BE WITH YOU"

Directed by David Lynch, Story by David Lynch & Mark Frost, teleplay by Mark Frost

Airdate September 30, 1990

Season two bows with this extended episode written by series creators Frost and Lynch and directed for the first time since episode 2 by Lynch. In-between seasons there was slight development in the form of THE SECRET DIARY OF LAURA PALMER, the book released in the summer of 1990 written by Jennifer Lynch, David's daughter. The strongest takeaway from this document is that Laura's bad girl persona is the result of fear, she's escaping however she can the malignant presence of BOB.

The show picks up precisely where it left off with Coop lying on his hotel room floor, three bullets in his chest. That warm milk he ordered from room service finally arrives, delivered by an older and somewhat out-of-touch waiter (played by veteran western actor Hank Worden, THE SEARCHERS, RED RIVER). Coop asks him to call a doctor, but instead the waiter hangs up the room phone, which had a concerned Deputy Andy on the other end of the line. The waiter doesn't seem to understand what Coop wants or obviously needs, and rather than trying to sort it out, he makes Coop sign for the milk. Then the waiter leaves, but not before telling Coop he's heard about him and flashing him a thumbs up. He returns twice more in the same half minute to flash the thumbs up again before ultimately leaving for good. Coop isn't left alone long, though, because a bald, bow-tied giant materializes over him. The giant has a message for Coop and it consists of three things, but before he tells them, he wants to know if these things come true, will Coop believe him? That depends on who he is, is the gist of Coop's reply. The Giant says to think of him as a friend. Coop asks where he comes from, to which the Giant retorts the real question is – where has Coop gone? Then he reveals the three things: 1) there's a man in a smiling bag, 2) the owls are not what they seem, and 3) without chemicals he points. The Giant then takes Coop's ring and promises to return it when Coop finds these clues to be true. The Giant says "they" want to help him, and one last thing: Leo's locked inside a hungry horse; there's a clue at Leo's house. The Giant dematerializes. Welcome back to Twin Peaks, everybody, and welcome back David Lynch.

At One Eyed Jacks Ben Horne is closing in on the new girl, not realizing she's his daughter Audrey. In other quarters his brother Jerry is with Blackie, who's hankering for some heroin, which he provides. Back in the boudoir Audrey's running out of places to hide from her horny father. She dons a mask at the last second, but Ben only finds her perceived playfulness all the more alluring. He pleads his case as the brothel's owner, but before he can discover her true identity, Jerry calls him away. But now Audrey knows her father was involved with Laura, sexually at least, and at worst, murderously.

Back in Coop's hotel room, he's still lying on the floor bleeding and unattended. He reveals while talking to Diane via his microcassette recorder that only one of the bullets wounded him, in his abdomen, the bureau-required vest stopped the other two from doing any greater harm. In the midst of this conversation he notices his ring is actually gone. He then cites a wishlist should he survive this ordeal: he wishes to treat people with more care and respect moving forward, he wishes to climb a tall but not too-tall hill and sit in the cool but not too-cool grass with the sun on his face, he wishes he'd cracked the Lindbergh kidnapping case, he wishes he could make love to a beautiful woman he has genuine affection for, and he wishes to visit Tibet and see it free. That's a pretty beautiful list, man. And this is when Truman, Hawk, and Andy finally arrive.

Coop comes to in the hospital later and is asked about his assault. The gunman was masked, he says, so unidentifiable. Truman has Lucy bring the Agent (and the audience) up to date on everything that's happened in town since last night (deep breath): Leo Johnson was shot but is alive if comatose, Jacques Renault was strangled to death, the mill burned to the ground, Shelly and Pete have been hospitalized for smoke inhalation, Catherine and Josie are both missing, and Nadine is in a coma of her own from her overdose suicide attempt. Coop can't help but wonder how long he's been out.

Shelly is in her hospital bed watching a newscaster (played by Frost) report from the scorched ruins of the mill. She's in tears because she doesn't yet know if Leo held true to his promise to murder Bobby.

Coop when being discharged sees orderlies wheeling away Jacques Renault in a body bag. He wonders if it's smiling.

And even elsewhere in the hospital, Ronette Pulaski almost comes out of *her* coma. "Soon," the scene seems to say...

Maddy and Sarah are having some coffee at home. Maddy shares with her aunt a dream she had about the living room rug. Leland interrupts with a song on his lips and shock of stark white hair on his head, changed overnight from its normally rich, walnut hue. He does not acknowledge this whatsoever. Sarah runs off to confront him but Maddy stays behind and sees the bloody stain from her dream appear on the real living room rug at her feet. She screams. This house is fucked up.

Ben and Jerry are preparing to tie up the last 24 hours' loose ends. They need to know where Catherine is and if she's primed to take the fall for orchestrating the mill fire, and then they need a medical update on Leo's condition and a reason from Hank why that condition isn't "deceased." Then Leland sings his way into the scene. Ben and Jerry are shocked but decide to just go with it. Leland announces he's all better now and ready to return to work.

Investigating the crime scene at Leo's house, Coop and Truman determine that the shot came from outside. Coop pieces the scene together, down to the struggle *inside* with another male. They don't think Shelly is involved. Hawk found a copy of Flesh World and a gas-stinking duster, but no cocaine. Agent Albert Rosenfeld returns and Andy in his desperate attempt to alert the others steps on a loose porch board that strikes him square in the head and makes him walk around like a Raptor for a few moments. Albert predictably mocks the Deputy, but the loose board reveals hidden boots and a whole lot of cocaine under the porch.

Donna and Maddy meet up at the diner. They play with eyewear while discussing James and how he spent the night in jail. They don't know if that's because of their prank on Jacoby, so pledge to stay silent until more is known. Norma stops by with a note for Donna delivered yesterday. It reads LOOK INTO THE MEALS ON WHEELS, and nothing more, no sender info, nothing. In a corner booth the Log Lady chews her pitch gum with obvious dissatisfaction.

Albert has returned to Twin Peaks to check out Coop's injuries as per Gordon Cole's orders. Andy comes in with an answer to the last thing the Giant told Coop: he called Hungry Horse, a town in Montana where Leo was locked up on February 9th, 1988, which is the same night Teresa Banks was murdered. Teresa, you'll remember, is the hooker who turned up dead in a fashion similar to Laura Palmer, down to the typed letter embedded under her dead fingernail. These murders were thought connected, but with Leo definitively in the clear for the one, doubt is now cast over his culpability for the other.

Phillip Gerard the one-armed man appears at the Sheriff's station looking for Truman, there to sell him some boots. Truman is busy at the moment, listening with James to the tape "found" at Jacoby's. Truman knows the cocaine in James' gas tank was planted, and James remains focused on the "mystery man" Laura mentions on the tape, the man with the red corvette. Truman knows this is Leo, but James disagrees, he thinks it's someone else, not Leo at all, and not Jacques either. She said on the tape that the dude really lights her fire, which reminds James of the poem she told him back when they started secretly dating and she was all hopped up on booze and drugs. It's the "Fire Walk With Me" poem he's referring to, which he says she concluded by asking if him he wanted to play with fire, if he wanted to play with BOB? James thinks this BOB fella is the mystery man. Coop enters the room and immediately asks James for the other half of Laura's heart necklace. James hands it over and tells them where he found it – in Jacoby's coconut with the cassette – then is escorted back to his cell.

Shortly thereafter Donna arrives at the station wearing Laura's sexy sunglasses and affecting Laura's sexy attitude. She's come to see James. She wants to know what he told the authorities about the Jacoby situation, and what they're thinking moving forward. James, however, wants to know how Maddy's doing. Donna jealously takes note and kisses him forcefully and desperately. It's totally weird, and Donna is definitely in the middle of a SINGLE WHITE FEMALE moment.

Cooper tasks Lucy and Andy with searching back issues of Flesh World for pictures of Teresa Banks. He's curious if there's a parallel between her and the ads of Laura and Ronette placed by Leo and Jacques. Given Lucy and Andy's cooled romantic status, looking through pornography makes for one uncomfortable situation.

At the hospital, Coop and Truman pay Dr. Jacoby a visit. He's still recovering from his assault and subsequent heart attack. They want to know how he came into possession of Laura's necklace. He reminds them of his original statement in which he admitted to following a man in a red corvette the night Laura died, losing him out on the logging road. That's where he found Donna and James burying the necklace. He took it merely as a keepsake of his troubled and beloved patient. He reiterates that Laura was living a double life, but the last time he saw her she'd found a kind of peace. He wonders now if that peace was the resolve to die, to let herself be killed. Coop has one more thing he wants to know: Jacoby was in the hospital's intensive care ward with Jacques Renault when the latter man was killed; did he see anything? He didn't, they had him drugged, but he did remember an odor from that time, the smell of oil, like scorched engine oil.

Down the hall, Bobby pays Shelly a visit. Both are happy to see the other still alive. Shelly explains what Leo did to her, to the mill, and how he knows about them, how he's vowed to kill Bobby. Bobby's still not worried, and to prove it, they make out and say their first "I love you"s. This relationship is quite touching for all its illicit origins, and their love is second only to Norma and Ed's in its genuineness.

Speaking of Ed, Coop runs into him at the hospital. Nadine's still comatose. Ed recounts their love story: he graduated high school involved with Norma, everyone thought they'd get married but Norma got cold feet and ran off with Hank, which left Ed devastated and primed to fall into Nadine's willing arms. When it turned out Norma's romp with Hank was anything but frisky, Ed tried to get his marriage annulled, but while on their honeymoon he accidentally shot out Nadine's eye while hunting, so felt obligated to stick with her. Hawk brings James by to console his uncle. Coop sees a body bag hung up to dry and can't help but notice it looks like it's smiling. That's two things he was told by the Giant that he's since found to be true (with the Hungry Horse/Leo info). Something about this clicks and Coop announces he's ready to lay this all out, "all this" being the murder of Laura Palmer.

After his visit with Shelly, Bobby runs into his dad at the diner. They actually have a normal conversation until Bobby dares to ask what the Major does for work. This of course is classified, but the Major does share a vision he had just the night before: he was on the veranda of a vast estate with a light emanating from inside it. He knew the place, had been born and raised there and was returning after a long absence. Wandering the house he noted additional rooms that blended coherently with the original design he remembered. A knock on the front door came and it was his son, Bobby, happy and harmonious. They embraced warmly. It was a transcendent moment that ended when the Major woke feeling optimistic and confident in Bobby's future. Given that's it's happening between the most opposing characters on the show, who just happen to be father and son, this moment is truly touching, and makes for a nice emotional pairing with the soft side of Bobby we just saw with Shelly. The Briggs' cap this with well wishes and a firm handshake. Then Bobby sees Hank, causing him to remember it was he who shot Leo.

In front of a vast and varied buffet of doughnuts, Coop verbally sketches for Truman, Hawk, Andy, Albert and Lucy the night Laura Palmer died: the girl had two appointments that night, the first with "J," or James, who she was nervous about seeing because she was going to end their relationship. Before she left her house for this rendezvous, she got a call from Leo to set up her second appointment of the night with him, Jacques Renault, and Ronette Pulaski for a go-round of hard drugs and gross sex. After Laura broke James' heart and jumped off his motorcycle at a stoplight, she ran into the woods to meet with the others. The foursome walked past the Log Lady's cabin to Jacques' where they partied down. Laura was bound by her arms and Waldo the mynah bird pecked her neck and shoulders. At some point Leo and Jacques fought, resulting in Jacques passing out outside, and when he woke everybody else was gone. The way Coop sees it, Leo left the cabin alone, leaving Ronette and Laura still inside. He thinks this because of the third man that the Log Lady mentioned walking past later that night, and because of the other set of footprints Hawk found outside Jacques' cabin. Whoever this person is, he took the girls to the train car, tied them up, knocked out Ronette and then started in on Laura, his rage so focused on her that he didn't notice Ronette wake up and escape. Once Laura was dead, the killer then built the mound of dirt, put the half-a-heart necklace on it, put the letter R under Laura's left index finger and scrawled in blood "Fire Walk With Me" on a scrap of paper. Interesting forensics note here: the blood used to write these words doesn't match Laura's, Ronette's, Jacques', or Leo's, which most likely means it belongs to the killer. The type is AB negative, and matches blood on a towel that was found down the tracks from the train car, where there were also several more scraps of torn paper. That, Coop concludes, is how it all went down. The only question that remains is: who's this third man? How Wellesian.

Truman delivers Pete home from the hospital. Josie is still missing after the mill fire, but there's a letter waiting that might hold the answer. Sure enough it's from Josie, saying she had to leave town on a business emergency and is in Seattle. This is regular behavior, Pete says, she goes quite often for business and shopping, so that's one case closed. Truman begrudgingly has to mention that they still haven't found Catherine, and tells Pete he should prepare for the worst. Pete takes this news a helluva lot harder than Catherine would were the situation reversed. An Asian man calls the house from The Great Northern looking for Josie. She of course isn't there and he doesn't give any further details, merely hangs up then immediately calls Hong Kong.

Ben and Jerry Horne are discussing their favorite subject – food – and find Hank waiting for them in Ben's office. They want to know where Josie is. He gives them the same Seattle story as the letter, seemingly proving it true. Then they want to know what happened with Leo, why he isn't dead? Hank says he's as good as, he's stuck in a coma with significant brain damage. Hank reveals here he doesn't know Bobby was inside the house, he thinks Leo had the axe because he was chopping wood. Inside. Even Jerry thinks this is ridiculous, but somehow it's accepted as truth because Leo is nuts. Ben wants to know about Catherine's fate, and while Hank doesn't know for sure what happened to her, he's pretty certain she was inside the burning mill. This pleases Ben, as it means she and Leo should take the heat for this, pun intended.

Audrey's still at One Eyed Jacks and reporting back to Blackie after meeting with the owner. Blackie tells her the owner was very disappointed with how that meeting went, of course not knowing she was his daughter. Audrey tries to talk around it, but Blackie isn't having it and issues the girl an ultimatum: put out or get out.

Over the phone, Donna arranges with Norma to take over Laura's Meals on Wheels route, based on the note she got. Then there's a musical interlude by Alicia Witt (TWO WEEKS NOTICE, DUNE) as one of Donna's younger sisters meant to entertain the family plus their dinner guests Maddy, Sarah and Leland, who's dressed in a tux for no given reason. Donna's other sister Harriett also contributes by reading a poem about Laura. Over dinner Doc asks about Leland's stark white hair. He says it just changed, like he has now: he feels he's finally turned a corner in his grief, and this makes him feel like singing. So he does. "Come On Get Happy" is the song he picks. This time, though, it isn't so creepy, everyone seems buoyed, until he starts speeding up too much, loses the thread, and passes out. He comes to, but only physically; mentally, he's not all there.

Coop's in bed talking to Diane. He's now blaming the Giant vision on the combination of his injury and sleep deprivation. He turns off the light. Simultaneously at One Eyed Jacks, Audrey is trying to reach her Special Agent telepathically to let him know she's in trouble. She's hoping by now he's seen the note she slipped under his door last night telling him where she is and what she's done, but of course, it got lost in the confusion of his shooting and is now hiding out of sight under the bed.

The Giant returns to Coop that night. Coop knows this time he isn't dreaming. The Giant forgot to tell him something: don't search for all the answers at once. He says one person saw the third man the night Laura died, and three have seen him since, but not his actual body. Only one of these, known to Coop, is ready to talk now. And one last thing: you forgot something. The Giant then creates a ball of light that goes into Coop's throat, and the Giant is gone.

At the hospital, Ronette has truly terrifying visions of Laura being viciously murdered by BOB in the train car, and awakens.

All in all, then, season 2 opens with a big damn bang. Right from the first scene they're tackling all the loose ends from the season 1 finale, *and* they take giant strides – pun intended – towards starting to wrap up the case of Laura's murder. Lynch returns to direct and he and Frost collaborated on the script for the first time since episode 3, and as such this is a re-establishment of the narrative and visual aesthetics that make TWIN PEAKS TWIN PEAKS. They bring back the expected quirks – for example the local who hollers, "Hot damn that's good pie!" in the first diner scene – and they throw a heap of the unexpected on us by turning a major corner in the central mystery. This was the first full season order the series received, meaning unlike season 1, there were 22 episodes to air this time around, three times as many as had already aired, and with 21 still to go, audiences were starting to realize that they were on the verge of a solution. The final sequence of the episode – which for my money is the most frightening TWIN PEAKS ever gets with the shrieking and screaming and killing and that terrible, terrible eye contact from Laura – made it a certified fact that BOB was Laura's killer. That would be like THE X-FILES finding definitive proof of aliens a dozen episodes in to its 10-season run. The only questions left, it would seem, are who exactly is BOB, and where is he? That is, those would be the only questions left if in revealing them, Lynch hadn't also asked a much larger question, one that would set the tone for the show past the "resolution" of Laura Palmer's murder: sure, there's an ending coming, but what the hell is it going to be?

The decision to wrap up the central mystery sooner than later came from the network, not Lynch and Frost, and this for many folks is the central executive decision that tanked the show. If the creators had been left to their own devices, who knows how or for how long they might have let the case play out. But that wasn't what happened, as even with phenomena the bottom line trumps the narrative, and as a result we got this episode, which can be viewed, I think, as almost like the other side of the coin of the quiet and atmospheric pilot, or a negative version. There's so much information crammed in here the characterization is mostly expository, in contrast to the pilot, where the info was scant and the characters took center stage. Wherever we're being led at the end of the season 2 premiere, we know it's nowhere expected, which is precisely what we were expecting.

EPISODE 9: "COMA"

Written by Harley Peyton, Directed by David Lynch

Airdate October 6th, 1990

This is another episode directed by Lynch, but the last until episode 14. We open with Coop and Albert breakfasting at The Great Northern as a jauntily-clad barbershop quartet sings behind them for no reason. I mentioned this was directed by Lynch, right? They are discussing Ronette Pulaski, who has awakened from her coma but is still in shock and not speaking. Coop plans to show her the sketches of Leo and BOB – the latter drawn from Sarah's vision – to see if that jars anything. Albert has the results of the autopsy on Jacques Renault: the man wasn't strangled, he was smothered; furthermore his wrists were bound with hospital tape. That's all there is down that avenue, but Albert also has conclusive evidence that the mill was an arson job he thinks Leo set. They'll need a statement from Shelly to verify this. Meanwhile, Albert's men are still trying to figure out who shot Coop in the season one finale. These findings, however, could have been delivered over the phone and are not really why Albert returned to Twin Peaks. He speaks a name that sucks the color from Coop's cheeks: Windom Earle. Agent Earle, that is, one Albert refers to both as Coop's former partner and "retired." Agent Earle had formerly been confined to a mental institution, but he's gone now, escaped. This isn't good. As Coop silently ponders the ramifications of this news, across the room an Asian man watches him discretely but quite intently.

It's Donna's first day taking over Laura's Meals on Wheels route, a move that was prompted by an anonymous note telling her to look into the program. Her first client is elderly Mrs. Tremond and her tuxedoed grandson Pierre, who reminds Donna that sometimes things can happen just like *this* and snaps his fingers. It's worth noting that Pierre looks like a little David Lynch, down to the hair, because here he is a little Lynch, Austin Jack Lynch, to be precise, one of David's sons.

Back in the current narrative, Mrs. Tremond doesn't care for the creamed corn included in her meal, and as though this displeasure is an incantation, instantly it's gone, transported across the room into her grandson's hands. Donna is bewildered, but the curiosity is explained away as the boy practicing magic. Mrs. Tremond wants to know who Donna is, but at the mention of Laura's name, the old woman shuts down evasively. All she'll say is Donna might inquire of the agoraphobic Mr. Smith next door, he was Laura's friend. Pierre speaks in French: "Je suis une ame solitaire" ("I am a lonely soul."). This is all just weird enough to get Donna out of there, and when she tries Mr. Smith next door there's no answer so she leaves him a note. Smith is absolutely home, though, and watches her go through the blinds.

Ronette is still in shock but is now responsive. After some trouble adjusting the heights of their chairs, Coop and Truman get down to the business of showing her a few sketches. Leo's first: she indicates he is not the man who hurt her. Then she's shown the BOB sketch, and him she knows. She starts seizing and trying to say something in her distress: "train car." I think we all know what that means.

Meanwhile, Ben and Jerry Horne are in Ben's office with both of Catherine's mill ledgers, the real one that shows the mill's decline into bankruptcy at Catherine's hands, and the fake one that shows the mill turning a healthy and hearty profit. The brothers are trying to figure out which one to burn to best suit their plan, which is to buy the ruined mill land from their co-conspirator Josie and transform it into the Ghostwood Estates development. It proves too tough a decision to make in the moment, however, so instead they toast marshmallows.

BOB posters – Have You Seen This Man? – are going up all over Twin Peaks, he's now officially the main suspect in Laura's murder. At the diner the Log Lady has coffee with Major Briggs. Her log has something to tell him: deliver the message. As vague and brusque as this is, Briggs immediately understands.

Andy demands an audience with Lucy to explain his reaction when she told him she was pregnant, why he was so pissed: he's sterile. And that doesn't mean he can skip baths, it means he can't have babies, so he wants to know how she's having one? She doesn't answer him.

Hank shows up at the station to sign in with Truman, a condition of his parole. He does so flippantly and leaves. Coop interprets from the iciness between them that Truman and Hank used to be friends. Truman says they grew up together and Hank used to be a Bookhouse Boy, one of the best. I know TWIN PEAKS' fans are a little skittish on the idea of prequels, but man oh man what I wouldn't give to see a STAND BY ME-esque series or film about Truman, Hank, Hawk, and Ed as adolescents. Call me, Mr. Frost. Speaking of the telephone, a call from Ben Horne interrupts this disappointing stroll down Truman's memory lane: Audrey is missing, and maybe has been for two days.

Ben and Leland are meeting when Jerry shows up at The Great Northern with Catherine's insurance policy, unsigned. It seems she had some concerns – rightfully so – about Josie being named her chief beneficiary. This is a minor problem to Ben; Catherine's dead, that's all that counts. They call their development investors to make sure everything's copacetic, but the Icelanders are upset about the mill fire, which they aren't supposed to know about but do know about because Leland called them and let them know about it. As Ben and Jerry smooth this over, Leland notices the wanted flyer for BOB and becomes quite transfixed by it. He knows this man, he says, this man lived next door to Leland's grandfather's summer place on nearby Pearl Lakes when Leland was a little boy. Leland is certain of this and leaves immediately to tell Truman. Jerry then asks the truest question of the entire series, the same question the audience has been asking itself for nine episodes: "Is this real, Ben, or some strange and twisted dream?"

Doc Hayward is updating Shelly on Leo's condition: he's still in a coma after being shot. The bullet was lodged by his spine and while they were able to remove it, they can't tell yet whether Leo is paralyzed. He lost a lot of blood, which led to the coma and probable brain damage, but it's tough to get a complete and accurate assessment of his condition just yet.

At the station, an anonymous call comes for the Sheriff, but Lucy won't transfer it without the caller's name, so instead she hangs up.

At One Eyed Jacks, Audrey is finally seeing a client. She arranges to take over the playtime of Emory Battis, Horne's Department Store manager. Battis particular fetish involves toenail polish, restraints and a blindfold, a running vacuum, and a bucket of ice. God only knows. Once Audrey and Battis are alone, she removes his blindfold and reveals herself. She threatens to go to the cops unless he tells her everything he knows about Laura, Ronette, the department store's perfume counter, and One Eyed Jacks. Literally in no position to do otherwise, he confesses Ben has him picking girls from the counter and sending them up here to work as "hospitality girls," Laura and Ronette included. Laura only came once, she was using drugs so got kicked out and never came back. Audrey wants to know if her dad knew Laura was here. He knew, and he *knew*, the italicized one connoting the Biblical sense. She wants to know if Laura knew Ben was the owner of One Eyed Jacks. She did. That's not going to help Audrey's daddy issues one bit.

Bobby and Shelly are parked by the river listening to some tunes and plotting their future together. Leo's looking at a lot of disability pay coming, a cool 5k a month, so long as he stays out of prison. As a near-vegetable, this is a possibility they can help along. Shelly doesn't care, she's glad Leo could be out of her life, but Bobby sees easy money. As long as Shelly doesn't give a statement about Leo and the mill fire to the authorities – which as his wife she can't be compelled to give – then they can't arrest him, and he comes home with all that money. Shelly relents, and they seal their scheme with some hot making out.

51

In Coop's room at The Great Northern, he still hasn't found the envelope Audrey left for him the night he was shot which tells him where she is. He's talking to Diane about the escape of Windom Earle and how troubling it is to him, as is the news Audrey is missing. These are both emotional bothers, we can tell, not professional ones. He's interrupted by a knock at his door. It's Major Briggs, there to deliver the message the log "spoke" of. While he can't reveal to the Special Agent the exact nature of his line of work, he can divulge that among his many duties is the maintenance of deep space monitors aimed a galaxies far, far away. Routinely these monitors receive communications, which are almost always dismissed as space garbage but they have to scan them nevertheless to be sure. He shows Coop a spreadsheet of gibberish, descrambled radio waves that were received by the monitors right up until the moment Coop was shot. At that point the readout changed. Among the gibberish appeared a single sentence in English: "the owls are not what they seem." Coop is fascinated, of course, because this is one of the things the Giant said to him last episode, but he can't figure why Briggs knew to bring this to him. Because of the second message, Briggs points out, delivered later the next morning: "Cooper." Over and over again.

James, Donna and Maddy cut a track in Donna's living room called "Just You and I," a haunting twist on 50's doo-wop that was entirely improvised by Lynch, Angelo Badalamenti and James Marshall ("James") on set while shooting. It's creepy if well-meaning and involves a lot of longing stares between what is slowly becoming a love triangle, because it looks like James might be falling for Maddy, or at least the memory of Laura he sees in Maddy. Donna picks up on their burgeoning connection and flees melodramatically, forcing James to rush after and assure her of his devotion with copious smooches. Donna then gets a call from Harold Smith, who has found her note and wants to meet tomorrow to talk about Laura. While Maddy's in the Hayward living room waiting for her friends to return, she slips into a vision of BOB coming to kill her. The ethereal calm of the scene's beginning is violently shattered with another song at the end, that of Maddy's unbridled screams.

The end is a series of images from Coop's subconscious: the Giant waving, Ronette seizing in her hospital bed, BOB blurred against a background of nothingness, "the owls are not what they seem," repeated flashes of the Giant standing over him, of Coop sleeping then awake in a wash of white light, of a hiding BOB with his face turning into an owl, of Sarah coming down the stairs at the Palmer house, of a laughing BOB slowly coming into focus, then a real phone call wakes him. It's Audrey. Instead of just doing the obvious and intelligent thing of telling him precisely where she is, tells him instead only that she saw him in his tuxedo, he looked like a movie star, and she's been in trouble but she's going to come home now. Unfortunately, that's as far as she get because Blackie kills the call, having overheard everything she just said. Furthermore, Battis is with her and has spilled the beans on her true identity and reason for coming to One Eyed Jacks. The jig, as they say, is up.

Another episode under the direction of Lynch lends to the continuing re-establishment of the TWIN PEAKS' aesthetic, and him at the helm of the season's first two episodes meant the weird-quotient got turned way up, but this time it was not just technical but narrative: this is the episode that starts looking beyond Laura's murder, this is where we get the first mention of Windom Earle, some specifics on Major Briggs' mysterious job, and a whiff of the scheme Bobby & Shelly are cooking up involving Leo and his money. These are the storylines that give us our first glimpse of what TWIN PEAKS looks like after its central mystery is solved, and all indications are that there are as many secrets surrounding this town as there are trees. While at the same time, however, the strange appearance of the Tremonds, the mention of misleading owls, and the intro of Harold Smith – among other things – says that while we might know it was BOB who killed Laura, there are still myriad things about that night and this girl that have yet to come to light. Problem is, at this point we're not sure we want to know what they are...

EPISODE 10: "THE MAN BEHIND GLASS"

Written by Robert Engels, Directed by Lesli Linka Glatter

Airdate October 13th, 1990

This week's episode opens on a frantic note with Ronette Pulaski thrashing about violently in her hospital bed, seizing and ripping out her IV. She has to be restrained and sedated, and only then is it determined by Albert that her IV has been tainted by someone, someone who, Coop discovers, also slipped a small typed letter under her fingernail, the same sort as was found on the bodies of Laura and Teresa Banks, which indicates this attack was meant to be fatal. The letter is B. Truman doesn't understand how any of this is possible as there's been a guard on the room 24 hours a day, but the proof can't be denied. Since the letters were never made public, Coop knows this can only be the work of the one true killer. He tells Albert and Truman about his visit by the Giant and the three things he told Coop. They take this odd news as well as anyone would.

Donna meets with Harold Smith, the agoraphobe on Laura's Meals on Wheels route and the man she was told by the mysterious Mrs. Tremond who might know something about Laura. Harold is a surprise – not the old shut-in Donna was expecting but a younger, handsome man – and furthermore reveals he knows who exactly Donna is, Laura had wanted him to get in touch if anything ever happened to her. His apartment is unusually warm because he grows a ton of orchids inside. He wonders if Donna might do him the favor of taking one of the flowers to lay at Laura's grave. Of course she will, and he steps away to prepare it. While he's out of the room, she spies a piece of paper sticking out of his bookshelf and moves to investigate. Before she can learn anything, though, Harold re-enters with the orchid. She takes it and leaves but says she'll return, which he obviously likes the sound of.

At the station, Coop is going over with Truman the three letters they have – R, B, and T – from the three victims of BOB – Teresa Banks, Ronette Pulaski, and Laura Palmer, respectively. As far as Coop knows, there are only four people involved with the investigation who have seen BOB: Sarah Palmer and Maddy Ferguson in visions, himself in a dream, and Ronette in person. Albert proceeds with his latest findings: the cocaine found in James' gas tank matched the traces found in Jacques Renault's apt and at Leo Johnson's house. The supposition is Leo planted it on James, but they can't exactly ask Leo because he's pretty much a vegetable after being shot. The boots found under the porch at Jacques' cabin haven't been worn, and the letter planted under Ronette's fingernail was taken from an issue of Flesh World. Pictures of the BOB sketch have been sent nationwide but so far no one has him in any database. And lastly, Coop was shot with a Walther PPK, best known as 007's gun, but that's all there is to know about that situation. Albert and Truman have yet another clash of personalities that leads to a minor scuffle during which Albert reveals himself to be an aggressive pacifist whose philosophy, like Gandhi and MLK, is based on a foundation of unconditional love. He tells Truman he loves him, then he leaves. It's the most beautiful moment of male bonding I've ever seen.

James is released from jail, but Coop's tired of the boy's interference and sternly tells him so. James goes, and Dick Tremayne (Ian Buchannan) enters. Apparently he's another paramour of Lucy's, as well as the menswear designer for Horne's fashion store. Lucy's a little miffed at him and he notices so offers to take her to lunch. Dutch, of course.

Then Leland Palmer shows up at the station with the wanted poster of BOB he saw at The Great Northern. He tells Coop, Truman and Hawk that he knows this man from when his was a little boy, he was Leland's grandfather's neighbor at Pearl Lakes; he thinks the man's name was Robertson. This aligns with the three letters pulled from the girls' fingernails. There's one last thing Leland remembers: Robertson used to flick lit matches at him and asked if he wanted to play with fire. This aligns with what James told Coop Laura said her mystery man often asked her. This was revealed in the conversation Laura and James had the night she recited the "Fire Walk With Me" poem to him, and the same conversation, we all remember, when she also said her mystery man asked if she wanted to play with BOB. Adding all this up, Coop's convinced this Robertson is their man.

Dick and Lucy dine at the Double R. He's a self-absorbed bore and no kind of gentleman. Lucy reveals they had a thing – a romantic thing – but it's been six weeks since he called her. He lamely claims he lost her phone number, but she's not letting him off the hook that easy. She says they'd been going out for three months, he'd made promises to her, including a trip to Seattle. They were intimate. Then he ghosted her. He offers to buy her a dress to make up for things. She thinks that's a grand idea, and suggests one from the maternity department. Dick falls uncharacteristically quiet.

In a booth nearby, James is asking Maddy if Donna seems a little different lately; she's been smoking, acting all tough, and wearing those sunglasses of Laura's, not to mention the way she kissed him in jail. Maddy doesn't care for this last detail but James doesn't notice, as he's too preoccupied with his own angst, and is contemplating taking a bike trip to clear his head. Maddy consoles him by taking his hand, and this is the opportune moment when Donna happens to walk in. Naturally, she misreads the situation and proceeds to play up Harold Smith as a handsome, charming, smart man, "completely unlike" anyone she knows. James, ever the dullest tool in the shed, doesn't catch her drift, but Donna doesn't bother to explain it to him and instead bolts in a huff.

Audrey is still at One Eyed Jacks where she's been revealed as Ben Horne's daughter and as such is bound, gagged, and being drugged by Blackie and Emory Battis. Battis wants to get rid of her because she knows Laura briefly worked there and she knows it's her own dad who owns the joint. It's because of all this, though, that Blackie's willing to bet Ben will pay handsomely to get his daughter and his secrets back, and with that kind of money she could buy him out of One Eyed Jacks and own the place free and clear. In the meantime and for good measure, she's going to turn Audrey into a heroin junkie, just like Ben did to her.

Phillip Gerard the one-armed man is showing Truman some of the boots he sells. While talking up his product, he sees the wanted poster of BOB and gets lightheaded. He asks to use the bathroom so that he might take his "medication. "

Truman takes this opportunity to meet with Shelly, who is waiting in his office at his request. She saves him the pitch, though: she's not going to make a statement against Leo regarding the mill fire and her abduction/attempted murder. Truman tries to talk her into it, saying they already know the truth, they just need her to verify it, but she sticks to her stubborn guns. Coop jumps in and gives it a reverse-psychological go, but that doesn't work, either. The girl's mind is made and that's where it's staying. When she leaves, Coop says he knows her refusal is part of an insurance scam, he just can't figure out who's helping her.

In the bathroom, meanwhile, Gerard's trying to shoot up something but starts having an episode, twitching, contorting, grimacing and groaning, but then stops as suddenly as he started. He emerges from the stall calm and calling for BOB, saying he knows the man is near and to beware, for now Gerard is after him. This transformation is reminiscent of at least two other Lynchian plot points: the abandoned film scenario ONE SALIVA BUBBLE that Lynch and TWIN PEAKS co-creator Mark Frost were working before the series that was supposed to be an "identity-switching comedy," and the transformation that takes place halfway through LOST HIGHWAY; in both instances, one man enters the scene, another man leaves.

At The Great Northern, the Asian man seen earlier is still lurking and observing as Coop is asking Ben if he's heard anything further from Audrey. Ben hasn't. Coop has, though. She called him last night and though she didn't say where she was, she referred to his tux, which he was wearing in this very hotel the night he got shot. He was also wearing it at One Eyed Jacks that same night but somehow seems to miss this connection, which is certainly odd for Coop, and one of his only investigative blindspots in the entire series. Ben, however, isn't too concerned because he says Audrey is willful and goes missing on occasion. Coop reminds Ben that missing girls in Twin Peaks are kind of a problem at the moment. Ben can't help but wonder if the Special Agent's interest is more than professional, which of course it is. Ben tries to warn him off, tells him men often fall under Audrey's spell; Coop should try and steer clear. The Asian Man, who has seen and overheard all this, follows Coop when the conversation ends.

As for Audrey, she's coming out of her dope haze in her room at One Eyed Jacks. A new man and woman are at her bedside. By his accent, the man is French Canadian. He gives her candy because post-heroin she needs the sugar. He says his name is Jean, then dopes her up again. He next appears as Battis and Blackie are watching Coop on a security tape. Battis recognizes Coop as the FBI agent assigned to the Palmer murder. That's when Jean – Jean *Renault*, brother to Jacques and Bernard as Blackie identifies him (and played by Michael Parks, KILL BILL, RED STATE) – decides he wants Cooper for himself because of the Agent's hand in the loss of both his brothers. He'll act the go-between for Blackie in obtaining Audrey's ransom so Horne won't know who's really responsible. In exchange, Battis just has to bring Coop to Jean. Battis, jellyfish that he is, agrees and goes to get the ransom tape he and Blackie made earlier. There's an insinuation that Jacques and Blackie used to be a thing, but now he's with his new lady, Nancy, who happens to be Blackie's younger, better-looking sister, which means there's some pretty bad blood between the three of them, but not bad enough they can't do business. Once Battis is gone, Jean adds the stipulation that Audrey can't be returned alive, she knows too much. No one has a problem with this.

Fun note here: as I mentioned, Jean, unlike Jacques or Bernard, speaks with a decidedly French-Canadian accent. According to actor Michael Parks, who played Jean, as quoted in Brad Dukes' book *REFLECTIONS: An Oral History of TWIN PEAKS*, he was asked to do a regular Canadian accent, but being an innovator, he thought the French Canadian had more "flavor" to it, so went with that. When he was told by episode director Lesli Linka Glatter that the other Renaults hadn't used French accents, he said, "That's their fucking problem." Easy to see why Parks was cast in the role, dude is the same hardcore, stone-cold, devil-may-care badass as the man he portrays. The issue was taken directly to Lynch for resolution. Lynch told Parks he could do whatever he wanted.

Back to it: Truman gets a call from Pete saying Josie will be home tomorrow. She's wanted for questioning in the mill fire, so the Sheriff goes to Coop for a favor: he wants to see Josie first, alone. Coop agrees. Deputy Hawk confirms there's a property at Pearl Lakes that matches the locale and description given to them by Leland as this Robertson's place. The house is boarded up and abandoned, but the Deputy has people looking into the history of its ownership. Truman asks Hawk if he's seen Gerard, the one-armed man, as he still isn't back from the bathroom. Coop reminds Truman that Gerard appeared in his dream/vision as an acquaintance of BOB, then they rush out to find him. The bathroom is empty, but the syringe with which Gerard attempted to inject himself is lying full on the floor. Coop remembers the Giant's third clue: "Without chemicals, he points."

Nadine is still in her coma but has to be restrained because according to Doc Hayward she's pumping a shit-ton of adrenaline through her system and already ripped through a set of leather cuffs. He suggests Ed sit with her, sing to her, try to soothe her troubled and damaged mind. Ed takes her hand and starts in on a few bars of "On Top of Old Smoky." It works, but only to a degree. She nearly breaks his hand then snaps the chains of her restraints and rises in bed clapping and cheering, like cheerleader-cheering. That's because she for some reason thinks she's an 18 year old high school senior. The only thing that has survived this mental schism is her love for Ed.

Jacoby's got his hospital room tricked out like a luau and is chilling with his Hawaiian wife when Coop and Truman arrive to hypnotize him, because of course they do. Coop leads the session. A little golf visualization and Jacoby is under a spell, (Truman too, almost). Cooper places Jacoby back in the ICU, in the room he shared with Jacques Renault. He reminds him of the burnt engine oil he reported smelling, but Jacoby goes back to the park where he saw Laura/Maddy, where he was assaulted and had his heart attack; he smelled the engine oil there, too. Coop tries to keep him focused on the ICU, asks him if anyone else came into the room that night. Jacoby remembers the sound of ripping tape waking him, seeing Jacques being smothered by a pillow, seeing him die and looking then to see the killer's face... Who does he see? they implore. Jacoby says only, "I know him."

At Laura's grave, Donna delivers the orchid and tells her dead friend who it's from. She then admits to the romance between her and James, but adds it isn't working now because she thinks there's something developing between him and Maddy, which would mean Donna ends up losing both Laura and James, her two best friends. She further admits to once wanting to be courageous like Laura, but look where that got the girl. She says Laura was selfish, always focused on her own problems, and those problems are still the only ones everybody's trying to solve, even though she's dead. Jeez, Don, jealous much?

As Donna is worrying about James' feelings for Maddy, though, she's really driving him into her arms, because at that very moment James is at the Palmers confiding in Maddy because he can't find Donna. His mom came home, loaded. This leads to James and Maddy sharing a sweet kiss, which Donna arrives just in time to see. What timing she has this episode. She bolts and James runs after her. Leland appears to see what all the hubbub is, and finds an upset Maddy. She's upset because people keep treating her like Laura, but she's not, she's completely different, and people keep expecting her to know something about the real Laura but she doesn't, she hardly knew the girl at all, she just came to town for a funeral. Leland consoles her, but is interrupted by Coop and Truman, who have let themselves in. Seems Jacoby said a little more after we left the scene. They're here to arrest Leland for the murder of Jacques Renault.

Donna runs right to Harold's, for some reason imposing her emotional issues on a man she's met once, for about ten minutes. Of course, Harold knows all about her, her issues, and her friends through Laura. He goes to get her something to drink. She goes to take a look at a pretty orchid but what she finds instead is a notebook with the following words handwritten on the first page...

"This is the diary of Laura Palmer..."

Once again, this episode is directed by Lesli Linka Glatter, who last helmed episode five, "Cooper's Dreams." Among Glatter's greater strengths, I think, is how she handles the playfulness of TWIN PEAKS from a technical perspective. There are lots of little cues and camera tricks that dispense TP's particular form of dark whimsy. Twice we think a conversation is occurring between two characters only to discover well into the scene that a third person is in the room; a reveal like this is startling to the point of near-absurdity, and it's a reminder that in TWIN PEAKS, out of frame never means insignificant.

Robert Engels returns to scripting duty, his first since episode 4, "The One-Armed Man," and like that episode, this one too is narratively enigmatic and dispenses clues that are as mysterious as they are revelatory. When you watch his episodes, it's easy to see why Engels was chosen to co-write FIRE WALK WITH ME with Lynch; he really seems to understand how to craft a plot that simultaneously satisfies and confounds. It's a delicious if heady cocktail.

After the dark excitement of the season's first two episodes under the direction of Lynch and the scripting of Frost, this first episode without the creators can feel a little lackluster, but that's only because equal measure is being given to the life after the solution to Laura's murder as to the solution itself. The harvest of season two is a long way off, and to ensure its bounty a score of seeds have been planted: Leland's murder of Jacques, the ransom of Audrey, the mysterious Asian man, Josie's involvement with the mill fire, Shelly and Bobby's insurance scam, the Donna-James-Maddy love triangle now with a fourth leg in Harold, Lucy's baby daddy drama, et cetera. The solution to the central mystery is within our grasp, there's not lot of road left between us and it, so the side streets are getting some attention, drawing our focus away from the main drag to the city surrounding it.

EPISODE 11: "LAURA'S SECRET DIARY"

Written by Jerry Stahl and Mark Frost & Harley Peyton & Robert Engels, Directed by Todd Holland

Airdate October 20th, 1990

This episode was troubled from the get-go. That first writing credit belongs to former drug addict and subject of Ben Stiller's PERMANENT MIDNIGHT Jerry Stahl, and as you can tell just from all the other names up there, his episode needed some help. That's because Stahl, who was by his own admission on heroin while writing the script – going as far as to shoot up in the bathroom during meetings – barely wrote anything, and what he did has been called "an absolute car wreck," and "completely incomprehensible, unusable, incomplete…with blood stains on it" by Mark Frost. This episode has more writers credited than any other, and in fact twice as many as it took to create the entire freaking series. No fault to Frost, Peyton or Engels and every ounce of it on the back of Stahl, who even had the gall to rag on his TWIN PEAKS experience in his own memoir despite being paid by the show for doing nothing. As a result this episode is a little disjointed and definitely feels cobbled together and rushed. There's a lot of information contained, and the execution isn't flawless, but the off-episodes make the on-episodes that much more enjoyable, and either way episode 11 still sets a lot of things in motion.

We open on a zooming and spinning frame that pulls out of a pinprick hole in the perforated ceiling of the interrogation room in which Leland Palmer is being read his rights for the murder of Jacques Renault. It's like the maddening gyre that starts the scene is a visual representation of Leland's internal mental chaos. He waives his rights and confesses to killing Jacques, "the man who killed my daughter." Truman asks why Leland thinks Jacques killed Laura? Because they arrested the man, he says. Leland is upset at having killed a man with his bare hands, but doesn't have any regrets.

Coop and Doc Hayward arrange to have a psychologist look at Leland in regards to a temporary insanity plea. Doc tries sympathizing with Leland's situation, but Coop won't have it: murder is murder no matter the motivation. Doc then runs into Andy, who has a question about his "sperms." He wants to know if he could take the fertility test again. Doc gives him a cup. Andy tries to be sneaky about all this, but Lucy busts him on the way to the restroom with a copy of Flesh World in-hand. This does not help her opinion of him.

Truman meanwhile says the Judge, Clinton Sternwood, will arrive in town that afternoon. He's a travelling judge making a circuit of towns throughout the county. On his docket today is Leland's bail hearing and Leo Johnson's competency examination. Truman wonders aloud if Leland will even get bail. That's for the DA to decide, Coop says. That DA is Daryl Lodwick, who is also on his way to town. Not forgetting their primary investigation, the murder of Laura Palmer, they discuss new information from Hawk, who called in from Pearl Lakes. Despite what Leland remembers, no one named Robertson ever lived next to the Palmer property there. The most recent owner lives in Montana now. Andy interrupts all this by bungling his semen sample, causing the cup to roll under a chair. As he retrieves it, Coop notices his boots, which are exactly like the ones they found under the porch of Jacques Renault's cabin. He asks where Andy got them. From Phillip Gerard, the one-armed man, of course.

As he strolls through his hotel, Ben Horne gets a tip from one of his employees that M. T. Wentz, a famed and esteemed travel writer, is coming to town. He or she always conceals their identity, pays only in cash, and is notoriously unknown, even by his or her coworkers, but a good review of The Great Northern could translate into a boom of new business. Ben agrees and wants an hourly update on any cash-paying new customers. He proceeds to his office, where he finds Jean Renault waiting for him. Jean shows Ben the video of Audrey bound and gagged, then says her captors require a large sum of money for her return, but he will require something as well. He tells Ben that One Eyed Jacks is being run by thieves and that Ben needs a partner always on premises to make sure everything's clean. Ben has no choice but to relent. Oh, and there's one last thing: Jean wants Special Agent Cooper to deliver the ransom. This is a dealbreaker. Ben, again, relents.

Donna's at the diner picking up meals to deliver in her wheels. As she leaves, Norma shares with Hank the news that M. T. Wentz is coming to town. She too recognizes the financial opportunities a good review could present, and wants to make sure they're in tip-top shape. Hank gets excited and runs out to buy some flowers, tablecloths and whatnot to spruce up the place. As he's leaving, he slyly suggests Norma should give Big Ed a call, maybe if this Wentz fella stops for gas Ed can steer him their way. She keeps her adulterous cool, says that's a good idea, she'll call him.

At Harold's abode, he and Donna toast to the memory of Laura. Harold brings out the diary Donna saw the night before and reads an excerpt from it about Laura's fantasies and nightmares and how she felt unable to share them with Donna because she was afraid Donna wouldn't hang out with her anymore if she knew what Laura was like on the inside: black and dark and soaked with dreams of big, big men and the different ways they might hold her and take her into their control. Whoa. Donna wonders if they should give this secret diary to the Sheriff. Harold says no, he's read it and there are no solutions in its pages, and besides, Laura gave it to him for safekeeping. He collects this kind of thing, people's secrets, and wonders if someday Donna might share hers. All in all, even for TWIN PEAKS this is a pretty creepy way to try and pick up a high school girl.

Ben shows Coop the video of Audrey and relates to him everything Jean said, leaving out all the parts that incriminate himself, of course. Coop wants to know why Ben is telling him instead of Truman. These people will kill Audrey, he counters, so he came to Cooper, knowing the Special Agent understands "her value." As the captors understand it, her value is a cool 125k in cash, which Ben has amassed. He asks if Cooper will deliver it, but the scene ends before an answer arrives.

Josie has returned from Seattle laden with boxes and bags of designer fashions and other big city frills. Pete's there and has to break the news to her that Catherine died in the mill fire. Josie already knows this, of course, as it was a part of her plan, and furthermore the reason she left town so suddenly and unexpectedly: to distance herself from suspicion involving the arson-murder. Pete says they're trying to plan a funeral service, but Catherine's body still hasn't been found.

Emory Battis – Horne's Department Store manager and One Eyed Jacks' recruiter – drags a drugged Audrey in front of Jean Renault because she's refusing to take her heroin like a good little hostage. It looks like Battis has gotten a little rough with the girl. Jean tells her arrangements for her release have been made and are in motion, then he kills Battis with a pistol, and swallows Audrey in an embrace perhaps meant to be comforting, but which comes across as threatening as the gunshot.

Back at the station, Andy approaches Lucy. She's still sore about the whole catching-him-on-the-verge-of-masturbation thing, though, so Coop separates them and demands to know what's happening with her. She says she and Andy dated for a year-and-a-half until she started getting a little fed up with his idiosyncrasies, such as not owning a sports coat, so she took time off from the relationship, during which she dated Dick Tremayne of Horne's Department Store, a man who by virtue of his profession owns a good deal of sports coats. But Dick was a dick, and that fizzled out, too. Coop asks if she wants to get back with Andy. She tearfully doesn't know, and rushes off. Truman catches the tail-end of this and assures Coop "she'll right out." Coop changes the subject by telling Truman he needs a Bookhouse Boy, Truman's best, but the less Truman knows, the better. Truman agrees and says he'll set a meeting at The Road House for later that night.

At the Double R a corpulent cowboy traveler comes in, and Norma and Hank assume it's M.T. Wentz. While "Wentz" is in the bathroom and Norma's in the kitchen making sure everything is perfectly made, Hank does his part by stealing the man's wallet. Meanwhile, over in the corner, Maddy's trying to make peace with Donna after smooching James. Donna's laying down Laura's whole "who said we were exclusive, I never did," too-cool-to-care bullshit then further demeans herself by intimating she's seeing someone else, too. She then tells Maddy about Laura's secret diary and asks for her help; she wants to nab it. Rifling through the wallet, Hank learns that the cowboy isn't Wentz, it's Lodwick, the District Attorney.

As a storm rages, Josie's showing off a new dress to Truman. He likes it but he's distracted. He has to know if she was really in Seattle. She swears she was and reminds him that she was afraid of Ben and Catherine. Yes, he knows, and now Catherine's dead, the mill's gone, and there's a lot of insurance money coming her way. He's got her dead to rights but she cries in mock offense until he apologizes, then she distracts him with sex. Sneaky one, that Mrs. Packard. Neither realize the Asian man who's been snooping around The Great Northern is outside the window watching them.

Judge Sternwood arrives at the Sheriff's station. He's a kindly, amiable soul, and almost as perceptible as Cooper, who Truman introduces. They all go off to confer. Dick Tremayne arrives to tell Lucy he's been miserable since they last spoke (last episode at the diner when she told him about her pregnancy) and he wants to do "the right thing," so gives her $650 for an abortion. Lucy tells him, in her own way, to cordially fuck off.

The Judge decides he won't grant Leland bail, despite knowing Leland as both a lawyer and a decent man. Leland is taken back to his cell. Then Syd comes in, a beautiful woman who is also Sternwood's travelling law clerk. They leave together and Coop asks Truman if the Bookhouse Boy is set for their meet later. Truman assures him the man will be there.

At The Great Northern, Ben sees a strange, round, mustachioed Asian man staring him down. This same man, "Mr. Tojamura," pays the desk clerk in cash. The supposition is, this is M.T. Wentz. The clerk passes him the Double R's card then calls Norma once he leaves to let her know the eagle has landed.

Josie introduces the other Asian man – the one last seen watching her and Truman get it on through the window – to Pete as her cousin Jonathan. When Pete leaves, Jonathan breaks this ruse and tells Josie her job of six years will be over once the mill insurance money comes in and the land gets sold. She says all she needs is Pete's signature, and in two days everything should be done. Good, Jonathan says, because they are both expected back in Hong Kong, where someone named Mr. Eckhardt is anxious to reunite with Josie. She claims to be ready to go and that Harry means nothing to her, but her eyes betray another truth.

At The Road House, Coop's Bookhouse Boy arrives: Truman himself.

The episode ends late at night in the diner. Everyone's gone home but Hank, who is currently sleeping in the back room. He's awakened by the sound of someone banging on the front door. He goes to answer it but no one's there, because they're somehow already inside. It's Jonathan, and he proceeds to handily beat the crap out of Hank. When he's done, he calls Hank a Blood Brother, and tells him next time they meet, he'll take his head off. There is something very believable about his tone, especially as punctuated with one last bash from a flashlight.

We've already talked about the clusterfuck behind the script for this episode. At the helm holding it all together is Todd Holland, here making his first of two appearances as director. Holland was discovered when his student film was seen by some dude named Steven Spielberg, who then hired him to write for AMAZING STORIES. Holland also directed 52 episodes of one of the greatest sitcoms ever, THE LARRY SANDERS SHOW, and won an Emmy for the series finale. Following this he moved onto MALCOLM IN THE MIDDLE where he won another pair of Emmys for directing – one for the pilot – and settled into a role as executive producer. Bottom line, Holland knows television, and can be considered one of the best director's the medium's seen in the last 30 years, so he was the perfect guy to be at the head of this derailing train of an episode. Holland keeps the various threads of narrative from getting tangled in each other, and deals out new developments alongside established stories in a way that verges on overwhelming but thankfully never gets there.

Subplots take the spotlight here, most notably the Leland arrest and the Josie deception. While the former is open ended, the latter seems to come with a definite and fast-approaching deadline. The only mention of the Laura Palmer case is a throwaway – no Robertson owned property at Pearl Lakes – but given the episodes to come, this was likely an intentional break meant to set up storylines that would survive beyond the mystery of Laura's murder.

EPISODE 12: "THE ORCHID'S CURSE"

Written by Barry Pullman, Directed by Graeme Clifford

Airdate October 27th, 1990

Morning breaks in Coop's room at The Great Northern. He dreamt he was eating a gumdrop and woke chewing an ear plug. He records a message to Diane asking her to send some replacements. Now, to stray from the narrative a moment, there's a fan theory that perhaps Diane isn't real, perhaps she's merely a creation of Coop's wounded psyche – wounded for reasons I won't spoil – and this is the scene that lends the most credence to this theory. By the next day, narratively, Cooper will be thanking Diane for the ear plugs. How he mailed the tape, it travelled across the country, reached her desk, was transcribed and complied with in time for the same day's post that then got the ear plugs back across the country to a remote corner of Washington State all within 24 hours is borderline impossible, and would seem to suggest Coop got them for himself, per the reminder he left for "Diane." Whether this is true, a fabrication, or an intentional confoundment slipped in by writers is yet to be proven, but with rumors that Diane could be played by Laura Dern in season 3, seems we could get a definitive answer soon. But I digress. Coop does his calisthenics, starting with a headstand, which causes him to locate the envelope Audrey slipped under his door the night he was shot, the envelope he lost in the ensuing chaos, the envelope that is the thing the Giant told him he forgot, and the answer to where she's being held against her will: One Eyed Jacks.

At the Sheriff's station, Hawk returns with word that two old ladies live in the house next to the Palmers at Pearl Lakes, and neither one of them is named Robertson. Lucy's on her way out of town to visit family; there's a temp on the way. Coop shares his newfound information about Audrey with Truman; this gives them an advantage.

Insurance rep Tim Pinkle (David Lander, best-known as "Squiggy" from LAVERNE & SHIRLEY) is showing Shelly and Bobby the equipment they'll use to move Leo around, as he's pretty much an immobile, unresponsive vegetable. His competency exam is set for later in the day, and if all goes well, he'll be on his way home with a big fat check soon to follow. As usual, Shelly and Bobby celebrate their windfall with some copious making out.

Court is in session at The Road House with Judge Sternwood presiding. First up is Leland, who has plead not guilty to murdering Jacques Renault by reason of temporary insanity. This is his bail hearing. The Judge reverses his earlier decision and releases Leland on his own recognizance.

Meanwhile, Donna delivers Harold his daily meal. She also delivers him a deal, more tantalizing even than Norma's meat loaf and mashed potatoes: she'll share with him her life story – becoming another chapter of his "living novel"/shut-in spank bank – in exchange for him allowing her to read Laura's secret diary, which the dead girl entrusted to him for safekeeping. He counters with a compromise: he'll read the diary to her, here, it cannot leave. Figuring half a deal is better than no deal, Donna agrees. Harold then reveals a hidden compartment in a bookshelf where he keeps his living novel notebooks, as well as Laura's diary. Donna gives him her scant biography, then plays at seduction. When that doesn't really work, she instead just snatches the diary out of Harold's hands and steps outside with it, halfheartedly attempting to pull the agoraphobe out of his element. It almost works, but then it really doesn't and Harold collapses, fetal and shivering, only present enough to reclaim the diary.

Make a point to remember how Harold's right hand trembles just before he collapses, and how he looks up and off into the distance, away from Donna. It'll be a while, and it won't involve Harold again, but this becomes a thing.

Back in court, it's time for Leo's competency exam. After hearing the arguments for and against putting Leo on trial, Judge Sternwood takes a brief recess to confer with Truman and Coop at the bar over a round of something called Black Yukon Sucker Punches (2 ounces bourbon, 1 ounce coffee-infused sweet vermouth, 1 teaspoon crème de cacao, topped with blue curacao whipped cream; Cheers) which are made by his clerk, Syd, who is also an expert mixologist, it would seem. Sternwood wants to know if Leo is the murderer of Laura Palmer. Coop doesn't think so, so Sternwood decides that Leo is not competent to stand trial, and will be sent home to Shelly as soon as medically possible. Truman informs Shelly of this. She acts pleased, but she isn't; the money might not be worth it. Judge Sternwood meanwhile cryptically advises Coop to keep an eye on the woods.

Ed brings Nadine home from the hospital. She still thinks she's an 18-year-old high school senior, doesn't recognize James, her nephew by marriage, and wants to know where her parents are. James is described to her as a schoolmate and the parents are said to be out of town. Doc Hayward told Ed there was nothing he could do to help his wife but indulge her delusions, so he's going with it. Nadine's super strength continues to manifest; this time she pulls the refrigerator door off its hinges.

Ben Horne has a meeting with Mr. Tojamura, the Japanese man everyone suspects of being travel writer M.T. Wentz in disguise. Tojamura says he represents an Asian investment group who would like to make a superior offer than the Icelanders on the Ghostwood Estates development plan. He has all the necessary documents, including commitment letters from Tokyo banks and a check for a cool five million, so on their end, everything's ready to go. Ben can't help but entertain the notion. They part and Hank enters through the office's back entrance, but is interrupted by Coop arriving for Audrey's ransom call. The call comes, the drop is set for midnight in Canada at an abandoned amusement park behind a bar called the Columbian, specifically at a horse with no head on the merry-go-round. Pretty creepy setting. The call ends and Ben hands over the 125K to Coop. Coop says nothing of what he knows about Audrey's whereabouts. He leaves, and Ben dispatches Hank to make sure both the money and Cooper are delivered to Jean Renault, while Audrey is brought home.

Donna and Maddy are at the diner where Donna's giving Maddy the rundown on the layout of Harold's apartment, including how to open the secret compartment where Laura's diary is kept. The plan is for Donna to lure Harold out of the room, then signal Maddy to come in, get the book, and get out.

At One Eyed Jacks preparing for the meet with Cooper, Jean Renault is being outfitted with a spring-loaded blade that attaches to his wrist and hides under his coat sleeve. The plan is to kill Coop then kill Audrey and use the ransom money to buy out Ben.

Andy calls Doc Hayward's office to get the results of his semen analysis. *Oligospermia* had been his diagnosis, or plainly put, "too few sperms." His latest test confirms he had it, but now he doesn't, he's good as new, he's fertile. And therefore, he's excited.

Coop and Truman are going over a layout of their own, that of One Eyed Jacks. Hawk comes in and they hide their plans (it is an unsanctioned and in fact illegal operation, after all). He's been tracking Gerard, the one-armed man, who has been staying in an area motel, but no one's seen him in a day or so. In Gerard's room, Hawk found more drugs like those found in the station bathroom, which Albert is currently analyzing. Truman dismisses Hawk and he and Coop continue to plan their rescue-raid. Andy calls Lucy at her family's, or so he thinks, but the number she left rings an abortion clinic.

Maddy, on her way to do Donna's dirty work, pops in the diner for a coffee to go. James is having dinner alone, He approaches and asks if she's seen Donna that day. She lies, says no, acts generally standoffish, then leaves. James, dumb not stupid, follows her.

Outside Harold's place, Maddy hides in the trees awaiting the signal. Inside, Donna continues sharing her story. She tells about a time when they were 13 that she and Laura put on tight skirts and went to The Road House to meet up with some older boys, "Josh, Rick, and Tim." After a while everyone wanted to go party, and Laura led the way. They went out to the woods where dancing, drinking, skinny-dipping, and kissing all ensued, with Laura at the center of it, the star to Donna's black hole. Donna got a kiss from one of the boys, Tim, but she never saw him again. She says it was the first time she ever fell in love. This story bears some resemblance to the sequence in FIRE WALK WITH ME when Laura and Donna went to the Bang Bang Bar, aside from the age of the girls. It could be that what Donna is telling Harold was the first of regular risque outings for the best friends, though given Donna's character is seems doubtful it was that regular.

Coop and Truman cross the Canadian border under cover of darkness and successfully infiltrate One Eyed Jacks. An owl hoots at their entrance. They get into the underbelly of the place, where the "hospitality girls" entertain their Johns. They spy Jean and Blackie and see them preparing the needle of smack that is to be Audrey's adieu. Harry stays put to keep an eye on them as Coop continues the search.

While they're looking at orchids, Harold finally makes a move on Donna. They kiss. He then immediately excuses himself for a minute – not weird at all – and Donna takes advantage of his pervy absence to signal Maddy.

Coop stumbles upon and apprehends Nancy, Blackie's sister and Jean's lover, and has her lead him to where they're keeping Audrey. He finds the girl in a drug-induced haze. Nancy tries to get the drop on him with a concealed knife, but he smoothly takes her down and throws Audrey over his shoulder.

Truman watches as Jean kills Blackie with his hidden blade, then Jean notices Truman and starts shooting. Before Truman can fire back, Jean disappears. Coop carrying Audrey links up with him and they make a run for it, but encounter a One Eyed Jacks' henchman with a pistol. It looks like their collective goose is all but cooked when Hawk shows up and ends things with a well-thrown knife. He saw through their hidden plans and followed them up here just in case. They all make it out unscathed, but Hank sees them and calls it into Ben. As he does, he's grabbed by Jean. In borrowing Hank's ID to see who he is, Jean grabs the badge of Lodwick instead. As there's no photo on the ID, Jean assumes Hank is the D.A.

Back at Harold's, Donna's directing Maddy to the diary while waiting for Harold to return. He does, unexpectedly. She tries distracting him with talk of orchids, but her erratic behavior betrays her, as does Maddy clumsily spilling the contents of the hidden compartment. Harold sees her take the diary, knows Donna has been playing him, and corners the two girls with a rusty garden tool. He's upset. He says if the girls want secrets, if that's all they're after, he's got the ultimate secret for them: the secret of knowing who killed you. Then he slowly rakes his own face with the tool. Creepy getting creepier.

A couple new names are running this episode, writer Barry Pullman and director Graeme Clifford. This was the first of four episodes Pullman wrote in the second season, and only his third job in the industry. After TWIN PEAKS he stuck to the realm of television, writing for shows like CRACKER and ROSWELL, and producing others such as SAVED and NEW AMSTERDAM. Clifford you might know as the director of Jessica Lange's Oscar-nominated turn, FRANCES; if you're an 80's punk like me, you know him as the director of the bitchin' Christian Slater skateboard thriller GLEAMING THE CUBE. This will be his only time at the helm of a TWIN PEAKS episode, but together with Pullman he creates a tense if largely uneventful episode. Audrey's storyline is the only thing that gets resolved, while everything else only inches along. Outside of the secret diary and Judge Sternwood's question about Leo as Laura's murder, no mention of the central mystery in made this episode, instead the spotlight is shone on burgeoning plotlines like Nadine's post-coma reversion, the mysterious Japanese offer on Ghostwood Estates, the pairing of Jean and Hank, the unfurling mystery of Harold Smith (who hasn't that much further to unfurl, truthfully); all these would seem to indicate that a resolution of Laura's murder can't be too far off.

Written by Harley Peyton & Robert Engels, Directed by Lesli Linka Glatter

Airdate November 3rd, 1990

This episode picks up right where the last one left off, with Donna and Maddy cornered by Harold Smith, his freshly-self-wounded face, and his rusty garden tool. He declares Donna a liar like the rest of them, calls her "unclean" and says she's "contaminated" him, then he charges at the girls. That's when James, who wisely followed Maddy from the diner after running into her last episode, rushes in and saves them. Donna goes for the diary but Harold snatches it back as they flee. She and James have a lovely-dovey make-up snuggle outside, to Maddy's scorned chagrin. Inside, Harold howls like BOB.

Coop, Truman and Hawk get Audrey safely to the Bookhouse, where Coop is able to deduce from her vital signs that she's been given heroin. Up until now she's been delusional, but comes out of it at Coop's touch. They have a moment of intense chemistry. It's a real pity the Cooper/Audrey romance wasn't allowed to flourish. The viewers wanted it, the writers wanted it, Lynch and Frost wanted it, but as most tellings have it, Kyle MacLachlan put the kibosh on the deal. Officially, it's said that he objected to the age difference between the characters and thought a man like Cooper would find such a romance inappropriate. Unofficially, rumor has it that Lara Flynn Boyle, who was romantically involved with MacLachlan at the time, was very much opposed to the characters hooking up, perhaps out of jealousy over Audrey's storylines trumping Donna's. Whatever the reason, the planned romance never came to be, and the ripples of this would affect more than just the arcs of Cooper and Audrey, but in fact all of the entire second season. More on that a few episodes down the line...

James and Donna send Maddy home. Donna is wearing James' jacket, so everything between them seems healed. They seal it with some good, old-fashioned teenage necking.

Truman's in his office going through mugshots looking for the man he saw kill Blackie at One Eyed Jacks. He finds him quick enough, shows Coop the shot, and explains the man is Jean Renault, Jacques and Bernard's older brother and an all-around bad dude. Truman mentions that before all the shooting started, he saw Jean and Blackie looking at video footage of Coop from the other time he'd been in the casino, which tips off Coop that he wasn't just a money-delivering middleman in this scheme, he was an intended victim, and Audrey was his bait. As much as Coop can get pissed, he gets pissed. He went outside his professional code to help Audrey, he says, then makes a quick but interesting allusion to another instance in which his personal feelings caused another for whom he cared harm. More on that later for sure. In this moment, Truman talks him back from the ledge. Their bromance is getting serious, there is no hierarchy between them at this point in the narrative, they are pledged as equals towards the same end, and increasingly that end isn't just the solution of Laura Palmer's murder, but also the safekeeping of all of Twin Peaks.

Back at The Great Northern later that night, Coop runs into Ben Horne and returns to him the ransom money. He tells Ben where Audrey was being held, but Ben feigns ignorance of One Eyed Jacks. Coop of course sees through this and tells Ben Blackie's been killed, and by who. More ignorance. So Coop tells Ben about the near-fatal amount heroin his former business-partners gave his daughter. This conjures the first genuine emotion Ben has shown during Audrey's abduction. He hugs Cooper, and his gratitude seems true, if everything else about the scenario is a lie.

Leo's been released from the hospital and has come home. Tom Brockman (Ian Abercrombie) the insurance man delivers him, along with the paperwork and a giant check for Shelley and Bobby. Only it's not so giant. It's only $700, not the 5K they were expecting. Brockman attributes this difference to taxes, fees, the usual bureaucratic rundown. This situation has just become a much, much bigger job for the two lovers. Leo groans from inside his vegetative state, but not too deep inside, it sounds like.

Donna is at the Sheriff's station telling Truman about Harold Smith and Laura' secret diary. Truman doesn't quite believe her, he thinks she and James are just up to hijinks. Why? Because the secret diary of a brutally-murdered teenage girl is typical fodder for teenage amusement? Ever seen THE BLOB, Harry? Cops thought those kids were fooling with them, too. Just sayin'. In Truman's defense, though, Dr. Jacoby's heart attack and the circumstances under which it was induced don't help Donna's credibility. She's insistent though, and eventually he relents and says he'll have it looked into. They're interrupted by the one and only David Lynch himself in his first on-screen appearance as Gordon Cole, FBI Regional Bureau Chief. Until now, his character has only been heard over the phone. He's revealed to have severe hearing impairment, complete with ancient-looking aids, and thus shouts everything he speaks and rarely registers responses correctly. It's pretty hilarious, and the best acting Lynch has ever done. Cole steals every scene he's in, and even in serious situations the humor of his performance can't be ignored. He and Truman have a semi-private conversation: he's there because Coop got shot and Albert wasn't too sold on the idea of returning to town, so Cole has the results of the other agent's lab analysis. The fibers found outside Coop's room the night of his assault match a Vicuna coat. Also, the drug in the one-armed man's syringe is unlike anything Albert has ever seen, some strange combination of stranger chemicals. And the papers found near the bloody towel down the tracks from the train car/crime scene, they were from a diary. Just then Hawk walks in with the one-armed man himself, Phillip Gerard, in custody. They have some questions for him and adjourn to Truman's office, forgetting Donna is just around the corner and has heard everything.

Ben is taken by Coop to see Audrey at the Bookhouse. It's the first time she's seen him since – unbeknownst to him – she discovered everything about the connection between him, One Eyed Jacks, the perfume counter, and Laura. Oh yeah, it's also the first time she's seen him since he unknowingly tried to bang her. She doesn't wait long to hint at this knowledge. But Ben is smart enough to calm her in front of the Fed. Audrey tries to get Coop alone to take her home, but Ben intercedes there, too, and Coop allows it.

Nadine is still convinced she's a teenager, and is stoked her parents have been gone so long, leaving she and Ed the whole house to themselves. Ed's still indulging her delusions as per Doc Hayward's orders. She's also still freakishly strong. And apparently a little randy. As Ed's about to find out off-screen, that's not a great combo.

Josie and her associate Jonathan are apparently associates-with-benefits, or so it seems as we find them dressing after implied fornication. He's gloating, she's disgusted. As a post-coital gift he gives her a one-way ticket to Hong Kong on a flight that leaves that night. She tries to stall for a couple more days, which Jonathan sees straight through as an attachment to Truman; despite the fact that she intentionally played the Sheriff for a fool, her feelings for him are real. Jonathan twists these feelings to his advantage and says either she leaves tonight as instructed, or he kills Truman. Midnight's the deadline.

Maddy and James have a lakeside conversation in which he apologizes for the emotional run-around he's put her through. She knows she was always just an echo of Laura to him, though, and that's cool, she kinda liked it. She's cool with him and Donna, too, and says it's time for her to leave town and go home to Missoula. They say their goodbyes.

Next we see her, Josie's at The Great Northern meeting with Ben. She's got the contract with Pete's signature for the mill land, and she wants her money. But it's not that easy, Ben says, as he's waiting on payments from Iceland. Josie doesn't care, she wants her money NOW. Ben senses her desperation and plays his hand: a dossier on her that holds the truth of her husband Andrew's "accidental" death. His ownership of this information means she should play ball his way. Josie counters by revealing that any harm to befall her would cause the cops to discover a safety deposit box containing enough evidence to send Ben up the river until he's old and gray. Mutually-assured destruction is a helluva game to play, but play it they do. He signs over to her the $5 million check he got from Tojamura. This concludes their business.

Bobby and Shelly are celebrating Leo's homecoming with a three-person party, complete with streamers, party hats, kazoos, and full-on getting it on in front of Leo. It's all fun and games until Leo moves; just a little bit, but enough to kill the amorous mood. Though Leo does end up facedown in a sheet cake, and that's pretty funny.

At the Sheriff's station, Cole and Cooper reunite. Cooper is told that today he reminds Cole of a small Mexican Chihuahua (pronounced *chee-wow-wow*) with no further no explanation given, though apparently it is a compliment. They retire to Truman's office to have a "private" conversation. It seems Albert told Cole that he thinks Coop's in over his head on this one. Cole mentions Coop getting shot in Pittsburgh. This is obviously a spot of shame for Coop, who explains that Pittsburgh was a different situation, and he's A-okay out here. Cole takes him at his word and the matter is dismissed. But that's not all Cole has come to talk about. Truman is invited in for this next part. It's an anonymous letter that was sent to home base addressed to Cooper. Cole comments it looks familiar and Cooper sighs, says it is. He opens it. It's a card with only a chess move typed on it, Pawn to Knight's 4. This is an opening move from Windom Earle, Coop knows. Cole says they're going to have to watch Coop's back from now on. Earle, you'll remember, is Coop's former partner and was previously mentioned in episode 9 as having escaped from an institution. His plotline – destined to be the second major one behind Laura Palmer's murder investigation – officially starts now.

Ben has decided it's time to bring Leland back into his professional fold, disregarding that the man is on bail for murder. He explains to Leland the interest in Ghostwood Estates from the Japanese party represented by Tojamura, despite the fact that he's already taken payment from the Icelanders. This means that before all the I's can be dotted and the T's can be crossed, they need to buy time. Leland has multiple solutions to this, he's on point and sharp as a tack, except for a single, small incident where he plucks fur from a stuffed white fox in the office. The look on his face makes him seem like he's hypnotized. Overall, though, Ben is pleased with Leland's efforts, and counts the meeting a success.

Truman visits Josie and finds Jonathan taking her packed bags outside. She tells him she's leaving but she won't say why, only that she sold the mill and she's going home. He tries desperately to convince her of his love, but it isn't enough, or maybe it's too much. Either way, she goes.

Ben and Tojamura are having dinner at The Great Northern. Tojamura is anxious; he's already paid Ben, after all, but no paperwork is forthcoming. Ben spins his bullshit, but Tojamura doesn't fall for it. Leland livens the tense scene by taking the microphone there in the lounge and belting out "Getting to Know You." Ben tries to coax him off stage but it turns into a forced duet. Meanwhile Pete tries to strike up a conversation with Tojamura at the bar but finds Tojamura isn't a conversationalist.

At the station, Coop, Cole, Truman and Hawk are in with Gerard, who's begging for his medicine, he can feel "the change" coming. As learned from Albert's analysis, Gerard's "medicine" has traces of various drugs dispensed to persons with multiple personality disorders. They're just about to administer him the drugs when the change happens. Gerard seizes, gags, but comes out of his fit calmer, and different. Coop asks him who he is. He says MIKE, an inhabiting spirit who's using Gerard as a host. MIKE admits coming to Coop in a dream and talking to him about BOB, who he calls his familiar, which in this context most-closely resembles the definition of a demon obeying or attending a witch, warlock, or other practitioner of the dark arts that is often assumed to take the form of an animal (remember the owl superimposed over BOB's face in Cooper's dream?). MIKE can't or won't say where BOB comes from. When Coop asks what BOB wants, MIKE says BOB is eager for fun, and to him fun is killing: "He wears a smile, and everybody run." He says BOB is a parasite feeding on fear and pleasure, and thus he needs a human host. He reminds Coop that he and BOB were once partners and then MIKE and Coop recite together the same poem: *Through the darkness of future past/The magician longs to see/One chance* out between two worlds/fire walk with me.* MIKE says he was saved from his own evil ways at the cost of Gerard's arm. MIKE says he still stays close to Gerard and enters him whenever he needs to for a single purpose: to stop BOB. He says the face they have on the poster is BOB's true face and only the gifted, or the damned, can see it. Coop asks if BOB is near now. "For nearly 40 years." Yikes. Where? MIKE describes a great house made of wood with many different rooms but all alike, and inhabited by many different souls each night. We end on a shot of The Great Northern cloaked in red light.

First up, that asterisk. The line in the poem "One chance out between two worlds," is cause for some discrepancy because depending on who you ask or where you look, the word "chance" might be "chants." According to an interview with WRAPPED IN PLASTIC magazine, Al Strobel, who plays one-armed Gerard, says the poem was originally shown to him by Lynch as handwritten, and the word was "chants," as though the way out from this place between two worlds is some form of incantation, the words to which would be: "Fire walk with me." In his book THE ESSENTIAL WRAPPED IN PLASTIC, WIP co-publisher John Thorne postulates that this means once you're in, the only way out of whatever quandary the poem suggests is to make a deal with the devil. Or a demon. Or a familiar. However, the word has also appeared as "chance" in scripts and other documents, and is in fact the presumed correct word. But following the idea that the poem's last line and most memorable refrain is some form of releasing spell, "chance" doesn't really set it up as well as "chants" does. I myself prefer "chants" and all its wonderfully dark implications, which is why at the beginning of this collection I quoted the poem using it instead of "chance."

This episode offers another stellar bit of directing from Lesli Linka Glatter who, for my money at least, is the second best director the series had behind Lynch. She maintains the atmosphere and the aesthetic tone of the series most consistently, and her own personal stamp on the material deviates the least from that aesthetic while still broadening it at the same time. It really says something, I think, that Lynch trusted her to direct an episode in which he acted.

Harley Peyton and Robert Engels wrote the script, and as we've come to expect, it's a deft balance of intrigue and taut characterization. Despite covering a lot of different ground and interacting with several smaller subplots as well as the Laura storyline, the episode is well-paced and crackles with kineticism and instills a feeling almost like gravity pulling us towards some kind of climax.

At the same time, this is the episode where all the theories went out the window and it was made crystal clear that any solution we were going to be given to Laura Palmer's murder wasn't going to be straight. The mystical elements that had been at the fringe all along now move into the center of everything. BOB and MIKE are the demons of the title, one reformed, one still lurking inside someone, where he'd been for 40 years, meaning BOB could be any of the show's adults. We're closer to the truth, all right, but we're a hell of a lot further from an answer.

EPISODE 14: "LONELY SOULS"

Written by Mark Frost, Directed by David Lynch

Airdate November 10th, 1990

This is the best TWIN PEAKS ever got. Episode 14, "Lonely Souls," is the pinnacle, the peak, not just of TWIN PEAKS but of all crime serials. Narratively, technically, and performance-wise it is a nothing short of a revelation, a tour-de-force of creativity, and one of the most memorable hours of television in the medium's history. It is also the single most important episode of the series, ahead, even, of the finale. Everything that has happened and everything that will happen in TWIN PEAKS hinges on episode 14. As such, it was entrusted to the only two men it could have been: Mark Frost on the page and David Lynch behind the camera.

As per Gerard/MIKE's revelation in the last episode, he, Coop, Truman, and Andy are fueling up on some java before hitting The Great Northern, where BOB's presence has been sensed. Hawk's there too, but he's headed to Harold Smith's house with a search warrant for Laura Palmer's secret diary, which they know from Donna Harold is in possession of. Gordon Cole's in the mix as well, and reminds Hawk about the torn pages found near the train car where Laura was murdered; they were from a diary, but not the one the police have, so maybe this new one is the match. Cole himself is off to Bend, Oregon, on a "hush-hush" assignment. Oh, if only the anthology series had been popular in 1990, TWIN PEAKS could have survived after Twin Peaks in small towns all over the Pacific Northwest.

Once they arrive at The Great Northern, Coop et al are joined by Doc Hayward and the hotel guests are lined up and paraded past MIKE to see if he can recognizes BOB's spirit in any of them. Most of these guests are seamen bouncing rubber balls, and none of them set off MIKE's BOB-dar. But then Ben Horne enters the room to find out what all this hubbub is, and MIKE collapses in a seizure. Tough to ignore a reaction like that.

Hawk arrives at Harold Smith's to find the place a mess and all the orchids cut to ribbons. The secret diary too has been shredded. Harold himself is hanging dead from a noose tied around a ceiling beam.

Coffee time at the Palmer house. Maddy tells Sarah and Leland that she has to return home tomorrow. They're distraught but of course they understand. Leland is a stronger man than we've seen him, emotionally-speaking. He seems to have really turned a corner in his grief, and while there might be some lingering wackiness, he's not the puddle of despair we've seen him until now.

As Harold's body is brought down, Coop and Truman find a note written in French pinned to it: "J'ai une ame solitaire," which in English translates into "I am a lonely soul." You'll recall this is the same thing said by Mrs. Tremond's grandson when Donna visits them; it was the Tremonds who directed Donna to Harold. Was the grandson predicting how their encounter would end? Among the debris Hawk locates what's left of Laura's secret diary.

Contrary to Shelly and Bobby's plan to make it rich off Leo's disability pay, the money coming in barely covers the money going out. They go through their options, and there aren't a lot of them. But Bobby figures Leo, with his illicit drug trade, must have been stashing cash somewhere other than a bank. Just then Leo starts screaming wildly from inside his vegetative state. He translates this into actual words – "New shoes" – then spits. Leo always loved him a fresh pair of kicks. Bobby wants to see this as a clue, however, and wonders if Leo might have bought any new shoes lately. Shelly says no, but he did have her take in a pair of boots to get repaired. Bobby has her get the receipt, he's got a feeling about this.

Audrey, recovered from her near-fatal heroin overdose, tells Ben she knows everything about One Eyed Jacks – meaning the connections between him and Blackie, Emory Battis, Ronette, and Laura. She also tells him she was "Prudence," the new girl behind the white mask he tried to bang. These revelations leave Ben uncharacteristically speechless, and compliant. She wants to know how long he's been the owner of One Eyed Jacks? Five years, he says. Did he know Laura had worked there? He did. Was he the one who sent her up there? No, Battis did that without his knowledge. Did he bang her? Ben attempts to let silence answer for him but Audrey won't allow it and repeats her question. He confesses to being intimate with Laura and gazes at a picture of her on his desk. Now, I'll admit I'm a naturally paranoid person, but I don't think you need to be paranoid to connect a picture on Ben's office desk of a teenage girl who isn't his daughter to an inappropriate relationship. Has no one ever seen this picture before? We're 14 episodes in, and he's not exactly trying to hide it, it's *on his desk*. Audrey then asks her father if he killed Laura. Ben says he loved Laura...and that's all he says. The episode is definitely being painted his direction.

Shelly very tearfully resigns her position at the diner to take care of Leo. Norma's cool about it, because of course she is, she's unflappable. She tells Shelly that no matter how much time passes, her job will be here waiting for her if ever she wants it. Then this comforting mood is shattered when Ed and Nadine – still a high school senior in her mind – arrive for some chocolate shakes. Norma doesn't understand why Ed's going along with it, but ever the good mistress she plays along as well, even when Nadine checks to make sure Norma isn't mad that she and Ed are going together now, what with Norma being his ex and all. It's a weirdly awkward encounter, even for TWIN PEAKS. The climax comes when Nadine crushes her milkshake glass with her bare hands. Blood and ice cream cover the counter, but Nadine is enthused if anything. She gives Ed a painful kiss on the lips.

Bobby and Mike Nelson show up at Shelly's with Leo's repaired boots, but she's at work. Leo's just kicking it by his lonesome in his chair. The boots aren't "new shoes," but Bobby's sure there's something to them. With a hammer he knocks off the heels and finds a microcassette tape in one of them.

Coop is at the Sheriff's station discussing the remains of Laura's secret diary with Diane via a microcassette of his own. Most of it has been destroyed, but Coop's found multiple references to a one-armed man and BOB, who seems to have been a presence in Laura's life since around adolescence (remember this is the diary published for real between seasons 1 and 2, the one started on her 12th birthday), and there are intimations of frequent molestation and abuse. BOB is referred to on more than one occasion as a friend of her father's. This is another scene geared towards the Ben Horne angle, and if you still have doubts about it, Coop concludes his analysis with the mention of an entry dated two weeks before Laura's death in which she writes "Someday I'm going to tell the world about Ben Horne. I'm going to tell them who Ben Horne really is." That's the makings of a solid case right there, and just in time to hammer the final nail in Horne's coffin of innocence, Audrey shows up to tell Coop about Ben and Laura's intimate relationship. Coop ties all this new information together with MIKE's collapse at The Great Northern. He proclaims it's time to get a warrant. You can practically hear 1990 collectively gasping.

In his office, Ben and Tojamura are finishing up their business, as Ben has accepted Tojamura's offer on Ghostwood Estates. But then the authorities interrupt. Ben tries to be Ben about it, all cavalier and dismissive, but they drop the reason they want him: for the murder of Laura Palmer. He angrily refutes the claim then tries to shoo them off, as though the matter is simply his word against theirs. When this doesn't send them away, Ben then tries to flee and has to be apprehended. They cuff him and drag him out kicking and screaming.

At the Palmer house, a record on the phonograph has ended but still spins. The camera lingers at the foot of the stairs until Sarah's hand enters the frame. This is an utterly terrifying moment. She is crawling down, obviously in some form of distress, and disoriented as well. She's calling for Leland but there's no answer.

Ben is taken to a holding cell. The Log Lady has been waiting for them because she, or rather her log, has a message for Coop and Truman. She say her log doesn't know what will happen or when, but there are owls in The Road House. Coop says knowingly, "Something is happening isn't it, Margaret?" She only says, "Yes."

Pete's making a late night cup of coffee when unexpectedly Tojamura appears in his kitchen. The Japanese man throws his arms around Pete and plants a sloppy wet one right on his kisser. Tojamura proclaims that since they met he's been strangely attracted to Pete. Pete's not having any of this, but then Tojamura's voice changes to one more familiar. And feminine. Tojamura, turns out, is Catherine in heavy disguise.

Sarah is still crawling, across the living room now. The record still spins silently. She sees a vision of a white horse manifest then disappear. She passes out. Mere feet away, there's Leland ignoring her plight and straightening his tie in the mirror with a satisfied smile on his face.

Julee Cruise and the band has them packed in at The Road House. Donna and James are there talking of Harold's suicide. Coop, Truman, and Margaret arrive and take a table. James tells Donna Maddy is leaving town. Beers and peanuts all around at Coop's table. Despite the log's warning, all is chill. And then it most certainly is not. The room goes still and silent. The band dissipates and is replaced by the Giant standing in a white-hot spotlight at the microphone. He tells Cooper "it is happening again." He says it twice.

At the Palmers, Leland is still smiling into the mirror. In the mirror, though, smiling back is BOB. Take a moment to let that really settle in. He turns from the mirror, reveals a pair of plastic gloves and gently, contentedly pulls them on. Sarah is still on the floor, still unconscious. Maddy begins to calling to them from upstairs, she says it smells like something's burning. Engine oil, perhaps? She comes down – stepping into her own spotlight – and sees Sarah. The next thing she sees is Leland/BOB charging at her, hands raised, and her death begins. The scene is brutally playful, a predator toying with its prey, taunting its helplessness. It is terrifying and horrifying, frightening and appalling. Maddy's screams are fucking real, the terror in them can't be faked. In reality, this scene was shot three times over several hours on the same day: once with BOB, once with Leland, and once with Ben Horne; actors Sheryl Lee, Frank Silva, Ray Wise and Richard Beymer have each acknowledged at one time or another that this was an extremely dark and emotionally-difficult day on set, and not a fond memory. Maddy pleads for help as Leland/BOB pummels her. He dances with her limp body and calls her Laura over and over and over. This is the Leland peeking through his inhabiting spirit, but BOB regains control, says he knows she's leaving, and smashes her face into the wall. She drops, dead. With an Exacto knife he cuts under the fingernail of her right hand.

Back in The Road House, the Giant disappears and the bar returns to normal. From the bar itself the elderly bellboy from The Great Northern (the one who delivered milk when Coop was shot) comes over and pats Coop on the shoulder, tells him he's so sorry. Everyone in the place – Donna, James, Margaret, Bobby – can sense an unknowable sadness. Donna begins to cry uncontrollably, as she did in the pilot when she realized – also untold – that Laura was dead.

Cooper stares off into space as over his expression red curtains are superimposed until they take over the frame. With this single frame, Lynch is telling us, yes, something has ended. But in its place something else has begun.

Being that this episode was directed by Lynch, there are some significant standouts, visually. Firstly, he reinforces the aesthetic he put in place by recreating images from the pilot and early episodes, both in terms of type of shot – like long, slow, pull-away tracking shots and lingering close-ups – and mirrored scenes like Donna crying, or a car racing along the curve of highway.

Then there's the revelation of BOB as Leland in the mirror, their faces switching positions from reflecting to reflected, either in both, with the eerie ticking of the record skipping in the background like the calm heart of a practiced killer. And the death sequence. So beautiful and horrible at once, a real production as hinted by the

70

spotlight that falls on Maddy when she comes downstairs and will follow her to the end of her life. The constant shifting back and forth of Leland to BOB, BOB to Leland, the shifting of film speed from slow motion with murky sound to the stark, unaccompanied, real-pace of the horrific moment: it is the kind of thing you never want to see but can't look away from, and as real as Sheryl Lee's performance feels, that of Ray Wise, too, is so convincing that it will take you out of the artificiality of the moment and plant you in it as though it were real. If you can get through this without your jaw dropping and every single hair on your body standing on its end, then you scare me. The second season would be dismissed by critics in an overall sense, but both Lee and Wise deserved Emmys, Golden Globes, and any other award they could have carried for their respective work in this episode.

ABC wanted a solution to the murder of Laura Palmer. They pressed for it to the point of insisting, and while Lynch and Frost delivered what was asked of them in a literal sense, figuratively they opened onto a broader mystery with their solution. And as for that solution, it turned out to be even more heinous than TWIN PEAKS had led viewers to expect. After all, the murder of a beautiful young woman is horrible, but the murder of a beautiful young woman by her respected father is much, much worse. And what's worse than that? A father murdering his daughter after years of incestuous torment. After the reddest herring possible in Ben Horne, Lynch and Frost jerked the rug out from under everyone with the darkest twist in TV history. Demonic possession, incest, filicide – this is not your conventional network murder mystery, and though we all knew that going into the series, none of us suspected it was going to go this direction. Understandably, the content turned off a lot of Middle America and from here the ratings would begin their gradual decline, but whether people were fatigued, disgusted, or disillusioned, this is the peak of TWIN PEAKS, and in closing one door it opened a very ominous pair of curtains.

Whatever it was going to be from here on out, the TWIN PEAKS we knew was over, and what was to come next was anybody's guess, even after it happened.

EPISODE 15: "DRIVE WITH A DEAD GIRL"

Written by Scott Frost, Directed by Caleb Deschanel

Airdate November 17th, 1990

In TWIN PEAKS' opening credits, Piper Laurie has always been billed last. While she had been absent from the last few episodes, given episode 14's more minor revelation she's returned to the credits, billed as playing both Catherine Martell and Mr. Tojamura. "Fumio Yamaguchi," who had been previously billed as playing Tojamura, is now gone.

The episode opens right back at the Palmer house, but it's the next morning now. Leland is chipping golf balls in the same living room where only hours ago he viciously murdered Maddy. Donna and James show up to say goodbye to Maddy, but Leland tells them she's already left, he dropped her at the bus station himself. He says she was disappointed they didn't come by last night like they were supposed to, although given what went down there last night, I think we all can agree it's probably for the best they didn't show up. Leland gets called away by Sarah – who is now alert, fine, and seemingly oblivious about everything that has transpired – leaving Donna and James alone with the dozens upon dozens of golf balls scattered around the room. They think it's funny. It isn't funny, it's a deviant mind occupying itself between kills. When Leland looks at himself in the mirror after showing them out, it's BOB he sees. He then heads out himself, making sure to take his golf bag with him. Maddy's corpse is stuffed inside, wrapped in plastic. Leland drops his niece in the trunk. It's such a nice day out, he decides to drive to work with the top down so that spring breeze can tickle his stark white hair.

Ben Horne is still sitting in jail under suspicion of Laura's murder. His brother Jerry shows up. Since Ben's regular lawyer, Leland, is himself under indictment for murder (Jacques Renault's), Jerry will be handling Ben's legal defense himself, which for some reason Ben's fine with. First order of business, Jerry needs to know where Ben was the night Laura died? We recall that Jerry doesn't appear in TWIN PEAKS until episode 2 because he was out of the country when the murder occurred, in France specifically, eating multiple brie and butter baguettes per day. Ben says Catherine is his alibi, they were together that fated night, but he still thinks she's dead, so that will be tough to prove. The brothers get distracted by the cell's bunk beds, which reminds Jerry of their first room together, and specifically of watching their babysitter Louise Dombrowski dancing on the hook rug with a flashlight. An extended memory sequence follows in which the girl dances sultrily in their lurid shared memory. Fun fact: though she's silhouetted and her face is never seen, Louise Dombrowski is played by Emily Fincher, sister to David, who directs movies, some of which you might be obsessed with.

Lucy shows up to work with her sister Gwen and Gwen's infant son in tow.

Coop and Truman are at The Great Northern when they come across Leland dancing in the lobby. He apparently hasn't heard about Ben's arrest. Harry breaks it to him. This news is especially distressing because it means Jacques wasn't the culprit and therefore Leland killed the wrong man, but Leland steels his emotions and resolves to let the law handle things this time. As he walks away, his crying turns to malicious snickering, BOB rejoicing in the framing of another for his crime. Cooper almost catches him, but BOB is a clever chameleon. Cooper still senses a strange wind, though, even if he can't tell from where it's blowing. BOB dances himself out.

Ben's blood is being drawn by Doc Hayward for purposes of trying to match it to that found at the crime scene. Cooper meanwhile shows Ben Laura's secret diary and tells him how it documents everything about One Eyed

Jacks and Ben's involvement. Coop reads the line about Laura yearning to reveal who Ben really is, and tries to use it to leverage a confession. Ben and Laura were lovers, is Coop's thinking, but she became a threat to all he had and had to be eliminated. Ben is greatly offended by this suggestion. Jerry takes a moment with his client; he tells Ben the case against him is too good, he's going to need a better lawyer.

Bobby is listening to the microcassette he found in the heel of Leo's repaired boots. It's the conversation from last season between Leo and Ben arranging for the mill to be burned down. This pleases Bobby, as Ben Horne's a great person to blackmail, what with all that money he's got.

Norma's mother Vivian (Jane Greer) surprises her by showing up at the diner out of the clear blue (or THE PAST, if you know Ms. Greer's filmography). She's there to introduce her new husband, Ernie Niles, a "financial analyst" who dresses like a used car salesman in 1975. The relationship between Norma and her mother seems a little strained, and when mom reveals herself to be more than a little nitpicky and superficial, we can see why. As if all this wasn't enough, Norma's still a little distracted because of the impending arrival of mysterious food critic M. T. Wentz. Mom and Ernie leave her be and go to check in at The Great Northern. In collecting Ernie's financial newspaper, Norma finds the sports page hidden inside, all marked up with betting notes. So then Ernie is a gambler, which isn't quite the same thing as an analyst. More importantly, he hasn't been in Twin Peaks/on TWIN PEAKS five minutes and he's already proven himself deceitful and duplicitous.

At The Great Northern under a nurse's care, MIKE/Phillip Gerard the one-armed man comes to because he can sense that BOB is close. He asks the nurse for a glass of water, and for some reason instead of just ducking into the bathroom, she has to leave the entire hotel room to get it. When the deputy steps into to check on things, MIKE bashes him over the head and escapes out the window.

Hank returns to the diner after disappearing for two days without a word. Norma's understandably pissed. Hank tries to explain it away by saying his past is always trying to catch up to him or some other such bullshit, but somehow it works. Hank then notices Norma's mom. Vivian seems to like him more than her own daughter, despite the whole prison-stint thing. Vivian invites the two of them to dinner at The Great Northern with her and Ernie. Norma's not too stoked at the prospect but Hank is and accepts for them both.

At the Sheriff's station, Truman and Pete engage in some birdwatching before Pete breaks the news that Josie has gone. Truman of course already knows this. Pete then gets something off his chest: he loved Josie. Truman can't blame him for that, he totally gets it. He mentions meeting her assistant, but Pete doesn't know of any assistant. When Truman describes the man, Pete recognizes him as Jonathan, the fella Josie said was her cousin. This confusion of identity, along with the haste of Josie's departure, gives Pete a bad feeling, and it's one Truman shares. Coop comes in with the news that Gerard is missing. He and the Sheriff depart immediately. At the same moment, Andy returns and sees Lucy watering the plants with an infant in her arms. It's her sister's, but he doesn't know this, and faints because he thinks it's hers. Pete meanwhile sneaks back to the holding cells to have a boisterous laugh at the expense of Ben Horne, and to deliver a taped message from Catherine, who is not dead, and who knows she is his alibi for the night Laura Palmer died, though she might be confused as to just when they were together. That is, unless he helps jog her memory in his favor by signing the mill back over to her, along with the Ghostwood Estates development. He can keep the hotel, she says, but it's a pittance comparted to what she's taking. She'll be sending a representative by with contracts in the next 24 hours, and she suggests he sign them. Pete, ever the willing cuckold, is loving this humiliation. Ben realizes he's been played. *Out*played. Pillows are destroyed.

Leland/BOB is driving and swerving gaily all over the road with Maddy still in the trunk. After running Truman and Coop onto the shoulder, they pull him over. He says he was just on his way to the country club to try out a new pair of irons and must have gotten distracted thinking about Ben and Laura. He says he remembered something about the night his daughter died, says he was working late that night with Ben at The Great Northern when Ben got a phone call around 10 o'clock that made him pretty angry; Leland can't remember the details, only that Ben mentioned something about "a dairy." That doesn't make any sense until Coop suggests it might have been "a diary." Now BOB's just straight-up toying with Coop. When Harry gets called back to the cruiser by Lucy on the radio, BOB asks Coop if he'd like to see those new irons. Coop isn't too curious but is politely obliging. BOB gets out of the car and opens the trunk. Cooper gets within mere feet of Maddy's body, but then Truman calls to him: Hawk's found Gerard. It almost looks like BOB is going to bash Coop's head in with his golf club right there in the middle of the road, in broad daylight with the Sheriff watching, but the Agent jogs away before anything can happen. The implication is clear, though: BOB isn't afraid of anything or anyone and is willing to murder them all indiscriminately.

When he's conscious again, Andy tells Lucy – despite her sister's interference – that his sperms are operational, but they weren't before. This is why he reacted the way he did, because he didn't think it was possible he could get her pregnant. But now that everything has been proven to be in working condition, he thinks he's the father of her baby-to-be. Lucy isn't exactly as happy as he is, because unlike him she knows about her dalliance with Dick Tremayne.

Coop and Truman have MIKE sniffing around Ben for traces of BOB. This isn't him, MIKE declares, but he knows him, he's been very close to him. Truman charges Ben with Laura's murder regardless. Coop asks for an aside, he doesn't think Ben killed Laura, he thinks Ben should be released. Truman has been a good sport through all the hocus pocus Coop's come up with until now, but there's solid evidence against Ben and it's Harry's responsibility to Laura, the Palmers, and everyone else in Twin Peaks to pay attention to that. Coop completely agrees and backs off. But the seed of doubt has been sewn.

At dinner, despite Vivian's minor complaints about the food, everything seems to be playing out in a civil fashion. Norma and Vivian excuse themselves and go to the little girls' room, leaving Hank and Ernie alone together for the first time. As it turns out, they know each other from prison where Ernie's nickname was "The Professor." Hank wants to know what his angle is with Vivian. Ernie says there's no angle, he's trying to go straight. He is in fact a financial analyst, albeit crooked (he robbed a Savings and Loan), but that's all behind him, he says. Hank senses an opportunity for blackmail, as Vivian has no idea about Ernie's past. He starts applying the pressure immediately.

Cherry pie and milk before bed for Coop, but a knock at the door interrupts him. It's Audrey. She wants to know if they arrested her father. He tells her they did. She wants to know if Coop thinks he did it. Coop says only that's not for him to decide. She wants to know if the information she uncovered helped arrest her father. In part, yes. While they're clearing the air, she wants Coop to know that when she was being held at One Eyed Jacks she was never with anyone in "that way." She wants him to know, in essence, that she is still pure and sexually untainted should he want to avail himself of her love. Before he can respond, Coop's phone rings. Whoever it is, it's important, he has to go immediately, and tells Audrey she must go too, back to her room, and she should lock her door. He won't say anything else. He does however take his gun when he leaves.

Police cars crowd the side of the road, their lights swirling red and blue and piercing the darkness with urgency. Truman and Cooper march with purpose through the trees to the rocky shore below the falls where another body has washed up wrapped in plastic. Truman pulls the sheeting away from a face. It's Maddy.

Emotionally, this is a tough episode. Leland/BOB is in peak form and it is a gut-punch of a performance by Ray Wise, who has always been on-point but between this episode and the next he reveals himself as perhaps the strongest actor in the cast. The range of emotions and the scant time he has to transition between them is mesmerizing to watch.

The script for this episode comes from Scott Frost, Mark's brother and the author of THE AUTOBIOGRAPHY OF FBI SPECIAL AGENT DALE COOPER: MY LIFE, MY TAPES. It's one of two episodes he'll write, and definitely the better one. With the mystery of who killed Laura Palmer "solved," Frost takes the investigation to strange new heights, as for the first time in TWIN PEAKS history we know more than the authorities about what's going on.

On the directing side of things, Caleb Deschanel returned for his second episode, and brought with him some excellent framing, particularly the scene in which Cooper almost catches Leland/BOB snickering after being told of Ben's arrest. The distant and dropped focus between characters is emblematic of the blurred truth between them as well.

As mentioned, this first episode post-killer-reveal manages to keep the mystery alive, although it's roughly solved, and even broadens its scope. We all know who did what, but what we don't know, what we can't even conceive of at this point, is how it will all come to light and if it can ever be resolved. Leland/BOB is now a ticking time bomb, he could do anything – maybe literally – and it's tough to figure how he's going to be outed, especially with such a strong case against Ben. Outside of this central storyline, only a couple of additional plots are advanced this episode, which is a nice change of pace after the last several in which there was a lot of information on a lot of fronts being tossed around. Even the addition of the Vivian/Ernie storyline doesn't feel new as much as it feels like another aspect of Hank's general shadiness, which is still unfurling now that it's out in the free light of day again.

TWIN PEAKS will never again be as focused as it is this episode and the next, and while that isn't all negative – it allows for deeper delvings into supporting characters and the town itself, what the show was always about – there is a twisted sense of nostalgia at play here, as well as a definite sense of closure, or at least "closure" as TWIN PEAKS defines it. While I myself am more fascinated by the ideas of the second half of the series, the writer in me is in constant awe of the way the first half unfurls, especially knowing the pressure Lynch, Frost et al were under from the studio to make things more mainstream. There's never been a mystery like the murder of Laura Palmer, from its reveal to its details to its ultimately unimaginable origins, and the way in which it was told, the way the clues were produced and followed, the way it was subverted at every turns by a plethora of red herrings, is nothing short of masterful and should be studied by anyone who aims to write television or any other sort of mystery.

Written by Mark Frost & Harley Peyton & Robert Engels, Directed by Tim Hunter

Airdate December 1ˢᵗ, 1990

Brace yourself for a powerful and confounding hour of television, and the climax of the Laura Palmer storyline.

Maddy has been found dead and wrapped in plastic, the same as her cousin Laura in the pilot. The next morning Coop, Truman, Hawk and a returned Albert are going over the details of the crime scene. Based on the typed letter O found under Maddy's right ringfinger, Albert is convinced this is the work of the same killer as Laura and Teresa Banks. Maddy was also clutching fur in her hand that belonged to a white fox with traces of embalming fluid in the fibers, so then a taxidermied fox. We recall, of course, the stuffed white fox in Ben Horne's office that so transfixed Leland in episode 13, the fox he tore fur from, though the authorities have not yet discovered this connection. Truman starts to call Leland to get in touch with Maddy's folks in Montana, but Coop asks him for 24 hours before any calls are made. For what? To finish this, he says, although admittedly he has no idea where to start. "You're already on the path," Hawk reminds him, "You don't need to know where it goes, you just need to follow it."

Donna and James meet for coffee after an evening of implied coitus. He presents her with a ring that he slips on her left hand. It isn't an out-and-out proposal, but it isn't not one, either. Norma serves her mother an omelet and is met with the woman's typical, nonplussed attitude. Norma calls Vivian on it, but it's kinda like calling a bear a bear: the bear doesn't give a shit. Donna and James overhear Andy saying *"Je une ame solitaire"* over and over again. Donna has heard this before from Mrs. Tremond's grandson, but Andy tells her he read it in Harold Smith's suicide note. Donna has to find Cooper immediately, and takes off without explaining why.

Donna takes Coop to Mrs. Tremond's house and explains to the Special Agent about her and her grandson, how the boy said the same French phrase as the one in Harold's note. Donna is convinced there's some eerie connection. When they get there, however, Mrs. Tremond isn't inside, or rather she is, but she's not the Mrs. Tremond Donna was expecting. This one is younger and lives alone, her own mother is deceased and she has no children. Coop says Donna's name aloud, and this Mrs. Tremond recognizes it. She presents a letter addressed to Donna that she found in her mail the day after Harold died. Donna recognizes the handwriting as Harold's and opens it with Coop. Inside is a page from Laura's diary dated February 22ⁿᵈ, her penultimate day alive. The passage describes a strange dream Laura had which mirrors exactly the dream Coop had earlier in season 1, where Laura/Not Laura whispered the killer's name in his ear, the name he forgot upon awakening. Laura describes Coop as an old man she thinks can help her. She further says BOB is only afraid of one man, MIKE, and wonders if Coop is him, but hopes whoever he is, even though it was a dream, that he heard her and will help her. There's an entry from the 23ʳᵈ as well: *"Tonight is the night I will die. I know I have to because it's the only way to keep BOB away from me, the only way to tear him out from inside. I know he wants me, I can feel his fire. But if I die he can't hurt me anymore."* Cooper has to see Phillip Gerard, a.k.a. the one-armed man, a.k.a. MIKE, stat.

At The Great Northern MIKE is feverish without his medicine and in distress but Coop needs him like this, he knows it's the only way MIKE can sense BOB: "without chemicals." He tells MIKE that BOB has killed again, and asks MIKE about the dream he and Laura shared, he needs the answers to its mysteries. MIKE cryptically describes his symbiotic relationship with BOB back when they were killing together as a golden circle, like a ring, Cooper's ring, the one taken by the Giant, who MIKE says "is known to us here," and thus real, or at least as real as MIKE is.

MIKE says the Giant can help find BOB, but you must ask him first. Coop want to know how? "You have all the clues you need," MIKE says, adding that the answer isn't in Coop's head, but his heart. This clears up little.

Cooper is confounded. He strolls into the corridor where he sees the same elderly bellboy who brought him hot milk the night he was shot. The waiter repeats what he said that night about the milk getting cool, but adds that it's getting warmer now. Coop – and the audience – catches his drift.

In Ben Horne's office, all clues are still pointing his direction. Phone records indicate he called Laura the night she died, and a stuffed white fox in the room seems to indicate that Maddy was there at some point before she died. Truman theorizes that Ben killed Maddy in the office then took her body to the waterfall below the hotel where it was found. Albert confirms that the time of death fits this timeline as Maddy was killed sometime before midnight, the time at which Ben was arrested. Furthermore, Albert has the results of Ben's blood test. They are read by Coop and Truman, but not revealed to the audience.

At the station, the sprinklers are getting tweaked up to code. Andy wants to talk to Lucy about their baby but Lucy isn't sure it is *their* baby, seeing as how Dick Tremayne was in the mix as well. She gauges the odds at 50/50. Andy goes right to the phone and calls Dick, says they need to have a talk. Meanwhile Ben is still sweating it out in a holding cell when he is visited by Tojamura. Tojamura has the Ghostwood Estates contracts ready for Ben to sign, but Ben says he can't right now. In that case, Tojamura concedes, Ben can just return the $5 million check he was given. But as he's already signed that over to Josie, Ben has to stall, and tries using his current predicament as an excuse. Tojamura takes this moment to reveal himself as Catherine in disguise. In the end, a few painted toenails is all it takes. Ben begs her to tell Truman about their night together, the night Laura died. She's happy to, as long as he signs the mill and Ghostwood Estates over to her. He does, thrilled by the prospect of freedom. Problem is, she's still not sure she's going to do it. She leaves Ben with even less than he had when she entered.

Donna is at the Palmers'. She has a tape of the song she and James and Maddy recorded, and wants Leland to mail it to her in Montana. He says he will but then gets distracted when he recognizes the sunglasses Donna is wearing. They were Laura's. She asks if he's heard that the cops found Laura's secret diary. Of course, they took it from her room. Nope, Donna says, wrong diary, this was a secret one given to Harold Smith for safekeeping. Leland is alarmed by this, he had no idea of its existence. He moves in close to Donna, too close given what we now know about him, but then the phone rings. It's Maddy's mom, Sarah's sister. She says Maddy hasn't arrived home yet and she's concerned. He says he'll look into it and gets off the phone. As he straightens his tie in the mirror before re-entering the living room, BOB is looking back. Donna is in real danger now, Maddy-danger, Laura-danger. Leland gives her a glass of lemonade and tries to calm her frazzled nerves by putting on a record. This is a terrible sign, and even Donna can sense it and is starting to feel a little nervous. Leland is fully BOB now, and moves to dance with Donna. She for some reason accepts his invitation. Already creepy in any context, in this one it's a blatantly-predatory gesture. Leland grabs Donna and pulls her to him. She's afraid, but gets saved by the doorbell. It's Sheriff Truman, thank god. He needs Leland's help, but all he can say is that there's been another murder. They leave without paying Donna another moment's notice.

As she's walking home, Donna knows between the phone call from Maddy's mom and the Sheriff's announcement that Maddy is dead. She calls James to meet her and breaks the news to him. This is the straw that breaks the back of what James can emotionally withstand. He won't even discuss it with Donna, it doesn't matter, the world will go to hell no matter their happiness, he says. He peels out on his motorcycle, leaving Donna alone and crying.

The Road House. A stormy night. Ben Horne has been taken there by Coop and Albert. They are the only three in the place until Truman arrives with Leland. Leland wants to know why they've all gathered there. Coop says they're waiting for someone, possibly the killer but he doesn't know for sure. All is very hush-hush and baited. Ed shows up too. Coop has them clear a large space in the center of the room. Lightning flashes outside. Hawk and Bobby arrive with Leo. Coop brings everyone up to speed on Maddy's murder, how it was perpetrated by the same killer, and how he believes that killer is in this room. He says he's exhausted every deductive method he knows from the practical to the metaphysical, and all that's left is to rely on magic. He's not sure what comes next, he says someone is missing. That's when Major Briggs walks in escorting the elderly bellboy. Briggs says he found the old man walking here and gave him a ride. The old man offers Coop a stick of gum. Leland recognizes it, it's a kind he used to chew when he was a kid, his favorite brand. The old man tells Leland that gum he likes is going to come back in style, which is also what the Man From Another Place said to Cooper in his dream. Like an incantation, this takes Coop back in memory to the red room and finally he hears what is whispered to him by Laura/Not Laura: "My father killed me." In The Road House, the Giant appears to Coop and returns his ring. Coop chews the gum, picks up the ring, then tells Ben he's taking him back to the station, and that he might want to bring along Leland as his attorney. They depart, but not before Coop thanks the old man with a hearty thumbs up. Then the dénouement begins...

Back at the station they take Ben down to an interrogation room. Leland asks if Ben's going to be charged. Coop says he is, but as Leland follows his client – who apparently he still intends to represent despite the crime he's accused of being the murder of Leland's own daughter – Coop whispers something to Truman, who only nods wide-eyed in response. They open the door and instead of leading Ben in, they bum-rush Leland, push him inside and lock the door. This is all it takes. BOB is loosed in an insane frenzy. Harry is dumbfounded and wants to know how Coop found out. He says Laura told him in a dream. Truman, however, is going to need harder evidence than that, so Coop suggests a confession.

Leland is bound and kept under the gun of Hawk. He's being read his rights. He's laughing, grinning madly. He admits to killing Laura and Maddy and says he has a thing for knives, "like that thing that happened to you in Pittsburgh that time, eh, Coop?" Coop's taken aback but holds his calm. BOB praises Leland as a good host but says he's just about all used up. Coop wants to know if Leland is aware of what BOB has done? Not yet, but when BOB leaves him, he will become aware, and it will be exquisitely horrible. This is enough solid proof for Truman. They leave BOB/Leland to his insane self.

Meanwhile Dick Tremayne has shown up for his conversation with Andy, but Lucy steps in and takes control. She tells them she's going to keep the baby, and that they will take a paternity test after the baby is born. She expects complete cooperation from them both until then. Dick lights a cigarette; its smoke drifts towards the smoke alarm. This is a startlingly out-of-place scene in the midst of arguably the series' most dramatic moment. Why it's there can only be speculated as comic relief, albeit unnecessary.

Outside Leland's cell, Coop is explaining to Albert, Hawk and Truman how his dream makes sense now: the little man danced, and so did Leland, compulsively so, after killing Laura; Cooper was told BOB was a gray haired man, and after killing Jacques Renault, Leland's hair turned white; Leland said the name of the man who looked like BOB who lived next to his grandparents' place in Pearl Lakes was Robertson, while MIKE said the people BOB inhabited were his children – Robertson, son of Robert, Robert BOB; and the letters under the fingernails of Teresa, Laura, Ronette Pulaski and Maddy were R, O, B, and T, which likely means BOB was spelling his name. Truman wants to know why Leland/BOB would kill Laura? Because she was onto him, Coop says, she wrote about his true identity in her diary. Leland found it and ripped out the pages, and Leland was the one who called Laura from Ben's office the night she died. Leland was also the third man outside Jacques' cabin that fateful night. It was he who took the girls to the train car, and it was his blood found outside that car, not Ben's. This is what Albert's report revealed. Truman isn't done questioning, though: if Laura was dead and BOB's secret was safe, then why kill Maddy? Any number of reasons, Coop posits, none of which are good. Truman just can't believe it, it can't be real, this possession, surely Leland's just crazy? As if refuting this, Leland/BOB starts reciting the "Fire Walk With Me" poem. That's when the smoke alarm goes off, triggering the newly-attuned sprinklers, and BOB's exodus from Leland begins. He starts to smash his head into the wall over and over again, trying to kill himself. When they finally get into the interrogation room, Truman, Albert and Coop can only comfort Leland beneath the torrent from the sprinklers as he comes back to himself and remembers the horrible things BOB made him do, from the sexual abuse to the murders. He is as distraught as a human can be as he reveals how BOB came to him in a dream when he was just a boy and asked if he wanted to play. That was all it took: Leland said yes and just like that BOB was inside him. For decades this went on, and whenever BOB would relinquish control, Leland could never remember what had happened. He says BOB wanted lives to use like he had used Leland's, especially Laura's, but she was too strong, she wouldn't let them in. So BOB made him kill her. Or rather, she made BOB make Leland kill her because she would have rather died than let BOB have her soul. This is an anguishing scene drowning in regret, the last chance at penance for a dying man. Albert and Truman rise and step away as Cooper leads Leland's soul towards its afterlife. He tells Leland in this moment to know himself and abide in that state, to look to the light, find it, and enter it. Leland's last words are of seeing Laura there in the light, beautiful and safe, then he dies in Coop's grip. The sprinklers cease. The mystery, at least in this realm, is over.

Outside, Coop, Truman and Albert are trying to make any sense they can out of what just happened. Truman is still sticking to the insanity defense, but Albert points out that other people actually saw BOB, Coop among them. Briggs interjects with the old Shakespeare line about how there's more to heaven and earth than what figures into our philosophy. Coop agrees with him, but Truman still isn't able to believe it. Coop asks if it's any more comforting to believe that a man for no reason whatsoever would rape and murder his own daughter. It most certainly is not. Briggs isn't sure the nature of evil is ever worth lingering over, as it exists regardless to our opinions of it, but Coop says knowing the nature of evil helps to stop it, which is their job. Briggs can't argue with this. Albert suggests maybe that's all BOB is, the evil men do personified. Then Truman closes things with the scariest question yet: if BOB can't be killed, if he was really here in their world and they had him in the body of Leland but now he's gone, where exactly did he go?

A red-tinted, frenetic and clumsy perspective rushing through the woods would seem to answer this. It comes to a sudden stop at a white glowing portal from which an owl escapes

As was the last episode, this episode is anchored by an unbelievably powerful performance by Ray Wise. I have seen his death scene a dozen times and I am always – *always* – covered in goosebumps by its conclusion. It's more than the connotation of what Leland is saying, it's how he says it, with a potent mixture of limitless shame, disbelieving terror, and unbridled anguish. Kyle MacLachlan is a great actor and perfectly deserving to carry the mantle for TWIN PEAKS, but for my money, and again, this is as the biggest Kyle MacLachlan fan it the world, Ray Wise is the strongest member of the cast and this episode right here illustrates how and why. He completely loses himself in both halves of his dual roles and takes us with him down deep into the pits of their despair/sadism.

Frost, Peyton and Engels scripted the episode, as evident by the taut storytelling and adherence to the series' mythology. Tim Hunter directs for the second time, and his aesthetic is marked with low-angle character shots, tilted frames, P.O.V. shots and even a freeze frame. For an episode so reliant on narrative, Hunter balances his visuals accordingly, making them separately interesting and ominously foreboding.

Overall, this episode is another of the series' finest hours, the episode that brings to a total conclusion the murder of Laura Palmer, if not a total resolution to the question of what or who is BOB? The effect of the last 15 minutes are so complete and engulfing that we're not left wondering what happens next – maybe for the first time – because wrapping our heads around all the revelations in this episode occupies our minds fully. This story has resolved itself, as it were, darker and weirder and more chaotically than I think anyone could have expected, and while it doesn't offer a lot of light as to where things are going, once again the show has passed another sign post from which it can't double back. This is the new starting point, the new atmosphere, the new city where our show is set. Nothing was ever safe here, but now nothing is sacred either, not even a father's love for his daughter. Everything in Twin Peaks can be corrupted, everything can be controlled. There are no limits, there is no safety, and not even the natural law of the universe as you understand it can protect you. There are indeed more things in heaven and earth than what figure into our philosophy, and apparently they all live in TWIN PEAKS.

EPISODE 17: "DISPUTE BETWEEN BROTHERS"

Written by Tricia Brock, Directed by Tina Rathbone

Airdate December 8th, 1990

The episode begins at the Palmer house three days after the death of Leland. Sarah passes on the sedative Doc Hayward offers her because she wants to be clear-headed for Leland's funeral. Coop is there also and explains to Sarah that Leland did not do these things, not the Leland she knew, at least, he'd fallen prey to one of the world's dark, unexplainable things and it corrupted him, it used him. Sarah knows this, she knows it was BOB who did all these horrible things, she saw him. Regardless, she says, this knowledge doesn't bring anyone back from the dead. Coop tells her that Leland renounced his deeds and the pain he caused his family, and then he passed away in peace to visions of Laura. This is little but some comfort.

Following the funeral – which in contrast to Laura's in not shown onscreen – everyone is at the Palmers' for a reception: Nadine and Ed, Hank and Norma, The Haywards, Audrey, a healed and rested Dr. Jacoby, Major Briggs, The Mayor Dwayne Milford, Pete...they haven't allowed the scandal of these tragedies stop them from showing their support for Sarah. That's small-town living for you. Ed and Donna discuss how James isn't around because somehow he thinks this is all his fault and took off on his motorcycle to clear his head. Major Briggs asks Coop what he's going to do now that the case is concluded. Coop says he has some vacation time saved up and now might be the time to cash him in. Briggs invites him nightfishing. Who says no to that? Nadine the 18 year-old in the 35 year-old's body is concerned her shoes are too reflective and people can see her underpants in them. Ed patiently dissuades this notion. Sarah, conversing with Audrey and Eileen Hayward, is despairing but still lucid, the most so we've ever seen her. The Mayor gets in a small brawl with his brother Dougie, who runs the town newspaper. Truman and Ed break it up before either elderly man can be injured. It's explained that theirs is a long-running and frivolous feud, nothing more than another helping of small-town shenanigans, which are exactly what Coop says he's going to miss about Twin Peaks, this and everything else going on at the reception, just people being people, and more important, being a community.

At Twin Peaks High School later that day, Ed and Jacoby are negotiating with the assistant principal to get Nadine admitted to the senior class; they think it will help her present mental condition. For some reason, the assistant principal concedes.

Audrey visits Cooper in his room at The Great Northern. She wants to know if he's leaving. He is. She tries one more time to make a pass at him, but their age difference and their past professional involvement prohibits him. She supposes he must have been hurt by someone once, but he says it's the other way around: someone was hurt by him and he will not let that happen again. Audrey asks, jokingly, if she died or something. As a matter of fact she did, she was a material witness to a federal crime, and he and his partner, Windom Earle, the man who taught him everything he knows about being an agent, were supposed to protect her. When the attempt on her life was made, Coop says he wasn't ready because emotion clouded his senses, he loved her, and as a result she died in his arms. In the same attack Coop himself was badly injured, and Earle lost his mind. He wonders if this is enough to satiate Audrey's curiosity? It is, but Audrey isn't done growing, so she agrees to table the conversation for a few years, though not before telling Coop the one problem with him: he's perfect.

Bobby is at Shelly's trying on one of Leo's suits for his meeting/blackmail attempt with Ben Horne based on the tape he found in Leo's boot on which Ben is heard hiring Leo to burn down the mill. Shelly's got a bad case of cabin fever, all she's been doing lately is staying in and taking care of Leo. Bobby tells her to just hang in there until this Horne thing is settled and they're on Easy Street.

Truman enters his office to find Catherine waiting for him in the garb of an LL Bean catalogue model and decidedly not dead. She wants to know if she's under suspicion for the mill fire. That depends on her answers to his questions, he says. She says she was saved from the fire by angels, a lie, but then tells him the truth about the call she got that night telling her to come to the mill, about seeing Shelly and untying her, then becoming lost in the conflagration of smoke and flames. She doesn't know how she got out but somehow she found herself in the woods. She grew afraid because it was obvious someone had lured her there with the intention of trying to kill her, so instead of returning home, she just kept going through the forest. At daylight she stumbled across her family's old summer cabin at Pearl Lakes, led, she reiterates, by her guardian angel. The house was stocked, so she waited there for her would-be killer to find her. But she ran out of food first, so here she is.

In the station lobby, Dick Tremayne has come to talk with Lucy about her baby. He is suddenly very convinced the child is his and is very into the idea of being a father, so much so he has become a mentor to an at-risk youth to help train himself in the ways of child-rearing. Andy overhears this and interjects, says that until it's known for sure who the biological father is, they should all just try to get along for the sake of Lucy and the baby. Lucy's torn between the debonair responsibility of Dick and the animal magnetism she feels for Andy. And all this happens on a ladder. Dick and Andy shake hands, and Andy leaves them to talk, but as soon as he gets around the corner Hawk stops him and suggests he's crazy for not fighting harder for Lucy. But Andy knows what he's doing – even if it hurts him – because he knows what will ultimately win Lucy's heart: "moral and manly behavior." The balance actor Harry Goaz strikes between Andy's childlike sensitivity and particular sense of masculinity is never more charming than in this scene; if Laura is the soul of TWIN PEAKS and Cooper is its intellect, dare I suggest that Andy is the heart?

Coop, on his way to go nightfishing with Briggs before leaving town, stops in to say goodbye to Truman. Truman's made him a going-away present, a fishing lure called a green butt skunk. Coop is enamored with the token, and touched by it. Truman also has a Bookhouse Boy patch for the Special Agent, which makes him an official member. Coop is honored beyond his ability to express himself. It's a misty-eyed man-moment between these two, the culmination of their bromance until now, a thing comprised of equal parts respect, admiration, trust and healthy skepticism. They brought out the best in one another as men and officers of the law, and there's never been a partnership like them in all the history of crime procedurals. I weep at the thought of Michael Ontkean not returning for season three. Coop then says his adieus to Hawk – if he's ever lost, Coop hopes Hawk is the man they send to find him (is this season 3 foreshadowing?) – then Andy – whose bravery is only exceeded by the size of his heart – and finally Lucy – to whose wedding he wants an invitation, no matter who the lucky groom turns out to be. It's a very WIZARD OF OZ moment, reminiscent of Dorothy saying goodbye to her travelling companions. Knowing David Lynch's fascination with this film (see WILD AT HEART), this is hardly unintentional. As Coop is about to depart, though, Canadian Mountie Preston King walks in with Agent Roger Hardy of the FBI. Coop knows Hardy, but not why he's here. Well, it seems that effective immediately, Coop is suspended without pay from the Bureau. Dum-dum-dum...

Three fun facts: Agent Roger Hardy is played by Clarence Williams III, who is most famous for starring in the TV series THE MOD SQUAD alongside Norma Jennings herself, actress Peggy Lipton. And RCMP Preston King is played by Gavan O'Herlihy, whose father Dan O'Herlihy will show up in later episodes as a character whose name would be a spoiler if I said it at this point. Furthermore, the name "Preston King" is actually the real name of Harry Goaz, born Harry Preston King.

Hardy is with the Bureau's Internal Affairs Division, and the Mountie is there, Coop assumes, because of the trip he made into Canada to rescue Audrey. By not informing the Canadian authorities about their mission, Coop technically committed malfeasance. Hardy says that isn't all, though: there's also an allegation about Coop's methods and motive for rescuing Audrey. Hardy won't elaborate right now as he's still waiting on evidence, but he says he and Coop will reconvene in an hour...alone.

Bobby is waiting to see Ben but mostly he's getting the run-around. Audrey encounters him and tries to figure out what he's up to. He gives her a little song and dance of his own, but she decides to help him anyway. She says she'll need ten seconds to get him into see her father; she only takes five. Bobby owes her one but not much of one, because he isn't in there ten seconds before Ben has him tossed out. In his anger at this mistreatment, Bobby shouts out that there's more than one copy of the tape he sent Ben. Audrey saves him from the security guys, and in exchange he offers to buy her ice cream. He asks if she wants a cup or a cone. And then comes the most blatantly seductive line of the series: "A cone: I like to lick." In the wake of the disallowed romantic storyline between Audrey and Cooper, it seems the writers were flirting with the idea of pushing Bobby and Audrey together. Spoiler alert, but this only lasts a couple or few episodes and thankfully goes nowhere. More on the circumstances surrounding this at the end.

Coop and Hardy reconvene. On his first visit to One Eyed Jacks, Coop explains, he went undercover to question Jacques Renault, who dealt blackjack there and who Coop believed had knowledge of Laura Palmer's death. Hardy interrupts to point out that Coop used this trip to lure Jacques back to the States where he could be arrested and then subsequently killed in the hospital. Leland killed Jacques, and Leland's dead, so problem solved, Coop thinks. His second trip across the border, as mentioned, was to rescue Audrey. On neither excursion did he alert the Canadian authorities. Coop understands this and he isn't trying to explain his way out of it, he just wants to know if the Bureau holds him personally responsible for the deaths of Jacques Renault and the people killed in the raid of One Eyed Jacks. Hardy says that's what they're trying to figure out. The real problem, however, is that Coop's rescue mission botched a six-month RCMP investigation into Jean Renault and left them with two dead, no Jean, and none of the cocaine they were using for bait. There's an implication that the drugs might have disappeared with Cooper and company. Coop knows nothing about the cocaine, but says they've miscounted their dead people: there's Emory Battis (who Jean killed), the bodyguard (who Hawk killed when he was about to kill Coop, Truman, and Audrey) and Blackie (who Jean also killed). They didn't know about Blackie but that's fine by them, more trouble to heap on Coop's already-full plate. Coop cops to the border crossing, but says he didn't kill anyone, and Roger should know Coop better than to suspect him of being involved in drug trafficking. Roger won't know anything until Coop proves it...to the DEA, who will be sending an agent within 24 hours. In the meantime, Hardy is going to need Coop's badge and gun. Dale hands them over. Truman's up for interrogation next, but as the Sheriff understands it, what with him being a fellow law enforcement authority from a separate organization with its own protocols to follow, they're going to need extradition papers and a subpoena to get a statement out of him; until they have that, he's mum, and not politely, either.

Cheerleading tryouts are happening at Twin Peaks High School and Nadine's up. To put it mildly, she's an athletic powerhouse.

Shelly's brushing Leo's teeth when the phone rings. She knows it's Bobby but she's resolved not to answer it because it's been a whole day with not one word for him. She's weak, though, and answers the phone anyway but still gives him an earful. As she's doing so, Leo starts rolling forward in his wheelchair. Shelly notices. Ordinarily movement from within a vegetative state would be a thing to celebrate. In this instance, it is the opposite.

Norma's taking down all the frills at the diner. The great restaurant reviewer M. T. Wentz has at last spoken, and the words weren't nice. This gets even harder to take when Norma's mother Vivian reveals that she's actually M.T. Wentz. She defends her review by explaining she's not mean, Norma's just not a good cook, and standards must prevail, after all. Norma, however, could give a shit about standards. This is her business, her livelihood, and now it's been threatened and by her own mother, no less. She tells Vivian to hit bricks, not just now but from now on.

Meanwhile, the ladies' better halves Hank and Ernie are having fun at One Eyed Jacks. They are pulled aside to private quarters by Jean Renault. Jean still thinks Hank is a district attorney thanks to the badge (Daryl Lodwick's) he found in Hank's pocket the night of Audrey's rescue. Hank's playing the role crooked and using it to his advantage. Hank introduces Ernie as The Professor, his criminal nickname. Jean has a problem he's been told by Hank that Ernie can handle: he needs 125k cash quick and all he has is a bunch of cocaine; he needs someone to broker a sale. Ernie can sort that out for them. Jean then has a man bring in the suitcase of drugs. The man is King, the Mountie, and the cocaine is that which disappeared during the raid. So the Mountie's in on framing Cooper. Hank and Ernie leave, but Jean and King continue talking. Seems the real plan is that four of the five kilos they have are to be sold, and the fifth is to be planted in Coop's car. If Jean can't kill the Special Agent, he'll at least ruin him.

Truman is awakened in the night by a noise outside his house. He gets his gun. The noise is Josie, bruised and dirtied, crying and barely able to stand.

The episode ends bucolically with Briggs and Coop by a campfire after fishing. The men wax poetical about the various forms of evil and darkness, and how all man can do is react to them. Most do so with fear, Briggs says, but Coop was blessed with special gifts, and he is not the only one. Briggs then asks if Coop has ever heard of the White Lodge. Coop has not, but he's intrigued. Something is sneaking up on them through the brush. Coop takes a break to drain the main vein, but says he looks forward to hearing more about this White Lodge. Briggs gives a wink and a thumbs up reminiscent of the elderly bellboy at The Great Northern. Coop is urinating on a tree. Directly above him, an owl hoots. Then a blinding white light comes through the trees. Briggs begins calling for Coop. The silhouette of a third someone, hooded it seems, is seen against the light. Cooper comes running back but the light, the silhouette, and Briggs have all vanished.

This episode is the first of two during the series' original run to be both written and directed by women, Tricia Brock and Tina Rathborne, respectively. Brock is primarily now a television director, having worked on other acclaimed series like BREAKING BAD, 30 ROCK, THE WALKING DEAD and MR. ROBOT. She would write one other episode of TWIN PEAKS, episode 23, which many consider to be the episode that picks up the series out of its second season slump (conversely, many also consider this episode to have started said slump). This is Rathborne's second and final episode as director; she last helmed episode three.

In many ways this is a hinge episode where TWIN PEAKS swings from its primary storyline – the murder of Laura Palmer – into its next storyline, which you might have noticed is a little fractured and unrealized as yet. That's because the plan for the second season had always been to bridge the narrative gap between Laura and Windom Earle with a Cooper-Audrey romance. Everything else that's going on – the Bobby/Shelly/Leo triangle, the Bobby-Ben Horne blackmail, Norma's mother troubles, Ernie and Hank helping Jacques, Nadine's head injury, the Mildford dispute, et cetera – was always intended to be background, just side-plots to balance out the main narrative. But when the romantic storyline was vetoed by MacLachlan, these side-plots were all the writers were left with. So the next six episodes are not the series' finest, but they're also not as off-putting as people like to pretend they are. Sure, there's a main thread missing, but the fabric of TWIN PEAKS is still intact and in fact a lot of the seemingly mundane stuff that will happen over the next half-dozen hours actually informs the final seven hours, which are phenomenal.

As case in point take the scene towards the beginning of the episode with Audrey and Cooper in his room at The Great Northern. Though it fails to give us what we really want – some hot smooching – the scene is the most revelatory of the episode. By Coop recounting the story of his lost love for the first time, albeit not completely, he sets up the next mystery: who was she? Why was she in danger? Who from? And why did her death make Cooper's partner, Earle, lose his mind? This story also makes perfectly clear what Cooper's greatest fear is: someone he loves being hurt as a result of his own actions. This might seem like a passing note of virtue here, but in the episodes to come it will take on increasing importance.

Episode 17 is the Rubicon of TWIN PEAKS: you either crossed it or you didn't. Sadly, most people did not, and this is when the ratings start to drastically and steadily drop. But that also makes this the defining line between TWIN PEAKS' fans and TWIN PEAKS' fanatics. This was never television for the casual viewer, but now it has become niche, directed at a thinner audience who wants more than to just watch, they want to engage, they want to be challenged, and they want to be surprised. This thinning wasn't intentional of course, no doubt the writers, producers and actors wanted to keep their larger audience, but this is what happened, and I think ultimately all of us will agree that TWIN PEAKS is a show better celebrated by the few and the informed than by the masses at large, as this exclusivity allowed the show to defy industry and narrative expectations, which for better or worse is exactly what it went on doing.

EPISODE 18: "MASKED BALL"

Written by Barry Pullman, Directed by Duwayne Dunham

Airdate December 15th, 1990

We open on a scene of James easy riding through Washington State, hitting the open road to clear his clouded head.

Meanwhile back in Twin Peaks, Coop and Truman are informing Major Briggs' wife Betty about his odd disappearance, but she's not too concerned, she says it happens a lot, especially if it's in regards to his work. She asks Coop if it seemed like it was. He can't be sure. She asks then if the Major disappeared suddenly. Coop says yes. Betty says the fact that they were in the woods is very significant as the Major talks about them constantly. Coop asks if the Major has been attempting to contact some force in the woods as a part of his work. Betty knows the drill, though: that's classified, she says. There's not much more they can do, then. She says Briggs left some notes she can go home and get for them. When she leaves, Coop says he isn't convinced the Major just walked off on his own, and he shouldn't be, not after what he saw at the end of the last episode. Andy and Hawk arrive with wedding presents for Dougie Milford and his new bride. Lucy's out helping with the wedding so there's a temp at the desk. She breaks in with a call for Coop; it's Gordon Cole, wanting Coop to know he's got his full support in the investigation against him, which Cole says is going to be starting soon, as the DEA is sending down a top dog to head it up, Dennis Bryson. Coop knows the name.

Coop reports for his interrogation with Roger Hardy and the other Internal Affairs agents. Coop says he has no defense for his actions in Canada because he is certain of their rightness. He'll of course accept whatever penalties come from breaking jurisdiction, but he did nothing wrong criminally and will represent himself in court if need be. Roger voices his admiration for Coop's standing up for himself. Coop starts talking about a bigger game, wind, animals, darkness, love, and Roger is lost. He reigns it in by telling Coop he's likely to be extradited on the charges. Coop can't alter this, so won't worry about it. How very Zen of him. Roger says Coop's suspension will continue and the DEA will start their investigation today. Furthermore, given all he's been through, Roger might recommend Coop for a full psychological evaluation. Dale appreciates his candor.

At Twin Peaks High School, everyone is humoring Nadine's delusions. She asks Donna if she's still going out with Mike Nelson. She isn't, which makes Nadine happy, because she thinks there's some major chemistry developing between them. Mike of course is oblivious to this. Donna asks her about Ed, isn't she still seeing him? Nadine says sometimes Ed acts like he's old enough to be her father; for now, she's content being young and free.

James stops off for a beer at a roadside bar. There's a cherry Corvette convertible in the lot, and an equally alluring woman sitting by herself at the bar. She's very weird, and very forward. She asks if he's handy with cars as she tweaked her husband's Jag and needs it repaired before he comes home. She lives just up the road. So now we know she's rich, horny, and her husband's out of town. James, like any teenage boy would, jumps at the chance to help out. She introduces herself: Evelyn Marsh.

Andy's leaving flowers for Lucy at her desk when Dick Tremayne shows up with Little Nicky, his charge from the Happy Helping Hand organization. They're on their way to get a malted and wanted to see if Lucy could join them. Andy has to remind Dick that she's helping with the Milford wedding. Drat, this means no malted, which upsets

Little Nicky but Dick doesn't budge, so Andy offers to take them instead. Dick begrudgingly obliges. I should note that the "Little" I'm putting in front of Nicky isn't to allude to the Adam Sandler film, but because that's what they call him. Every time. This is likely alluding to the same thing Sandler's film is, that since a prominent alias for Satan is "Old Nick," his son therefore would be "Little Nicky." That might spoil a little of this Little Nicky's behavior to come, but it had to be done.

In Truman's office, Coop asks him and Hawk if they've ever heard of the White Lodge. They obviously have, but first Hawk wants to know how Coop heard about it. From Major Briggs. Hawk tells Coop that he may be fearless in this world, but there are other worlds; his people believe the White Lodge is where the spirits who rule man and nature reside. He then presents Coop with the idea of the White Lodge's counterpart, the Black Lodge, which legend tells is the shadow self of the White Lodge. Hawk says every spirit must pass through the Lodges on its way to perfection, and while there it will meet its own shadow self, or what his people call the "dweller on the threshold." Hawk closes with a stern admonition: enter the Black Lodge with imperfect courage and it will annihilate your soul. Sounds like a great place. The temp interrupts to let Coop know that DEA Agent Dennis Bryson is here to see him. Coop isn't at all intimidated by this, as he and Bryson are old friends. Then Bryson walks in, and he's a she, Dennis is Denise (and both are David Duchovny).

Mike Nelson is working out at the school gym when Nadine saunters in and starts hitting on him by lifting more weight than he can. Mike is perplexed, but the wrestling Coach is impressed and wants to know if Nadine's ever thought about going out for the team.

Josie is still staying at Truman's, recovering from her ordeal, whatever it was. Truman needs to know what happened, and he needs it to be the truth. Josie explains she used to work for a man called Thomas Eckhardt in Hong Kong. He took her off the streets, taught her about life and business, and became like her father, her master, and her lover. Then she met Andrew Packard, and though she was afraid to cross Eckhardt like that, she accepted his proposal of marriage anyway. Truman wants to know who Jonathan Lee – who she's passed off as her cousin and her assistant, separately – really is. Josie says he works for Eckhardt and would have killed her if she hadn't escaped him, because Eckhardt wants her all for himself, he always has, and whereas Andrew had the resources to protect her, she doesn't think Truman is any match for Eckhardt's wrathful influence. She lies and says she thinks Eckhardt is responsible for Andrew's death – if he is, he's not solely responsible, because we know Josie and Hank arranged and executed the murder – and says she'd rather die herself than go back to him, another reason she escaped from Jonathan, but now she's worried that by doing so she's doomed both herself and Truman.

There's a 2/3rds MOD SQUAD reunion at the Double R when Norma (Peggy Lipton) serves Agent Hardy (Clarence Williams III) some coffee. It's interrupted by Hank and Ernie returning from their "hunting expedition," a.k.a. the trip to One Eyed Jacks to set up a drug deal with Jean Renault. Norma tells Ernie that Vivian's gone back to Seattle, which is just as well what with the four kilos of cocaine he has to move in the next few days. Andy, Dick and Nicky are at the counter enjoying coffees and a malted, respectively, until Little Nicky reveals his devilish side by pranking them both.

James is working under Evelyn's hood. That's not a metaphor, he's literally working under the hood of her husband's Jag. She calls the car just another unique, perfect toy that Jeffrey owns, and counts herself as a part of that collection. James starts rambling about straddling his bike, revving the throttle, and rocketing into the darkness. These are metaphors, and very, very thin ones. Evelyn offers him the room over the garage while he works over the next few days. James accepts because of course he does: a femme fatale is only worth her weight in wiles.

Ben Horne, meanwhile, is reveling in old Super 8 movies of how simple life at The Great Northern used to be before his father died and Catherine robbed him of the mill and Ghostwood Estates. He's a bit broken, Ben, he's shaggy and unshaved, his physical appearance a mirror to his unsteady mental state. His life has reached a crossroads, and he seems either unwilling or unable to decide how to proceed. His mother comes on the screen.

He approaches her image and kisses it as the film ends. Hank enters. Ben wastes no time proclaiming Hank is a failure, because Catherine's alive and responsible for his downfall, the exact opposite of what Hank was contracted to arrange. Not to mention in the meantime Ben was arrested for murder and his lawyer was publically revealed to be an incestuous psychotic: neither are great for the reputation of one in the hospitality business. Then he goes on a bit about Feng Shui, but Hank cuts this nonsense out. He informs Ben that he's out of One Eyed Jacks, it's one more thing Ben doesn't own anymore. Hank says it's been taken over and also, he doesn't work for Ben anymore. That's when Ben figures out it's Jean Renault calling the shots now. Hank says it doesn't matter who is calling them, only that Ben isn't; he's a mess, and he's out. Hank goes, and Ben proves this "mess" comment correct by making shadow puppets of bucks in the light of the projector.

In his room, Cooper gets a letter from Windom Earle – another chess move – and a microcassette. On the tape we hear Earle for the first time, talking about how their chess game is leading them towards a classical confrontation, and taunting Coop about his next move, mocking how Coop is patterned in his thinking, and thus vulnerable. Earle explains how his knights and rooks will advance his influence, how his pawns and even his queen will be sacrificed in the obtaining of his goal: to kill the king. There's a lot of crypticness to what Earle is saying here, but one thig is crystal clear: dude is not talking about chess.

Dougie's wedding begins at The Great Northern. His bride Lana is quite beautiful, quite young, and TEEN WITCH (Robyn Lively). When objections are asked for, Dougie's brother Dwayne, the Mayor, calls Lana a gold digger. Truman walks him out before another geriatric brawl can ensue.

Denise calls Coop over for a drink at the wedding reception. She gives him the bad news first: cocaine residue was found in Coop's car. Denise admits it looks like a frame, but she'll needs evidence to prove it. They segue into Denise's change: seems she went undercover as a transvestite for a bust, and it just felt right. This came as a complete surprise to everyone, including Denise. Dancing ensues, Coop with Audrey, and Andy with Denise.

Josie is telling Catherine that Andrew was killed by Eckhardt, and now Catherine is in danger. Catherine knows this, just like she knows that Josie had a hand in Andrew's death, and her near-death in the mill fire. What she doesn't know is why Josie would want to save her now? Josie says she was forced into all of those things and now she's come to Catherine because she has nowhere else to go, she's at her sister-in-law's mercy. This is not a good place to be. Catherine makes Josie an offer she can't refuse: from now on Josie is her maid, and if she disobeys in the slightest, Catherine will contact Eckhardt and hand her over to him. Josie agrees and leaves. As she does ... Andrew Packard (Dan O'Herlihy) enters, not at all dead. Everything is going according to plan, he says, and now all they have to do is wait for Eckhardt to come seeking his true love. When he does...they'll be waiting.

A reminder here that O'Herlihy is the father of the actor Gavan O'Herlihy, who plays the crooked Canadian Mountie Preston King. Both are quite Irish, so do a fine job hiding their accents.

The episode was the second written by Barry Pullman, after episode 12. He would write two more episodes, 24 and the penultimate, 28. Behind Mark Frost, Robert Engels, and Harley Peyton, Pullman contributed the most scripts to TWIN PEAKS, and unlike those others, each of his episodes was a solo gig. Series editor Duwayne Dunham directed, his first episode behind the camera since the very first episode (not the pilot), and given that Dunham was involved with the series more than most all of the other directors owing to his status as editor, his episodes are very closely akin to the aesthetic Lynch established, and having that here in an environment that narratively wasn't so familiar helped give the disparate plotlines a visual link with the series up to now.

This episode marks the first aural appearance of Windom Earle, the arrival of Denise Bryson, and the return of Andrew Packard. These characters are central to the three biggest subplots propelling the narrative at this point. Though the first and the last are just starting, the middle is progressing as expected, slowly and with the introduction of many new characters besides Bryson: Agent Hardy, RCMP King, Ernie Niles. In the meantime, though, the episode neglects several of the main characters whose own subplots are ongoing: there's no Shelly, no Bobby, no Leo, no Ed, no Sarah, no Lucy. And then there's the James subplot. You guys know I love TWIN PEAKS, blindingly-so to a degree. But even I can't convince myself that the Evelyn Marsh story is a high point of the series. In fact, I can't tell which subplot is worse, by which I mean more pointless: the James/Evelyn noir or the Andy/Dick/Little Nicky atrocity. On the one hand, James' is the more egregiously-useless because it is the only subplot in the series to take place entirely unconnected to the town of Twin Peaks (One Eyed Jacks is connected through Ben and others), but the Helping Hands story is so off-tone, even for the quirky brand of comedy TWIN PEAKS' employs, that it's never anything but angrily distracting. Both, of course, are the result of the writers having to scramble for content after being made to drop the idea of a Cooper-Audrey romance, but still, there had to be other directions things could have gone.

There are some highlights too, though, namely in the brief discussion of the Black and White Lodges. These spiritual locales become central not just to the second half of the second season but to the series overall, and the pace at which this story is parsed out over the next 11 episodes is an example of TWIN PEAKS' plotting at its finest.

For some viewers, though, episode 18 is where the narrative starts to get muddled. There were already a score of characters to keep up with, and now there were more, even weirder ones. It can feel a tad bit desperate at times, like the writers were trying to expand their particular brand of weirdness, which is fine, except that weirdness is Lynch's, and he's not the one doing it. Still, this episode is more streamlined than the last, perhaps owing to more concentrated plot management, and of course the stuff about Earle and the Lodges. Perhaps if there'd been another scene or two of those stories rather than, say, Dougie Milford's wedding, old viewers would have felt the Twin Peakiness a little more and stuck around.

EPISODE 19: "THE BLACK WIDOW"

Written by Harley Peyton & Robert Engels, Directed by Caleb Deschanel

Airdate January 12th, 1991

Bobby Briggs pays Ben Horne another visit to try and blackmail him using the audio tape on which Ben is heard hiring Leo to burn down the mill. Ben however has sunken further into his state of shabby mental disarray following his arrest and the usurpation of his business assets by Catherine. This disarray is best represented by a tall, teetering stack of objects from Ben's office that he has erected on his desk. Ben asks Bobby bluntly what he wants. A job, that's all. So Ben gives him one following Hank and chronicling his movements. Upon leaving, Bobby sees Dougie's young new bride Lana running down the hall screaming.

Coop – now out of his typical black suit and dressed in more environ-friendly attire like a flannel and cargo pants – is picking out property to possibly purchase in Twin Peaks. In trying to decide which house to have the Realtor (Irene) show him first, he flips a coin. It lands on a particular file that the Realtor thought she'd taken out, a place quaintly named Dead Dog Farm that she further describes as a puzzle and a place where no one who moves in ever stays too long. Coop, of course, would like to see it immediately.

Dick Tremayne shows up at the Sheriff's station on his way to take Little Nicky on a camping trip. There, he meets with Lucy, Andy, and Nicky's case manager from Happy Helping Hands (played by a pre-SNL Molly Shannon). She's there to let them (all, apparently) in on Nicky's background. Why this wasn't done before the boy was paired with an adult is unknown. Seems Little Nicky has been plagued by "persistent random misfortune" most of his life, which has caused him to bounce from foster home to foster home. He's an orphan, you see, his parents were killed. Dick's curious how they died? Under mysterious circumstances, that's all they know. This meeting is interrupted when Andy is called away by Truman for an emergency at The Great Northern.

That emergency is Dougie Milford, dead in his wedding bed. If the lovemaking guide and other similar texts strewn about the room are any indication, it would seem that Dougie's heart couldn't keep up with his libido. The Mayor arrives to see his brother. Though their relationship was contentious in life, in the wake of Dougie's death Dwayne is heartbroken and crestfallen. As for Dougie's new bride Lana, Dwayne considers her his brother's assassin and tells her so, then calls her a witch. Hawk doesn't like to hear such talk aimed at a lovely young lady, but Lana tells him the Mayor is right, she's cursed, Dougie isn't the first man to get hurt in her loving embrace. Hawk tries to comfort her, and impress her. The first part goes okay, but the second part, not so much.

At Twin Peaks High School, the wrestling coach is introducing Nadine as the newest member of the team. It's groundbreaking, he knows, but she has a right to compete the same as any of the guys on the team. Coach asks for his top wrestler, Mike Nelson, to come forward. Nadine proves she's the new alpha by taking him down several times, but retains her feminine side by asking him out. She eventually ends the match by bench pressing him, tossing him to the ground, and pinning him. She still wants an answer about that date, though.

Later, looking pretty stiff and banged up, Mike approaches his ex, Donna. He needs her help, because the only thing worse than Nadine's aggression is her affection. He wants Donna to pretend she's still his girlfriend or he's afraid he's going to end up in traction.

Outside of Twin Peaks, James is still staying at Evelyn's house while he "fixes her car." He meets her brother Malcolm, who is also Evelyn's husband's driver. Malcolm's a bit of a tipsy louse and an obvious cad, and he goes on about how Evelyn getting married changed both their lives for the better, even if she has to deal with a little physical abuse now and again from the old man. There's a cycle at play between Evelyn and her husband, he says, where every couple of weeks Jeffrey gives her a thorough beating, and in exchange she gets back at him by destroying one of his precious things. This time it was the car James is working on. This is a lot of info for a guy to give in the first 60 seconds you meet him, but that's a pointless expository scene for you.

Dead Dog Farm is a dilapidated shithole. The Realtor says only the best and the worst are attracted to the place, and most end up turning away; only the purest of heart can feel its pain. This is before, you know, she tells him the square footage of the place, or how many bedrooms it has. In Twin Peaks, apparently, even the real estate is cryptic. Coop asks if she's shown the place to anyone else recently. Not this year, she says. That's odd, because he notices three fresh sets of tire tracks in the drive: a jeep, a four-wheeler, and a luxury sedan. Furthermore, the front door is unlocked. There's no one inside but Coop can tell there's been a meeting there in the last few hours because there's a full ashtray on the kitchen table and baby laxative in the sink. His conclusion? Someone was cutting cocaine here.

Dick Tremayne is attempting to change a flat on his Mercedes and has the car jacked up, but Little Nicky's in the driver's seat messing with stuff. Dick orders him out of the car. Nicky obliges and Dick goes back to changing the tire but then suddenly the car falls off the jack, almost crushing Dick. This sets off the waterworks in Nicky because he's afraid Dick will die like others Nicky has been placed with. Dick is, too, no doubt remembering the phrase "persistent random misfortune."

Coop is introduced by Truman to Colonel Riley, the investigator sent by the Air Force to look into Major Briggs' disappearance. Riley wants to know if Coop noticed any wildlife in the area when Briggs went missing, specifically owls. In fact yes, Coop heard and saw one just before. Truman wants Riley to cut to the chase, Briggs is a friend, and Coop tells him they already know about the monitors and the messages from space pertaining to Coop. Riley says he's got it half-right: the monitors are pointed into space, but the messages they got about Coop came from the Ghostwood Forest; where or to whom these messages were going is another, unanswered question. Coop wonders if this has anything to do with the White Lodge? That, naturally, is classified. Truman still needs more to go on. All Riley can say is that Briggs' disappearance has implications that go so far beyond national security, they make "the Cold War seem like a case of the sniffles."

James has Evelyn's engine purring again. He brings up with her the conversation he had with Malcolm earlier. He tries to get to the truth, but she won't answer his questions, so instead they kiss. Evelyn at least admits that she's afraid of her husband, but says she can't leave him. They kiss again. Then her husband Jeffrey pulls into the drive, and Evelyn goes to greet him.

Bobby runs into Audrey at The Great Northern as he's handing over photos of Hank to Ben. They continue their burgeoning flirtation, with Bobby even being bold enough to suggest a celebration later, just the two of them. Audrey however has other ideas about their coupling: she thinks they should go into business together. He tries to kiss her. She evades. Then he goes into Ben's office and she goes into her crawlspace between the walls to eavesdrop. Ben has set up a scale model of Gettysburg and is fighting the battle move by move, dressed in the coat of a Confederate General. Bobby shows him the pictures of Hank. Ben is pleased.

Pete and Catherine are popping champagne, celebrating their victory over Ben. Josie is in her maid's uniform being politely derided by Catherine. Pete tries to get his sister to go easy on her, but Catherine's pissed because Josie had a hand in Andrew's death (or rather the attempt, as both she and we know as of last episode that

Andrew is still alive) and in turn stole the mill from her. Pete can't believe that, not about his beloved Josie. Catherine doesn't care if he believes her or not, she's on her high horse about vanquishing her enemies.

Coop is talking to Diane. His response to Windom Earle's opening chess move was just printed in the personal column of a nationally-distributed newspaper left unnamed. However, Coop has already received a response, he received it yesterday in fact, which means that Earle perfectly predicted his move. This also means that Earle is toying with him and hiding his real plan. Coop talks about the property he saw and how a man could settle down and have a family there. He's fully invested in Twin Peaks, even if "this bucolic hideaway is filled with secrets" that may be connected to his current legal troubles, which if they aren't resolved in his favor could lead to serious jail time. Audrey knocks at his door. She has the photos Bobby took of Hank, she stole them from her dad and thinks Coop needs to see them: Hank, Ernie, Jean Renault and RCMP King meeting at Dead Dog Farm. This could be exactly the exonerating evidence he needs. Then Denise shows up. Audrey is more impressed with the fact that there are female agents than she is aware that Denise isn't entirely female. She's so bolstered by this moment of female empowerment, in fact, that she boldly plants a firm wet one on Coop's lips before skedaddling. Coop shows Denise the photos as well as cocaine samples he took from the Farm, and assumes the latter will be a match to that found in his car. Denise is very pleased with Coop's innocence and everything, but would much rather talk about the young hottie who just smooched the Special Agent. An important social moment here, as Coop says he wouldn't have expected Denise was still interested in women. This is, according to my research, the first time a transgender character appears on television on a major, recurring role, and also the first instance on TV of someone clarifying that being transgender doesn't necessarily equate to being homosexual. Coop doesn't really get it, but at least it was said.

Ed's at the diner, bummed out and bending Norma's ear about plans versus life. They hold hands and she talks of making new plans, both of them completely unaware that Hank is around the corner watching them.

Dick returns to the Sheriff's station, not to see Lucy, but Andy. He needs a word, he thinks there's a problem with Little Nicky. Problem is, he thinks the kid's homicidal, and possibly the devil. This creates the single worst moment in TWIN PEAKS history, a moment so jarring and out of place it should be slapped. Andy produces a *freaking thought bubble* of Little Nicky in a red devil costume with fake flames flickering around him. Seriously. Adam Sandler's LITTLE NICKY was better than this moment, and that movie is terrible. At least this is brief, as Dick pops the bubble by stressing that they need to find out the truth about what really happened to Little Nicky's parents.

Doc Hayward has the results of Dougie Milford's autopsy and is telling brother Dwayne that he died of natural causes. Dwayne asks if the good doctor checked for signs of witchcraft, which of course he did not. Dwayne wants to press charges against Lana anyway, he says she killed Dougie with sex. Truman can't arrest her for that. So Dwayne says he'll sue her civilly to make sure she doesn't get any of Dougie's money. He storms off as quickly as an old man can. Hearing he's gone, Hawk pops out of the coffee room with the Widow Milford – in a skin-tight, eye-catching black dress – looking for some whisky to put in her warm milk. Dick, Truman, Andy and Doc all gawk; Dick even recites poetry at the sight of her. Sometime later, Lucy gets a call for Truman but can't find him, or anyone for that matter. She goes looking and finds all the men and the Widow Milford having a ball in the Sheriff's office. All the men are enamored, while Lucy is just pissed

Ernie's eating chicken at the diner when Denise sits down at his table. She says she has proof Ernie's broken parole, and unless he does what she says, he's going to go away for a very long time. Cut to Ernie confessing on the record to being hired to find a buyer for the drugs for Jean Renault and RCMP King. He says he was physically threatened by them, his wife was too, and that's why he did it, but no one believes that. Denise asks if he's found a buyer yet. He says no, but she says yes he has, her, and tells him to set up a meet at the Farm tomorrow. Looks like we got us a good, old-fashioned sting operation.

James wakes in the night to the sound of shouting and glass breaking in the main house. Malcolm comes in and confirms it's Jeffrey wailing on Evelyn. He plants the idea of killing Jeffrey.

Bobby comes home during a thunderstorm to find his Mom waiting up, sitting alone in the dark and missing the Major. She's not sure he'll come back this time. Bobby recalls the conversation he and the Major had at the Double R about Bobby's future and his happiness. He says it was nice between them then, and Bobby and Betty both agree that Garland is an exceptional man. Then the power goes out. And the Major appears in the shadows wearing a bomber jacket, a white scarf, and aviator goggles. He asks how long he's been gone. Two days, he's told. He says it seemed much shorter. He and Betty embrace, and he tells Bobby to put out that cigarette and fix him a strong cocktail. When Bobby leaves the room, Betty asks Garland if everything is all right. He says no, not exactly.

Caleb Deschanel returns to direct his third and final episode of the series, off a script from Harley Peyton and Robert Engels. It's a shame, somewhat, because though this isn't the weakest of the second-season slump, it is the weakest of Deschanel's episodes, the other two being episode six, just before the season one finale, and episode 15, the one right after Leland kills Maddie. Still, as mentioned, it's far from the weakest in this weak stretch, thanks largely to the increasing mythology and importance of the Black and White Lodges, and the ramping up of the Windom Earle storyline, which will be the dominant narrative of the remaining episodes. As for the other plot involving Coop, this drug-trafficking nonsense, the whole thing turns out to be much ado about nothing as an obvious solution presents itself without Cooper even really having to go look for it, the chance for absolution just sort of falls in his lap. If it wasn't for the character of Denise and the performance of Duchovny, this storyline would be largely pointless, in my opinion, but it's far from the most egregious in the episode. I don't know about you, but at this point I'm pulling for Little Nicky to just kill Dick Tremayne.

But the return of Briggs is another sort of return, a return of focus. These middle episodes are what they are and what they are now is winding down, with the Black Lodge/Windom Earle story moving into the spotlight, and therein lies some of the most intriguing aspects and episodes of TWIN PEAKS yet.

EPISODE 20: "CHECKMATE"

Written by Harley Peyton, Directed by Todd Holland

Airdate January 19, 1991

The episode opens with a truly trippy sequence that involves fire, space, and a stone throne in a jungle setting. These images reflect the memories of Major Garland Briggs, who is attempting to recount his time away but he remembers nothing of his disappearance other than returning two days later to the same spot from which he went missing. All he can recall with clarity is the image of a giant owl. Briggs is stirred from his trance when Doc Hayward takes a photograph of a new mark, like a scar, behind his right ear. The mark is three triangles with their points touching, similar to the symbol for radioactive material. Coop and Truman continue to question him, but there isn't much he can tell them because his work is, as we know, mostly classified. But as the Major thinks about it, this doesn't matter as much to him now. He seems to be suffering a crisis of conscience. Coop has him start at the beginning. He asks if Coop is familiar with Project Blue Book? Coop is, it's the Air Force investigations into UFOs. Briggs reveals that though the project was officially disbanded in 1969, there are some who continue the investigations on their own; elsewhere these people look to the stars, but here in Twin Peaks they look below the Earth because they are searching for the White Lodge. No sooner does Briggs mention the place than two military police come in to claim jurisdiction over him. He leaves with them. The sprinklers are leaking again, just as they were the day Leland died.

Elsewhere in the Sheriff's station, Ernie Niles, at DEA Agent Denise Bryson's behest, makes a call to set the fake cocaine buy with Jean Renault.

Deputy Andy and Dick Tremayne have a secret meeting in reference to Little Nicky's background. Dick found out that the boy's records have been sealed and sent back to the orphanage, which means if they're going to find out the truth about what happened to his parents, they're going to have to go there and steal them.

Meanwhile, Coop has Lucy checking the personal columns of every single nationally-distributed newspaper for any chess moves or mention of Windom Earle. So far she's found neither.

At the Double R, Ed gets his coffee refilled by Norma. They're warming up to each other again after all the literal craziness with Nadine in the wake of her suicide attempt. Ed surreptitiously sets up a secret rendezvous.

Leo's still a handful for Shelly, especially with Bobby not helping out like he's supposed to. He won't feed Leo, he won't clean the place, and all because he doesn't think he has to, he's Ben Horne's "Golden Boy" now and all this is beneath him. But not beneath Shelly, apparently, so he leaves her to it.

James calls his Uncle Ed to ask a favor: he needs all the money from his savings account sent to him, but he won't say why. Ed begrudgingly agrees. Evelyn overhears this and enters, in large sunglasses, and asks if James is homesick. Not particularly, he replies. She asks if it was a girl he left town over. In a sense, yes, and then he tells her about Laura and Maddy, both dead despite his efforts. This is why he left, he says, because he had to. So much unfounded angst in that Hurley boy. Evelyn kisses him. He takes off her sunglasses and sees the black eye she's hiding, then they kiss again. Jeffrey, her husband, is heard leaving. Evelyn says she needs James' help but runs off before saying what for exactly.

93

Nadine finds Mike Nelson at the diner and persists in throwing herself at him. Mike very plainly makes his point to her: he's not interested. Nadine asks him out again anyway, then kisses him right out of his seat. She leaves him be, but not without making an impression.

Norma's leaving too, to rendezvous with Ed, but Hank stops her on her way out, curious as to her plans. She says she's running errands, but he knows better.

Truman shows up at the Packard/Martell homestead to see why Josie hasn't moved into his place like she said she was going to, but she has changed her mind and decided that this is where she's the safest, and also where he's the safest if she is. They smooch sadly.

Audrey discovers her father has gone off the deep end. His preoccupation with the Battle of Gettysburg has turned into a living, breathing, mental break wherein he believes he is actually commanding the Confederates in The Civil War. He knows Audrey, knows she is his daughter, but given his unwavering focus on the war and the adoption of a Southern accent, it would seem most of his mind is stuck in 1863. Audrey's trying to get him on his metaphorical feet again so he can save the family business, but he won't be shaken from the field of battle. Audrey calls the only person she can think of who might be able to help get through to Ben: Jerry.

Norma shows up at Ed's house – Nadine's in school – and professes her undying love for him. She says to hell with their troublesome situations, she only wants to be with him. They begins to kiss but she wants him to respond first. All he says is "later" and keeps up the kissing.

Ernie's getting wired for the fake drug buy. His mission is to introduce Denise to Jean Renault and walk everyone through the buy then scoot so Truman can swoop in and make the arrest. Coop won't be able to participate because he's been suspended from the bureau, but Truman fixes this by deputizing Coop, which pleases the former Special Agent as much as you would expect it to, which is to say, tremendously. Denise shows up, but as Dennis.

At the Dorritt Home for Boys, Andy and Dick are breaking into the office while everyone's at lunch. They locate Nicholas Needleman's file, before they can learn anything from it, an adopting couple comes to visit with their future ward. Dick has to think on his feet, which isn't his strong suit.

Donna drops by Ed's looking for James. Ed tells her about the money James asked for, and the bar on highway 96 he's supposed to send it to. Donna offers to take it instead. Once she's gone Norma slips out, their conversation still unresolved. Hank though has slipped in without being noticed, and starts to beat the crap out of Ed for sleeping with his wife. That's when Nadine comes home, though, and proceeds to beat the ever-living shit out of Hank.

Ben is talking military strategy with an uninterested Bobby. Ben seems to be confusing Bobby for General Meade of the Union Army. Bobby gets exasperated and scoots. Audrey's outside waiting for him. She says Jerry is headed home and Jacoby is coming tomorrow. As they walk away, Catherine comes to see Ben. She had come to gloat over his ruination at her hands, but her desire for him proves stronger than her spite.

James reveals to Evelyn that he's finished fixing her husband's car. They celebrate with champagne and sweet talk. She asks where he'll go next. He's not sure. She doesn't want him to go anywhere, she wants more time with him. They kiss, and are seen by Evelyn's brother Malcolm who seems suspiciously happy at this entanglement.

At Dead Dog Farm Ernie, Jean Renault and the RCMP King are waiting for Hank, but they can't wait anymore. Ernie's so nervous he shorts out his wire with flop sweat, revealing the sting and forcing Jean and King to take Ernie and Dennis hostage. Coop knows what Jean really wants, though, so trades himself for the other men.

Post-coitus, Evelyn leaves James sleeping. Malcolm is waiting for her in the hall. They kiss in a way that should suggest they aren't really brother and sister, but this is TWIN PEAKS so it's tough to say for sure right now.

Back at Dead Dog Farm, the State Police have showed up to lend assistance, but Jean and King are still barricaded inside the house with Coop, who has been beaten and bound. Coop points out that their options are but one: surrender. Jean completely agrees, but adds that the only decision is whether or not to go quietly or in a blaze of vengeful glory after killing Coop. Jean is more than willing to die if it means the death of the Special Agent who turned a simple place complicated, fucking with his business, and setting in motion the death of both his brothers. Coop's arrival changed Twin Peaks, Jean believes, and so he figures maybe Coop's departure in a body bag will change it back. Out the window, King sees a waitress bringing them food. That waitress is Denise, but they think she's "just a girl." She and Coop take control of the situation, which involves Coop wounding Jean and Hawk finishing the job. Renault dies. Coop thanks Denise for her intervention, but Denise reveals it was all Truman's plan.

Back at Leo and Shelly's, the power is flickering on and off. Shelly gets up to investigate, and discovers Leo isn't in his bed. A weird wind-up clown is instead. Leo isn't in his chair either. She turns to find him standing, face covered in cake and wearing a party hat. He says her name. She screams.

At the Sheriff's station, the cause of the town-wide power outage is revealed: Lucy got an anonymous call from someone saying there was a bomb in the woods, then there was an explosion, then the lights went out. There were also a couple of fires at the power station. Coop senses something is beyond normally wrong. He walks through the station and stops in Truman's office. He calls Truman over to see what he's discovered. There's an unidentified dead man tied to Truman's chair and posed to point at a chess board. This is Windom Earle's next move, and it's a doozy.

Fun fact: the dead man in Truman's chair is played by Craig MacLachlan, Kyle's brother, who also has small roles in Lynch's FIRE WALK WITH ME and HOTEL ROOM.

This episode is where the slump turns towards the light at the end of the tunnel. Director Todd Holland returns for the second and final time – the first being episode 11, "Laura's Secret Diary – and like his former episode, this one launches and closes plotlines. The Earle narrative begins to blossom as a character who has only been intimated to be a threat is revealed to be a very real one, and The White Lodge mystery also starts to deepen, but ultimately we're left with no more information at the end of the episode than the little we already had when the episode began. And on the opposite end of things, the Coop's suspension/Denise storyline is all but wrapped up, while the surprise return of Leo sets in motion another potentially violent storyline.

This, to me at least, signals the end of the no-man's-land that exists between the Laura Palmer murder and the Windom Earle mystery, which are the two central plots of TWIN PEAKS. There are still a couple episodes to go before we're completely out of the woods, a couple more painfully-silly subplots that need to be wrapped up, but at least now they're revealing themselves as merely set dressing for what would be – until 2017, that is – the final act.

EPISODE 21: "DOUBLE PLAY"

Written by Scott Frost, Directed by Uli Edel

Airdate February 2nd, 1991

We pick up minutes after last episode's cliffhanger, with Coop and Truman gathered around the dead man tied to Truman's desk chair. There's a chesspiece in the man's mouth. Coop gives it to Andy to dust for prints, then assumes the man was killed by a very precise puncturing of his heart. Doc Hayward's preliminary investigation confirms as much. This is something Coop has seen before. In searching for bloodstains on the carpet they find instead the small, thin branch of a Lodgepole Pine. Hawk reports he found two sets of boot prints outside, both made by the same boots, one time coming and one time going, the coming-set pressed deeper because the wearer was carrying a body. Truman asks how Coop can be sure this is the work of Windom Earle. Coop paints them a very visceral picture of this crime: the man is a drifter, a vagrant who would have been picked up by a friendly traveler and taken over the ridge where he was stabbed, the car will still be there; the man managed to escape from his attacker but obviously didn't survive his wound. This accomplished, Earle then set off the bomb in the woods that took out the power station and set the fires, drawing everyone away from the Sheriff's station so that he might slip in through Truman's office window and arrange this macabre tableau. Coop can feel Earle all over this scene, but warns they won't find any evidence of him. The man is a genius, Coop surmises, and this is him taking the first pawn of his sick game.

Audrey and Bobby are forging their business relationship in the candlelit lounge of The Great Northern. She says their surest route to getting rich is to bring her father Ben back from the brink of madness before he loses everything.

At Shelly's, she's still hiding from a suddenly-able and cake-plastered Leo. He's here one second, then as the lights flicker he disappears from view. As she cowers by the refrigerator, a jar of jam comes flying out of the darkness and smashes next to her. She screams and runs for the front door but it's locked. The owls outside hoot along with her calls for help. She runs for the backdoor, but the wheelchair is launched into her path, tripping her up. Then Leo is there, leaning against the fridge, barely able to stand but enraged. He calls Shelly a bad girl. She gets a knife. He's gone again, so she starts to cut her way through the vinyl sheeting perpetually serving as an exterior wall, but there's Leo again, jerking her back and throwing her over the kitchen table, causing her to lose consciousness, and the knife. Bobby shows up as Shelly's getting her senses back and Leo's grabbing an axe. Bobby hears her scream and tries to get inside as Leo is saying, "goodbye wife" and lifting the axe over his head. That's when Bobby rushes in and grabs the axe. They tussle and Leo gets the upper hand and starts to choke Bobby with the axe handle until Shelly ends it all by stabbing Leo in the leg. He screams and stumbles away through the rift Shelly cut in the vinyl sheeting and into the woods, howling like a wounded animal the entire time.

The long night has passed and as Coop suspected, there's no evidence of Windom Earle or any other perpetrator in Truman's office. There is good news, though: the FBI and the DEA won't be pressing charges against Coop, but until he hears from Gordon Cole his suspension still stands. Truman reminds Coop he's still a Twin Peaks Sheriff's Deputy, and if Coop wants this Earle case, it's all his. Of course Coop wants it. Hawk returns with news that they did indeed find the car that Earle used to pick up the drifter right where Coop said it would be, and it too was clean. Hawk also bears the news that Hank Jennings missed the drug buy at Dead Dog Farm because he was in the hospital claiming he got hit by a bus. We know he means a bus named Nadine. Hank's been booked for parole violation, and there's one more thing Hawk has to tell them: Shelly called about the Leo incident. Busy day in a small town.

In the lobby, Andy shares with Lucy his and Dick's theory that Little Nicky murdered his birth parents, despite being only six years old at the time of the supposed crime. Lucy thinks they're nuts, and says she's going to get to the bottom of this right away.

Out at Evelyn's, James is working on Jeffrey's car when he finally get the chance to meet Jeffrey. The latter man dressed in a *sweet* Air Jordon track suit, and seems like an okay guy. James is still wary, and excuses himself from the scene as swiftly as possible. When Jeffrey leaves in the car James was working on, Nadine watches him go, having an aural premonition of a violent crash.

Ed is talking with Doc Hayward about Nadine because she wants to start dating high school boys and he doesn't know what to do about that, as he hints that she's incredibly frisky in the boudoir and he's afraid given her absurd strength, she'll kill some poor kid. All Doc can offer him – as the father of a teenage girl and not a medical practitioner – is a prescription for patience and the virtue of an early curfew. Now it's Doc's turn to bend Ed's ear: he says Donna left that morning to go find James and wants to know if he as that same father has anything to worry about. Ed explains the sitch, says not to worry, it seems fine. After Doc leaves, Norma drops by with some extra mashed potatoes for Ed (that's how you know it's love) and news that Hank is in the hospital, apparently a tree fell on him. Ed knows better and tells her about the brawl yesterday after she left his place. She couldn't care less, because either way, Hank is heading back to the big house. This signals a new start for her, for them, and it means no more hiding, no more lying.

Evelyn finds James packing to go. He feels icky after meeting the dude whose wife he's banging. Evelyn tries to distract him with further amorous advances, but he doesn't want her like that anymore. So she plays the sympathy card and pleas for his help against Jeffrey, the brute. James leaves to check his bike, but his resolve is shaken.

Coop is studying the chessboard Earle left at the crime scene. Truman asks how the game factors into their relationship. Coop says Earle is a big fan, he believes life can be inferred from the patterns of the game, and so every day for three years while they were partners he and Coop would play. Problem is, Earle always won. Coop doesn't know what else to do but publish his responding move in the Twin Peaks Gazette. This sounds as nuts to Truman as it does the rest of us, so he asks for some background and context. At last we learn Cooper's secret: four years ago Earle and Coop were assigned to protect a federal witness, a woman, beautiful and gentle, named Caroline. Coop and Caroline fell in love. One night during the assignment he failed in his vigilance and an attack was made. He was wounded and when he came to Caroline was dying in his arms. It's the same story he told Audrey a few episodes back, but this time there's a little more detail to it. Caroline had been stabbed to death, her wound identical to the one on the vagrant. Her killer was never apprehended, and though Cooper's physical wound healed, Earle went mad and had to be institutionalized, where he remained until his recent escape. Truman's still not making the connection, so Coop slips him the last piece of the puzzle. Caroline, the witness, his lover, was Earle's wife. So Earle holds Coop responsible for her death? Nope, worse: Coop thinks Earle killed his own wife, and furthermore he thinks Earle committed the crime she witnessed. He thinks Earle faked insanity in the beginning, but now it's overtaken his cold, hard, and brilliant mind, making him capable of anything.

Donna makes it to Wallie's Hide Out on highway 96 where James wanted his money delivered. She's looking for him, but finds Evelyn instead. Evelyn mentions James recently did some work for her, but says he's gone now, headed for the ocean, she thinks, Mexico maybe. She suggests Donna go home, she's too late. The doo-wop ditty James and Donna and Maddy recorded plays over scenes of the separate but comparative angst of Donna and James.

The Civil War rages on in Ben's office. Audrey enters with Jerry, at long last returned to see about his brother. Dr. Jacoby is in the corner observing and scribbling notes. He tells Jerry to address Ben as "General." Ben recognizes

97

his brother, but as General Jeb Stuart. Seems in Ben's version of the Civil War, the Confederates are about to march on Washington and claim victory. According to Jacoby, this is a good thing: by reversing the historical outcome, Ben perhaps will also reverse his own emotional setback. All he needs now is the understanding of his loved ones, and a Union surrender.

Major Briggs enters the Sheriff's station exhausted and asking urgently to see Truman. Then he collapses. After a tall glass of water, he's cognizant again and explains to Coop and Truman that when he was questioned by his own people about his disappearance, their suspicion of him was palpable, paranoid, even. He is now forced to admit that their quest for the White Lodge is not as ideologically pure as he once thought, and thus his allegiance to them is tarnished, allowing this disclosure. Briggs believes he was taken to the White Lodge when he disappeared, though he has no memory of it, only the sense that there is much trouble ahead. He doesn't know the form this trouble will yet take, but he'll come when it emerges, and until that time he'll be in the shadows if they need him. He leaves as Andy enters, needing to show them something: Jacoby is there with Lana Milford, Dougie's delectable widow, and he can attest, having spent the last 24 hours in her company, that she is not cursed to kill her lovers, she's just a nympho with mad skills, which raises the temperature of every man in the room. Lana and Jacoby leave to go bowling, but they don't get out of the building before they're accosted by Mayor Dwayne Milford, Dougie's brother, and his very large shotgun. Dwayne wants vengeance for his brother's death. Coop suggests he talk with Lana alone, just the two of them. No one bothers to take the shotgun from Dwayne as they enter a conference room and close the door behind them. It takes about a minute before Lana has charmed the Mayor's hard heart with her warm kisses. The Mayor proclaims they've decided to adopt a child together. For her part, he reminds her so much of Dougie that she can't help but love him. They're both allowed to leave, because threatening to kill people isn't that big of deal in Twin Peaks.

Catherine has something she wants to show Pete. She asks if Pete ever considered how she survived the fire and rose, in obscurity, to take the mill from Ben. Now that she mentions it, he has. She reintroduces him to Andrew Packard, not dead at all. Pete's in disbelief, he saw the boat on which Andrew was killed. But it was a faked death to thwart an assassination attempt coming from Thomas Eckhardt, an old business partner of Andrew's who became vengeful when Andrew one-upped him on a deal. Josie has been Eckhardt's agent all this time, attempting a long con meant to lead to Andrew's death. Eckhardt is coming to Twin Peaks, they've learned, and now they'll see if Josie works for him still.

At just that moment a woman is checking into The Great Northern for Thomas Eckhardt, who's waiting by the hearth. He's got fire in his eyes, kinda literally.

Lucy is demanding an audience with Andy, Dick and Doc Hayward. In the meantime, Truman needs Coop's help with Jonathan Lee, who Josie told him she slipped away from in Seattle. News just came in over the wire that he's dead, and Truman needs to know if Josie was involved. Coop's all over it. Back with Lucy and Doc, she's told him about Andy and Dick's ideas about Little Nicky murdering his parents so he called the orphanage himself and cut through the red tape. Nicky's mom was an immigrant chambermaid at The Great Northern and his dad was a rapist. She died in delivery and Nicky moved from state home to state home until a loving couple finally adopted him. All was well until an icy road killed both of them, leaving Little Nicky all alone yet again. There isn't a dry eye in the house, but if there was, it would be rolling.

James it turns out, hasn't left Evelyn's, not yet at least, but he's finally finished packing. Their affair is wrong, he says. She says she loves him. Then the sound of sirens. Evelyn tells James Jeffrey is dead. James correctly guesses the man was killed in a car accident, which means he's been set up to take the fall. She admits he has, but not by her, by Malcolm, who is not her brother. She tells James to flee, to go find that young girl who loves him. James makes a break for it and manages to elude the cops, stumbling into Donna in the process. She followed Evelyn home from Wallie's and helps him escape.

We end on Leo in the woods, wounded and disoriented. An owl screeches past. Wind whistles in the trees and low-hanging clouds rumble with thunder. There's a cabin out here, somewhere Leo's never seen, and inside that cabin there's a light. Leo goes to it and enters, looking for Shelly. Instead he finds a man in a black suit who invites him to sit and offers to help him. The man then introduces himself: Windom Earle.

Episode 21 is a return to form for TWIN PEAKS that sees Coop start back on the road to his black suit, expands the lore of the Lodges, and begins the Earle plotline in earnest with the first (visual) appearance of the man himself, as played by Kenneth Welsh. And thankfully, the episode also brings to a needlessly depressing end the worst subplot of the series – the Andy-Dick Tremayne-Little Nicky debacle. These twists of plot comes courtesy of writer Scott Frost, and the episode's direction – which is notably stylized – was from German director Uli Edel who at the time had just directed the outstanding film LAST EXIT TO BROOKLYN, and had yet to direct the terrible erotic-legal-thriller/Madonna vehicle BODY OF EVIDENCE. Seems TWIN PEAKS caught him in a sweet spot between the two, because his time at the helm here created some powerful and in some instances foreshadowing images. For example the rift in the vinyl sheeting through which a wounded Leo escapes into the night can be inferred as the rift between two worlds soon to open in the series, and perhaps is suggesting that it's the power of the Lodges that "resurrected" Leo to lead him violently into the clutches of Windom Earle.

Furthermore, in the scene where the image of Caroline is appears transparent over Cooper's own, note the red tint to it, a sure sign of things to come. These visuals, along with inserts of totem poles, waterfalls and trees swaying in the night wind are all standard for TWIN PEAKS, but here take on an extra-menacing tone to rival Lynch's own. Edel did a fine job of balancing the tragic with the comic here, especially for a one-time series director.

And I'm not accusing anyone of anything other than a brilliant homage, but there are striking visual and tonal similarities between Windom Earle's cabin in TWIN PEAKS and Jacob's cabin in LOST.

Anyway, bottom line, the final act has begun. And instead of opening wide at its inception, we're seeing the curtains close around Twin Peaks, tighter and tighter...

EPISODE 22: "SLAVES AND MASTERS"

Written by Harley Peyton and Robert Engels, Directed by Diane Keaton

Airdate February 9th, 1991

Actress Diane Keaton (ANNIE HALL) makes her television directorial debut with this episode, which she opens with a close-up of chess pieces. Worse yet, these are thematic chess pieces, not even ones that are a part of an active scene. This is just Ms. Keaton letting we the audience know that she's seen the show, and she gets it: it's weird, right?

The narrative itself opens with Evelyn in mourning, or so it should appear. She and Malcolm are giving the cops info on James, describing him as the man who fixed the car that killed her husband Jeffrey. Evelyn lies about how she met James, making it sound like he sought her out, and not the other way around. The cop promises to check out James then leaves. That's when Malcolm, Evelyn's lover not her brother and Jeffrey's real killer, tells her to keep it together so they can pull off their scam.

At Wallie's Hideout, Donna and James are going over their limited options regarding James' legal situation, and the bottom line is: they need help. She wants to call Ed, he wants to get Evelyn to tell the truth. When Donna asks why he's so sure Evelyn would save him like that, his silence is the answer, and she responds by going to call Ed and giving him the skinny. Ms. Keaton plays the weird/quirky card again in the form of a half dozen cigar-smoking bus drivers all in the same uniform and sitting the same way at the bar.

Another set of chess pieces marks our entrance to the Sheriff's station conference room, where Bobby and Shelly are being interviewed by Coop and Truman about the incident with Leo last night. Truman wants to know what Bobby was doing there in the first place. Bobby spells it out, all of it, their entire relationship. Coop asks him where he was the night the mill burned. Bobby wonders why. Because Leo tried to kill him, Coop says, so it could be you who shot him in retaliation. Bobby tells the truth here as well: Hank shot Leo. Shelly has no idea where Leo could be, but Truman promises to keep deputies on her house. Albert returns as they leave. He and Harry hug robustly, the best of friends now following Albert's declaration the last time he was in town (episode 10) that the foundation of his method for living is love. He's there on direct orders from Gordon Cole to assist Coop with the Earle investigation. He shows them a map of the U.S. with a giant C spelled out on it when one connects the dots of a series of deliveries to police stations, each one designed to look like a mailbomb but in fact harmless and containing individual pieces of clothing: a white veil here, a garter there, a pair of white slippers somewhere else, a pearl necklace, a wedding dress – all Caroline's, Coop knows. Each of the deliveries were paid for with a credit card signed by Windom Earle. Law enforcement everywhere is looking for him, but he's only interested in Coop. Furthermore, the dead man in Truman's office died as Coop suspected, of a stab wound to the heart. Earle waited until rigor mortis partially set in before posing him then moved on to cause the explosion at the power station. All they found at that crime scene was the map Albert just produced.

Speaking of Earle, he's in his cabin in the woods playing a jaunty tune on a wooden shakuhachi flute for Leo. The place is decorated like the Devil's junk drawer. Earle has learned all about Leo and the various crimes for which he is currently wanted. Leo tries to leave but Earle takes him down with the flute, says he owns Leo now, and punctuates the point by fitting him with an electric shock collar. It's effective, and Earle is revealed to be truly and crazily sadistic.

Ed and Norma are in bed together, post coital, talking about their long and beleaguered relationship, the wasted years and opportunities they've lost, the pain they shielded even from themselves. But it's over now, now it's about the future, their future, and what they're going to do with it. No more hiding, no more pretending, there's still plenty of time left for them. Nadine is heard to come home and Norma starts to bolt but Ed keeps her next to him; they have to talk about it some time. Nadine nonchalantly tears down the door and gets into bed with them. She's upset because she was disqualified from a wrestling match because of an illegal move. She then notices Norma, but only to apologize for beating the crap out of Hank. She then gets out of bed and starts to leave but not before telling them she knows about them and it's really okay, she's in love with Mike Nelson. She says it's really serious between them, so Ed and Norma can do whatever they like, she's completely cool.

Coop and Truman are talking to Josie about Jonathan Lee's death. The Seattle police know she's connected to him. She asks how he died. Not well, he was shot three times in the back of the head. Truman says she has to tell them the truth and Coop goes hunting for coffee to give them privacy. Pete comes in while he's doing so loaded to bear with dry cleaning, he's been helping Josie out. When the phone rings, Coop takes the dry cleaning while Pete goes to answer it. It's for Josie. Coop tells Pete where he can find her then removes from the dry cleaning a thread from a Vicuna coat, along with a black leather glove. On the phone is Thomas Eckhardt, Josie's secret employer. He's in town. He's heard about Jonathan. And Catherine has heard all of this on another extension.

Ben Horne is in the throes of his Civil War insanity and has now added a saddled, stuffed donkey and his son Johnny in full Native American regale to the tableau. Jacoby, Audrey and Jerry are standing by humoring him. Jerry tells the others there are some benefits to Ben being crazy, namely that it leaves Jerry the opportunity to develop some projects on his own. Audrey clues him in that if Ben is declared incapable of running the business, according to his will it's she who becomes the executor of his estate, not Jerry. She tells Jacoby to fix her father. So Jacoby says it's time to implement the Appomattox Scenario.

Evelyn's back in the bar, wasted with sorrow, when Donna approaches her. She wants to know why she's doing this to James *Why not?* is the best answer she has, as she's become bitter and fatalistic in her conflicted emotional distress. Malcolm shows up to collect her and level a blatant murder threat at Donna.

Albert has analyzed the thread from Josie's coat: it matches the thread found outside Coop's room the night he was shot. The gloves are still being checked for gunpowder residue. As for Seattle, cops are looking for an Asian woman in connection with Mr. Lee's death, the sketch of whom looks a lot like Josie. Jonathan – Kumagai is his last name – has an Interpol rap sheet as long as Coop's arm and Albert's willing to bet the three bullets pulled from the back of the man's head will match those in Coop's vest. All signs point to Josie as Coop's would-be assassin, but for Truman's sake, Coop hopes it isn't true.

While keeping this info to himself, Coop goes to see Truman, who has an ID on the dead guy, Erik Powell, a transient as Coop suspected. Coop knows the name, the last name at least, it's the same as Caroline's maiden name. This Powell isn't a relative but he is a message, Earle's way of telling Coop that he hasn't forgotten a thing. It also means that whenever Earle takes a piece from the chess board in the game with Coop, someone in the real world dies, pawns first then up through the more meaningful pieces. And Coop, remember, has never beaten Earle, so stands to lose a lot of pieces, including his king, which we can presume represents his own life. Truman however, can take him to a chess expert living right there in town: Pete. He learned from a Spaniard, and he is indeed a master. So Coop enlists his services: he can't tell him why but he needs Pete to arrange a stalemate losing as few pieces as possible, preferably none. Pete's happy to help.

Shelly stops by the diner to see Norma. She wants her job back and Norma's glad to give it to her. Truman interrupts the happy reunion with some sour info: Hank's almost ready to leave the hospital. Norma doesn't want him back. With the attempted murder of Leo and his various parole violations, there's no chance Hank's coming back, Truman assures her, he's going to jail for a long time. This pleases her verily.

Eckhardt arrives at the Martell house at Catherine's invitation and to Josie's stunned chagrin. Catherine and Eckhardt discuss his history with Andrew, which was sunny at first and sour in the end, when, you know, Eckhardt had Andrew killed. Eckhardt says that wasn't about business, it was about love, his for Josie. Catherine wants to broker a trade, Josie for something very valuable TBD.

Evelyn's blowing smoke rings past her lying lips when James storms in demanding to know why she set him up. Did Malcolm make her do it? Short answer, she's just a manipulative bitch who used him for her husband's money. But she was still into him, despite all the lying pretense. They kiss, and Malcolm sneaks in and knocks him out. Now they have to kill him, it's the perfect ending: jilted lover kills husband, breaks in to finish the job. All that's left is for Evelyn to shoot him, Malcom suggests.

The Appomattox Scenario is underway, in which Audrey, Jacoby, Bobby and Jerry all in costume help Ben believe that he has won the Civil War for the South, thus reversing history. The hope is that this symbolic victory will reverse Ben's attitudes about his own losses of late. And sure enough, as soon as he signs the papers he collapses and comes to as though out of a trance. He says he had the strangest dream, it's another very WIZARD OF OZ moment. But he seems happier, healed, even.

Earle is applying a disguise as Leo is writing some kind of letter under the command of his shock collar. The letter, as Earle describes it, is composed of "pretty words for pretty girls" and it is revealed Leo is writing it beneath pictures of Audrey, Donna, and Shelly. Earle wonder alouds which will be his queen.

Malcolm and Evelyn are preparing to shoot James when Donna rushes in, just to be immediately apprehended by Malcolm. Donna pleads with Evelyn to spare James' life, and it works, Evelyn shoots Malcolm instead.

We see Caroline in a picture Coop carries in his wallet, which also causes him not to see Earle, in costume, who passes him on his way to The Great Northern's front desk, where he says he has a delivery for Audrey.

In his room, Coop finds a present on his bed: a death mask of Caroline hooked to a tape recorder of Earle professing his love for his wife, acknowledging Coop's, and informing him that it's his move…

In the effort of full disclosure, this is my least favorite episode. In addition to Keaton's blunt direction (TWIN PEAKS is never good when it's trying to be TWIN PEAKS), this episode is too heavy on the horrible James-Evelyn subplot, which at least it resolves, but still, not the best hour the series ever produced. The script by Peyton and Engels is sound enough and sets in motion the first machinations of Earle's overall plot, but the rest of it is somewhat drab and/or convoluted. The Eckhardt-Josie-Andrew subplot seems forced, and the Nadine-Ed-Norma subplot seems dragged out. And unfortunately, I wasn't the only one feeling a little, well, fed up at this point.

It was after this episode finished 85th out of 89 programs for the week that ABC decided that after the next episode aired, they were going to put the show on indefinite hiatus. The lack of a singular, suspenseful plot between Laura's resolution and Windom's entrance had driven off too many viewers, as had the Gulf War: because of the event, TWIN PEAKS was preempted from its timeslot six times, making it hard to keep up with the show even if you wanted to. A letter writing campaign organized by C.O.O.P. (Citizens Opposed to the Offing of PEAKS) managed to get the show back on the air six weeks later, for the final six episodes of the series, but the damage was done and the scramble for the exits had begun.

It's fans only from this point forward, but it's also from this point forward that we learn the true mystery at the heart of TWIN PEAKS, one that will certainly be at the forefront of season three.

EPISODE 23: "THE CONDEMNED WOMAN"

Written by Tricia Brock, Directed by Lesli Linka Glatter

Airdate February 16th, 1991

Cooper is playing the tape left in his room by Windom Earle (along with Caroline's death mask) for Truman, which is the same message we heard at the end of the last episode, plus a little bit we hadn't heard yet: "make your next move tomorrow or I'll make it for you." They call Pete and ask him to head over. He'll be on his way just as soon as he finishes serving breakfast to Catherine and Andrew. The playful, brotherly dynamic between the two men has returned, to Catherine's disgust. Pete splits, and Josie returns. She hasn't seen Andrew yet and in fact has no idea he's still alive. As such, she's pretty surprised, and faints.

Truman is ruminating over the death of Jonathan Kumagai and Josie's likely involvement when Hawk brings in a hobbled Hank, who is there to plead his case but Truman isn't hearing it and informs him it isn't just a parole violation he's being charged with, it's also the attempted murder of Leo Johnson. Hank says he has an alibi for that, but Truman says he has an eyewitness. Hank tries to strike a deal, trade his freedom for information leading to the arrest of the murderer of Andrew Packard. He means Josie, but Truman either doesn't know or doesn't care, because he's not making any deals. Hank lays it all on the table, explicitly accusing Josie, in response to which Hawk kicks out his crutch and sends Hank crashing onto Truman's desk.

Albert is sharing with Coop the latest forensics on Kumagai: the bullets from him match the bullets from Coop's vest. Same gun means same shooter – Josie Packard. Albert's ready to pounce but Coop is urging caution. He'll talk to her himself, maybe she'll confess and come in of her own accord. Albert doesn't think so but it isn't his call.

At The Great Northern, Audrey is given a letter by the concierge that was left for her at the desk last episode by Windom Earle in disguise. She's interrupted from opening it by a dreamy fella (Billy Zane) who she doesn't recognize, but who certainly knows her, and has since they were children. He doesn't give his name, but he does drop that he owns his own plane, and that smile says he's definitely DTF. She's flustered and he makes a smooth exit. Once her pulse slows down, she remembers the letter and opens it. Inside is a torn piece of paper, what looks like a third of a page, along with a card that reads "Save the one you love. Please attend a gathering of angels tonight at The Road House, 9:30."

Nadine comes home from school early, obviously distraught. Ed asks what wrong and she spells it out for him: she and Mike Nelson are in love, and she's sorry, she didn't want to hurt Ed, but on a recent wrestling trip she and Mike had a long night of robust sexual activity. Long, gross story short: she's breaking up with Ed. It's sweet and weird and wonderful for them both, because man, this was a terrible relationship.

Coop is confronting Josie about Seattle, and she's sticking to her story about losing Kumagai at the airport. Catherine's listening in and loving every second. Coop tells Josie if she won't be honest for her own sake, she should do it for Harry's. She remains obstinate. So Coop tells her it's talk or be made to talk: she has until 9 pm to come to the station with the truth or he comes looking for her. Catherine shows herself and rubs salt in Josie's wound by telling her Eckhardt wants to inspect the merchandise before he pays for it, so she'll need to go see him tonight, alone. Josie knows he will kill her. Catherine further frays Josie's unraveling sanity by wondering what he'll do when he finds out Andrew is alive, because that looks like Josie betrayed Eckhardt and didn't kill her husband like she was supposed to. Josie is losing her marbles like there's a hole in the bag. Serving her own needs,

103

Catherine reveals to Josie a gun that she might take along on her meeting. Funny how focused crazy can get when it has a gun in its hands.

At The Great Northern a mentally-renewed Ben Horne is getting back to business with a healthier attitude, celery instead of cigars, a track suit instead of Brooks Brothers, and a more congenial spirit, as evidenced by him inviting Bobby to sit in on a board meeting. They're joined by Audrey and Jerry. Typically, Ben says, these meeting are boring affairs but today's is special, and that's when Audrey's handsome man from earlier enters and is embraced by Ben. He is John Justice Wheeler, Ben explains, an old family friend and a self-made man who Ben has asked to join the board. It seems Ben invested in JJW when the guy was just starting out, and JJW turned that investment into an empire, and now that Horne Industries is in dire straits, JJW has come to return that kindness. So Ben explains the sitch: Catherine owns the mill and Ghostwood Estates. Since they have no legal recourse, Ben plans to protest the development on the grounds that it would wipe out the habitat of the endangered pine weasel.

At the Double R, Earle in disguise is paying his bill and leaving an envelope addressed to Shelly. Norma is on the phone with her younger sister Annie, who's coming for a visit tomorrow from the convent she's fleeing. Clearing the counter, Shelly finds her envelope. It has the same contents as Audrey's: a torn piece of paper with poetry on it, and the invitation. Then Big Ed walks in. He comes behind the counter, takes Norma in his arms, talks all lovey-dovey then proposes marriage. They kiss a "yes."

In the woods, Leo's sharpening sticks when Earle returns to the cabin. Earle puts an arrowhead on one of the sticks.

Hank gets a visitor in jail: Norma. She's come to ask for a divorce. He'll give it to her in exchange for one last favor: say she was with him the night Leo was shot. She refuses. He calls her Ed's whore. And Norma delivers the most empowering line of her run: "I'd rather be his whore than your wife." Daaaaaaaaaaaaaaamn, dude.

Pete's going over the chess options with Coop and Truman. There's only five minutes before the deadline to post in the newspaper, so the move has to come now, and it has to be made so that none of Coop's pieces are open to take, because each piece lost will represent a real person murdered. Albert appears with some private news for Coop: the powder from the gun that shot him is match for that found on Josie's gloves, and a new witness in Seattle saw her leaving the car where Jonathan was found dead. The time to move is now, but Coop asserts that he has control. Truman knows something's up and takes off.

At Josie's, she's getting ready for her rendezvous with Eckhardt when Andrew comes to see her with an offering of champagne. She apologizes for trying to murder him. There's no need, he's aware of Eckhardt's persuasive powers, and he did love her once upon a time, which is why he tells her if she doesn't act soon she'll be arrested. Ever the dependent, Josie asks him what she should do? See Eckhardt, leave with him. All this talk of chess between Coop and Earle, and Josie's the biggest pawn in TWIN PEAKS.

Donna and James meet out in the woods. He's back from clearing his name with the cops in regards to Jeffrey's murder. Evelyn's going to trial and he'll be a witness. Donna's made a picnic for them. She starts it by saying she knows about him and Evelyn making the beast with two backs, but she gets it, he was taken advantage of. Sure, yeah, that's what happened. She wants him to come back to Twin Peaks, but he still isn't ready. She understands that too, she needs something new in her life as well. She tells him to go, to stay away as long as he wants. It's a passive break-up but it's sweet, and it's a fitting final chapter in a love affair that should have ended episodes ago. They make promises they'll never keep and kiss sweetly for the last time.

Pete and Catherine are enjoying some down time at the house when an insistent visitor comes knocking. It's Truman to see Josie, but he's too late, she's gone. Catherine tries to be vague about where but Pete knows she's at The Great Northern to see an old friend. Who? Catherine tells him. He bolts.

Eckhardt, in heading to the rendezvous, finds himself in the elevator with a ghost: Andrew Packard. Andrew lies to Eckhardt and tells him Josie betrayed him and saved Andrew's life because she loved him. This really gets Eckhardt's goat because Josie was his lover first, and thus his property. Andrew winds him up and leaves him with a warning: Josie might be coming back to him tonight with a vengeance.

In The Great Northern restaurant, Ben is dining with Audrey and JJW. It turns out JJW flips corporations for a living, and living is good. He's also an environmentalist; complete package much? Ben is called away, leaving the young folk to converse. Audrey doubts JJW's motivations, but he's really just doing a favor for man who once did a favor for him. Audrey's independent though, fiercely so, and thinks Hornes can fend for themselves. JJW is inclined to agree, but in a romantic sense. She melts a little, asks him about where he's been living. All over the far flung corners of the world. This is also alluring to starry-eyed Audrey. It isn't Coop chemistry, but it's palpable.

At The Road House, Shelly and Donna run into each other. It seems Donna got the same letter as Shelly and Audrey, the latter of whom appears just as the girls are piecing together their separate papers. Complete, it's a poem: "See the mountains kiss high heaven/And the waves clasp one another/No sister-flower would be forgiven If it disdain'd its brother/And the sunlight clasps the earth/And the moonbeams kiss the sea/What is all this sweet work worth, If thou kiss not me?" As they read it aloud, Earle is down the bar in disguise, watching them.

In his room, Coop is practicing fly fishing when he gets a call from Catherine telling him not to come bother looking for Josie, as she's at The Great Northern right now in Thomas Eckhardt's suite. The trap is complete: Josie's been convinced to try and shoot Eckhardt, Eckhardt's been convinced Josie will try to harm him, and Coop's on his way to witness it all. He takes his own weapon. Outside the suite he hears cries and shouts, then a gun shot. He bursts in to find Josie and Eckhardt in bed. Eckhardt gets up with a hole in his chest and blood soaking through his pj's. He falls dead, revealing Josie upright now with her own weapon pointed at Coop. She plays the self-defense angle. Coop wonders if she'll play the same after shooting him. She admits to killing Jonathan because he was trying to take her back to Hong Kong, then admits to shooting Coop because she was afraid of being found out and sent to jail. This is when Truman enters. His gun is drawn as well. She apologizes to him for everything, then has some kind of episode, a cross between a seizure and a heart attack, and collapses on the bed. Truman rushes to her, but she's dead. It's pretty a pretty weird death, but this is TWIN PEAKS, so it gets even weirder. Coop sees a bright spotlight shine on Truman and Josie's body, then they fade away, leaving just the light on the bed. That's when BOB appears for the first time since Leland's death. He crawls over the bed with a question: "Coop, what happened to dead Josie?" He screams laughter. He fades and The Man From Another Place appears. Then the spotlight fades and Truman is back, crying with dead Josie in his arms. *Then*, in the weirdest moment of an already weird series, the camera pans to the knob of the nightstand by the bed, in which Josie's screaming face appears. It presses against the wood but can't break free.

WTF?

Another episode both written and directed by women, Tricia Brock and Lesli Linka Glatter, respectively, that features the final appearance of TWIN PEAKS' most deceptive femme fatale, Josie Packard. If the demise of Josie seems abrupt and out of the blue, that's because it was. At this point in the series, Joan Chen, the actress who played Josie, wanted out to focus on her film career, which the writers obliged. The result is an odd death made cryptic by the three-fold curiosity of the return of BOB, the question he poses as to what killed Josie, and the appearance of Josie's soul in the drawer knob. In regard to the first two curiosities, it is popularly-believed that Josie was killed by fear, the fear of being found out, the fear of being at the end of her deception with nowhere to turn but the truth, and the fear that this truth would cause the one she loves, namely Truman, to turn away from her. Josie lied herself into a corner, and in the end, her fear of coming out of it killed her. This is what caused BOB, a spirit who feeds on fear, to manifest. As to why Josie wound up in the drawer knob, most of us strike that up as TWIN PEAKS being TWIN PEAKS.

There's a lot of closure in this episode, not just the Josie storyline, but the Donna/James romance (it's his final episode as well, at least in the flesh), and even the Norma/Ed engagement is an end to the turmoil that has defined their relationship from the first time we met them. But there are also a lot of new beginnings here what with the JJW/Audrey stirrings, Earle incorporating the girls into his game (posing the possible question who will be the next dead young thing from Twin Peaks?), but mostly this episode was about getting Josie out of here. And mission accomplished.

EPISODE 24: "WOUNDS AND SCARS"

Written by Barry Pullman, Directed by James Foley

Airdate March 28th, 1991

This was the series' first episode back after a six-week hiatus. Only the diehards were watching at this point, and there was a pervasive feeling among them that things were coming to an end; even if cancellation wasn't certain at this point, the writing was on the wall all the same.

We open on Sheriff Harry S. Truman drowning his sorrows over Josie's strange death in some whiskey and imagined sax at the Bookhouse. Hawk brings him some breakfast from the diner, because apparently the Sheriff has been drinking all night. He's reticent enough to ask how things are at work. All about Earle, Hawk says, but they're holding it together for now with Coop at the helm. Hawk leaves Truman to wallow because he knows the Sheriff needs to get this pain out of his system his own way.

At the diner, Norma's little sister Annie arrives. My lifelong appreciation for Heather Graham began right here, following a major infatuation directed her way after seeing LICENSE TO DRIVE. Annie, we recall, has returned to Twin Peaks after leaving her life in a convent. The sisters reunite but Annie is quick to note she doesn't want charity, she wants to work for her keep. Beautiful and honest, what a combo. Down the counter Major Briggs is visited by the Log Lady, who notices the new mark behind his right ear. She seems distraught by it.

Hawk is reporting Harry's condition to Coop, who's a little overwhelmed with being in charge of the department, not to mention having seen BOB again when Josie died. Speaking of Josie, her autopsy results came back and Doc Hayward was unable to determine the cause of her death. Furthermore, she weighed an impossible 65 pounds. As for Earle, Coop's just waiting for his response to the latest chess move.

In his cabin in the woods, Earle at that very moment is reading Coop's move in the town paper's personals column. When he realizes the move doesn't allow him to claim any pieces, he knows what Coop is up to, and furthermore knows he's being helped. This counts as cheating to Earle, and he vows many people are going to regret this then plays a jaunty tune on his shakuhachi flute. His wedding ring is prominently featured.

At The Great Northern, Audrey is running various tasks when JJW appears and they awkwardly but cutely apologize to each other for last night's dinner, then set up a nice picnic for the weekend. Each seems equally smitten with the other.

Coop visits Harry with some cold truth: in addition to killing Eckhardt, killing Jonathan in Seattle, and trying to kill Coop, Josie was also wanted by Interpol for a long, long list of felony charges, two of which were for prostitution. Coop says Truman needs to know all this, who she was, he needs to know the person he's making her to be in memory isn't the person she was in reality. But Harry isn't hearing it.

Catherine, meanwhile, is going about her business when Thomas Eckhardt's lovely executive assistant Jones (Brenda Strong, SEINFELD) comes to see her. She's there to expedite Eckhardt's body back across the Pacific and says he and Josie are to be buried side-by-side. Catherine pulls a casual pistol on Jones to help her hurry to the point. Jones has brought a gift for Catherine from Thomas. It's a black box. Jones says she'll be leaving town that night and wishes Catherine good luck, then saunters out of the room. I wish there'd been more of Jones, she's intriguing in a way Eckhardt was not, and there seems to be broad potential for the character. Alas, she's all but done with TWIN PEAKS.

Earle, in disguise, shows up at Donna's looking for her parents, who aren't there. He claims to be a fellow doctor and an old friend stopping by for a surprise visit. So Donna, apparently unscarred by the murder of her best friend, her best friend's cousin, and her own near-murder at the hands of Harold Smith, invites this strange adult male into her completely empty house. Small talk is made, then Earle says he has a gift for her dad for the occasion of the 30th anniversary of their med school graduation, but she can't open it. He also gives her a card with his phone number. Not at all creepy, Donna, don't worry about it.

Pete is keeping his chess skills sharp by plotting future hypothetical moves. He's gone through every stalemate match in recorded history, and there's no way to arrive at one without sacrificing a minimum of six pieces, or six people in the real world. Coop suggests they prioritize protecting royalty, that's Earle's real prize. Major Briggs and the Log Lady show up needing to talk with Coop about the mark Briggs got when he was missing. The log noticed it, and caused Margaret to remember something: she has a similar mark on the back of her right leg. It isn't exactly the same, instead of three identical triangles it's two irregular ones, symmetrically side-by-side. If you're watching the series on the Gold Box Set, you'll recognize Margaret's symbol as the same as the episode indicator on the DVD menu. She says she got it when she was seven and went walking in the woods. It only felt like she was gone a few hours to her, but when she returned people told her she'd been missing for a day. All she could ever remember about her time away was a flash of light and the mark on her leg. Coop draws it on the chalkboard next to a sketch of Briggs' mark. The Major points out that all three of them, Coop included, have seen this white light. Margaret adds that she heard the call of an owl at the time of the light, as did Briggs and Coop. She also says the only other time she heard that sound and saw that sight in conjunction is when her husband died in a fire the night they were wed. Looking at the symbols together, everyone can sense that they connect to something, but they're just not sure what.

It's picnic time for JJW and Audrey. He's serenading her with acapella cowboy songs, and dude's game is on point because she's gobbling it up. These are two very beautiful people; the children they could've had. Audrey at this point is way over Coop and pretty much says so out loud, laying a clear emotional path for JJW.

Doc and Mrs. Hayward return and are told of their visitor. They know the name he gave, Gerald Craig, but say isn't possible the man was actually there. Donna tells them the whole story and shows her father the card and the gift Earle left. Doc is unsettled, and rightfully so because Gerald Craig was his indeed roommate in med school but he died, drowned in a rafting incident, Doc knows for certain, he tried to save his friend's life but failed. Eileen calls the phone number on the card: it's a cemetery. Doc opens the gift: it's a chess piece, a black knight, with a written move tied around its neck, Knight to King's Bishop 3. Doc knows the danger this denotes and heads directly for Coop.

Meanwhile the other Doc in town, Jacoby, is brokering the relationship dissolution between Ed and Nadine. She thinks it's a dating break-up, so Jacoby's trying to get through to her without freaking her out that it's a divorce they're talking about. He's not getting through, though, Nadine's wounded mind just isn't ready to handle the truth. So Jacoby puts it to her plainly. Her response is to instantly lose the imagined vision in her already dead eye, a sign she's returning to the Nadine she was.

Back at the Hayward's there's a knock at the door. When Donna starts downstairs to answer it, she sees her mom is already there. Talking hushed tones, Ben Horne leans into view and takes Mrs. Hayward's hand in a loving gesture, then gets on his knees so they are face to face – she's in a wheelchair you'll remember – and he places a finger over his lips then leans in tenderly and whispers something to her. Their body language betrays an intimate knowledge of one another. Donna watches everything undetected.

At the diner, Norma shows Shelly a flyer for the Miss Twin Peaks pageant and suggests Shelly enter, there's cash and a scholarship up for grabs. Earle, in disguise as a biker, overhears and seconds the suggestion. Shelly is, after all, a bombshell in every way. Then Cooper enters. Earle sees him but Coop doesn't recognize his former partner so pays him no mind. He can't help but notice, however, the exquisitely beautiful young woman who comes to take his order: Annie. He's instantly flustered and captivated in a way we've never seen him. He deduces who she is and introduces himself. She seems a little smitten as well. Coop notices a cut mark on Annie's wrist, and Earle sourly notices their innocent flirtation. Cooper senses this ire, perhaps, but when he glances Earle's direction the man is gone. But Hawk is there, telling Coop they have a problem at the Bookhouse.

Once there, they see Truman has torn the place apart in rage. He's drunk as a skunk and down as a goose, and more than a little crazy with grief. He's got his gun out. Even Coop can't calm him at first. This is the single best scene Michael Ontkean ever performs in the series, and his portrayal of Truman at his lowest delivers us to a place of unexpected emotional depth. The anger and desperation tearing this strong, stoic man apart is heartbreaking, but in time Harry crumbles into his friend's embrace and the corner is turned.

Mike and Nadine are checking into The Great Northern for one night only, under assumed names, and in costume. Kinky.

Ben is in the lounge hosting a Stop Ghostwood campaign meeting aimed at halting the development from hastening the extinction of the pine weasel. The highlight of the evening is a fashion show hosted by Dick Tremayne with models including Lucy and Andy as prepped by Audrey. At the bar, Catherine pops by to say hello to Ben and openly doubt his newfound sincerity. He's been changed, he claims, fundamentally altered as a person, and now he needs to thoroughly scrub his conscience clean, hence the do-gooder attitude. He hopes the same can happen for her, and she almost believes him. Almost. Pinkel (David Lander again, the medical supply salesmen last seen at Leo's) brings out a live pine weasel in an attempt to implore donations from the audience. He takes it out of its cage and starts extolling the creature's virtues and traits, such as its attraction to bright shiny objects, like the studs of Dick's tuxedo shirt, and the smell of cheap cologne, like whatever Dick is wearing. I think you can see where this is going. Dick is persuaded to give the weasel a kiss for the audience at which point it bites him square on the nose, which incites a room-clearing panic that ends with Audrey and JJW kissing amidst the chaos.

At the Bookhouse, the unknown deputy left to watch over a passed-out Sheriff Truman is knocked out by Jones, who then undresses and gets into bed with the Sheriff...

This episode is the third of four written by Barry Pullman; he'll be back for episode 28, the penultimate. Directing the episode is James Foley, who at the time was known for his early films RECKLESS, AT CLOSE RANGE with Sean Penn and WHO'S THAT GIRL? with Madonna, for whom he also directed some music videos, including "True Blue" and the uber-cinematic "Papa Don't Preach." If you're catching a Penn-Madonna-Foley connection, it goes even deeper than you think: at the wedding of Penn and Madonna, Foley was the best man. After TWIN PEAKS his career would really pick up on the big screen – with films like GLENGARRY GLEN ROSS, THE CHAMBER, and CONFIDENCE – and in television shows like HANNIBAL, HOUSE OF CARDS, and BILLIONS. This would be the only episode of this series he would direct, and in fact it was his first foray into television. For a debut, Foley handles a mid-stream show with myriad plotlines adeptly enough.

The White Lodge gets a tad bit of exploration this week, namely through its connection to Margaret the Log Lady. By all accounts, it would seem she too has visited the White Lodge (as a child), so is another attuned to its particular vibrations. We also get the most information to date on her husband, who though still unnamed is also revealed to have had experience with the Lodge – it's the only other time Margaret saw the white light and heard the owl together, the seeming announcement of the White Lodge – but given that his experience ended with a fire that killed him, it seems safe to say it wasn't just the White Lodge he encountered. This thread won't be sufficiently answered, if ever, until a certain scene in FIRE WALK WITH ME involving a certain cultural and musical icon.

The overall atmosphere at this point is a chess match, not just between Coop and Earle, good and evil, but also between the network and the show, the network seeking to wrap things up, and the show trying to claim as much narrative territory as possible before this happens. You can almost feel the series and its cast and crew fighting for their show, or at least looking to solidify themselves in the public mind before moving on to the next job.

And while the mirrored Coop/Annie and Audrey/JJW romances are charming in their own ways, ultimately they're a hurtful substitute for the love between the Special Agent and Miss Horne that should have been.

Written by Harley Peyton & Robert Engels, Directed by Duwayne Dunham

Airdate April 4th, 1991

Picking up on the heels of the last episode, in the Bookhouse a non-descript deputy is still unconscious on the floor with a knot on his head, and Sheriff Truman is right where we left him, drunk and out cold in bed with Eckhardt's lovely assistant Jones crawling all over him in a silky black teddy. She takes a vial from her stockings and rubs whatever it contains all over Harry's lips, then her own, then she kisses him. He's barely cognizant of any of this and delusionally assumes it's Josie who's with him. Jones snaps this illusion by pulling some piano wire from her bracelet and using it to strangle Truman. This brings the good Sheriff to his senses and he manages to knock her out. There is no indication whatsoever why she needed to strip down for this assassination attempt, but no one is complaining (except maybe that deputy).

At The Great Northern, John Justice Wheeler is working when Audrey brings him breakfast. The sexual chemistry between the two of them is mounting. Pun intended. Also, it's hard to tell which one of these lovely people has better lips. They make a plan for a sunset rendezvous. Thinly-veiled innuendos flitter about like the butterflies in young Audrey's stomach.

Meanwhile, Truman has returned to his duties as Sheriff with Jones in tow, but she ain't talking, not to him at least. She does ask to speak with the closest South African consulate; they'll get right on that. Truman can't figure why Eckhardt would want him dead, but Coop points out the obvious: "sexual jealousy." Coop furthermore teaches his friend a surefire hangover technique: being grossed out to the point of nausea. Doc Hayward is waiting for them in Truman's office, as is a bonsai tree, which is reportedly a gift from Josie. Doc cuts past this awkwardness with the news that Windom Earle came to his house. He shows them the chess piece and move he left with Donna. Coop says they have to publish their responding move immediately. That's when Gordon Cole shows up. He's got the classified portion of Earle's dossier for Coop to look over. We learn here that the bonsai isn't from Josie, it's from Earle, and at this very moment he's in his cabin listening to their conversation via a device hidden in the tree. Cole explains that when Earle went AWOL from the mental institution he was hopped up on haloperidol, which is the same drug the one-armed man Phillip Gerard used to curb his MIKE-ness. There's an interesting mention in the file that Earle was loaned out to Project Blue Book in 1965 for a couple of years, but the records of his time there are still blacked out as a matter of national security. This links him quite curiously to Major Briggs. As the others head out for breakfast, Cole pulls Coop aside and says with Earle on the loose, the Bureau needs him back in ranks. Cole returns Coop's badge back and upgrades his sidearm to a 10mm. Earle has heard all of this and has his indentured servant Leo select three cards from a fanned deck. All three cards he chooses are queens, one with Donna's face, one with Audrey's, and one with Shelley's. Earle then tells Leo to try and find the king. Leo picks another card: a king with Dale's face. I'm thinking this has to be a loaded deck. Earle then pulls the Queen of Hearts from behind Leo's ear. The face on this card is blank. The gist of all this is, Earle's got something sinister planned for the Miss Twin Peaks pageant, namely some killin', and he intends to make sure Coop is there to see it.

The next day Donna follows her mother to The Great Northern because she's suspicious after seeing Eileen with Ben Horne earlier. She sees the two adults greet each other, then Ben wheels her mom away. At the same time,

Donna's ex Mike and Nadine are at the reception desk checking out after their illicit night together. Both seem quite satisfied. Donna runs across Audrey and asks if maybe she knows the connection between their parents. Audrey doesn't, but she knows how they can find out, and takes Donna to her peephole between the walls that looks in on Ben's office.

In the office, Eileen is trying to return a thick stack of love letters Ben sent to her 20 years ago. He is refusing to accept them. It would seem that back in the day these two had a thing going, and now, all these years later, Ben has finally realized the error of his ways and wants Eileen back as his lover. She protests, but not convincingly. This is when Donna and Audrey start observing. The first thing they hear is Ben asking Eileen if she's "told her." Eileen vehemently denies this, saying she never will, and telling him he must stay away from "her," he must promise he will. He does. She leaves. Audrey and Donna are confused, and Donna swears to get to the truth at the bottom of all they've seen. The obvious conclusion to draw here is that Donna is Ben's daughter, not Doc's, and thus Audrey's half-sister. Another mini mystery stirs...

Coop and crew stop in the Double R for breakfast. Coop's dressed once again in his standard dark suit and beige trenchcoat; it's a sight for sore eyes. Cole spies Shelly and goes over to pitch woo. He's yelling as usual, and when she quietly asks him to lower his voice, he hears her perfectly. Being that he's all but deaf to every other sound on Earth, being able to understand her voice clearly when at a normal level is nothing short of a miracle, he declares. This increases his infatuation with Miss Johnson to mythical levels. Coop meanwhile is sketching on a napkin the mark on Margaret the Log Lady's leg – side-by-side symmetrical twin-peaked triangles – and is adding three vertical diamonds between them, like those that make up Briggs' mark, just rearranged. Then Annie stops by his table and steals all his attention. They flirt in a truly beautiful and odd fashion, and Truman notices, especially when Coop tries to tell her a joke. It's not at all funny, but she laughs: true love for sure. Annie notices Coop's sketch and says it looks like the marking in Owl Cave. Coop doesn't know what she's talking about, but Truman does and takes a look. She's right, the Sheriff says, it's an exact match, which is odd as Coop has never seen or heard of the mark or even the cave. He wants to fix this, stat.

Donna gets a postcard from James. He's in San Francisco on his way to Mexico. A regular Kerouac, that one. Her dad passes by and she asks him how mom knows Ben Horne. When he says she doesn't, Donna reveals Ben came by the house yesterday and the two of them seemed friendly enough. Doc revises his lie, says they must know each other from charity work. Donna mentions mom went to see Ben today, too. Must be charity work, yeah, that's the ticket, she told me this morning she was going, I just forgot, whoops. Bad poker face, Doc. Doc is saved by the doorbell, sort of. It's a delivery with package for Mrs. H, a dozen roses but no card to go with them. Doc sighs knowingly.

Audrey's at the library doing research on civil disobedience when she runs into Windom Earle in disguise as a poetry professor. This is a happy coincidence, she thinks, because recently a poem was sent to her. This poem was, of course, sent by Earle, and he continues the charade by analyzing its meaning for her. It was written by the great Percy Shelley, he says, then comments Audrey looks like a queen. She doesn't interpret it as a threat directly, but she senses enough bad mojo to skedaddle.

During a slow moment at work, Annie asks Shelly what she knows about Agent Cooper, under the veil of not being even remotely interested. That Dale is a tough one to read, Shelly says, but even she can see he's interested in Annie.

Andy's all geared up for some spelunking at Owl Cave, and Lucy, recently turned on by Andy's heroic actions at the fashion-show-turned-weasel-riot (and turned off by Dick's cowardly showing at the same) tells him to be careful. Coop's ready to go but Truman tells him Pete has the next chess move ready. The move will expose one of their pawns, but taking it would expose one of Earle's bishops, so strategy says they should be safe. This resolved, off they go.

Ben, continuing his tour of regrets, apologizes to Audrey for the kind of father he's been all these years, the mistakes he's made along the way (his affair with Laura Palmer among them), and says he wants to repent, to build their family into something good, but only if she'll serve as his second-in-command. She will. That's excellent, Ben says, and tells her she's on a plane to Seattle in an hour to confab with environmentalists about taking the pine weasel campaign national. This assignment derails her later plans with JJW, who arrives in this scene just in time to be rejected. He ends up chatting with Ben instead about the nature of being good. This conversation causes JJW to reveal that he's falling in love with Audrey. This pleases Ben verily. He offers the young suitor a carrot.

At Owl Cave, Coop, Truman, Hawk and Andy are spelunking. Hawk leads them to the marking, a petroglyph carved into the cave wall. It's a perfect match to what Coop drew combining the marks found on both Major Briggs and Margaret the Log Lady. The only difference is an addition, a curl of flame above the topmost diamond. An owl calls and flies through the cave. Andy for some reason takes a swipe at it with a pickaxe but instead strikes the petroglyph's flame in its center, causing a small but bright flare. The pickaxe won't come out but the center diamond pushes out from the wall until its face falls away, revealing another, smaller symbol on the face of a slender pole that is also moving outward. This smaller symbol is a single diamond with two wings. As Coop peers closer, he sees this symbol is coming out of yet another painted flame. Make sense? No? You're not alone. While he too has no idea where this clue will lead them, Coop is certain it will be "a place both wonderful and strange." He's giddy like a kid on Christmas morning about it. The same owl that buzzed them flies free from the cave.

Annie pops into The Great Northern for her first-ever alcoholic beverage just as Dale is passing through the room having returned from the cave. He's regaling Diane via tape of the night's adventure but stops cold when he notices Annie. On a side-note, another bit of evidence, if you're looking for it, that Diane might not exist can be found here, I think, in the way Coop instantly dismisses his tape recorder when he encounters Annie. It's like he doesn't need Diane tonight, like she's something he might have found a real, actual substitute for, like she's a convention created for his sake and thus can wait, rather than an official recorder of investigative events that would need to be expediently documented. Like I said, if you're looking for it. Coop and Annie talk. He's amazed at how the world is all new to her, something she's a little thrown by, but nevertheless excited by as well. He notices again the scar on her wrist. She notices him noticing and gives a vague peek into her backstory, saying she's "failed before." Coop is his typically chivalrous self. To describe their chemistry isn't possible, but if you've seen it you know that MacLachlan and Graham did an outstanding job of building their dynamic without obvious handholds or definitive statements, instead rather by crafting a separate and singular relationship persona forged of their two idiosyncratic characters.

Back in Owl Cave, Earle is creeping around and finds the petroglyph. He notices something Coop and the others did not: across the cave from the petroglyph is another wall painting of the smaller symbol with wings, but inverted. So Earle turns the slender pole poking out of the wall until its symbol matches that on the opposite wall. This causes Andy's discarded pickaxe to fall out of the wall and the cavern to start calmly collapsing

This episode was the last directed by series editor Dwayne Dunham, and it really started the ball rolling in terms of pushing the Earle-Cooper-Lodges narrative down the homestretch. Speaking of the homestretch, given that's where the series was, especially with official cancellation looming, you'd think they'd be streamlining and trying to tie up loose ends, but when you look at the Ben-Donna paternity mystery, and the blossoming romance between Audrey and JJW, you can see how there were seeds of a season 3 being sewn into these final episodes, just-in-case plotlines that could carry over into uncharted territory. The only thing that's new but that doesn't feel it is the Annie introduction, partially because of how easily her character fits into Coop's narrative of love, and partially because you know she likely to factor into the Earle narrative as his faceless queen. Normally I'd lament about how it should be Audrey in that position as Coop's ultimate love and thus his ultimate vulnerability, but the character of Annie and the performance by Graham are compositely more innocent and pure than we would ever want Audrey to be, and so heightens the sense of foreboding. The poor girl just got out into the world, after all, and *this* is the pocket of it in which she emerged.

But make no mistake, subplots aside, TWIN PEAKS is all about Earle now, what exactly his nefarious plans include and how exactly Coop can stop them. Add to this the looming mythology of the Lodges bolstered by the findings in Owl Cave and the intuitive nature of Coop leading them to it, we can tell there's something larger than life coming to Twin Peaks, we just have no idea what it is. But with four episodes to go, we at least know some kind of answer is coming soon.

Written by Mark Frost & Harley Peyton, Directed by Jonathan Sanger

Airdate April 11th, 1991

The episode opens with Coop, Truman, Andy and Hawk returning to Owl Cave for further exploration of the petroglyph they discovered last episode, but when they get there they find someone's already done the work for them. Part of the wall has crumbled away, revealing an even larger, more detailed petroglyph than they originally found. Hawk notices a boot print in the dirt and says it matches the one he found outside the power station the night it exploded, which means the person who was here and who unearthed this larger petroglyph was Earle. The image itself looks like a map with mountains that have swirling vortices inside them, and trees arranged in a circle. There are also a pair of figures, one giant and one very small, standing next to each other. Coop tells Andy to work up a large-scale drawing of it.

At that very moment, Earle is back at his cabin hidden in the woods telling Leo about the White Lodge, "a place of great goodness" where animals and spirits frolic together. He makes it sound basically like a naturalist's heaven where the souls of man and beast, indeed all living things, are in perfect harmony, which of course is disgusting to Earle, all that unhindered goodness and overflowing well-being. Fortunately, though, there is an opposite place, he says, a Black Lodge, a place of unimaginable power full of dark forces and vicious secrets. The spirits there are malevolent and violent and if harnessed can offer a vast power to whoever summons them, a power that can shape the world to their will. Earle says he intends to find this Black Lodge, and he intends to have its power. Turns out Leo isn't alone in the audience, there's a long-haired metalhead in the cabin too (played by Ted Raimi, Sam's brother) who was lured here by the promise of a party and beer. He's not sure what all this means but as Earle attempts to soothe him with some lovely flute music, we see a picture of the petroglyph on Earle's computer, one step ahead of Coop.

Pete is at home simultaneously plotting his next move in the chess match with Earle, and crafting poetry in Josie's memory. Catherine comes in looking for a hand opening the box Eckhardt had Jones give her after his death; she's been trying for days to get into it but can't figure how. Pete realizes it's a puzzle box, which means the trick to opening it is to fit the pieces together just so. She wants to know how long it will take to figure out. He says by design, it could take years.

At the diner, Bobby is talking to Shelly about their future. He says the secret of success has at last occurred to him: beautiful people get whatever they want. And Shelly is very beautiful. So he wants her to enter the Miss Twin Peaks pageant. She's not really into the idea but Bobby wasn't asking, he wants her in it so she's going to be in it. Across the room, Lana is talking about the very same thing with her husband, Mayor Milford, but unlike Shelly, she's very into the idea, so much so she wants Milford's help. He thinks she means by way of coaching her, but she means by way of rigging the pageant in her favor, as he's on the judging committee. He's wary of course, but she's a temptress and a sexual dynamo to boot, so there's not really much resistance he can offer. Then Coop swings by to grab coffee and donuts for the gang, and to very formally ask Annie if she would like to accompany him on a nature study that afternoon. It's pretty cute how nervous he is. She of course accepts. Shelly mumbles the last line of the poem Earle sent her (and Donna and Audrey) and Coop overhears it, he knows it. Shelly spills the details and

Coop says he needs to see this poem immediately. Shelly has her piece in her purse and gets it for him, explaining how each girl got her own section. Coop, very serious now, says he needs to keep her piece.

In the privacy of the Sheriff's office, Coop lets Truman in on the poem, the girls it was sent to, and the person who he knows sent it. It seems Coop himself had once sent the very same poem to another lovely lady, Caroline, Earle's dead wife. Therefore he thinks this is a threat of some sort. Hawk shows up with Donna's piece of the poem, says Audrey's out of town with hers. As he's leaving, Coop asks Hawk to bring him Leo's arrest record.

In the conference room, Major Briggs is watching Andy draw the petroglyph on the chalkboard. Briggs knows this image. Coop enters, says they need Briggs' help, but they can't say why. This doesn't bother the Major. What a badass. Coop says they currently have three investigations open in Twin Peaks: the disappearance of Leo Johnson, the whereabouts of Windom Earle, and the discovery of the Owl Cave petroglyph. Coop thinks all three are related. He needs from Briggs everything there is to know about Earle's time with Project Blue Book. Briggs can tell him plenty, but he has a few moral considerations first. He asks if the info will prevent loss of life. Yes. He then asks if the drawing on the board is the Owl Cave petroglyph. It is. Briggs has dreamt of it, and a flash of this dream involving the silhouette of a hooded figure (last seen before Briggs disappeared while nightfishing with Coop), an owl, and a bit of fire convinces him: he'll do as Coop has asked. Hawk brings in Leo's arrest report. After closely analyzing the handwritten statement it contains, Coop concludes the poem sent by Earle was transcribed by Leo. As they already knew Earle had been in Owl Cave by his bootprint, this bit of info about Leo connects all of the open investigations.

Dick Tremayne's nose is still bandaged from the pine weasel attack at the fashion show two episodes back. He's at The Great Northern waiting to see Ben because he can't find Audrey, who's supposed to be coordinating with him about a wine-tasting benefit to be held there that evening. Ben informs him she's out of town and directs him to the concierge. Ben does offer to pay for medical expenses regarding Dick's nose, seeing as it happened at his hotel, at an event he sponsored, and Dick attempts to exploit this generosity by finagling some worker's comp out of it as well (Ben's also his employer at the department store). It pushes Ben's resolve against doing bad to its limits, but he grants this as well.

Earle, aproned and dirty, pops a bottle of beer for Leo to take to the metalhead, now willingly incased in a giant *papier mache* chesspiece, a pawn to be precise. Dude's all for helping out, he's just not sure how he's supposed to get out of this thing. That's when Earle produces a crossbow, tells the metalhead he's not supposed to get out of it, and asks Leo for an arrow. Leo, though, refuses. This is too evil even for him, apparently. So Earle fiddles with Leo's shock collar until he complies. Earle loads the arrow, then after an eloquent speech on the afterlife, kills the metalhead.

The Miss Twin Peaks rules committee – Doc Hayward, Mayor Milford, and Pete – are meeting at The Road House for the pageant sign-up. Ben has asked to address them. He wants to convince them to class-up the pageant a little bit by incorporating all of a woman's beauty, not just physical but mental, spiritual, and moral as well. This is pretty weird coming from a whoremonger, but they hear him out. He says the pageant needs a theme, and that theme should be how to save our forests. Pete of course mentions Ben's opposition to Ghostwood as a possible motivation for wanting such a theme, but Ben says the issue is much bigger than that, and leaves with them taking his idea under advisement. As he goes, he stops by a table where Bobby sits with Shelly and Donna to remind the boy of a chore. On his way out, his vision lingers ever so slightly on Donna, but enough she notices.

The pageant registration begins, and Shelly is all nerves, especially about the public speaking aspect. Nadine and Mike show up amidst this, she's signing up too. Bobby and Mike break away to chat, something they haven't done in a while because Mike's been preoccupied with Nadine. Bobby ribs him about dating a fossil, but Mike counters with a one-two punch of Nadine's sexual maturity and superhuman strength that sufficiently KOs Bobby's kidding.

Truman is so desperate to understand Josie that he's gone to Catherine looking for any information on why she did what she did. Catherine thinks Josie learned early how to survive by being a chameleon, whatever people wanted her to be; the girl was more lies than truth and she believed them all. But there may be a clue from Josie's past that could benefit them both: the puzzle box. Pete returns home and in attempting to help them he accidentally drops the box, which opens it. But all that's inside is another box with a clock of moon phases and symbols on its face.

Coop and Annie are in a rowboat on a lake on a beautiful afternoon. They're gently delving into her past. She mentions a high school boyfriend. Coop asks if the guy had anything to do with her entering the convent, and she backs off, so he does as well. All she'll say is that she's done hiding from the world, it's why she came home, to face the fear of her past failures. Coop takes her hands and lovingly traces the scars on her wrists with his fingertips. She admits she cut herself because of that boyfriend. He can relate to the feeling because of Caroline, and maybe also because of this similar experience he can help her with feelings like that. They kiss, then row ashore and leave hand in hand. Earle sees all of this through binoculars, and it pleases him in a most sinister way.

The wine-tasting benefit has begun. Dick is hosting, Lana and Lucy are pouring, and Andy is among the tasters. Dick's nose bandage soaks up some of the red wine when he takes in its bouquet.

Gordon Cole is at the diner regaling Shelly with normal-volume stories of his exploits (we remember her voice is the only sound he can hear without mechanical aid) when Coop and Annie arrive. Side note: these scenes between David Lynch and Madchen Amick are so much fun to watch. He's never been more playful and her affection/admiration of him is so genuine. It really speaks to the family atmosphere behind the scenes of TWIN PEAKS, and the very real gratitude all the cast and crew had for the show's creators. These scenes are happy pockets among the plot's mounting darkness. Anyway, Cole's on his way out of town and asks the new couple to join him and Shelly for a whole lot of pie. While doing so, he musters the courage to tell Shelly if he doesn't kiss her before he leaves he'll regret it all of his days. Shelly obliges him with a chaste smooch, but Bobby walks in on it, and he is not pleased. He wants to know what the heck is going on, and Gordon, unaware of who Bobby is to Shelly, tells him it's a tender moment between two adults and he should keep looking cuz it's going to happen again. And it does. So awesome.

Later, Coop is enjoying his nightly glass of warm milk by the fireplace in The Great Northern lobby when he is joined by a lovelorn John Justice Wheeler. The two men discuss the perils and peaks of love, JJW on the former and Coop on the latter. They're both at the beginning of what could be beautiful things, and both looking forward with varied perspectives. JJW is delivered a telegram and whatever it contains causes him to immediately prepare for departure.

At the Hayward dinner table, Donna flat out asks her mom how she knows Ben Horne. Doc jumps in with the cover story about charity work, but Donna counters with the roses that were sent to mom without a card. Mom tries to distract her with peas and Donna plays along with talk of entering the Miss Twin Peaks pageant, but when asked why, she says she wants the money for studying overseas, a not-so-veiled threat to abandon her parents if their secrets hurt her.

Coop's been called to a strange occurrence at the gazebo by the lake where he was earlier with Annie: a giant wooden crate has been placed in it. Truman thought it was a bomb, but it isn't ticking. On the box there is a large ring tied to a rope and a sign that says "Pull Me." Coop knows this is the work of Earle, just as he knows Earle is adjusting his game to the adjustments Coop is making, meaning his foe has become unpredictable. Coop has everyone back away and uses a rock, crime scene tape, and his new gun to pull the ring from a safe distance. The box opens and inside is the completed chess piece, a pawn, with the dead metalhead inside and a note around it all that reads, "Next time it will be someone you know."

Jonathan Sanger directed the episode, his first and only of the series. Primarily a producer, Sanger knew Lynch from THE ELEPHANT MAN, which he helped put together. He would later direct an episode of Lynch/Frost's short-lived ON THE AIR series. For having to jump in at such a complex place, Sanger does a fine job making his episode fit seamlessly into the aesthetic and narrative. Helping this latter regard, the narrative, is the fact that the episode was co-written by Mark Frost, marking the first time his name has appeared on a teleplay since episode 16, the one where Leland dies. There's a lot of mythology and set-up for the finale in this episode, and he and Harley Peyton do an excellent job juggling all the storylines that are up in the air while simultaneously stopping them from colliding in confusing ways. There's a renewed atmosphere to TWIN PEAKS in this episode, and it is one that will remain with the series for the next four hours.

But don't be mistaken, it's not going to be a happy ending. Things are getting pretty dark. At this point we all know Earle is going to try and do something terrible to Annie, and each episode he seems to get a little crazier, which only broadens the horrors of which he's capable. To top it all off, he's now actively seeking the nefarious power of the Black Lodge, you know, the place that made BOB. The kind of visceral terror this knowledge provokes in the viewer hasn't existed since the height of the Laura Palmer storyline. Something heinous is coming, maybe the worst thing yet. Like Coop and the connection between the Lodge and Earle, we just can't see it yet, but we can feel it.

Alas, there was another feeling that TWIN PEAKS fans acquired the day this episode aired: anguish. After this episode the series was officially cancelled. ABC would allow the last episode in April to air as scheduled, but after that the network would push what were now the final two episodes of the series to summer, after May sweeps. Furthermore, as the series had already finished shooting those final episodes a month before this announcement, there would be no chance to tie up any storylines, even the ones still starting up like Ben's rebirth and possible relation to Donna, Audrey and JJW's burgeoning love, Coop and Annie's, The Ghostwood struggle etc., not to mention whatever was set to unravel in the three remaining episodes. The rest was silence. What was done was done and would now serve as a coda for better or worse.

But only for 25 years or so...

EPISODE 27: "THE PATH TO THE BLACK LODGE"

Written by Harley Peyton & Robert Engels, Directed by Stephen Gyllenhaal

Airdate April 18th 1991

We're back with the dead metalhead in a giant *papier mache* pawn that was left by Earle in the park's gazebo at the end of the last episode. The authorities are moving the body with noted difficulty. According to a fellow metalhead (actor Willie Garver, for fans of SEX AND THE CITY and WHITE COLLAR), the dead dude's name was Rusty Tomaski and he was part of a band on their way to a gig in Knife River when a tire on the van blew. Coop can piece it together from there: they met someone. Dude says yeah, a guy in a suit came right out of the woods and asked if they wanted some brews. Rusty left with him and that was the last time he was seen alive. As Rusty's friend is led away, Coop remarks to Truman that Earle took another pawn but without telling them his move, meaning he's playing off the board now, where there are no rules.

Coop, Truman and Andy get back to the station and are told by Lucy that Hawk is waiting in Truman's office with a "sad man." They go, but Lucy calls Andy back and asks what he knows about saving the planet, because (deep breath here) in 24 hours she will decide who the father of her baby is, and furthermore she's decided to run for Miss Twin Peaks because her new family will need the money, and therefore she needs to know what Andy knows about saving the planet because that's what the theme of the pageant is, and she'll need to write a good speech if she's going to win. All Andy knows for sure is that one, people need to stop sinking their beer cans in Pearl Lake, and two, Styrofoam lives forever. That's a start.

John Justice Wheeler is on his way out of town, trying to wait for Audrey to return from her business trip to Seattle, but she's not back yet and he can't hold off any longer. He sends a man to collect his bags.

In Ben's office, he's getting a physical from Doc Hayward for insurance purposes, but Doc has an axe to grind about Ben stirring up trouble with Eileen and Donna. Ben says he understands Doc is angry, but he's trying to do what's right. He mentions a lie that survives between the two of them, and he and Eileen. Doc declares goodness in Ben to be a time bomb, he knows that lie revealed will only ruin lives. Ben will not be thwarted, though, and JJW's arrival interrupts any further conversation. Doc simply asks that Ben please be careful. Instead of angry, the good doctor is imploring, the last ploy of a desperate man. JJW, in the meantime, has come to say goodbye, and reveals why – his partner has been murdered. This is really all we ever get about this. Must have been a season 3 hook.

Donna is in the attic of her house checking out her birth certificate. While her mother's name is there, the father's name has been left blank. Furthermore, in old photos a mustachioed Ben Horne is seen paling around with Eileen and Doc. They appear to be the best of friends. The phone rings and her mom yells up: it's Agent Cooper for her, he says it's important.

Audrey at last returns to The Great Northern and is greeted by several messages left by JJW, as well as Deputy Hawk who's there because Coop wants to see her toot suite. She leaves, missing JJW who is still in with her father. Ben is worrying about how JJW's departure will affect the Ghostwood protest but JJW can't care, his partner and friend is dead and he must take his place. He gives Ben a letter for Audrey and begrudgingly leaves.

Major Briggs meets with Truman and Coop to tell them what he's gleaned from reading up on Earle's time with Project Blue Book. Earle was the team's brightest member until the focus shifted from outer space to the woods around Twin Peaks, at which point Earle became obsessed and possessive of assignments, and violent to the degree he was dismissed from the project altogether. So Earle knew of this place decades before Coop arrived. Briggs shows them a video of Earle from that time discussing "dugpas," dark sorcerers who "cultivate evil for the sake of evil, nothing else," and who have access to a secret place that increases and strengthens this evil they do exponentially. This place is tangible and thus it can be found and utilized. It is called The Black Lodge. Coop self-corrects an earlier assumption: when Earle came to Twin Peaks, Coop had assumed it was to wreak vengeance on him alone, but now he sees it's all been camouflage for what Earle was really after: the power of The Black Lodge. So then the new objective, as Coop sees it, is to figure out what The Black Lodge has to do with the petroglyph in Owl Cave. They'll work while Briggs catches some shut eye, which he'll do right after he takes a quick stroll through the woods to clear his head. No one's figured out yet that the bonsai tree on the table is a device planted by Earle that allows him to listen in on everything they're planning. He's pleased with their progress or lack thereof, because he knows something they don't, but before he reveals just what that is, he first wants to speak with Briggs, have a little reunion and try to learn a thing or two. He suggests to Leo they take a stroll through the woods as well, and doesn't notice when Leo pockets the remote for the shock collar.

At the diner, an unknown woman suffers a brief tremor in her right hand that seems to catch her by surprise (remember when this happened to Harold Smith?). Elsewhere in a booth, as a part of his plan to secure riches from Shelly's beauty, Bobby is having her read the speech he's written for the pageant. A couple tweaks are all it needs. Bobby then apologizes for the way his attitude shifted after he started working for Ben, and how he hasn't been paying attention to her the way he should. When he saw her kissing Cole last episode, it just all snapped back into place for him. His apology works, and they reconcile with a kiss of their own. Then Shelly gets a call from Cooper, who needs to see her immediately.

At The Road House, construction is under way for the pageant and Mayor Milford is meeting with Lana to tell her the other two judges besides himself will be Norma and Dick Tremayne, so her victory is all but assured. She wants it totally assured, though. All they need is Dick, the Mayor says, and so if they orchestrate a little alone time between the two of them, Lana's charms are certain to do the rest. Those charms distract the Mayor and he pleads with her to elope with him, but she won't agree to marry him until after she's won the pageant.

Meanwhile, Coop is meeting with Audrey, Donna and Shelly about the poem they received, as well as the invitations to The Road House. Audrey says they went but no one met them. Coop asks if they've had any contact recently with strangers that struck them as odd or puzzling. Donna tells about Earle posing as a friend of her father's, Shelly got a $10 tip on a cup of coffee from a male customer the same day she got the poem, and Audrey serendipitously ran into a poetry professor in the library. Coop asks Shelly if the handwriting looks familiar. It does, it's Leo's. He wants each of them to check in with the Sheriff twice a day at 9 and 9, he wants their parents to know their whereabouts at all time, and he doesn't want them going anywhere alone because they're in danger, all of Twin Peaks is.

Earle is telling Leo about the dugpas. He likens them to Kali worshippers and other such bloodthirsty zealots. The queen cards are tacked to the wall and Leo notices Shelly's face on one of them, says her name. Earle asks if Leo would mourn her death, seeing as how she was cheating on him; the reason he wants to know is because if Shelly wins Miss Twin Peaks, she dies. So that's his big plan. Leo though, despite everything, still cares for Shelly and doesn't want her killed. So he comes at Earle with the remote, not realizing it's the collar that does the shocking, and he's still wearing that. Earle plays frightened until Leo presses the button, shocking himself, and then the joke's all on Leo.

Audrey returns to The Great Northern and just misses JJW yet again, now for the last time. She goes to see her father to ask if he's seen her would-be lover, but he's got another item on his agenda: he wants her to be the spokesperson for the Stop Ghostwood movement by winning Miss Twin Peaks. She just wants to know where JJW is. Ben breaks it to her that he had to leave. For good. He gives her the letter JJW left. She runs out, racing for the airport to try and catch him before he takes off, pausing in the lobby just long enough to recruit Pete into driving her.

Coop, Truman and Andy are studying and hypothesizing about the Owl Cave petroglyph. Coop says the symbols suggest a time, but for what he doesn't know, it could be an invitation. They pause to wonder where Major Briggs is, as he should have been there by now. Andy calls his house. In the interim, Coop lets his mind wander to Annie, which Truman happily notes is not at all like the Special Agent. Coop admits he's smitten, in love, which Truman is happy to hear, if also disheartened. The wound of Josie is far from healed. Coop's right hand, prying apart the blinds to look outside, trembles just like the woman's in the diner did.

Briggs is still strolling through the woods when the mark behind his ear tingles and he turns to find two men in a horse costume approaching him. The head has a tranq gun and shoots the Major with it. It is, of course, Earle and Leo in the costume.

JJW is boarding his private jet at the airport, still searching the landscape in vain for a sign of Audrey.

Coop visits with Annie while she's working. She notices he's troubled, and he tells her he can't stop thinking about her. She has the same problem in regards to him. It's a cute conversation, one they both enjoy, but all isn't well. There's no tangible threat present, but the way the camera pulls away from them oh so slowly while that haunting TWIN PEAKS music builds beneath their conversation gives the distinct impression that while life is happy between the two of them, the world in which they exist is dark and conspiring. They kiss. Annie knocks plates to the ground. They break. Syrup drips malevolently.

Pete gets Audrey to the airport as JJW's plane is taxiing away. She gets ahead of it and she and JJW have the most romantic runway goodbye this side of CASABLANCA. They each profess their love for the other, and Audrey offers him her virginity, right there, right then. Thank god it's his jet. Pete gets misty watching the lovers embrace, and as he wipes away the tears, his right hand trembles uncontrollably.

Earle has Briggs tied against a giant target on bales of hay and is loading his crossbow. He wants to know when Briggs first saw the symbol in Owl Cave? Briggs is not at liberty to divulge any information. Earle sinks an arrow right by his ear and asks what the petroglyph means? Briggs repeats his refusal like a good soldier. Earle grazes his leg with another arrow, then asks a test question: what's the capital of North Carolina? Briggs can answer that, Raleigh, so then he's capable of telling the truth, he's just not willing, therefore Earle gives him truth serum. He asks his questions again: Briggs first saw the symbol in dreams, and the petroglyph means that if Jupiter and Saturn meet in alignment then "they will receive you."

Catherine is sharing the contents of the puzzle box Eckhardt left her to her brother Andrew (reminder: it's another box with a face like a clock of moon phases and astrological symbols). They're trying to open it and as they fiddle they distract their frustration with talks of foreign investors ready to throw money at the Ghostwood Estates development, despite Ben's interference, which Andrew notes is ultimately ineffectual because of work Ben himself did when the project was his; all the hurdles and studies have been cleared and filed, there's no stopping them now. Andrew presses the moon phases like calculator buttons, entering various dates. When he enters the date the gift arrived, the box pops open. Inside is yet another box, which Andrew smashes open. Inside that is a seemingly-solid, metallic rectangular cube.

Annie's at The Road House waiting on Coop. He arrives and they dance. Coop gets a little forward in talking about the feel of her body against his and she rewards his boldness with an impassioned kiss. She wants him. She tells him so. Then she segues somewhat unexpectedly into announcing that she's going to enter the Miss Twin Peaks pageant like Coop and several others have suggested. The TWIN PEAKS doomsday clock just ticked another minute towards midnight. Coop calls her a queen and that's enough to trigger the powers that be in the White Lodge. The room goes black but for a hot white spot on Coop, and another on stage where the Giant has appeared and is

121

frantically waving both his arms, mouthing a silent "No" over and over again. For a being we've only seen as calm and stoic, this display of emotionality and even fear is quite unnerving.

It's after dark when Pete wakes in his truck to the sound of JJW's jet taking off. Audrey's still there, a full-fledged woman now. She's sad her lover is gone but Pete says if the man promised he'd come back, he will. Audrey says he also promised he'd take her fishing but that never happened. This is an area in which Pete can help, he's got tackle in the truck right now, and suggests fishing is the best cure for a broken heart.

In the cabin in the woods, everyone is freaking out. Leo is screaming, shaking and holding his head. Briggs, still restrained, is having some kind of spiritual seizure. And Earle is singing and laughing and looking at the petroglyph with the information Briggs gave him in mind. It's a clock he realizes now, a clock and an invitation. He teams this with the thing he mentioned earlier he knows that Coop doesn't: that the petroglyph is also a map. On his computer he transposes the cave painting onto a scale map of Twin Peaks. Now he knows not only when the entrance to The Black Lodge will open, but where it will as well.

Back at The Road House Coop's vision fades, but everything has changed. All over town, something is wrong. In the forest, in a circle of trees there is a smaller circle of white power with what looks like a pool of oil at its center. A spotlight shines over this pool and reaching out mid-air from the folds of time and space is the denim-clad right arm of BOB, clawing for a grip on our reality, and finally manifesting. The pool reflects a red curtain, and the music of the Man From Another Place is heard, that salty saxophone. The way the curtain folds in the circular pool makes it look like the eye of some great, ravenous beast peeking into our world for something to devour.

Another first-time director helmed this episode, the last of the series: Stephen Gyllenhaal. And yes, before you ask, it's not a coincidence, he is the father of Jake and Maggie, and also an accomplished director (_side note_: with a 200+ person cast, how come none of the acting Gyllenhaals or Deschanels are in TWIN PEAKS season 3? And what about Rashida Jones ((Peggy Lipton's real life daughter))? Missed opportunity, you ask me.). At the time, Gyllenhaal was coming off the feature PARIS TROUT starring fellow Lynch-collaborator Dennis Hopper. There's an elegance and refinement to the episode that can be attributed to Gyllenhaal's direction, and the result is a smooth and polished, subtly-stylistic hour. Peyton and Engels scripted the episode, which finally starts to pay out some of the IOU's they've given us in terms of the connection between Earle, the petroglyph, and the Black Lodge.

At the same time, the way they've looped the Lodges storyline back to the Laura Palmer storyline via the re-emergence of BOB harkens to the series' early days when the mysteries were more attractive than the answers, and hints that the resolution this time around will not be so cut and dry as that other plot's. There's also a lot of sadness that starts to creep in, for me at least, for the things we'll never get to see, not even in the upcoming third season: JJW and Audrey's love (she's back for season 3, Billy Zane is not on the cast list), Audrey and Pete's friendship (Jack Nance is dead now), and the increasing bond between Coop and Truman now that Coop's sticking around town, maybe for good (Ontkean isn't returning, though the character might be in the form of Robert Forster). And I'd wager it must have felt that way to viewers at the time too, knowing as they did for certain now that the series had been cancelled.

After this episode, it would be seven weeks until viewers saw TWIN PEAKS again, and that would be the final two episodes aired back-to-back some throwaway night in June in an era when the TV season definitely ended in May. The show and its participants deserved better, as did the audience, but it was the hand both were dealt.

EPISODE 28: "MISS TWIN PEAKS"

Written by Barry Pullman, Directed by Tim Hunter

Airdate June 10th, 1991

Before we start, try and imagine what it felt like on June 10th, 1991 if you were a die-hard TWIN PEAKS fan: it was the best of days and the worst of days. The best because after nearly two months of being abruptly forced to wait, you were finally going to see the last two episodes of the series, but therein is the worst of it: these were the last two episodes of TWIN PEAKS *ever*, and there was no certainty whatsoever that there would ever be more. No one knew about Lynch's plans for a movie, no one back then was picking up other people's cancelled TV shows, and one letter writing campaign had already succeeded in resurrecting the show but failed to bring with it new viewers to keep the show alive. This was it, the deal was done, there were only two nails left to hammer into the coffin, and they were about to air back-to-back. Even now, watching for my sixth or so cycle, knowing there's FIRE WALK WITH ME, knowing – for the very first time – that there is indeed a season 3 on the horizon and that the story isn't over, I still feel a mix of sadness and dread on the precipice of these last two episodes. This ending wasn't meant to be, as the path to here hadn't been given the chance to unfold at the pace with which the creators wanted. But this was the ending we had, at the time, and it made for two of the most interesting, and certainly the trippiest hours of the entire series. Let's get started, shall we?

Leo Johnson and Major Briggs are still prisoners of Windom Earle. Leo, however, manages to get a hold of the keys to Briggs' shackles when their captor is away. He can't free himself, but sets the Major loose with one imperative: "Save Shelly." He's an asshole, that Leo, but not through and through, here at his worst he's at his best. Earle returns and discovers Briggs gone. But more worrisome: there's something different about the man. His face is paler, his eyes redder, his teeth and mouth and tongue black as night. He looks, in short, like a demon. Instead of punishing Leo, he suggests instead they play a new game...

At the Double R diner Norma is encouraging about the chances both Annie and Shelly have of being crowned Miss Twin Peaks. She says this is an important day for the town in a very important year; a lot of healing from Laura's murder could start today and it would be nice to see one of her girls up there representing that new beginning. Of course, neither she nor anyone else knows that Earle's plan is to execute the Queen, so careful there what you wish for, Norma. It's brought up that the reason Norma is one of the judges this year is because it's the 20th anniversary of her own crowning at the very first Miss Twin Peaks pageant. When Shelly remarks that Norma could still win today, she ain't kidding. Hubba hubba, Ms. Lipton.

Ben Horne finds daughter Audrey waiting for him in his office. Their moods are opposed: he's reading up on the great religions of the world as part of his continuing evolution, and she's lovelorn over John Justice Wheeler, the man who deflowered her then fled the continent. Ben is actually a positive father figure here and comforts his daughter in her moment of despair. When it passes, she updates him on her trip to Seattle: she learned there that the Packards are using a Savings and Loan to funnel money into the Ghostwood development, but it's being done real hush-hush because the bank doesn't want bad publicity from the pine weasel protest. If that's what they're trying to avoid, then that's exactly what Ben will give them, and he asks Audrey again if she's given any thought to entering the pageant and becoming the face of their protest. She thinks little of such contests, and isn't interested.

Ben pushes through her resistance and paints a picture of an educated and intellectual Miss Twin Peaks who could rebuke and obliterate the very standards by which Audrey is appalled. Unfortunately, she's now considering it.

Coop and Truman are watching Andy, who's been staring at the drawing of the petroglyph on the chalkboard all day. People are still on the lookout for Major Briggs, but Coop knows Earle had something to do with his disappearance because of their connection through Project Blue Book. Truman wonders what Earle would want Briggs for, and Coop speculates aloud, much to the glee of Earle, who's listening via the bug in the bonsai tree on Truman's desk. Coop says Earle's been looking for the Lodge a long time, since 1965, which means this chess game he's playing has more pieces than they might have originally considered. There's also the question of Josie's mysterious death. This especially piques Truman's curiosity. Coop believes Josie died of fear, and reveals that the night she died he saw BOB. He believes these things are connected and that BOB was drawn back into their world by the absolute, pure fear Josie was feeling in the moment she expired. Furthermore, Coop has deduced that BOB comes from The Black Lodge, or what the locals call "the evil in these woods;" if it's the power of The Black Lodge that Earle is after, like Coop thinks it is, then they have to get there first. But little does Dale know he's just solved the last piece of the puzzle for Earle. Earle already knows where The Black Lodge entrance is thanks to the petroglyph, and he knows when the lock will appear thanks to Briggs' drugged revelation about Jupiter and Mars last episode, but now, thanks to Coop, he knows the key – fear. Earle's appearance has returned to normal, but his soul is more corrupt than ever. He's off to collect his queen, whoever she may be, and start the final mechanisms of this monstrous machine. As if the moment weren't sadistic enough, Earle declares he hasn't felt this good since puncturing his wife Caroline's aorta. Before he departs, he has a final goodbye with Leo and leaves him a little present: a hand-wrought cage the size of Leo's head dangling just above him and filled with spiders the size of bagels. There's no bottom to this cage, meaning the whole thing could just drop onto Leo's head, spiders and all, if it wasn't for the twine held taut by Leo's teeth counteracting the cage's weight. As his hands and legs are bound, it's quite the predicament Leo's been left in.

The contestants of Miss Twin Peaks – including Lana, Lucy, Donna, and Nadine – are being led through choreography by Pinkle as the judges – Norma, Mayor Milford, and Dick Tremayne – are discussing the qualities they're looking for in a winner. They settle on some typical ideals and split up. The girls get a break, and Lana uses this opportunity to get some persuasive alone time with Dick as her fiancé the Mayor suggested. They go off to "find a prop." They find something.

Coop is meditating instead of sleeping and its working like gangbusters, he feels great. A quick update to Diane in which he mentions Annie for the first time, in most flattering terms, including the realization that he hasn't felt this way for anyone since Caroline. A knock on his door ends this conversation, which is the last Coop will have with Diane in season two. A moment of static cassette hiss in her honor. At Coop's door is Annie, as though by confessing his love for her aloud he somehow conjured her. She's nervous because the pageant starts in six hours and she hasn't written a word of her speech. She needs his help, especially as she's terrified of public speaking. Yet again this leads into how awkward Annie feels being back in the world, and yet again it ends with a passionate embrace and some grade-A smooching. And this time...some implied lovemaking.

Nadine is showing slides of her wrestling exploits to Mike, Ed, Nadine, and Dr. Jacoby. The Doctor has gathered them to talk through the "break up." Nadine, still convinced she's a senior cheerleader, is feeling a little guilty for being as happy as she is because she's worried Ed is equally as sad. Ed tells her this isn't so, he and Norma are going to get married. She says that's cool, she and Mike are getting married too, but then she squeezes her intended's hand so hard she breaks several of his bones.

Briggs is still trying to find his way out of the forest. He's disoriented, drugged, exhausted, but soldier that he is he presses on. Hawk comes upon him. Briggs asks which way is the castle and Hawk loads him into the car. At the station, Truman tells Coop they checked Briggs out and physically he's fine, but mentally, emotionally, not so much. Coop smells the Major and detects odiferous traces of haloperidol. Briggs is so zonked on the stuff he doesn't even recognize his own name. However he does know he's been in the woods, but other than that he's no immediate help. Andy comes back to resume staring at the petroglyph. As he does, Coop tells Truman it's not just about being in the right place to enter The Black Lodge, it's about being in the right place at the right time. Looking at one of the symbols, Andy asks if the 4H club could have anything to do with this. Probably not.

Pete, Andrew and Catherine are trying to get into the metal rectangular cube that is hopefully the last of Eckhardt's puzzle boxes. In frustration, Andrew shoots it thrice. That does the job. Inside is a key, no doubt to something valuable. Until they figure out where it fits, they'll store the key in plain sight on a cake tray. Seems Packards don't even trust each other.

Donna is all dolled up and leaving for the pageant. Her parents want to hear her speech, but she'd rather discuss the truth about Mom and Ben Horne, and if they won't tell her, then she'll ask Ben. They don't tell her. So she leaves, resolved.

Coop catches a break when he finds symbols in a book that match those Andy mistook for indicators of the 4H club. They stand for Jupiter and Saturn, and in this instance represent a conjunction of the two planets, a celestial alignment, which translates to a time. These particular planets when in conjunction can signify an explosive shift in power, both good and bad. Coop checks and the next conjunction is due sometime between January and June. It's March now. So they know when the Lodge will be open, they just need the where. Briggs interrupts with a reminder to "Protect the Queen," and "fear and love open the doors." The first part, of course, is an obtuse reference to Earle's plan for the pageant winner, and the second is in reference to the doors of the Lodges; we know fear opens The Black Lodge, and now we know love does the same to The White Lodge. Briggs is an obvious conduit of the latter realm and is transferring messages to Coop like the Giant tried to last episode when Annie announced she was entering the pageant. Coop is their Agent now, The White Lodge's, but the lines of communication aren't all the way open. Regardless Coop understands, even if he doesn't know immediately what it all means. Briggs mentions the queen again and it clicks: Earle's playing chess and in chess the queen is the most important piece, it's the one you take to get the king, so that's what Earle wants, a queen, like say the one crowned winner of Miss Twin Peaks, to take to the entrance of The Black Lodge and use her fear to open it. Andy is trying to interrupt but Coop and Truman are so wrapped up in this flood of revelations that they ignore him. He chases after trying to get them to listen, in the process knocking the bonsai off the table, breaking the pot, and revealing the bug. They instantly know who planted it, and realize Earle is way ahead of them. They have to get to The Road House immediately, the pageant has already started.

Donna. Audrey. Shelly. Annie. Lucy. Nadine. Lana. These are the names we know in the pageant. So it stands to reason one of these women will be Earle's queen. I think we all know what direction this is headed in, if perhaps we don't know how it's going to get there. Everyone in town is in the room except for the only ones who know everyone is in danger. The opening dance number ends and the talent portion begins. Lucy is an ace tapper, turns out. Bobby, backstage, sees the Log Lady lurking in the shadows only seconds after he saw her in the crowd. This backstage Log Lady is no Lady, though, she's Earle in drag, but his log is real enough to knock Bobby out. Coop and Truman arrive but in order to trap Earle they need the pageant to finish. Their plan is to grab the winning girl the second she's announced and give her around-the-clock protection until Earle can be stopped. Lana's also a dancer, of a much more exotic sort. There's not limp noodle in the place. Audrey meanwhile gives an intelligent, impassioned, and well-received speech.

Backstage, Donna comes across Ben and engages him. She wants the truth. He thinks they should all discuss this as a group, them and her parents. She doesn't. She wants to know what the hell is going on. He starts to talk, but she jumps ahead of his words and assumes he's her actual father then runs off crying. Ben doesn't deny it.

Annie's speech goes well, despite her nerves and because of Coop's influence and presence. Earle, still in costume, skulks above the stage on the catwalk. The pageant ends and the ballots are being counted, a winner will be announced any moment. In the unknown interim, Lucy gets Andy and Dick together for the revelation of which man she has chosen to be the father of her unborn child, regardless of who is biologically responsible: Andy. Duh.

125

No one's surprised or heartbroken, Dick included. For the happy (and TWIN PEAKS' cutest) couple, though, it's a new beginning. But Andy can't celebrate because despite somehow having been in the same room with him for at least half an hour, Andy still hasn't told Coop whatever it is he noticed about the petroglyph.

At long last it's time to crown Miss Twin Peaks. No one is surprised when it's Annie. Coop, however, is scared in his stoic way. Lana's pissed, as is the Mayor, but it was Dick who swayed his vote Annie's way, her speech was just too moving. It's a moment of celebration, and it is a quick one. The lights go out. The music dies. The applause halts, confused. A strobe begins to flash. Uncertain murmurs fill the room then turn to screams when smoke starts billowing from the stage. Panic. Chaos. Coop and Truman trying to navigate it, trying to get to Annie. Nadine gets knocked out by a falling sandbag. Doc leads Annie from the stage but loses her in the smoke. And at long last, Coop sees Earle and recognizes him despite the Log Lady disguise and the demon whiteface he's reverted to. The two men, former friends and partners now nemeses and rivals, stare at each other, Coop with primal fear and Earle with primal evil. Coop fights through the crowd but Earle uses a remote to detonate another flash of flame and smoke. Earle then chloroforms Annie and drags her away. When the lights come back on and the smoke drifts away and Coop and Harry find each other, Annie and Earle are gone. Truman goes to try and head them off and Andy finally tells Coop what he figured out and what we already knew: the petroglyph is a map of Twin Peaks.

Whew. That's certainly a set up for a series finale. Oddly enough, neither Lynch nor Frost had a direct hand in this episode. It was written by Barry Pullman, his last of four episodes, and directed by Tim Hunter, his final episode of three. The finale would see the last collaboration of the co-creators as well as second string plotters Harley Peyton and Robert Engels, but despite a lack of major players, this is a taut and suspenseful episode that paints by the numbers the perimeter of the bigger picture to come in the next episode.

Outside of the finale and the episode resolving the Laura Palmer storyline, the final act of "Miss Twin Peaks" is as tense and dread-inducing as the series ever got. Knowing what we do about Earle's preoccupation with The Black Lodge and his intentions for the pageant winner, not to mention the obvious parallels between Annie and Caroline, we can see shadows of what's coming from a mile away; it's the horrific details we can't discern. I was standing for the last ten minutes of this episode I was so nervous, and I've seen it five times before. Kudos to the pacing at which the narrative unravels, there were times it might have felt slightly redundant, Earle realizing things to have Coop realize them only scenes later, but that's what chess is, one move following another, sometimes applying the same strategy with the same result, and no other episode of the Earle storyline has more mimicked chess than this one. It serves as a microcosm of the whole plot in one compact and powerful episode that unnerves you in ways Laura's case never did: for one, with Laura we didn't have the burden of knowing what kind of evil BOB and The Black Lodge were capable of until after their horrors had been enacted, and two, Annie is a purer victim, more chaste and innocent, a former nun, even; Laura was no alter girl. Annie is clean as the driven snow, and her corruption would be most unsavory, not to mention it would utterly annihilate Coop's soul. But again, that's Earle's whole point...

EPISODE 29: "BEYOND LIFE AND DEATH"

Written by Mark Frost & Harley Peyton & Robert Engels, Directed by David Lynch

Airdate June 10th, 1991

Here we are at last, making one final trip – or so we thought for a quarter-century until about two years ago – into the woods. And it's the strangest trip yet. Here we go.

In the aftermath of the Miss Twin Peaks pageant, everyone is shaken. At the station Andy is consoling Lucy with amorous consequences. Coop meanwhile is at the end of his rope trying to figure out where Earle could have taken Annie. Truman says all available men are out there on the case, but no one can find a trace of Earle or Annie, it's like they've vanished. Coop knows the Owl Cave petroglyph is the only thing that can offer a solution. He sees the figure of the Giant, of the Little Man, of fire: "Fire Walk With Me." Pete interrupts with the incredible claim that the Log Lady stole his truck from The Road House and fled towards the Ghostwood Forest. Coop remembers Earle was dressed as the Log Lady at The Road House, and furthermore, he knows that the real Log Lady will be there with them in one minute. In the interim and knowing now that Earle has fled to the woods, Coop further intuits that The Black Lodge opening is somewhere in Ghostwood. When Pete mentions off-handedly that he had 12 rainbow trout in the bed of his truck, this jogs Truman's memory: in the petroglyph there's a circle of 12 sycamore trees, and there's a place like that in Ghostwood called Glastonbury Grove. Hawk jumps in and reminds everyone that Glastonbury Grove is where he found the bloody rags and the torn out pages of Laura Palmer's diary; this puts it within a stone's throw of the train car where Laura was murdered. The name Glastonbury rings a bell with Coop, and he realizes it's because it's the same as the burial place of King Arthur. King Arthur, of course, had 12 knights with whom he met at a circular table. Just then, as Coop predicted, the Log Lady arrives. She has a jar of oil Coop asked her to bring. She tells him her husband – who died in a fire in the woods on their wedding night decades prior – called it an opening to a gateway. This is the oil then, seen in the puddle at the end of episode 27 in which the red curtains were reflected. Coop smells it, lets Truman smell it. It reminds both of scorched engine oil, which is what Dr. Jacoby reported smelling at the park when he saw Maddy/Laura and was attacked from behind, what he smelled again in the hospital the night Lelan killed Jacques Renault, and also what Maddy smelled just before she was murdered by Leland/BOB. Then we get a real blast from the past as Coop has Hawk bring in … Ronette Pulaski. She's looking better than the last time we saw her a dozen or more episodes ago, if still a little shell-shocked. Coop asks if she recognizes the smell of the oil. She does, and it frightens her because she remembers it from the night Laura was killed.

Meanwhile in Ghostwood Forest, Earle and Annie arrive at Glastonbury Grove in Pete's pilfered pickup. Earle formally introduces himself. She's heard his name. He points out the 12 trout in the truck bed, and notes he likes the fear he's feeling from her. We remember, of course, that fear opens The Black Lodge. As he drags her towards the Grove, Annie begins to pray. They reach the ring of sycamore trees with the circle of white powder at its center, and Earle proclaims they have an appointment with the end of the world. They enter the ring of trees. He's a raving lunatic at this point, and she is paralyzed spiritually. Both are the first effects of the dark power of The Black Lodge. The shadows of the forest morph into the folds of a deep red curtain, which Earle is able to part and lead Annie through. They pass out of our world and into The Black Lodge. The curtains then fade to shadows again.

At Ed's, Doc Hayward is tending to Mike and Nadine, the latter of whom got hit on the head by a sandbag in the melee at The Road House. Despite these injuries, Ed is snapping a jaunty tune and smiling as he snuggles up to Norma, who at last he's free to be with. Mike is trying to comfort Nadine but when he professes his love for her and tries to steal a kiss, she freaks out, says she doesn't know who he is or why he's in her house. She's back in her right mind (if it can be called that) and she doesn't remember a thing about high school, cheerleading, Mike, or Ed and Norma. What really gets her goat is that her silent drape runners are gone. Suddenly the happiness of just a moment ago is shattered.

Donna has a suitcase and is on her way out the door of the family as her mother Eileen and Ben Horne try to talk with her about Ben being her birth father. Ben takes the blame for Donna finding out like this, then Doc comes home, figures out pretty quick what's going on and tells Ben to hit bricks. As Ben is asking Doc's forgiveness, Sylvia Horne – who hasn't appeared since season one – shows up on the stoop demanding to know what Ben's trying to do to this nice family. Doc snaps and punches Ben hard in the face, knocking him against the stone hearth and opening a giant gash in his forehead that drops him like a sack of potatoes to the ground, where he lays motionless. Doc is in anguish at his own rage and what it has wrought, and Donna is a blubbering mess.

At the Packard's, Andrew is taking a closer look at the key Eckhardt left Catherine. He recognizes it as belonging to a safety deposit box and replaces it with an identical one. Pete catches him in the act, though, but Andrew doesn't let that deter him.

Coop and Truman locate Pete's truck at Glastonbury Grove, but there's no trace of Earle or Annie. They make their way to the circle of sycamores, finding the way by Coop's intuition, or rather the messages he's being divined from The White Lodge. Halfway out, these messages tell him he has to go on alone. He won't explain why, he just goes. But then Truman starts creeping after. Coop hears an owl hoot and knows he's close. He comes upon the circle of trees. He enters the circle and sees the puddle of oil inside the smaller circle of powder. He recognizes it as the same brought by the Log Lady. He also sees footprints, and follows them to where Earle and Annie disappeared behind the red curtain. As Truman watches, the curtains appear and Coop disappears behind them as well. It should be noted, however, that the curtains opened for Coop, he didn't open them.

Coop is inside The Black Lodge. He enters into a hallway decorated same as the red room of his dreams. At the end of the hallway is a statue of Venus, armless. The song "Under the Sycamore Tree" is being sung from somewhere in a strong baritone. Coop walks down the hallway and parts the curtain at the other end. The light begins to strobe. He's in a room exactly like the one he dreamed about. The Man From Another Place enters as well and the strobing curbs but doesn't die. The Man dances across the room to a chair and has a seat. The singer – an elderly Hispanic man – is seen and finishes his song as the lights flash between white and red and darkness. The singer fades from sight. Coop's eyes are wide, as though he's hypnotized.

Back in the real world, Andy finds Truman in Glastonbury Grove. They wait until morning but Coop still hasn't reappeared. He's been missing going on 10 hours now. Andy leaves to get food and coffee.

Audrey shows up at the Twin Peaks Saving & Loan first thing that morning and very politely chains herself to the bank vault. This is an act of civil disobedience in protest of the bank financing the Ghostwood development project, and she won't leave until it is agreed that a town meeting will be held to discuss the effect of the development on the local environment. Amidst this modest chaos Andrew Packard and Pete arrive to check the safety deposit boxes, but of course there's a Horne standing in the way of that. Andrew admires her verve, but doesn't see a problem. She just chained herself to the door, after all, and that still opens. So in they go. Andrew has the elderly bank manager, Dell, locate the box that matches their key. Andrew and Pete open it, and at long last there's the bomb we've all been expecting, along with a note that reads, "Got you Andrew, Thomas." Then the bomb explodes, presumably killing all inside the vault.

Major Briggs and his wife are enjoying a lovely breakfast at the diner as Bobby and Shelly talk at the counter. Bobby thinks they should get married. Shelly reminds him technically she still is, and he says Leo is all but out of the picture. Bobby's more correct than he knows thanks to the spider cage hanging above Leo in Earle's cabin. Then Jacoby enters with Sarah Palmer, another character we haven't seen in forever. They're looking for the Major, Sarah has a message for him, and she's going to speak it in a voice that is most definitely not her own. It says: "I'm in the Black Lodge with Dale Cooper. I'm waiting for you."

In The Black Lodge Coop is still in the room with the Man From Another Place. The lights are normal again and both men are sitting. The Man tells Coop, "when you see me again it won't be me," and that this room is just the waiting room. Then he offers Coop some coffee and tells him some of his friends are here. That's when she walks in. Laura. Or the not-Laura of Coop's dream, the one who whispered her killer's name to the older version of Coop. She speaks backwards and snaps her fingers, then says the best line in all of television history because apparently it's 100% true: "I'll see you again in 25 years." Laura disappears and the elderly bellman from The Great Northern, the one who came to Coop after he was shot, right before the Giant did, appears in her place with a full cup of coffee. He and the Man exchange hallelujahs. The bellman serves Coop the coffee then turns into the Giant and takes his seat next to the Man, who clarifies these spirits are one and the same. The Giant disappears. The Man rubs his hands together sinisterly, and Coop goes to sample the coffee but one second it has congealed into a solid, the next it is liquid, and the next it is syrup. "Wow, BOB, wow," exclaims the Man, then levels his gaze on Coop and says "Fire Walk With Me." A vision of flames and a shrill shriek then the room goes dark and light starts strobing again. The Man is gone. Coop stands and walks across the waiting room and exits, entering the true Black Lodge, which looks just like hall he came down before, calm and serenely-lit. The same Venus statue waits at the hall's end. Coop walks toward it and parts the curtain there, entering another room. It is decorated exactly the same, there's no immediately discernible difference, so Coop turns back, walks back down the hall again, and re-enters the waiting room. The Man is still there and tells Coop he's going the wrong way. Coop returns again to the hallway and down it to the next room. In it the Man manifests laughing madly and sits down. But remember the promise made that when Coop saw the man again, "it won't be me." This then is the Man's doppelganger, which we can tell by his milky eyes. "Another friend," he says, laughing and disappearing behind his chair as Maddy enters across the room. Her eyes too, milky white. She warns Coop to watch out for her cousin, then fades from view. Coop returns to the last hallway, goes back to the waiting room. It's empty, completely, even of furniture, only bare floor and curtains. He crosses to the middle of the room and looks down. The Man's doppelganger is sneering up at him saying "Doppelganger." Laura is in the room again assuming the same pose she was when she disappeared minutes earlier, but now her eyes are white as well and her face is twisted in a snarl.

Then comes the single most terrifying sequence of the entire series.

The lights die and start strobing violently as Laura's doppelganger shrieks and contorts herself over furniture then rushes into the camera, her eyes insane, looking like some parasite in need of feeding, which perhaps she is. Coop runs from the waiting room back into the depths of the Black Lodge. The first room he comes to is also empty but he finds the gunshot wound in his stomach has suddenly and painfully reopened and is bleeding badly. He stumbles back into the hallway, following the path of his own blood. The Venus statue is notably absent, as though no beauty can be here. When Coop enters the next room, his hands slick with blood, he sees himself lying dead on the floor with Caroline in his arms. Then Caroline is Annie in the same dress, killed the same way as Caroline was, by a single stab wound to the heart. Annie sits up like a zombie. Coop says her name but she doesn't seem to understand. The light strobes yet again. Annie and the other Coop disappear. Our Coop is wandering the hallways now, calling Annie's name. He enters another room. His wound is healed. Annie is there, also healed and wearing the dress she wore in the pageant, the dress she was wearing when Earle absconded with her. She tells Coop she saw the face of the man who killed her. He doesn't understand. She says it was her husband. Coop calls her name but she doesn't know it, asks who's Annie and then morphs into a white-eyed Caroline, then back into Annie but in Caroline's dress, the dress we saw her dead in, then into Laura, white-eyed and still shrieking like a tea kettle, and lastly into Windom Earle. Annie appears separate, standing between the two men, then disappears. Windom laughs and tells Coop if he gives up his soul, Annie will live. Coop instantly agrees, so Earle instantly stabs him. A vision of flames, and then time reverses itself, or rather is reversed. Coop is unstabbed and finds Earle in the clutches of an enraged BOB. BOB tells Coop to go, tells him Earle can't ask for Coop's soul, so instead BOB will take Earle's. This involves, apparently, igniting said soul and extracting it from the top of Earle's head. It sounds like it hurts. Coop goes while the going is supposedly good. Then, out the opposite corner, Coop enters the room again, comes up behind BOB laughing maniacally along with him. The eyes, though, betray this new Coop isn't our Coop, it's "bad Coop," the doppelganger created by The Black Lodge. In the hallway, good Coop meets white-eyed Leland, who tells him he didn't kill anybody. Coop starts to move on, but sees his doppelganger enter the hallway. Good Coop scoots. Bad Coop follows him, pausing to snicker evilly with Leland. Good Coop is running, Bad Coop chasing after. Each hallway and each room they pass through looks the same. Good Coop makes it to the waiting room, and just as he's about to get out Bad Coop catches up and they tussle by the curtain as the light strobes again and BOB blocks our view, leering at us now, sniffing at the screen like a hungry dog that smells fresh meat. We don't see which Coop gets out or how.

In the woods, Truman sees the red curtain appear again and runs towards it, calling Coop's name. The Special Agent appears on the ground, unconscious, along with a bloodied Annie.

Back at The Great Northern Coop is in bed. He wakes, surrounded by Doc Hayward and Truman. He asks how Annie is. They tell him she's going to be fine. He says he needs to brush his teeth. They help him up and he goes into the bathroom, closing the door behind him. They both notice there's something off about him. In the bathroom, Coop squeezes all the toothpaste into the sink, then smiles into his reflection … which is BOB. Coop smashes his forehead against the mirror, cracking it. Truman and Doc hear this and call his name, try the knob but it's locked. Coop/BOB meanwhile is snickering madly, laughing at his own faux concern for the girl's well-being. He utters the episode's, and at the time the series' chilling last line in a mocking, depraved tone: "How's Annie?" He says it over and over and over, and each time he finds it funnier, while we find it more horrifying.

And that's it. That's how TWIN PEAKS ended. For good, at the time. If you listen carefully, you can still hear the echoes from 1991 of a quarter-million televisions being kicked in at once. The show didn't just end on a high note, it ended at the peak – pardon the pun – of its mystery and intensity, delivered by the strangest, most confounding and open-to-interpretation hour of television ever.

The script might say the finale was written by Mark Frost, Harley Peyton and Robert Engels, but the truth of the matter is that when David Lynch got his hands on the script, he altered most of it, including most notably changing the original ending to the looser, broader, more-obtuse ending that made it to air. In a nutshell, the writers saw the finale as a physical confrontation between Earle and Cooper, which makes absolute sense, and Lynch saw it as more of a metaphysical confrontation not between Coop and his nemesis, but Coop and his true greatest enemy: his own fear. The result is a confounding, confusing and probably intentionally-so sequence that is equally fascinating and flabbergasting, and which breaks down to Coop's fear of Annie being killed as a result of her involvement with him being so strong that it allows The Black Lodge to divide his soul into good and bad forms, the latter of which escapes into our world, leaving the former trapped in The Black Lodge. That still might not clear it up, but like I said it's up for broad interpretation.

Aside from the narrative, the whole episode is a technical highlight, but especially the last half hour once Coop enters The Black Lodge. If this finale is not necessarily the culmination of all the series' plot threads, it is absolutely the culmination of everything visual that makes TWIN PEAKS TWIN PEAKS. This is the one payoff we get for certain, we get to see The Black Lodge in all its weird, wild glory, and it's an incredible world unto itself. The chevron, the Venus, the curtains, the furniture, the light: it's perfect, visually speaking.

So then where does everything stand when the final credits roll? Ben Horne is Donna's real dad and possibly dead, which would make Doc Hayward a killer. We see Doc again, he shows up at the end of episode at Coop's bedside, but Ben is never seen again nor is any mention of his condition made. Mike Nelson is single again because Nadine is back in her right mind and still in love with Ed, who didn't get a chance to divorce her which means he's not married to Norma, like both of them were longing for. Audrey was in the bank when the bomb went off; until recently I'd wondered if this had killed her, but since Sherilyn Fenn made the cast list for season three, seems Audrey somehow survived. Andrew and Pete, however, most likely died, being right in front of the bomb when it blew. We don't know where Catherine ended up, and the other character in their realm, Josie, is a drawer knob in The Great Northern. We get no resolution for Andy, Lucy, Hawk, Truman, Shelly, Bobby, Major Briggs, Sarah Palmer or the Log Lady, but all but Briggs and Truman are returning in some form for season three, and even Truman might be, if Lynch recast the character; Michael Ontkean retired from acting more than a decade ago and Robert Forster, who was originally offered the Truman role but passed, could be playing the Sheriff in the new season.

Annie is somehow alive. What this means for her soul we do not know, and may not know, as Heather Graham in not listed as being a part of season three. Given that she seemed to be in mortal peril from Bad Coop/BOB, perhaps she didn't survive her return very long.

And Coop is not Coop. Rather, he's two Coops, and the one we know, the one we love, is trapped in that horrible place, and presumably has been since the first time this scene aired 25 years ago.

Love it or hate it, TWIN PEAKS certainly went out with a bang, if also with the most frustrating series finale in all of TV history. It could be argued that the show was approaching its apex, and it can certainly be considered that the pacing of the second season and the narrative after Laura, both of which turned away viewers in droves, rewarded those who stuck around by insidiously linking back to the original storyline in a way that gave it deeper, chillier, and even darker connotations than it originally had. Everything after Leland died that people thought was straying from what made TWIN PEAKS a phenomenon was really backstory of the mythical dimension that birthed the evil that led to the murder that started TWIN PEAKS. If you look at it that way, season 3, or what season 3 could have been at that time, might have been the point all along: season 1 you show the manifest of this ancient evil and introduce our hero; season 2 you reveal the nature of the evil, the origins of where it comes, and send our hero to confront it; season 3, our hero is the evil and must be saved from himself. But that's just speculation on my part.

For my money, TWIN PEAKS never got more interesting than it did in the last 20 seconds of the second season finale. I've seen the series all the way through many times now, and every single time it has been a gut-wrenching moment, usually followed by curses both colorful and condemning directed at ABC executives and mainstream American television audiences. This time, though, knowing the story isn't over, knowing, in fact, that with an 18-episode commitment for season three the story is barely half-way told, it was an exciting moment, it was a moment of renewed potential, even if or somewhat especially because it can't be linear anymore. We can't just pick up with Truman and Doc on the other side of that door (I don't think), Annie isn't around in season 3, or if she is, Heather Graham isn't playing her (Naomi Watts?) and Truman isn't back either (see above), but I think this makes it more interesting because in addition to whatever mysteries are swirling about when the third season starts up, there will be mysteries for a quarter-century before them to explore.

I've said before and I'll say it again here: I don't think a movie wrap-up would have been the satisfying thing fans thought it would be. I think what's opened by the finale is too big to wrap up in two hours, and in fact I think it's got the most room to grow of any plot TWIN PEAKS ever introduced. It's the biggest story yet, what's started here, the rest has just been leading up to it, this is the ultimate showdown. To wrap that up in a movie would have been disrespectful to all the work that had been done up until then. A prequel was the only way to go: layer the mythos, give people more room for their imaginations to extrapolate and hope one day the show could be given the room to finish correctly. They have that room now thanks to Showtime, and we're going to get the slowly-unfurling resolution we and the series deserve.

PERSPECTIVES

"She's filled with secrets"

The Man From Another Place

CANDLE IN THE WIND – LAURA PALMER & MARILYN MONROE

The story of how one iconic blonde came to inspire another

When it came to seeking a tragic inspiration for their centerpiece character, TWIN PEAKS' co-creators David Lynch and Mark Frost went straight to an iconic well.

Norma Jean Mortensen was born in the shadow of Hollywood in 1926 to a mother with emotional issues who never revealed the identity of the girl's father. There were siblings from a previous marriage, but the girl wouldn't know of them until her adolescence, and they would never be close. During her childhood she went by three different surnames and lived with a host of foster families following her mother's complete and permanent mental breakdown. At 16, facing yet another return to the foster system, Norma Jean dropped out of high school and into an arranged marriage of convenience with a neighbor boy five years her senior. The marriage would last four years, during which time the girl with a shifting identity started modeling and finally locked on the single persona she would inhabit the rest of her life: Marilyn Monroe.

The rest we know. Monroe became the prototypical blonde sex object of her era, her actual self often diminutized by the industry for the sake of what she could represent for them. She was more of a symbol than a person in the end, and that led to an array of issues with drugs, alcohol, sex, and commitment that helped paint her as one of the most – if not THE most – tragically beautiful women in American history and popular culture. At the time of her death from a suspected overdose, Monroe was only 36 years old, but in her short life she made an impression that is still reverberating more than half a century later.

In 1989, when television writer and producer Mark Frost met with provocative auteur David Lynch to discuss working together, it wasn't about TWIN PEAKS, not yet, at least. Their first project was going to be a biopic of Monroe based on the book GODDESS: THE SECRET LIVES OF MARILYN MONROE by Anthony Summers (not to be confused with the 2015 Lifetime miniseries THE SECRET *LIFE* OF MARILYN MONROE or the eponymous book it's based on). As they got into the script, however, and discovered their particular chemistry, the movie started to veer away from the realm of fallen angel into the more political and conspiratorial side of Monroe's life.

"I always, like ten trillion other people, liked Marilyn Monroe, and was fascinated by her life," said Lynch, *"So when this came along I was interested, but, you know, what's the drill? I got into it carefully...We met with Anthony Summers, who wrote the book. The more we went along the more it was sort of like UFOs. You're fascinated by them, but you can't really prove if they exist. Even if you see pictures, or stories, or people are hypnotized, you never really know. Same thing with Marilyn Monroe and the Kennedys and all this. I can't figure out even now what's real and what's a story."*

When Frost and Lynch blatantly stated in their script that they believed the actress had been murdered, and even went so far as to name a culprit (alas, unknown), the studio swiftly pulled the plug.

But the two had established a good creative rapport and wanted to continue exploring it. Next up was ONE SALIVA BUBBLE, which is purported to be a comedy about identity swapping – a funny LOST HIGHWAY, perhaps? – and which also never came to fruition for one reason or another. Word of the unlikely collaboration was rumbling through the industry, however, and eventually the bright idea was hatched to get the duo working on a television show. Their original idea dealt with the ancient and mythical underwater kingdom Lemuria – kinda like Atlantis –

whose descendants walk among humans and must be outed by federal agents. This too fizzled but the paranormal tone felt right to Frost and Lynch, and they expanded their discussions until the town and story of TWIN PEAKS were born.

There's nothing more uniquely American-tragic than the murder of a pretty young girl, went their thinking, and in setting up the persona of Laura Palmer, Frost and Lynch returned to the blonde who had brought them together. Both Laura and Marilyn suffered from issues of identity: who they were supposed to be versus who they actually were, and both self-medicated the stress from this dissociation with drugs, alcohol, and meaningless sexual encounters meant to validate the self but that in fact left an emptier space inside. Both women came from sexually abusive backgrounds, Laura at the hands of BOB, Monroe by various foster fathers and other older men, and both had their adult mindsets and self-image shaped by these horrific encounters. Both women used their sex appeal as a weapon, or at least as the only form of control they had over their lives, and both women were outed by their deaths as being almost the opposite of what they were perceived to be.

What I said about Marilyn above could be said about Laura as well: she was a symbol to people, not a real, fragile person, and when the symbol died, revealing that person, the world instead chose to preserve the illusion by elevating her memory to an iconic status. Death was the biggest thing to ever happen to Marilyn Monroe, as it was to Laura Palmer, and in each instance a tragic, beautiful, flawed young woman was transformed into something immortal.

Reflections in a broken mirror is perhaps how best to describe the connection between Laura and Marilyn, not identical personas but composed of the same flawed elements, outside and in, built of the same damaged pieces. It is this connection between them that allowed TWIN PEAKS to connect with its viewing audience in such an intimate and instantaneous way. This tragedy was designed to appeal to our most innate sympathies, while simultaneously indulging our deepest fears: innocence more than just shattered; mangled, corrupted, obliterated.

"I restore myself when I'm alone" is a quote for which Marilyn is famous, but it just as easily could have been taken from the diary of another troubled young girl trying to make sense of the chaos she somehow created just by being alive.

THE NAKED FOREST - FILM NOIR AND 'TWIN PEAKS'

How the series borrowed from the stylized genre (then twisted it)

While it can be extremely difficult to classify TWIN PEAKS – is it drama? Horror? A supernatural thriller? A crime procedural? Sci-fi? Dark comedy? – it's not so hard to determine that the one cinematic storytelling tradition from which the series borrows most heavily is Film Noir.

For the uninformed, Film Noir refers to a specific type of filmmaking – largely American – that came to prominence during the 1940's and 50's and was named by film critic Nino Frank, who saw the need to categorize the new wave of gritty urban crime films coming out of the States. John Huston, Orson Welles, Otto Preminger, Billy Wilder, Carol Reed, and Alfred Hitchcock are among the genre's greatest purveyors, and so powerful was the movement that it was co-opted by other countries at the height of its popularity – see the work of Frenchmen Jean Pierre Melville, Henri-Georges Clouzot and Jules Dassin, or certain films by Michelangelo Antonioni, Luchino Visconti, or Akira Kurosawa – and furthermore lived past its heyday as "neo-noir," which covers a hugely broad spectrum encompassing everything from BLOOD SIMPLE to PULP FICTION to BATMAN BEGINS, and pretty much every dramatic TV series of note lately, including BREAKING BAD, THE KILLING, and TRUE DETECTIVE.

Noir is a highly-stylized genre, and is known for its technical distinctions as well as its narrative ones. Speaking to the former qualifications, Noir is often shot wide, using the landscape – particularly urban settings – as another character; when there are close-ups, they are rarely straight on, and instead are off-center, low-to the ground, or coming from an odd angle like the Dutch to greater personify the uncertain atmosphere of the film. Furthermore Noir, as the nomenclature might lead you to believe, is designed around a specific lighting style, sometimes referred to as "chiaroscuro," that lays an emphasis on contrasting light with shadow and typically favors darkness. Light, when it does come, it itself rarely direct, rather hitting its subject from the side or behind, again, to heighten the mysterious tone.

In terms of its narrative distinctions, Noir always involves a crime, usually murder. This is because thematically, Noir's singular obsession is seeking, finding, and displaying the dark side of humanity, our basest selves, motivated by greed, lust, anger or other such deadly sins. As such, blackmail, adultery, double-crossing, and back-stabbing often factor into the narrative mix. Noir is often set in a metropolitan area, but really any place that can be considered labyrinthine or disorienting because of its arrangement – like, say, a forest that's also a portal into a dimension that consists solely of hallways and curtained rooms without windows – counts. To further add to this convolution, Noir rarely attacks its story head-on. There are flashbacks, flash-forwards, flash-asides, unreliable narrators, multiple versions of events, and a general air of confusion as to what the truth is, who knows it, and if that's what they're telling.

Even from this most basic of summations, you should already be seeing the Film Noir in TWIN PEAKS. But there's more to this connection than just a vibe or a few surface comparisons, and while some purists might argue that TWIN PEAKS is ultimately more Noir*ish* than Noir – the distinction being that it doesn't adhere to Noir's strict sense of resolution and leaves itself open to interpretation – from the get-go the design of this mysterious Washington town, the people who inhabit it, and the trauma that infects it were all drawn in some way from Noir.

Obviously, there's the basic plot: a pretty young blonde girl with more secrets than smiles washes up dead with no immediately-identifiable assailant. That's Noir through and through, from the attractive virtue of the victim to that virtue's unbeknownst impurity. Furthermore, as the story unravels it will come to include sexual perversity (on a few counts), fluctuating moralities, betrayal galore, and more melodrama than a soap-opera awards show on the Poseidon. And the series' second major plotline, the *tete a tete* between Dale Cooper and Windom Earle, is a take on the partner-turned-enemy stereotype. All of these elements are tried-and-true Noir staples.

Then there's the man sent to solve case: Cooper, a fed who works on his own, who speaks in voiceover narration to his Gal Friday Diane via a microcassette recorder, who obeys a strict moral code of his own devising often to the peril of his personal and professional life, and who has a dark secret or two of his own that makes him susceptible to corruption.

There's the cadre of Femme Fatales – devious temptresses who use their charms and wiles to entrap clueless men and lead them into compromising, dangerous, and often fatal scenarios – personified by Laura Palmer but also found to varying degrees in the characters of Donna Hayward, Shelly Johnson, Evelyn Marsh, and of course, Audrey Horne. While most crime dramas make victims of women, even in their victimhood the women of TWIN PEAKS fight back: Laura kept a diary exposing her killer and in some ways took ownership of her death, Donna starts off a pushover devastated by her friend's murder but finds her backbone through mimicry of Laura, Shelly is a victim of domestic abuse who deceives her abuser to her advantage (or tries to), Evelyn as well has been abused by her husband and plots successfully to have him murdered, and Audrey – who's been kidnapped, drugged, slapped around, possibly sexually assaulted, once almost by her father, generally ignored, underestimated, jilted, and deflowered then abandoned in the same five minutes – is perhaps the show's strongest character, both in terms of will and spirit; she is indefatigable and a pillar of independence. Strong women are one of the most distinguishing elements of Film Noir, and perhaps the one TWIN PEAKS borrowed from the most. There's even an old-school Femme Fatale among the cast (two if you count Piper Laurie's role in THE HUSTLER, which some do): Jane Greer, who plays Norma's mother Vivian for three episodes in the second season, was a Hollywood actress who came to prominence in the days of Noir with memorable turns in OUT OF THE PAST and THE BIG STEAL, both alongside Robert Mitchum. Additionally, Russ Tamblyn (Dr. Jacoby) was in the original GUN CRAZY, Dan O'Herlihy (Andrew Packard) was in LARCENY, and James Booth (Ernie Niles) started his career with a bit role in THE NARROWING CIRCLE. Seems Lynch didn't just borrow themes from Film Noir, he borrowed people as well.

And in some instances, the characters these people played had names that were derived directly from Noir: Laura gets her name from the Otto Preminger film, LAURA, which also features the names Waldo and Lydecker, which you'll note are the same as Jacques Renault's Mynah bird that bit Laura the night she died, and the veterinarian who treated said bird, respectively. Windom Earle's surname comes from Humphrey Bogart's in HIGH SIERRA, directed by Raoul Walsh and written in part by John Huston. Mr. Neff, the insurance agent who comes to Catherine Martell the night before the mill fire and tries to get her to sign a cooked life insurance policy takes his name from Billy Wilder's DOUBLE INDEMNITY, the plot of which centers on an insurance scam. Gordon Cole, the FBI Field Supervisor Coop reports to and who is played by David Lynch, comes from a minor character in another Wilder Noir classic, SUNSET BOULEVARD. Judge Sternwood, the circuit judge who denies then sets Leland's bail after he kills Jacques Renault, and who deems Leo mentally unfit to stand trial for burning down the mill, comes from Martha Vicker's character in Howard Hawks' THE BIG SLEEP, and the District Attorney who argues before Sternwood, Daryl Lodwick, is named for the D.A. in Preminger's ANATOMY OF A MURDER. If you count television Noir, Phillip Gerard, or MIKE, the One-Armed Man, shares the same name minus an "L" as the detective pursing Dr. Richard Kimble in THE FUGITIVE. And going back to cinema, Madeleine Ferguson, the doppelganger cousin of Laura Palmer, gets both her names from characters in Hitchcock's VERTIGO: Madeleine is the name of the first character played by Kim Novak, and Ferguson is the last name of Jimmy Stewart's character. Note here that in VERTIGO, Madeleine dies and grief-stricken, Ferguson "recreates" her in the form of lookalike Judy, also played by Novak; the idea of dual-identities, mistaken-identities, or heretofore unknown twins is also very ingrained in the Noir tradition.

Then there's the "Third Man." For most of the latter half of the investigation into Laura's murder, the suspicion was that the killer was a third man described by the Log Lady who was heard walking through the woods to Jacques' cabin the night Laura died *after* Jacques, Leo, Laura and Ronette, and whose boot prints were discovered both outside a cabin window and outside the train car where Laura was killed. THE THIRD MAN is, of course, the name of one of Noir's greatest accomplishments, directed by Carol Reed and starring Orson Welles. In Reed's version, the "third man" also refers to a possible witness to/perpetrator of a suspicious death.

As for the technical elements TWIN PEAKS borrows from Noir, certainly landscape as a character can be checked off the list. Not only is the show named for its location, the place itself ultimately becomes the most important character in the series and the reason for everything that happens. Wide-angle shots were something David Lynch insisted on and something series' cinematographer Frank Byers – who shot everything but the pilot – has said he found inspiration for in Welles' own TOUCH OF EVIL. In terms of close-ups, there's never anything straight about them, whether it's the framing, the angle, or even the duration of the shot. Think of the blood on the donuts seen from above at a slant after Waldo is shot by Leo, or the halves of the heart necklace shared between James and Laura, both revealed by wavering flashlight in otherwise impenetrable darkness, one in the woods being buried, one waiting on a pile of dirt at the murder scene. And you want to talk chiaroscuro? TWIN PEAKS is nothing if not aesthetically (and thematically) a struggle between darkness and light with darkness almost always winning. Think of the color scheme of TWIN PEAKS and how the brightest you get is blood red while almost everything else is dripping in deep blues or strobing between overwashed light and the densest of shadows, the kind out of which anything might crawl. Even the music of Angelo Badalamenti, the costuming, the set design and decoration – these things harken back to the era of Noir more so than they do the era the show existed in; I grew up in the 80's, and there weren't a lot of girls in saddle shoes and bobby socks around.

But TWIN PEAKS wouldn't be TWIN PEAKS if it strictly adhered to Noir principles, it would be, I don't know, L.A. CONFIDENTIAL or something like that. No, TWIN PEAKS twists the expectations of Noir and creates its own strange hybrid of cut-and-dry and the metaphysical. There's the fact that, as mentioned, while Noir always arrives at a clear, pointed and exact resolution, TWIN PEAKS "ends" nowhere near that; it could, in fact, be considered the most unresolved series finale in history, or at least it could have been until season 3 was announced. Then there are our protagonists, Coop and Laura. Coop is no Bogey, he doesn't define his masculinity in cigarettes, liquor, or sexual conquests, in fact the opposite. He doesn't smoke, is a coffee fanatic who only drinks alcohol rarely and in moderation, and despite more than one opportunity to bed a resident of Twin Peaks, all Coop really wants from life is "to make love to a beautiful woman I have genuine affection for." That's not hard-boiled, it's soft-hearted. And Laura, well, she fits inside the parameters of a Femme Fatale for sure; nearly every man in town – EVERY man – has been with her or has wanted to be with her, and while she uses her femininity and sexual allure to her benefit, it is also a curse to her, a thing she is a slave to. Her moxie is a put-on, a coping mechanism, and while it can be said that all moxie is to a degree, not to the degree Laura has a need for it. She's surviving not just a man's world but a demon's universe, and ultimately she is the most fragile person in the narrative, despite her wells of strength. Then lastly, there are the villains. Noir in no terms whatsoever would deal with a central villain of such vague and indescribable origins and nature as BOB, nor would his lair exist between dimensions. Even Windom Earle, the "straighter" of the villains, ends up in the same place as BOB, fluctuating between worlds and levels of consciousness. If TWIN PEAKS was pure Noir, BOB would have been an escaped con who murders Laura then hides out above a convenience store while MIKE, his cell mate, helps the cops track him down but Windom, Coop's disgraced partner, wants the glory for himself and will do anything – *anything* – to get it. In either scenario, Annie's toast.

So then while it might not conform strictly to the ideals and parameters of Film Noir, there's no denying the influence of the genre on TWIN PEAKS. Both are the product of a prosperous society faced with its own mortality, both reflect the hidden evils that hide in the heart of man, and both, at their lightest and darkest, are as uniquely American as, well, cherry pie.

BLUE ROSE SPECIAL: THE SYMBOLISM OF FOOD IN 'TWIN PEAKS'

The coffee, doughnuts, and cherry pie are not what they seem

One of the first things folks think about when they think about TWIN PEAKS – especially in terms of the show's quirky, off-beat nature – is food. Food is everywhere in TWIN PEAKS, and like everything else in the series, it means more than what you think it means. For Ben and Jerry Horne, food is a manifestation of their wealth, they feast on exotic, foreign, and decadent delights like baguettes with brie and butter brought all the way from France, or smoked cheese pigs; while for Norma Jennings, owner of the Double R Diner, food is a path to wealth, it is a reflection of her life, ordinary and everyday with hints of elegance. But the three biggest food referentials in TWIN PEAKS, as everybody knows, are delicious doughnuts, cherry pie to die for, and all those damn fine cups of coffee. And like everything else, they too are representative of themes and in fact people important to TWIN PEAKS.

As a food, doughnuts are a little silly. They're frosted in bright colors and dusted in sprinkles, powdered with sugar, filled with jams and jellies and creams, and are sickly-sweet to the taste. They're also stereotypical cop food. In TWIN PEAKS, this relationship is explored to the extreme. When you see a doughnut in TWIN PEAKS, you're usually seeing dozens of them, comically more than the two or three people in the room could possibly consume. This sucks the seriousness out of an otherwise serious place – namely the Sheriff's station – and helps create a colloquial vibe attributed to the Department that further paints them as quaint country folk perhaps unprepared to handle such a major case like the murder of Laura Palmer, which we remember at its incept is a serial killer case. This vibe also exists so that Truman, Hawk, and Andy may each rise above expectations in several instances, thus making them more heroic in the audience's eyes for overcoming their perceived limitations. As a metaphor then, doughnuts represent not only the quirky, silly, and simple side of the Twin Peaks authorities, but also the sweetness inherent to them as well, the kindness, the virtue, which further establishes them as on the side of right.

Doughnuts in TWIN PEAKS also serve as a kind of absurd visual equalizer, most notably in the death scene of Waldo, Jacques Renault's mynah bird and a possible witness to Laura's murder. While in police custody, Waldo is shot through the station window by Leo Johnson. Though we don't see the death itself, we are given the gist by the striking image of Waldo's blood and a few feathers spattered across the elaborate doughnut display set up in the room. It's a dark moment granted ridiculous levity by the contrast of death coating breakfast desserts.

Cherry pie is a little more lascivious as a metaphor. It too has a simplicity to it as a food, but beyond that cherry pie in particular has certain sexual connotations that reflect its balance between sweet (or innocent) and tart (or promiscuous). If you need a better understanding of the connotations I'm talking about, I'll direct you to the music video for Warrant's "Cherry Pie" on YouTube and leave it at that. Though she is never directly associated with it in the series, mostly on account of being dead, the TWIN PEAKS character cherry pie most directly reflects is Laura Palmer. Like the pie, Laura had her sweet, innocent side, and she had her "tart," promiscuous side. She was a powerfully sexual being but this was a side of herself also forged from violence and violation, so as such she was ashamed of her sexuality and hid it under the pretty, flaky crust of her exterior being: a wholesome, benevolent, uniquely-American teenage girl. The dichotomy of Laura's tarnished innocence is the essence of those mentioned sexual connotations of cherry pie – rebellion, recklessness, and wanton self-destruction among them – and Laura personified them to a T.

Cherry pie, or perhaps just the cherry part, is also representative of Audrey Horne, TWIN PEAKS' would-be sultry vixen. From her attitude, flirtatious nature, and alluring physical prowess, it might be assumed that Audrey is well-versed in the art of love. The pinnacle proof behind this assumption, of course, comes when Audrey goes undercover at One Eyed Jacks and proves her potential as a "hospitality girl" to Blackie by tying the stem of a cherry into a knot. With her tongue. This is pretty much as blatantly explicit as you could get on network TV in the pre-NYPD BLUE era, and it's also the single most sensual moment of the series. But here again, the cherry isn't all about sex, there has to be an innocent component to the metaphor as well. So then later in the second season, it's revealed that Audrey is a virgin, which certain wouldn't undermine her, um, tying skills, but does cause the audience to realize that she's more innocent than she's portrayed or portrays herself. The cherry is the perfect food to reflect this balance.

Lastly, we come to the biggest food metaphor of them all, coffee. And while coffee is tied to pretty much every character in the series from the fresh pots of the Double R to Pete's fishy percolator, we all know who the beverage's strong and dependable qualities are mirroring: Special Agent Dale Cooper. He is java's strongest advocate and greatest aficionado in the series, it is synonymous with him and the only seeming chemical vice in which he partakes (he does have the occasional drink, but never more than one is shown, nor does it seem to affect him whatsoever). Like coffee, Dale Cooper is a reliable go-to to get the job done. He is efficient, direct, and bold. He isn't complicated, he's always alert, and he is intellectually inexhaustible, his acumen able to be refilled endlessly. And how Cooper takes his coffee, "black as midnight on a moonless night," is a reflection of both his outward appearance – slick black hair, black suits with black ties – and how he will come to understand the hidden world within Twin Peaks. Furthermore, his choice of phrasing when describing how he takes his coffee is a reflection of the poet inside the stoic, and the man of whimsy tucked behind the man of reason.

When Cooper enters The Black Lodge in the season two finale, it is coffee that he's offered, much like Hades offers hungry Persephone pomegranate seeds that condemn her to annual residence in Hell, one month for every seed. Could it be that the Black Lodge would have an easier time obtaining the soul of Dale Cooper if some sort of elixir or potion was willfully taken by him while there, the way Laura or Teresa Banks had to willingly put on The Black Lodge ring to forfeit their souls? And if so, wouldn't coffee be the natural way to disguise this elixir or potion? If I was trying to poison Coop, that's exactly where I'd put it. By that logic, when Cooper accepts the coffee and tries to drink it but finds it either solid or syrupy and thus unable to ingest, that could be a manifestation of either his good side, The White Lodge, or both trying to save him from the inevitability of the path he has started down.

Sigmund Freud, father of psychoanalysis, is famous for once remarking "sometimes a cigar is just a cigar." Freud obviously never saw TWIN PEAKS – which is a shame, because I think he would have gone nuts for it – because nowhere in this town or series is that statement true. There is meaning everywhere, in everything, even on the plate.

AN OPPOSITION OF SELF – DUALITY AND 'TWIN PEAKS'

How TWIN PEAKS examines duality on nearly every single level

If it is about anything, TWIN PEAKS is a show about duality. Even the name suggests it, as does pretty much everything about the premise: its basic struggle is between the polar forces of good and evil, which manifest themselves in dark and sinister, and quirky and offbeat fashions in the people of Twin Peaks, and more so in the metaphysical realms into which the town provides passage, The Black and White Lodges, that themselves offer a dual reality in and out of which the show meanders. As for the characters who populate the cast, they too are often diametric, their public personas clashing with their private or internal selves. The theme of duality has become a prominent one in Lynch's oeuvre, with traces of it seen in BLUE VELVET and WILD AT HEART before moving to the forefront in TWIN PEAKS, LOST HIGHWAY, and most especially MULHOLLAND DRIVE. But nowhere is the theme of duality more heavily referenced than in TWIN PEAKS, in which Lynch explores opposing natures using such broad strokes as characterization and storyline, as well as more minute touches like setting, dialogue, and even costuming.

Laura Palmer, the show's entry point, is presented to us as two sides of a marred coin. Her psychiatrist, Dr. Jacoby, says as much when talking with Special Agent Cooper and Sheriff Truman in episode 8 after his heart attack: *"Laura...was in fact, well she was leading a double life. Two people."* On the one side, the side shown to the world, she was a bright and beautiful young girl, blonde-haired and blue-eyed, a homecoming queen dating a football player with two loving parents and a social network of caring friends. She tutored foreign speakers in English and the mentally-handicapped, delivered Meals on Wheels to shut-ins, and generally embodied everything her fellow townsfolk considered good, pure, and wholesome. But on her other side, the hidden side, Laura was also a chain-smoking, liquor-swilling cocaine addict, a one-time brothel worker and several-time participant in BDSM group-sexual experiences who was two-, three-, four- and more-timing her boyfriend; she was also a victim of sexual abuse and incest, an accessory to at least one murder (see FIRE WALK WITH ME), and her mental state could have best been described as "fractured," or split in two.

The duality of Laura is a perfect circle: it is created by both the wholesome nature and inherent depravity the town emits, the former crafting her in its own image and the latter ultimately setting in motion the forces that will so heinously destroy her. The opposing forces controlling Twin Peaks never begin and they never end, they simply always are, have been, and will forever be, and Laura is just a leaf like others caught in the cyclone they create, tossed from extreme to extreme by a volition not her own but that she can feel all around her, inside even. Perhaps the most telling manifestation of this dichotomy of self in Laura is her pair of diaries, the one she keeps hidden at home and the alternate one she gives to Harold Smith for safekeeping. The former is what we'd expect from a teenage girl's diary and the secrets it might contain – boys, partying, general if slightly-extreme rebellion – while the latter chronicles a harrowing and horrifying descent into madness propelled by unbelievable attrition and unimaginable perpetrators. In Laura, this duality cannot thrive and so it is extinguished – not entirely against her will – taking the girl with it.

From Laura Palmer however the duality echoes into other characters, most obviously that of her identical cousin Maddy Ferguson who comes from Missoula, Montana to attend Laura's funeral. Maddy signifies another side of Laura, the "what-could-have-been" side perhaps. Maddy noted that as children the girls were very close, but as they grew older they grew apart. In hindsight, we know that this is because as Laura entered adolescence, BOB's

142

torture of her truly began, along with her fracturing of self. This duality is flipped back on itself when James and Donna dress Maddy up as Laura to lure Dr. Jacoby from his office so they might ransack it for a tape Laura made. This confusion leads not only to Jacoby's assault and heart attack, but also serves to further fuse the two girls in the eyes of BOB. The ultimate irony is that though Maddy and Laura travelled life by different paths, and though Maddy's was mostly free of the influence of the forces at work in Twin Peaks, the lives of both girls ended in the same horrific way and by the same hand. All it took was Maddy entering town limits for those paths to reconverge; she would pick up where Laura left off and as a result lose a bit of herself along the way. During her stay in Twin Peaks Maddy changes from naively supportive to proactively skeptical, she assumes Laura's place in the Donna-James love triangle, and seems willing to change her personality to more mirror Laura's for the affections of James until it becomes obvious he doesn't want her to, at which point she plans to leave and stumbles into the same fate as her cousin. Even the name Madeleine Ferguson represents duality: it's taken from characters in Alfred Hitchcock's VERTIGO, which with its plot of an obsessive man trying to replace a lost lover in the form of a new woman is most certainly an influence on TWIN PEAKS and David Lynch in general.

Besides Maddy though, there's another resident of Twin Peaks who decides to use the revelation of Laura's duality to influence her own. Donna Hayward was the dandelion to Laura's rose, she was "the other one," the slightly-more demure and less-outgoing of the girls and thus relegated to Laura's shadow. As revealed in FIRE WALK WITH ME – which at essence is all about Laura's duality – Donna had been idolizing Laura's mischievousness and "maturity" long before Laura died, and the void that her murder opened was one Donna was all too willing to fill, starting by adopting Laura's secret boyfriend James as her own – pretty much immediately – then moving past James through Harold Smith into a frame of mind where she started chain-smoking and even wearing Laura's sunglasses to indicate her change of character from a docile little lamb into a would-be stalking lioness. Ultimately, though, Donna is too much herself to be Laura and reverts to her quivering damsel-in-distress persona, but the message of her brief jaunt into duality is clear: Laura occupied a role in Twin Peaks, she was emblematic of something the town required for balance, and this role would need to be refilled.

Annie Blackburn – Norma's little sister and Agent Cooper's love interest, fresh from the convent – would eventually come to occupy that role. Annie's duality isn't so much internal as it is reflexive: she represents both the purity and sacrifice of Laura, as well as the ability to act as a conduit for Cooper's love and fear much like his last lover, Caroline Earle. Like the former, Annie would be drawn into The Black Lodge by a man perverted by its influence, she was an innocent seduced by the depraved into a most unholy state, and like the latter any harm to befall her would ravage the steely emotional intellect of Cooper, causing his position in the balance of things to shift, thus tipping the duality of town towards darkness. In this way Annie is a reflection of both women, her personality strongest when it is a reinterpretation of theirs; instead of just being a goody-two-shoes like Laura is perceived to be, Annie was a the ultimate good girl, a nun-to-be, and instead of being Cooper's forbidden love like Caroline, she was his true. This is not to say, however, that Annie doesn't have her own inherent duality. Though she leaves it to come to Twin Peaks, Annie was following a calling that supports a belief in life eternal; she came to that calling by attempting to end her own life. Annie is an innocent, that much is true, but she is not one ignorant of guilt, shame, or regret. It is where these disparate halves become whole that Annie exists, and it is this combination of traits that makes her such delectable bait for luring Cooper into the ultimate manifestation of duality in TWIN PEAKS: The Black Lodge

The Black Lodge is comprised of basically two types of inhabitants, both dependent upon duality: parasitic spirits who need hosts to move around our world, and doppelgangers, shadow selves wrenched away from the persons they represent by the evil of The Black Lodge and held captive for time immeasurable. In terms of the former group, BOB is the most active. When he manifests in the world, it is in the body of Leland Palmer, a duality quite literally represented by BOB's reflection when Leland looks in the mirror at certain times, usually before bouts of violent murder. When Leland dies and BOB is expunged from his body, BOB returns to the Lodge where Leland's doppelganger, no longer half of a whole, will now roam the corridors for eternity, as will doppelgangers of Laura, Maddy, The Man From Another Place, and Caroline. It would seem death or some other similarly-traumatic experience generates the doppelgangers, some instance of absolute fear conquering perfect courage. Of the doppelgangers mentioned, only those of Laura and The Man From Another Place co-exist with their other halves. In Laura's case, this can possibly be explained by considering that The White and Black Lodges are open to spirits from both, and when Laura appears to Cooper in The Black Lodge she is merely strolling over from The White where her spirit is presumed to have gone at the end of FIRE WALK WITH ME, while her doppelganger resides in The Black Lodge because it was born of her fear of BOB. In the case of The Man From Another Place, this coexistence is because he is the only resident of The Black Lodge who is both in part an inhabiting spirit and in part a host. In FIRE WALK WITH ME it is revealed that The Man From Another Place is the result of MIKE cutting off the arm of his real-world host Phillip Gerard. MIKE amputated the arm to rid himself of a tattoo he shared with BOB, thus breaking their murderous bond. The essence of MIKE contained in that arm returns to the Black Lodge, where it becomes The Man From Another Place. The Man says so himself at the beginning of the movie – "I am the Arm" – and then demonstrates as much at the end when he and Gerard appear together in the Lodge, the Man's hand on Gerard's shoulder nub and the two speaking in unison to BOB. The other parasitic spirt who resides in the Lodge is known to the audience as the Giant who first appears to Coop at The Great Northern after he's been shot. In the real world the Giant is represented by the elderly bellboy who initially appears to Coop that same night, immediately preceding the Giant's appearance. Though the Giant appears to Cooper in The Black Lodge, he is generally thought to be an agent of The White Lodge. Again, his presence in the former could just be a visit.

And then lastly there's Cooper himself. If the duality of Laura was our introduction to TWIN PEAKS, then Cooper's fate was – until 2017, at least – our exit. Cooper's duality is unique in that it is physical as well as spiritual. Following his trip into The Black Lodge in hopes of rescuing Annie, Coop succumbs to his fear and has his soul divided in two, resulting in separate selves that can best be described, for lack of more complex terms, as "Good Dale," and "Bad Dale." Annie establishes as much when she appears to Laura in a dream in FIRE WALK WITH ME and tells her: *"The Good Dale is in the Lodge, and he can't leave."* The moment of Dale's division comes in the final episode when he enters the room of the Lodge wherein he sees himself lying on the ground next to Caroline, presumably dead. He blinks, and Caroline turns to Annie, wearing the same dress and sharing, again presumably, the same fate. It is at this moment that Coop is forced to face his most ultimate fear: that his own inadequacies will inhibit him from preventing the worst thing he can imagine, the death of a woman he loves as a result of his own actions; it happened once with Caroline – him loving her caused Windom, her husband, to murder her – and now, here, it would seem to be happening again with Annie. Coop's fear trumps his courage and these emotions are no longer able to live inside the same meat suit so they separate and race for the Lodge's exit and the real world beyond, knowing only one of them can exist in it. It is Leland's doppelganger that will delay Good Dale and cause Bad Dale to exit first, leading to the most climactic series finale in television history: BOB and Cooper as dual agents of the Lodge. In the end then, Cooper isn't only a diametric reflection of himself, he's also a reflection of the very spirit he'd been hunting all series. We opened with a girl who had a secret life, and we close on an Agent who has a secret soul.

Outside of these more obvious and developed instances of duality, there are other examples everywhere throughout the series: Catherine Martell posing as Mr. Tojamura to get what she wants from Ben Horne; Agent Dennis Bryson expressing his feminine side as Denise before reverting to his original persona at his/her arc's end; Josie Packard and her tri-duality as Andrew's unfortunate widow, Truman's caring lover, and Thomas Eckhardt's Mata Hari; Audrey and her Hester Prynne identity when she goes undercover at One Eyed Jacks; Ernie Niles as a financial advisor on the surface and a hardened criminal beneath, and his wife Vivian's façade as a judgmental mother masking her professional career as travel writer and restaurant reviewer M. T. Wentz; Nadine's personality schism brought on by head trauma that takes her from the mindset of a 35-year old married woman obsessed with silent drape runners to that of an 18-year old high school senior obsessed with cheerleading; Ben Horne's psychotic break after losing Ghostwood that transforms him from a greedy corporate scumbag into a caring and philanthropic do-gooder via a personal reenactment of the Civil War; Lucy's struggle between deciding which of her dueling beaus will be a better father to her unborn child, regardless of paternity; Donna's two dads; Leo's arc from an abusive monster to a helpless, crippled, and unwilling minion; the chess game in which Earle engages

Cooper; the alternating black and white chevron pattern of The Black Lodge floor; even Dr. Jacoby's trademark red and blue spectacle lenses. All of these cues and tons more reveal the ever-present struggle between opposing forces in TWIN PEAKS.

The universe is comprised of balanced diametric forces, forces that push when others pull, forces that create when others destroy. Without this balance, chaos ensues and reality becomes warped, fractured, or otherwise flawed. It is in one of these fractures that the town of Twin Peaks exists. The death of Laura Palmer caused an imbalance that set in motion the events of the series, and Cooper was the agent – pardon the pun – through which order could have been restored, making his role in the drama the polar opposite of hers. But as we all know, Coop's efforts only led to an even greater imbalance of the dual forces at work in Twin Peaks, one that has left the town, the series and its audience teetering on the brink of oblivion for a quarter-century now. Only (Show)time will tell if that balance can ever be restored, and if this duality will be the salvation or annihilation of TWIN PEAKS.

INVITATION TO LOVE – THE SOAP WITHIN A SOAP

The favorite melodrama of the characters in our favorite melodrama

TWIN PEAKS is, from a televisual narrative standpoint, a soap opera in that it is a dramatic series dealing with the daily events of a wide and set cast of characters in a central locale. It's a soap opera with super-dark, supernatural connotations, sure, kind of like PEYTON PLACE meets DARK SHADOWS, but it still conforms to the soap opera qualities of being melodramatic, sensational, and rife with idiosyncratic absurdities that make perfect sense within the context of the world the show creates.

Speaking of PEYTON PLACE, when Frost and Lynch pitched the initial, rough concept of their show, ABC executives recommended the series to them as an example of a soap opera set in a small, quaint town and the secrets behind its façade. Frost and Lynch, perhaps predictably, hated PEYTON PLACE and didn't even finish watching it, but perhaps in some small way it still influenced them, because the soap opera they ended up creating was as far from traditional as they could get while still, as mentioned, qualifying itself as one.

To balance this lack of traditionalism, Mark Frost came up with INVITATION TO LOVE, the soap-within-a-soap watched by certain characters in TWIN PEAKS, namely the Palmer and Johnson households. This is the sort of soap opera one expects from the term, complete with dysfunctionally-wealthy families, flashy archetypes and glamorous set dressings. There's a clip from ITL in the first seven episodes of TWIN PEAKS, or the entire first season, each directed by Frost and starring Lance Davis as Martin Hadley playing Chet, Erika Anderson as Selina Swift playing Jade/Emerald, Peter Michael Goetz as Evan St. Vincent playing Jared Lancaster, and Robert Giolito as Jason Denbo playing Montana. Davis and Goetz are former students of Frost's father Warren (Doc Hayward) at the University of Minnesota, and Giolito is Frost's brother in law. This assemblage of close friends and extended family made for a spirited shoot that lasted only one day and took place in the Ennis-Brown house in Los Angeles designed by revered architect Frank Lloyd Wright. By all accounts, it was loosely-structured to say the least, with a lot of improvisation, impromptu cut corners, and palling around. Though no real plot was ever established, rather a series of vignettes, the purpose of ITL was to parallel certain events in TWIN PEAKS and act as a mirror to the melodrama on our screens.

The best example of this parallelism lies in the connection between Maddy and Laura and Jade and Emerald. Each pair of characters is played by the same actress, Sheryl Lee and Anderson, respectively, and both characters are related: Maddy is Laura's nearly-identical cousin, while Jade is Emerald's identical twin sister. Furthermore, both pairs of characters are personality opposites: Maddy is sweet to Laura's sour, Emerald is a cold vixen while Jade is a warm and happy homemaker. Long-lost twins and mistaken identity are a tried-and-true, perhaps overused staple of soap operas, and while the Maddy-Laura dichotomy exploits this, Frost and Lynch also use it to set up a more insidious idea that won't come to fruition until the second season of the series: the idea of doppelgangers.

The other notable parallel between the action on INVITIATION TO LOVE and the action in TWIN PEAKS comes in the final episode of season one when Leo is shot through his window by Hank. As this is transpiring, ITL is on the boob tube in Leo's living room showing the same scenario happening to Montana.

Alas, INVITATION TO LOVE would never see a second season. Rumor has it David Lynch hated the way it looked, being shot on video, and with the expanding storylines of TWIN PEAKS' second season, not to mention new cast members like Kenneth Welsh, Billy Zane, Heather Graham, Ian Buchanan, Robyn Lively, Dan O'Herlihy, Michael

Parks, Brenda Strong, Jane Greer, and David Warner, there simply weren't enough resources to finance and plan a separate plotline for the meta-soap.

INVITIATION TO LOVE reflects TWIN PEAKS' narrative concept, even if to most viewers it came across as quirky background footage. By including a soap opera in their soap opera, Frost and Lynch were able to poke fun and then subvert the genre's conventions, adding yet another layer to TWIN PEAKS' densely untraditional makeup.

The full run of INVITATION TO LOVE, which totals just over 15 minutes, can be found with a simple search on YouTube, and even though some clips don't have any audio because when shown on TWIN PEAKS they were muted, when you see them together like that the parody is more obvious, of course, but so is the subtle parallelism Frost intended. With any luck, TWIN PEAKS season 3 will feature newer installments of INVITATION TO LOVE, or at least a little closure. I gotta know what happened to Montana.

SAVE OUR SHOW – C.O.O.P. & THE POWER OF PEAKIES

How a fan-based letter-writing campaign got TWIN PEAKS a brief stay of execution

Good things, by definition, never last forever. That's part of what makes them good, their finity, knowing that they must be appreciated in the moment because that moment is not eternal. It sucks, but such is life – literally. Sometime the end comes quick, and sometimes it dallies, lingering over you like a specter, haunting your final days. That's how it happened to TWIN PEAKS. The end could be seen looming like a thundercloud on the horizon for months before the rain actually fell and washed away one of the finest, most intriguing, most daring, and most unique shows in television history.

On February 15th, 1991, six days after airing the 15th episode of the second season, "Slaves and Masters," ABC officially suspended TWIN PEAKS from its primetime lineup. There were six episodes remaining in the season, and the network would say only that these would be aired "at an unspecified date." This wasn't a cancellation, per se, but it was a close as you could get, and by industry standards it was the first phase of just such a thing.

TWIN PEAKS had always been a niche program, and furthermore, in the beginning it was predicated upon a single mystery, Who Killed Laura Palmer? When that mystery was revealed in the seventh episode of season two – at the network's demand, not the desire of co-creators David Lynch and Mark Frost – the audience understandably dropped off. But narratively, the show's hands were tied. Like writer/producer Harley Peyton said at the time, "We couldn't just have another homicidal maniac arrive in town the next day," even though that's kinda exactly what they did by expanding The Black Lodge mythos and introducing Coop's former partner, the now-deranged Windom Earle. As the show began building towards these new crescendos, the path broadened and differed from what made the first season so appealing. Things got weirder, more esoteric, supporting characters were drawn closer to the spotlight, new characters were introduced, Coop became a civilian and citizen for a while; everything, in short, changed.

The show's positioning on the network schedule didn't help, either. TWIN PEAKS started airing its first season Thursday nights at 9 p.m., right up against the most popular show of the era, CHEERS. While it garnered record ratings for ABC in the beginning, it couldn't trump NBC's comedic powerhouse in the long run, especially since they shared the same audience demographic (men and women 18-35). This was frustrating to producers so they got the network to compromise and air the season one finale on a Wednesday night instead; it got the best ratings since the first episodes and led to a quick series renewal.

It's when that second season started airing that the juggling act began. The premiere was on a Sunday night, then the first 15 episodes were shifted to Saturdays at 10 p.m., also known as the worst possible slot on the television schedule. There it would remain until the suspension was dealt, with the added insult of being pre-empted from several of those slots for reports from the First Gulf War.

In a fit of uncharacteristic publicity, Lynch himself held a press conference following the announcement of the suspension. Addressing the world from the set of The Great Northern, he started simply: "We're in trouble, and we need help." He and Frost then asked fans of the show to write ABC's entertainment chief Robert Iger and demand a new time slot. That's all Lynch and Frost wanted: a new slot, and a shot. A shot to get their material in front of the most eyes possible, because they believed if people actually saw what the show was doing, they'd come back.

The slot they had in mind was the same where the season one finale had done so well – Wednesday nights at 10 p.m.

"Our audience doesn't stay home on Saturdays," Frost explained at the time, "We'd like to be on a weeknight – that gives people a chance to talk about it at work the next day."

To our younger readers, that might seem like a minor, almost insignificant point, but remember the time period: as far as the average American was concerned, the internet didn't exist in 1990, meaning word of mouth was still exactly that, things only went "viral" when people *actually* spoke to one another. Work and school were the logical places such things happened, but come Monday morning, if you're still talking about Saturday night, it isn't about what you watched on TV.

For reference, what was airing on ABC Wednesday nights at 10 during that period was an ensemble legal drama called EQUAL JUSTICE that itself only lasted 26 episodes – three less than TWIN PEAKS, to date – and is only notable for co-starring Sarah Jessica Parker, if that even makes a thing notable.

Two intrepid young men heard the call of Lynch and Frost and decided to take things to the next level. They were Michael R. Caputo and Keith Poston, and at the time they were a couple of young public relations executives in D.C. working 20 hours a day and still finding time to get hooked on TWIN PEAKS. As they were in politics, Caputo and Poston knew the only real way to motivate a lot of people towards a common, specific goal is to build a coalition, something they knew a thing or two about. So Caputo somehow got on the horn with Lynch, Frost, and their production company's C.O.O. Ken Scherer. He not only got their permission to fight the good fight, he also got permission to use a licensed image on a t-shirt that could be sold to finance the campaign. Again, remember the era: there were no social media sites, no email lists, every correspondence cost. And now that they had a means to fund their cause, all they needed was a name. It was almost obvious.

C.O.O.P. – Citizens Opposed to the Offing of Peaks.

Brilliant.

From there things rolled like a doughnut down a hill. Because he was the spokesman for a major lobbying corporation at the time, Caputo had to send Poston out to be the face of the movement while he orchestrated things from home, organizing clusters of C.O.O.P.ers in other American cities and arranging interviews with the press. In the very first C.O.O.P. news conference, USA Today asked Poston what he thought of Robert Iger:

"Bob, today you remind me of a small Mexican Chihuahua."

This, of course, is a paraphrasing of a line Gordon Cole (David Lynch) says to Dale Cooper (Kyle MacLachlan) in the series, and it was a pull-quote for the paper. While to the network this labeled C.O.O.P. as a little kooky, the fans understood and started responding in droves. Within four weeks the organization was 20,000 people strong, every single one of whom had reached out of their own accord to C.O.O.P. and paid for the privilege in postage. Now it was *on*.

Caputo ran the newsroom at the House of Representatives so knew folks at ABC, which afforded him access to the network's executive phone list. He passed these numbers onto his flock and would arrange specific dates and times to deluge specific people with calls and faxes. Thousands of stale doughnuts and several dozen logs also found their way to ABC headquarters. And you know what? It *worked*. Kinda.

ABC conceded somewhat and brought back TWIN PEAKS for its final six episodes on March 28th, 1991, which marked a return to its original timeslot of Thursday nights at 9. CHEERS, of course, still existed, but it was better than been stranded out in the no man's land of Saturday nights. The Windom Earle storyline had already been established by now, but things began swelling towards a tragic ending when Norma's sister Annie came to town, and when the final moves of the chess match between Earle and Coop started to reveal themselves. Alas, it wasn't enough to bring back audiences in large enough numbers, and just before the highly-polarizing, incredibly-unresolved season two finale, the show was officially and finally cancelled.

From there you probably know the gist: other networks were considered, foreign markets too, and eventually Lynch settled on the idea of taking things theatrical, with infamously divisive results. But whatever the series did to itself after it was repositioned in ABC's lineup, the thing to take away from all this is the resourceful devotion of TWIN PEAKS' small but firm fan base.

And sure, TWIN PEAKS isn't the only show to be saved by its viewers, Netflix and Hulu are pretty much making their livings at that kind of thing these days, but it is one of the most notable and most successful campaigns in memory. I've said it before and I'll say it again: there really isn't a legion of television fans as eternally-supportive as TWIN PEAKS' fans. We've kept this show alive and vibrant for a *quarter-century* between seasons, and our devotion and proselytizing was likely a large factor in network executives' decision to greenlight a third season after so long. That's amazing if you think about it. Will FIREFLY still have enough attention behind it to warrant a second season in 2027? Will ARRESTED DEVELOPMENT still have enough fans in 2038 to finally get that fifth season? The short answer is Hell No. Television is a fickle mistress who changes her preferences like she changes her underwear – often and thoughtlessly. What's funny or captivating today is overdone and passé tomorrow. But not TWIN PEAKS. TWIN PEAKS' tomorrow is more fascinating than even its yesterday, and the fact that we're going to get to see that tomorrow is owed in no small way to the dedication inspired by two guys who just wanted their favorite show to stop getting the short end of the network stick.

A PLACE BOTH WONDERFUL AND STRANGE – ORIGINS OF THE LODGES

Black or White, they're the most interesting facet of a fascinating show. This is where they come from.

The sum total of everything that's weirdly wonderful and uniquely brilliant about TWIN PEAKS lies in the warring juxtaposition of mirror-opposite spiritual realms, one good and one evil, and their ability to manifest their agents in real-world vessels. They are The White Lodge and The Black Lodge, they exist within the folds between reality and Another Place, and the portal into at least one of them lays dormant in Glastonbury Grove in the Ghostwood Forest outside Twin Peaks, waiting for the right time, conditions, and person to open it. Likely there are other portals scattered around the globe – FIRE WALK WITH ME indicates as much through the character of Phillip Jeffries (David Bowie) who is presumed to have entered one in Buenos Aires, Argentina – but over the course of the series, only the one was discussed, and it is as old as the land on which the town was built, and like that land, it is the basis for everything that Twin Peaks will become.

We only see inside The Black Lodge over the course of TWIN PEAKS, though Major Garland Briggs, Bobby's dad, claims to have spent some time in The White Lodge after his disappearance while nightfishing with Cooper in season two. An entrance to The White Lodge is never mentioned or revealed, though it can be presumed from the petroglyph in Owl Cave and the duality of the concept of the lodges that both places are in essence the same, and it is only how you enter that determines which one you wind up in.

To enter the lodge(s), a person must first enter the ring of 12 young sycamore trees that comprise Glastonbury Grove. Once inside this ring, a person can be affected in a matter of ways. It seems to either hypnotize the virtuous into a zombie-like trance as it did Annie Blackburn, or it further corrupts the wicked as it did Windom Earle. The brief scenes in the final few episodes when Windom appears with ghostly white skin, rotten teeth and black eyes are symptoms of his time within this circle. The next step is to walk around a pool of dark liquid that smells like scorched engine oil. This oil and its purpose was discovered off-screen but revealed in the series finale by Margaret the Log Lady, who brings it in a jar to Coop as he's preparing to head out to the Grove. Her husband, the Woodsman who died in a fire, brought it to her shortly before his death and described it as a key that opened a portal between worlds. Coop ends up not needing the oil because he has a metaphysical key, which is the primary means of gaining access to either Lodge. In the instance of The White Lodge, that key is overpowering love; in the instance of The Black Lodge, that key is infinite fear, of the sort someone who is being brutally murdered – or someone who fears their true love is being brutally murdered – might experience. Certain planetary alignments, specifically Jupiter with Saturn, also temporarily open the portal. Regardless of how one gets it open, when they do a red curtain appears and all that's left is to part it and step inside. The White Lodge seems to be a place one can exit unaffected, as Briggs appeared the same in appearance and disposition following his return, but The Black Lodge? Your soul is forfeit the second you enter, and to date no one has reemerged without being changed for the very worst.

Contrary to how it might sound up until now, this isn't a post meant to explain The White and Black Lodges to you, not in the sense you might be expecting. There are plenty of people online who have taken a load of time breaking down that particular mythology, and I don't see the need to rehash their excellent work. Instead, I thought I'd explain where the Lodges came from, the literary and narrative roots of the places, because it might surprise you to learn they weren't created for the series.

THE DEVIL'S GUARD by Talbot Mundy, published 1926

This pulpy bit of fiction set in Tibet was the primary source of inspiration for Frost and Lynch. Basically it's an adventure tale about a Brit named Ramsden – a virtuous, moral and loyal man (sound familiar?) – who is trying to rescue a friend that has become obsessed with a spiritual realm called The Black Lodge and the sorcerers who reside there (again, sound familiar?). These sorcerers are at war with The White Lodge, a place that like electricity is invisible but everywhere, one simply needs to know how to enter it. You might recall in FIRE WALK WITH ME that one of the two Woodsmen in the room above the convenience store, the one played by Jurgen Prochnow and believed to be the Log Lady's husband, introduced himself with a spark of electricity. This is probably not a coincidence.

The Black Lodge here is explained as being the opposite of The White Lodge and all that infers, including that it is far easier to enter The Black Lodge than it is The White. The sorcerers who live in The Black Lodge are called Dugpas, or spirits who eat souls, which is the exact term Windom Earle used to describe the spirits like BOB who reside in TWIN PEAKS' version of The Black Lodge. The Dugpas, Mundy explains, are failed initiates of The White Lodge who turned their rejection into ire, but he didn't create the concept. Mentions of Dugpas can be found in various Buddhist texts and histories of the Tibetan region, including THE TIBETAN TALE OF LOVE AND MAGIC by Alexandra David-Neel, in which the group is described as an evil sect of Buddhist monks who separated from the herd in the 16th century and who took their name from the Tibetan word for "thunder," as it was during a violent storm that they first established their monastery, and their dark legacy. So then from a TWIN PEAKS point of view, THE DEVIL'S GUARD is a kind of jumping-off point for Frost and Lynch when it comes to crafting a dualistic spiritual realm and its inhabitants for their television show. The book provides the basics – really everything it mentions about the Lodges I've mentioned here – and other sources will inform the development.

PSYCHIC SELF-DEFENSE by Dion Fortune, published 1935

This volume hits many of the same notes as THE DEVIL'S GUARD but because it is a work of nonfiction whose aim is to detect and defend against psychic attacks, it is less narrative and more instructional, the kind of book that Laura or Cooper could have really used. The White Lodge here is only mentioned in a metaphysical context once, at the very beginning, and is described as a gathering place for the "occult police force" that watches over all our spirits (as broken down by race, apparently), but there is plenty of talk of inter-dimensionality and the negative forces that hide below the surface of our reality waiting to step between the folds and snatch up innocent souls. Hence the police force. There are only four occasions, Fortune defines, when the flow reverses and we in this world have access to those other dimensions: when "we may find ourselves in a place where these forces are concentrated," when "we may meet people who are handling these forces," when "we may ourselves go out to meet the Unseen, led by our interest in it, and get out of our depth before we know where we are," and when "we may fall victim to certain pathological conditions." I don't know about you, but respectively those sound like pretty solid base descriptions for the town of Twin Peaks, aspects of Margaret the Log Lady, Major Briggs, Cooper, Laura, Sarah and Leland, the motivation behind Windom Earle's character, and the fates of Phillip Gerard, Leland, and Earle. Furthermore, when describing psychic attacks, Fortune tells the reader to be wary of immediate retaliation, as "the person from whom it emanates may not have originated it," or in plainer speak for Peakies, there could be a possessing spirit responsible. You can see how this book informs the narrative concepts of THE DEVIL'S GUARD and deepens the mythology, both of The Lodges and of TWIN PEAKS in general; when you're starting from a place this metaphysical, it ripples outward and informs everything about a story, from the plot points to the people who carry them out.

MOONCHILD by Aleister Crowley, published 1917

This is technically the first mention of The Black and White Lodges in western literature. The titular Moonchild is a messianic being impregnated in a woman by a society of White (good) Magicians to help defeat a society of Dugpa-like Black (bad) Magicians. The White Magicians, as you might imagine, reside in The White Lodge, while their counterparts dwell in the nefarious Black Lodge. This is perhaps where the idea of agency was added to the Lodge mythos, the idea that one of these soul-eating spirits or magicians might influence, effect, or inhabit an unwilling person. Like many of Crowley's works, MOONCHILD has its basis in reality, as the opposed factions depicted within are likely thinly-veiled versions of Crowley's own secret society, the AA – which was dedicated to the advancement of humanity by perfection of the individual on every plane through a graded series of syncretic (blending many schools of thought) initiations – and that society's defectors and detractors. You can guess who was meant to be White and who Black. Years after the book was written, Crowley revealed that it wasn't fiction at all, but the narrative retelling of an actual magical skirmish, which would mean that these Lodges were "real" places, and its inhabitants could in fact be walking among us, or for that matter *within* us, BOB-style. If that doesn't scare you, you're not alive.

Besides these works, there's also the general tradition within shamanistic cultures – like those of certain Native American tribes indigenous to the Pacific Northwest – of alternating spiritual realms, much like Eastern culture recognizes the duality of forces such as the Yin and the Yang, opposing but dependent entities that together create a cosmic balance, though they are each constantly struggling to tip that balance in their respective favor. The ethereal, ephemeral energy manifested in this way is like a perpetual-motion machine that powers the soul and in the process either strengthens or destroys it. The Lodges are inherent to the nature of existence and thus eternal and immutable. In TWIN PEAKS these traditions are embodied by Deputy Hawk, a Native American, who is the first in the series to explain the concept of The Black Lodge as it relates to the mythology of his people.

From all these disparate elements, Frost and Lynch composited their own take on the idea that good and evil aren't ideas at all, but forces of attraction and repulsion that pull at the souls of humans, and furthermore physical places between worlds in which belligerent spirits vie for ultimate and eternal dominance over reality. The Lodges are more than mere purgatories or spiritual penitentiaries, they closer resemble Earthly afterlives, active and potent kingdoms from which people are played like puppets and magic flows like wind through a forest of Douglas firs.

The Lodges are what TWIN PEAKS is really about, specifically The Black Lodge. Laura's murder is a symptom of it, as is everything else that happens from that moment until BOB returns in a Dale suit. Cooper is the character he is because The White Lodge requires a man of those qualities, while his storyline is what it is because that sort of man among the legions of The Black Lodge is a worst-case scenario, and TWIN PEAKS is nothing if not chock-full of worst-case scenarios. This single element is what elevates TWIN PEAKS over every other mystery/crime procedural in television history, and opened the door for other such programs of its ilk like THE X-FILES, AMERICAN GOTHIC, FRINGE, HARPER'S ISLAND, WAYWARD PINES, and to an extent SUPERNATURAL.

There's a common misconception that when you're alone somewhere dark and quiet, like the woods, it's being alone that frightens you. This isn't true. It's the idea that you're *not* alone that's giving you the willies. And in no woods are you ever less alone than Ghostwood Forest. There is indeed a darkness in those woods, older than man by eons and as such it considers us playthings for plundering. But there is a lightness as well, and perhaps if one can survive the former, the latter awaits.

INVESTIGATING THE LONELY SOUL OF HAROLD SMITH

There's more to the man than orchids and wine: namely a connection to the Black Lodge

Though he only appears in four episodes of the series and a single scene in FIRE WALK WITH ME, Harold Smith is a vital figure in the mythology of both Laura Palmer and TWIN PEAKS at large. An agoraphobe when we meet him in both the series and the film, Harold Smith is best described as bookish and sensitive, a soft-spoken dandy of a man who breeds orchids in his home and collects the stories of others in what he calls a "living novel." He is meek and mild, but he is also refined and charming in his mousy way, and there seems to be an allure to him that women of a certain age – albeit schoolgirl age – find attractive.

Harold enters the world of TWIN PEAKS in the third episode of the second season (episode 10) through Donna, who meets him when she takes over Laura's Meals on Wheels route. Donna is directed to Harold by elderly Mrs. Tremond and her magician nephew Pierre. While delivering their meals and making small talk, Donna learns from Mrs. Tremond that Harold and Laura were friends. The old woman further suggests that Harold might have information for Donna. This leads to Donna discovering that Laura and Harold were confidants, and that before she died, Laura entrusted Harold with a second, secret diary that holds further clues as to her murderer and the anguish surrounding her death. This happens right in the middle of Donna's "becoming Laura" phase, when she's wearing the girl's sunglasses and smoking too many cigarettes, and it also coincides with the weakening of her relationship with James thanks to the interjection of Maddy. Put them all together and the result is a light romance of sorts that develops between Donna and Harold, the courtship of which includes Harold bargaining for her story in exchange for sharing the contents – if not the object itself – of Laura's diary. But just the knowledge of what's inside isn't enough for Donna, so she conspires with Maddy to steal it from Harold, knowing he'll never leave his house, and in the end both the diary and Harold's life are destroyed.

While the character can feel like nothing more than a plot device used to reveal Laura's secret diary, there are some who see more to Harold Smith than just a demure and slightly-deranged botanist: they see The Black Lodge all over him.

The most obvious link between Harold Smith, The Black Lodge, and those who inhabit it wasn't obvious at all when it first aired, and in fact wasn't made so until several episodes later, after Harold was dead by his own hand. In episode 12, "The Orchid's Curse," Donna snatches Laura's secret diary from Harold and uses it to playfully lure him outside, seemingly testing the veracity of his agoraphobia. A step or two out and at first he's fine. But then his right arm, outstretched, starts trembling uncontrollably, he looks up and to the side with a vacant expression, as though staring at something that can't be seen, and then he collapses, having fainted. At the time, all this is passed off in the viewer's mind as symptomatic of his larger condition, this is the fit or attack he has when he goes outside. But 15 episodes later in number 27, "The Path to the Black Lodge," this same exact sudden and uncontrollable trembling of the right arm is experienced by a handful of Twin Peaks residents, including Special Agent Dale Cooper. In that episode, the trembling is seemingly linked to the occurring astrological alignment that is setting in motion the opening of The Black Lodge, which leads to the return of BOB to Twin Peaks at the episode's end, where he is seen entering our world at Glastonbury Grove from a fold between dimensions, *right arm first*.

This establishes the possibility, then, that Harold had a particular awareness of The Black Lodge that most others did not. After all, no one else was shown to be trembling around the time Harold was, suggesting that he was especially receptive to disturbances in our world by the Lodge. Whether this is from what he learned from Laura and her diary, or because of a personal encounter is a matter of fascinating conjecture. Could a brush with the power of the Lodge be what turned him agoraphobic? Or is he so sensitive, in fact, that however he knows of it, he cannot keep his fear of the Lodge from his mind, but is fortunate enough to know that this is the key to being captured by it and so hides himself and his emotions from the world to lessen his chances of being consumed? Though the source or even the duration of Harold's agoraphobia is never revealed with any certainty, it would seem that for a botanist, a man who has dedicated himself to the natural wonders of our world, this self-imprisonment would be an exquisite torture, of the sort one would only inflict upon oneself if it was an absolute matter of life and death. Fear of having one's soul consumed by the spirits of The Black Lodge would fulfill those conditions, I'd think.

Whatever his reasons and however he came by the knowledge, it's undeniable that the Lodge seems to want Harold, especially as it keeps sending agents – in the form of Mrs. Tremond and her grandson Pierre, and possibly Laura and Donna – to interact with him.

Once the Harold storyline is "resolved" – that is, once he's dead – the assumption towards the Tremonds becomes that they were placed in the narrative to guide Donna towards Harold so she might discover Laura's secret diary, which contains clues to both BOB's identity and his weaknesses (more on this below). But as we would later learn in FIRE WALK WITH ME, specifically during the Phillip Jeffries scene, Mrs. Tremond and her grandson are associated with The Black Lodge, as they are in attendance at the meeting in the room above the convenience store with the Lodge's other spirits including BOB and The Man From Another Place. It seems unlikely based on their actions and depictions that they are the same type of consuming, possessing spirits as BOB, but rather something like bait, or more minor agents meant to prep or lure spirits for consumption while BOB and his ilk are busy with bigger things. This would color the Tremonds' purpose for appearing to Donna a more sinister shade, especially when you take into consideration the second scene in FIRE WALK WITH ME in which the Tremonds – now going by the surname Chalfont – appear to Laura. In this latter scene, they gift the girl a picture of an open doorway in an empty room. This painting will hang on Laura's bedroom wall and at a later point become a pivotal prop showcasing her mental, emotional, and spiritual fracturing. Taking all this into retrospective consideration then, the Tremonds might not have intended to guide Donna to Harold for the sake of the case as much as they wanted Harold to meet Donna, someone with the potential to lead him out of his presumed safe haven and back into the world where the forces of The Black Lodge might conclude their nefarious business with him.

If this is true, then it can be considered also that perhaps Laura might have been led to Harold for the same purpose as Donna: to help the Lodge claim him. On the other hand, however, Laura could be the source of Harold's connection to The Black Lodge. In the former case, Laura wouldn't have been acting as an agent of the Lodge in the same sense of the Tremonds, but more so as someone under its influence, not completely ensnared but with enough of its hooks in her that it could pull a couple strings. The idea in this instance would be that Laura and Harold were being used to weaken each other's resolve through shared awareness of the evil inherent to Twin Peaks, thus making both their souls ripe for the plucking. The snag in this theory – that Harold was made agoraphobic by his fear of the Lodge before meeting Laura – comes in Harold's one scene in FIRE WALK WITH ME when he expresses disbelief in the real-life existence of BOB, something he surely would not do had he an actual experience with the Lodge at that point. Therefore it's the latter theory that makes more sense, that Harold's introduction to The Black Lodge and its powers comes from his connection to Laura. Laura did, after all, share her knowledge of BOB with Harold, so it could be that BOB was aware of this, and in the wake of her death before Leland was revealed as his host, the spirit was attempting to clean up all loose ends. Unlike Dr. Jacoby, who had been led to believe by Laura that her tormentor was a mortal man, namely one in a red Corvette (Leo), Harold was aware that there were some metaphysical connotations to Laura's tormentor, if only in her frazzled mind. BOB would want Harold silenced – the less people know about him and the Lodge, the easier it is to collect their souls – but as he had not been invited to Harold's world, he couldn't just barge in, which meant he'd need someone who could get close to Harold, someone he or his agents could direct Harold's way and possibly lure the man into BOB's clutches. But with Laura dead and Leland resisting him at every turn, BOB was forced to look elsewhere. Namely at Donna.

Donna's involvement, like Laura's and like most everything in TWIN PEAKS, is open to alternate streams of interpretation. She could just be an unlucky girl who stumbles across the wrong guy at the wrong time, an innocent, so to speak, who wanders into the lion's den, but given the role of the Tremonds in the Donna-Harold meet-cute, this doesn't seem likely. Rather it seems likely that Donna was being manipulated by forces beyond her control or even possibly her awareness. She is, in fact, the closest young woman to Laura, and unlike Ronette Pulaski or even Maddy, as Laura's best friend Donna would have spent more time in Laura's company than any other girl, and the same is true in regards to Laura's family. Therefore it makes sense that BOB would have a keen awareness of Donna, inside Leland he would have seen the girl regularly, almost daily, and he would know of the effect Laura had on Donna's sense of self, which would possibly make him able to exploit her. At the least, even if he couldn't directly manipulate her, BOB's awareness of Donna's emotional fortitude or lack thereof would have let him know she was ripe for manipulation of any sort, and he could have dispensed his subservient spirits, namely the Tremonds, to lead her into Harold's path while he dealt with restraining Leland and thwarting the authorities on his trail. The scene with Harold's shaking arm would seem to support this. Shortly after meeting him, Donna uses her wiles – which through Laura BOB might have known would be particularly appealing to Harold, this young girl in distress – to make Harold do the one thing he has sworn off for the rest of his life: go outside. As soon as he's there, the trembling begins. Could this be him sensing the power of The Black Lodge? And when he stares off into nothing yet still so focused, could he be sensing the Lodge sensing him back, getting a lock on his soul now out in the world? If so, this would certainly seem a revelation – that Laura was right, that there are predatory spirits in the world and now they want him – worth collapsing into unconsciousness over.

Furthermore, when Donna inevitably rejects Harold by orchestrating with Maddy the theft of Laura's secret diary, he becomes uncharacteristically violent – this mild, meek, weak, and dainty man – as though possessed. It's worth noting that in the original episode script, Harold was going to attempt and attack the girls before they would be rescued by James. Lenny Von Dohlen, the actor who played Harold, thought this act too uncharacteristic and suggested the self-hurt instead. This can still be interpreted the same way as perhaps the script intended: that the fear caused by this rejection weakened Harold's spirit to the point that for a second something was able to take over, possess him so to speak, and instead of giving in to it and hurting the girls – as the script would have had – he took a page from Laura's book (kinda literally) and resisted, hurting himself instead. This would make Harold's suicide the result not of Donna's betrayal, but rather of the knowledge that he'd at last let the Lodge in, that it had now tasted his fear in full and would not be satisfied until he belonged to it, so to thwart his ultimate corruption, he ended his life.

As a maudlin postscript to the theory that Harold Smith was aware of, hiding from, and resisting the power and spirits of The Black Lodge, we have his suicide note, which was composed entirely of the French phrase, "*J'ai une ame solitaire,*" which translates approximately into "I am a lonely soul." This is, of course, the same French phrase that was uttered by Pierre Tremond to Donna before she met Harold. Donna hears the phrase again as Andy is muttering it to himself in the diner following the discovery of Harold's body. This leads to her learning about the suicide note, which causes her to confront Coop about Harold and take him to the Tremonds' residence. Once there, however, old Mrs. Tremond isn't the resident, it's another, younger woman who goes by that name but has never heard of the other two. She has, though, heard of Donna, and has a letter for her that was left by Harold shortly before the hanging unpleasantness. The note is a page from Laura' diary talking about BOB's weakness: he is afraid of MIKE. This will indirectly help Coop use Phillip Gerard to detect BOB's presence and "resolve" Laura's murder at his hands. It is not a coincidence, then, that Harold wrote the words he did in his suicide note, it was his penultimate act of resistance. He knew the Tremonds had been sent to observe him, perhaps he'd been tormented by whispers of that lonely phrase in the deepest reaches of his spirit, and he knew that Donna would remember it and use it to find this most important clue from the diary. After all, as Donna says herself when pleading her case to Coop, "Harold's world was in his words. The suicide note has to be a message."

It is, and one Harold only could have known to write if he had knowledge of the spirits of The Black Lodge and their role in Laura's death, not to mention his own.

LOOK TO THE SKIES – PROJECT BLUE BOOK AND 'TWIN PEAKS'

A closer look at the very real, very classified work of Major Garland Briggs

Though The Black Lodge doesn't become a true plot point of TWIN PEAKS until halfway through the second season, the seeds were there all along. Sheriff Truman is the first to vaguely attempt to verbalize the essence and effect of the Lodge, describing it in episode three by saying: *"There's a sort of evil out there. Something very, very strange in these old woods. Call it what you want. A darkness, a presence. It takes many forms but... it's been out there for as long as anyone can remember and we've always been here to fight it."* Hawk, the Native American Sheriff's deputy whose people have inhabited Twin Peaks for centuries, gives perhaps the series' best account, calling The Black Lodge *"the shadow-self of The White Lodge. The legend says that every spirit must pass through there on the way to perfection. There, you will meet your own shadow self. My people call it 'The Dweller on the Threshold' ... But it is said, if you confront The Black Lodge with imperfect courage, it will utterly annihilate your soul."*

While the connotations and origins vary, one thing is certain: The Black and White Lodges are more than mere realms of the mind, they are metaphysical places that can be physically entered given the right set of particular circumstances of time, place, person, and intention. While we know by the second season's end that Dale Cooper, Windom Earle, Annie Blackburn, Leland Palmer, Laura Palmer, Maddie Ferguson, Caroline Earle, and BOB, The Giant, and The Man From Another Place all have entered, visited, or reside in The Black Lodge, the only person to have an active experience with The White Lodge is Major Garland Briggs, Bobby's father and an employee of the United States Air Force, though for the majority of TWIN PEAKS' initial run this employment was mentioned only as highly-classified. But after Briggs' trip/summoning/abduction by The White Lodge in episode 17, the nature of that work was forced into the spotlight.

Briggs, it turns out, is a member of Project Blue Book, which sounds like it's another quirky conspiracy theory invented for the program, but the truth is, Project Blue Book was very, very real, and it did exactly what TWIN PEAKS depicted it to do: study the skies for anomalous phenomena. But series creators David Lynch and Mark Frost, along with writers Harley Peyton and Robert Engels and through the characters of both Major Briggs and Windom Earle, extrapolated this weird slice of actual history into an even weirder slice of primetime television.

For 18 years between 1952 and 1970, Project Blue Book served as a systematic study by the Air Force with two guiding objectives: 1) determine if Unidentified Flying Objects were a threat to U.S. national security, and 2) scientifically analyze UFO-related data. During its official run, PBB collected more than 12,000 reports of UFOs and UFO-related phenomena, and their analytical results of these reports went into an even bigger report, The Condon Report, which was released in 1968 and determined that no UFO ever reported was a threat to our security, no report indicated the existence of technology in advance of our own, and no report indicated the UFOs in question were extraterrestrial in origin. Sure guys, suuuure.

In reality, this report led to the government cancelling Project Blue Book. In TWIN PEAKS, no such thing ever happened, and the Air Force kept its monitors tuned to the sky and continued to search for anomalous phenomena. In the second episode of the second season, Briggs comes to Cooper and for the first time reveals the nature of his work. He says normally all the info their monitors collect is gibberish, but at the exact moment

Cooper was shot (in the season one finale), something sensical emerged: "the owls are not what they seem." This, of course, is not a new message to Cooper, it was spoken to him by The Giant just the episode before. When Cooper inquires how the Major knew to bring him this message, Briggs points out the second message they received the next morning: Cooper's own name, repeated over and over. The crux of this scene, however, is the fact that these messages didn't come from the monitors pointed at deep space, but rather those for some reason pointed directly at the Ghostwood Forest surrounding Twin Peaks.

The connotation here would seem to be that whatever is in the woods is not of our Earth, which isn't to say it's extraterrestrial like the rest of Project Blue Book's pursuits, but that it falls into the same auspicious category as such phenomena: not of our experience, interfering with our experience, and possibly threatening. By attaching Major Briggs, the United States Air Force, and Project Blue Book to the Lodges, Lynch and Frost et al were taking the first steps towards transitioning these realms from places entered in dreams to places entered in reality, thus causing them to have a greater impact on the story beyond just providing clues; the Lodges could themselves be solutions. Later in the second season when Briggs enters and returns from The White Lodge, he is not affected in the way those who enter The Black Lodge are. In fact, he barely seems to be altered at all. How Briggs managed to survive the Lodge or Lodges is never covered, but it could have something to do with how he entered, that is, not of his own will but rather the Lodge's, he was summoned to be given the knowledge needed to help Dale (and inadvertently, Earle) enter The Black Lodge, and also possibly escape it. The ways in which Briggs' character was becoming more involved towards the end of season two seemed to indicate that if there had been a season three at that time, Briggs would have become a very major player in the post-Lodge storyline, and a possible savior of Cooper. Don S. Davis, the actor who played Briggs, hinted at as much in interviews, though no actual storyline was ever discussed. And unfortunately, whatever season three does hold, Briggs will not be an active part of it, as Davis passed away some years ago.

Project Blue Book is first mentioned by name by Briggs in episode 20 while he's being debriefed by Cooper and Truman upon his return from The White Lodge, but he is not the only TWIN PEAKS character who worked on the project. Four episodes later in episode 25, Briggs will provide a video tape that reveals that before he was with the FBI, Windom Earle – Coop's ex-partner and nemesis, murderer of the love of Coop's life (Caroline, Earle's own wife), and the madman with whom he is currently engaged in a deadly game of chess – was also a member of Project Blue Book, but was removed from the team because of his obsession with the woods around Twin Peaks, the entrance to the Lodges he found evidence of there, and the dark sorcerers who inhabited The Black Lodge, Dugpas, who "cultivate evil for the sake of evil and nothing else. They express themselves in darkness for darkness, without leavening motive. This ardent purity has allowed them to access a secret place of great power, where the cultivation of evil proceeds in exponential fashion. And with it, the furtherance of evil's resulting power. These are not fairy tales, or myths. This place of power is tangible, and as such, can be found, entered, and perhaps utilized in some fashion. The dugpas have many names for it, but chief among them is The Black Lodge... But you don't believe me, do you? You think I'm mad. Overworked. Go away."

Learning about, accessing, and acquiring this power would become the secret focus of Earle's life and would eventually unravel his psyche to the point that when he learned of his wife's betrayal with his partner, he murdered her, faked his own insanity to escape prosecution, and then when he heard Dale Cooper was in Twin Peaks, he orchestrated his escape so that he could make one last bid for the power of The Black Lodge and use it to destroy Cooper. We all know how that turned out for Earle: he got his soul turned into a top hat of fire and was never seen again, in this realm or any other.

By linking Earle with Blue Book and Briggs, we acquire the understanding that's what wrong with Earle has been wrong a long time, and that being in Twin Peaks with Cooper is a sort of destiny fulfillment for the maniac: he can have access to his greatest desire and simultaneously, vanquish his greatest adversary. As such, Earle gives in to his madness, he embraces it as his key into The Black Lodge, and he allows himself corrupted to the core, a decision that will ultimately thwart his destiny with his demise. Furthermore, this link helps create the perfect narrative circle of TWIN PEAKS' run (with FIRE WALK WITH ME bridging the final gap): the Lodges are the cause of everything that happen in the series, from Laura's murder to Coop's division of self, and while Coop came to the town because of the murder, in essence his destiny as well has led him to this place, as his association with Earle put him on the Lodges' radar long before they were on his.

From Briggs and Earle we learn the most tangible facts about the Lodges, and from their efforts access is granted – for better and worse. The writers of TWIN PEAKS didn't need to link this plotline to Project Blue Book, it stood well enough on its own and the monitoring bits of plot could have been easily explained away or written around, but by linking their fiction with history's fact, they added yet another layer of verisimilitude to their outrageous concept, and that is, after all, one of the reasons TWIN PEAKS is so appealing: despite its quirk and metaphysical leanings, it's just rational enough to be real, its flights of fancy or supernatural dabblings aren't as outlandish as they may seem upon first revelation; the deeper you go, the more you learn they are linked to real people, places, events, organizations, philosophies et cetera, which in turn makes TWIN PEAKS' story more fabular than fantastic, something meant to inform as well as entertain, something to learn from, a guide, almost, through the darker pockets of our perceived reality, whether those pockets hang over us in the stars, or lurk in the shadows that surround us here on Earth. Either way there's more in the darkness than we dare dream, and vigilance is the only – though not guaranteed – route to ensuring whatever is lurking there stays on the outside and doesn't get in.

GENUINE AFFECTION – THE LOVES OF DALE COOPER

Behind every Special Agent, there's a special woman. In Coop's case, three.

The character of Special Agent Dale Cooper as portrayed by actor Kyle MacLachlan is a many-faceted persona: he's a realist with metaphysical leanings, a poetic pragmatist, a hopeful fatalist, but above all else, he is a romantic. You can sense it in his zeal for knowledge and alternative schools of thought, in his passion for justice, his search for salvation via truth, and in his affection for the simple things in life like a slice of pie and a damn fine cup of coffee.

In the more literal sense, Coop's romantic side is best encapsulated by the man himself in the season two premiere when he is lying gut-shot on his hotel room floor telling Diane via microcassette recorder the things he would hope to do were he to survive his present ordeal, including this tidbit:

"I would very much like to make love to a beautiful woman who I had genuine affection for."

This is said with such longing and familiarity, as though Coop is describing something he's never had but has glimpsed before, perhaps a metaphorical sun to which his heart flew too close. Over the course of the series, Coop experiences three sorts of love in his quest to fulfill the above desire – forbidden, ideal, and true – as manifested by three women: Audrey Horne, Caroline Earle, and Annie Blackburn. What these woman and Coop's affection for them reveal about the Special Agent reinforces the idea that in his heart of hearts, Dale Cooper is a lover, and that's what makes him a fighter.

The loves of Coop are presented in the order they are revealed in the series, not chronologically. So you know.

AUDREY HORNE – COOP'S FORBIDDEN LOVE

From the first second they are on screen together, there is obvious and simmering chemistry between Coop and Audrey Horne, 18-year-old daughter of The Great Northern impresario Benjamin Horne. I made note of Audrey's age only because the show was sure to, letting we the audience understand that while the blatant flirtatiousness transpiring between the two of them was, yes, a little May-December (or perhaps more fairly May-September), it was also perfectly legal. Part of this chemistry came from the way the characters were written, and part was natural and came from the actors themselves, MacLachlan and Sherilyn Fenn. As the first season progressed, this flirtatiousness grew into stronger feelings, at least on the part of Audrey, and culminated in the climax of episode six, in which Coop returns to his hotel room to find a naked Audrey under the covers of his bed, lying in wait. This is the Rubicon of their relationship, a tipping point when words turn to the possibility of deeds, and thus Coop has to make a decision. He decides to err on the side of virtue and shifts his role in Audrey's life into something more like a protector.

A Cooper-Audrey romance was always intended by the writers of TWIN PEAKS and lingers into the second season, when it was set to come to fruition in the wake of the reveal of Laura's killer, but MacLachlan objected to the idea of it. As his line of thinking supposedly went, Cooper was too virtuous a man to give in to the temptation of Audrey, she was just too young. As a result, the romance was abandoned, but in doing so, the love of Audrey was definitively transformed into forbidden, something it hadn't really been up until then. Was it a little risqué, the idea of this professional, full-grown man wooing a nubile, virginal 18-year old girl? Of course it was, salacious, even, but literature and film are full of such scenarios, and as such it's not so scandalous. But it had never been *wrong*, and that's what Coop's refusal of the affair made it. The character denies himself the love of Audrey, which would have been physical, yes, but also would have been true, I think, she did love the Special Agent, and no doubt had the story been allowed to progress, that would have been the emphasis, not just the sultry physicality of the characters. Instead, refusing the love of Audrey serves as a kind of penance for Coop's hand in the loss of his ideal love, described below, and a penultimate preparation for his discovering true love.

CAROLINE EARLE – COOP'S IDEAL LOVE

I know, I know, it's a little strange to describe another man's wife as Coop's ideal love, but that's what makes her ideal: she comes with an asterisk, in a sense, she's socially and morally unobtainable, and that only elevates her idealness in the mind of the beholder.

Caroline was the wife of Windom Earle, Coop's former partner and current nemesis in the second season of TWIN PEAKS. Caroline was witness to a federal crime (eventually revealed to have been perpetrated by Windom) and placed under protective custody, which Coop and Windom oversaw. During this time, Coop and Caroline fell in love and began an affair. While the details and length of this affair are never disclosed, Coop does at one point call Caroline "the love of my life," further cementing her idealness in memory. As Coop tells it, one night in Pittsburgh he let his guard down and an attempt was made on Caroline's life. It was a successful attempt that left him injured and her dead in his arms, a stab wound to her heart the cause. As for the culprit, Coop learns after the fact it was Windom who killed his own wife, having found out about her betrayal with his young protégé. In the wake of Caroline's murder, Earle was said to have lost his mind and was committed to an institution (where he would plot his revenge and eventual escape) and Coop was left devastated on all fronts. He vowed to never again get involved with a woman who was a part of a case (this in part explains some of his hesitance to romance Audrey, though her involvement in the Palmer case was peripheral at best) and he insulated his heart in layers of fear to protect it from being hurt again.

Caroline was not Coop's true love like he wanted her to be. The asterisk attached to her idealness was a big one, and for better or worse, right or wrong, it tarnished their relationship. There was no honor to it, and as a man renowned for his honor, it was a love that made Coop someone he was not. But that does not invalidate the love between Coop and Caroline, it was real and by its tragic ending it became ideal, if only, again, because it was unobtainable, now permanently. But the loss of Caroline and the emotional walls Coop erected because of it were not all that came of this tragedy. They were also the final preparations for Coop's discovery of true love. Now that he was no longer seeking it, now that he thought himself in fact immune to it, it was ready for him.

ANNIE BLACKBURN – COOP'S TRUE LOVE

Though she doesn't appear until the second season's final act, Annie is the love that has the most profound impact on Coop's life, figuratively and literally. Annie is the younger sister of Norma, who owns the Double R diner, and she returns to Twin Peaks after a stint in a convent. As it was with Audrey, Coop's chemistry with Annie is palpable from their first meeting, but unlike that other relationship, it is Coop who is more immediately and obviously love-struck and Annie the one who seems hesitant to embark that direction. As their courtship progresses we learn that Annie's hesitancy isn't based on Coop but rather an ill-fated love in her own past that drove her to attempt suicide and landed her in the convent. In time, love triumphs and the two begin a passionate relationship that is thwarted by Windom Earle, who uses Coop's love of Annie to both wield her as a key to enter The Black Lodge and lure the Special Agent into following him there.

As Coop's true love, Annie combines the innocence of Audrey with the sense of emotional completion he found in Caroline without the illicitness of either. She breaks down the walls the latter caused him to build, which shut out the former, and allows him to let a woman into his heart in a way he had never been able to before, either because of his own limitations or the boundaries of morality. This love is pure, it is genuine, and it Is his, the one for which he has been longing. It is his ultimate desire, realized. Which is why it is also his ultimate downfall.

It is Coop's love for Annie that is the root of his greatest fear: that she too will be harmed because of her involvement with him. This fear is what drives Coop into The Black Lodge after her and Windom, and this fear, this vulnerability, is what leads to the division of Coop's soul into opposing "good" and "bad" halves, the latter of which escapes into our world at the second season's conclusion. But though once again marred, unlike his forbidden love or his ideal love, Coop's love for Annie is unchanged by escalation or tragedy, it remains the same no matter the situation and can in fact be said to be strengthening right up to the second season's final scene. This steadfastness is what makes it true.

To put it in Biblical terms, Dale Cooper would seem to be love's Job. It constantly tests his faith, as every time he acquires it, there are dire consequences: in one instance, he's forced to deny it; in another, it is killed; in another, it destroys his own soul. Yet it remains his strongest and greatest desire, to be with one whose beauty inside and out is unparalleled in his heart. Despite everything he's seen, Coop still believes love is the answer to the most elusive mystery he or anyone else ever encounters in this life: how to be happy. Love guides everything he does, everything he thinks, and thus it is being a romantic that makes Special Agent Dale Cooper his particular brand of heroic.

A RIVER RUNS THROUGH IT – WATER AND TWIN PEAKS

How various bodies of water reflect the various souls collected by The Black Lodge

Water is one of the most basic and at the same time most multifarious of narrative symbols. As one of the four essential elements, water has been a part of storytelling since the art form originated, factoring into myriad tales, legends, epics, mythologies, and even religions. Water is life, and water is death, and water is change, and water is stasis, so on and so forth down parallel but conflicting lines. While it is not one of the more obvious symbols in TWIN PEAKS, I do believe the series, either intentionally or not, creates a link between bodies of water and certain victims of The Black Lodge, specifically Laura Palmer, Maddy Ferguson, Annie Blackburn, Teresa Banks, and by proxy of intention, Ronette Pulaski. By analyzing what these links are and what they say about the mentioned women, greater insight into character is revealed and a pattern is established: water in TWIN PEAKS is an evil portent, a natural accompaniment to the supernatural harvesting of souls at the incorporeal hands of The Black Lodge.

Though it is not the first image of the series, water does factor prominently into the opening moments of TWIN PEAKS' pilot, in direct relation to Laura Palmer. Water, here a river, is transporting Laura's dead body, wrapped in plastic, from the shadows of night into the light of discovery. It deposits her on a rocky spot of shore for Pete Martell to find when he goes out fishing, thus launching the central mystery of TWIN PEAKS. As we learn from the evolution of the case and in even more graphic detail in FIRE WALK WITH ME, Laura was fluctuating between selves, constantly alternating her personality between the girl everyone wanted her to be – the homecoming queen who tutored the mentally handicapped and helped feed the less fortunate – and the girl she really was – a chain-smoking, booze-swilling, coke-snorting abuse victim and sex addict. This fluctuation, we learn, is because of the mounting predation of BOB, which caused Laura to change back and forth so much that eventually the division between these selves became a schism and her final unravelling began. In this way, Laura is like the river that carried her body, never the same from one second to the next, always moving, always changing, and impossible to stop. Rivers have destinations they can't help but flow into; Laura's soul did as well – The Black Lodge. As such, seeing the physical journey of her death in the pilot foreshadows the spiritual journey that led to it and that the series and FIRE WALK WITH ME will come to reveal.

Teresa Banks, Leland/BOB's first victim, also had her corpse carried by water, the Wind River outside Deer Meadow, Washington. Though there isn't much known about Teresa, we do know she was a prostitute – which itself indicates a constant state of change, being who each new John requires – and we know she hadn't been in town for very long, only a month or so, which also would seem to hint at a transient nature. Furthermore, she lived in a trailer, a house built to move. Teresa's river too would seem to be representative of a persona in flux, and again, fatally so.

In regards to Maddy Ferguson, Laura's identical cousin, after she's killed by BOB/Leland on the eve of finally leaving town, her body is discovered, also wrapped in plastic, at the base of the waterfall outside The Great Northern. Her stint in Twin Peaks was motivated only by familial concern – she came to pay her respects at Laura's funeral and assist her aunt and uncle in this difficult time – but very quickly the town piled its madness upon her. In Maddy's time in Twin Peaks she was roped into a murder investigation, fell in love, fell out of love, dressed up like her dead cousin to lure a psychiatrist out of his office, had a pair of terrifying premonitions, and of course, was murdered by her uncle, who was possessed by an ancient spirit specific to the region. Maddy's true self was drowned by Twin Peaks and what it, its citizens, and its otherwordly inhabitants wanted her to be: another Laura. When she wouldn't willingly become this and decided to assert her independence by leaving, The Black Lodge had

BOB kill her, thus keeping her there forever. But with no more use for her Earthly vessel, it was left at the bottom of a constant torrent of falling water, itself just a river running off a cliff. As such, like Laura and to any extent we know Teresa, Maddy too was changing because of the forces at play in Twin Peaks, but there was no willingness in it, there wasn't even an awareness of it. Like a leaf Maddy just let the metaphorical river of her life take her where it wanted until it swept her over the cliff and pummeled her from existence.

Annie Blackburn may or may not be a victim of The Black Lodge. In the second season finale we saw her alive in there, we saw her dead in there, and in FIRE WALK WITH ME we see her speaking from there though technically from a temporal standpoint she hasn't entered it yet. But when "Agent Cooper" wakes in his hotel room after returning unconscious from the Lodge, he's told by Doc Hayward and Sheriff Truman that Annie is at the hospital recovering and she's going to be fine. This would seem to indicate she survived the ordeal, but alive or not, no one who enters then leaves The Black Lodge is ever "fine." As the Cooper to whom this information is told isn't exactly the Cooper we all know and love, it stands to reason Annie might not be either. She could be some half of her whole like Coop, or possessed like Leland. Though her last chapter has yet to be written (or at least yet to be revealed), there is a symbol of the vast depth of murky possibilities awaiting her and her soul in the form of water. In episode 26, just before all the proverbial shit starts hitting that big ole proverbial fan, Annie and Cooper have their first proper date in a rowboat on Black Lake in Easter Park. It is in this scene – which opens with Annie languidly rippling the surface of the water with the fingertips of her *right* hand – when Annie finally opens up a little about her past to Coop, a series of revelations that culminate in Annie's reason for returning to Twin Peaks after all the personal trauma she suffered there: to conquer her fears. Of course she does not do this, in turn making herself a viable key for entering The Black Lodge, which when found can only be unlocked by fear. In this sweet moment on the lake, however, Annie is hopeful, she is floating on a current of positive emotions flowing Dale's direction, but she has no idea of the depth of the darkness below the surface of things, she has no idea that soon this current of emotions will drag her beneath that surface and into the black. This lake is like Annie herself, so pleasant by appearance but so dark where we can't see. It is also like what Annie represents to Cooper: stillness, an end to searching, to change. A lake, after all, unlike rivers or waterfalls, goes nowhere.

The last woman I mentioned above was Ronette Pulaski, who was abducted by Leland/BOB with Laura that fateful and horrible night, and was certain to share in the other girl's fate until some last minute divine intervention came along. Ronette avoided The Black Lodge, and as such the water symbolism she's linked to is also avoidant. The very first time we see Ronette in TWIN PEAKS is when she's roaming in a post-traumatic daze through the woods, specifically crossing a railroad bridge over a small river. It is never mentioned as such, but for all we know the river she's crossing is the very same Laura's body was set drifting down. Either way the symbolism is clear: Ronette is saved from the river by the bridge the way she was saved from The Black Lodge by the interference of The White Lodge.

There's only one last figure to connect to this water symbolism, and that's The Black Lodge's fiercest reaper, BOB. Obviously he's the spirit at work here: he (as Leland) murdered Teresa, murdered Laura, tried to murder Ronette, and murdered Maddy. Though there is no direct connection between BOB and Annie in the series – it's Windom Earle who takes her to The Black Lodge – the fact that she appears to Laura in FIRE WALK WITH ME would seem to position her in BOB's sphere of awareness. But if BOB is associated with any kind of symbolism, it's clearly fire. However, at the point BOB enters the greater TWIN PEAKS story – that is, not just what aired but the unfilmed backstory that came decades before – there isn't fire but water. When he is close to the end, Leland confesses he first encountered BOB when he was a young boy and implies he was molested by BOB to weaken his spirit so that BOB might take him over. The site of this horrible introduction? The Palmer house at Pearl Lakes (which are a stone's throw from Glastonbury Grove, where the entrance to The Black Lodge is). Leland originally perceived BOB as a neighbor before realizing him for the demonic force he truly was. Here it is the idyllic, serene qualities of water, especially placid lakewater, that are being perverted. A vacation at a family home, be it at a lake, a beach, a mountain, isn't like travelling to a city and staying in a hotel where you're perhaps more on guard. These other places are familiar, comforting locales where one can completely relax, completely trust in their safety, and thus completely let their guards down. Therefore they are the perfect sort of places for evil to insinuate itself. BOB might have burned through TWIN PEAKS, but he was washed into the world.

He's also washed out of it. In Leland's last living scene when he's been revealed as Laura's killer and is at the Sheriff's station detailing his history with BOB, as he starts to die the sprinkler system malfunctions and sends down a man-made storm that nearly floods the room. It doesn't stop until Cooper cradles Leland's spirit from this world to the next and Leland passes. The last thing we see that episode is the POV of BOB rushing back to The Black Lodge. As water brought BOB into Leland, water accompanies his exit. From a sinister perspective, this exit allows BOB the freedom to possess another. The next person we will see him reflected in is Dale Cooper in the season two finale. So water, then, has a hand in the series-to-then's tragic ending.

And speaking of Dale, I know that Cooper's soul like the women's above is also in The Black Lodge, or at least half of it is, but as an Agent not just of the FBI but also The White Lodge, I believe this makes him immune to the symbolism of water, unless you count the very abstract notion that he is there to extinguish the fire, so to speak, of BOB and The Black Lodge, and nothing puts out fire like water.

Fire gets all the glory in TWIN PEAKS. It burns down the mill, it's given tribute in cave art, dreams and poems, it gets a spot in the movie title, even. But I get it, fire's the cool one, the loud one, the kinetic one, the dangerous one. Fire's the good-looking guy with the bad streak, while water's just the quiet, average, more subtle guy you see everywhere and therefore hardly notice. But still souls run deep, to twist the saying, and while fire lives fast, bright and briefly, water keeps running, keeps telling its secrets while hiding others. Water as a symbol is just as important to TWIN PEAKS as fire, maybe even more so. After all, the title credits don't end on a shot of fire.

TWIN PEAKS:
FIRE WALK WITH ME

"It was a dream! We live inside a dream!"

FBI Agent Phillip Jeffries

'FIRE WALK WITH ME' EPISODE GUIDE

If you write off the film because it's a prequel, you're missing the point

Much maligning has been directed at FIRE WALK WITH ME, the prequel film to the TWIN PEAKS series, but honestly, if you're still bitching about this, you just don't get it. FIRE WALK WITH ME is the link that makes the narrative of TWIN PEAKS a perfect circle, it's the head of the snake biting its own tail and far from narrowing the story, it inflates the mythology of TWIN PEAKS, BOB, and The Black and White Lodges into something much larger with many more possibilities than the series ever even hinted at. FIRE WALK WITH ME is now, with season three on the horizon, more important than ever, and so is our need to understand it. Going into season 3 just knowing the first 29 episodes will leave you woefully unprepared, but recognizing that FIRE WALK WITH ME is still a complicated piece of cinema, use this very thorough guide to fill in the blanks and clear up some of the fogs. And by the way, I don't use "very thorough" lightly. Get a snack, we're going to be here a minute.

FIRE WALK WITH ME

Written by David Lynch & Robert Engels, Directed by David Lynch

Released August 28th, 1992

We open on a television full of static that is suddenly smashed as a woman screams "No!" Seconds later we see the implied source of the scream, 17 year-old Teresa Banks, dead and wrapped in plastic, floating down a river in Deer Meadow, Washington. From what we've been told in the series, we know this is happening a year before the murder of Laura Palmer. Cut to Regional Bureau Chief Gordon Cole (David Lynch), who is telling his secretary to get Agent Chet Desmond on the phone. Desmond (Chris Isaak) is in Fargo busting teeny-boppers when he gets the call. Cole assigns him the Banks case and arranges to meet him in Portland, OR, as soon as possible.

Side-note: from the series we'd been led to believe that Cooper investigated the Banks case; the only reason that differs here is that actor Kyle MacLachlan only had limited availability to give this project.

At a private airport, Desmond meets with Cole and Sam Stanley (Kiefer Sutherland), an Agent from Spokane. Cole then introduces them to a "surprise:" a woman in a red dress, a red hat and a strange expression on her face. She spins and blinks and opens and closes her left hand. Cole says her name is Lil and she's his mother's sister's girl, then Cole fans four upside down fingers over his face, which Desmond takes to mean Federal. Sam is confused. Later in the car, Desmond explains Lil was a living code system: her sour expression means there will be problems with local authorities; both eyes blinking mean trouble with the higher-ups who run the authorities; one hand in her pocket means these higher-ups are hiding something, while the other one repeatedly making a fist means they'll be belligerent, to boot; she was walking in place so a lot of legwork will be involved; the mother's sister's girl comment in conjunction with the four fingers means the uncle of a higher-up is in federal prison; and the dress Lil was wearing was taken in to fit her which means drugs are involved, and the flower pinned to it, a blue rose, means something Desmond can't tell Sam about. That's a lot for one lady.

In Deer Meadow, Desmond and Sam are trying to meet with Sheriff Cable but as forewarned, he's purposely keeping them waiting and in the meantime his deputies and receptionist are showing the Federal Agents open disrespect. So Desmond gives the deputy an attitude adjustment through his nose and shows himself to the Sheriff's office. He states his case to Cable, who doesn't seem to care for anyone honing in on his investigation. This is inconsequential to Desmond as his authority supersedes Cable's, so regardless of the Sheriff's feelings, he's going to need everything the department has on Ms. Banks. Cable gives it up along with his professional assessment that Banks was a drifter and her murder was "a basic kill."

Desmond and Sam go to the morgue to examine Teresa's corpse. Sam does the dirty work while Desmond pores through her file. Seems Cable was right about the drifter part, she'd only been in town a month at the time of her death. The file has her living out at the Fat Trout Trailer Park, and working the night shift as a waitress at Hap's Diner. No one has come forward to claim her body and no one is expected to, no known next of kin is listed. Sam says her skull has been crushed by repeated blows to the back of the head with a blunt, obtuse-angled object. She's missing a ring, they can tell from the tan line of it, but there isn't a ring listed among the personal effects in her file. This causes Sam to look closer at her finger, the third of her left. There's something under the fingernail there. Upon closer inspection, Sam extracts an object. It's a piece of white paper with the letter "T" typed on it. Of course, we remember other letters found under fingernails during the series: Laura's "R," Maddy's "B," and intended victim Ronette Pulaski's "O." We also remember these letters were spelling out "Robert," BOB's full name. Why they are delivered out of order, or if and/or where the "E" and other "R" victims are is never addressed.

They finish their examination in the wee small hours but instead of sleeping they head to Hap's Diner for some food and info on Teresa. The head waitress, Irene, tells them Teresa worked there a month, was nice enough if often tardy, had bit of a nose-candy problem, and her death was a freak accident, with no evidence supporting this last bit given. Oh, and one other thing, for a three-day period shortly before her death, Teresa's left arm went completely numb. Irene just assumed it was a drug thing, but Sam thinks it would have to be a nerve problem, but he'd need to take the body back to Portland to test for sure.

Once the sun comes up Desmond and Sam check out the trailer park. They meet with park manager Carl Rodd (Harry Dean Stanton, confirmed for season three) and get shown to Teresa's trailer, which Carl implies saw frequent and various male visitors. On the fridge there's a pic of Teresa and in it her missing ring is plainly seen, a gold band with some kind of green stone in the setting. Carl gets everybody coffee and as they drink it they're visited by an older woman, dirtied and hunched over on a cane, an icepack to her face. She looks around the trailer. Desmond asks if she knew Teresa. She leaves without saying a word. Carl seems respectfully fearful of her, and amidst this reaction a telephone pole with 6 on it is intercut. Carl offers no explanation for the old woman but to say timidly and cryptically that he's already gone places and just wants to stay where he is.

Desmond and Sam return to the Sheriff's station to receive Teresa's body and take it to Portland. The Sheriff tries to resist but Desmond ignores him and asks instead where Teresa's ring is. Sheriff plays smartass and nothing is learned. Desmond tells Sam to start to Portland with the body, he's going to check out the trailer park one last time. Sam knows whatever Desmond is doing there, it has to do with the blue rose on Lil's dress.

Desmond returns to the park at dusk. Carl shows him to Deputy Cliff's trailer, the Sheriff's lapdog with the aching nose. It's just down from Teresa's. Desmond is left alone outside it. He looks up at the telephone pole humming next to him, and notices the 6 on it. Then he notices a dirty, derelict trailer behind him and goes to inspect that instead. The lights inside come on as he approaches. He knocks on the door. There's no answer. He looks under the trailer and there, on a mound of dirt like the one (to be) found by Cooper and Truman in the train car with Laura's

170

half-a-heart necklace atop it, is Teresa's ring, the green stone bearing same mark found in Owl Cave in the final episodes of season two, the squared diamond with twin peaks coming off its upper sides. As Desmond takes the ring from the mound the scene goes dark.

Next thing we know we're in Philadelphia at 10:10 am on February 16th, and Special Agent Dale Cooper is meeting with Gordon Cole because he's worried about a dream he had pertaining to this exact day at this precise time. He then leaves the office to go and check if there is a time delay on the security camera in the hallway. He does this by standing in front of the camera for a few seconds then going to an adjacent room to check the camera's monitor. The first time he does this, he isn't on the monitor, so there's no delay. But he checks again anyway, and the second time he isn't on the monitor either, so there is still no delay. Down the hall, an elevator opens. The third time Coop checks, he sees himself on the monitor, so there is a delay. A man (David Bowie) in a white suit and tropical shirt briskly exits the elevator. While Coop is watching himself onscreen, the man in the white suit walks past his image into Cole's office. Coop rushes in as though danger is afoot. Albert Rosenfield (Miguel Ferrer) is there now, too. The man in the white suit is Phillip Jeffries, a long-lost agent who opens a passionate diatribe (in a Southern accent) with the cryptic statement: "I'm not going to talk about Judy. In fact, we're not going to talk about Judy at all. We're going to keep her out of this." He then points angrily at Cooper and asks the room "Who do you think this is there?" Jeffries is obviously in a state of mental distress, and possibly insane. It seems he was sent out on a case two years ago and that was the last anyone here has seen or heard from him. Cole asks where he's been, and Jeffries says he wants to tell them everything, but he doesn't have a lot to go on. At this point the scene dissolves to a dingy, boarded-over room that crackles with electricity. In the room are BOB, the Man From Another Place, a bearded man (Jurgen Prochnow), Mrs. Tremond and her Grandson Pierre from episode nine of the series ("Coma"), a man in a red suit and a white mask with a prolonged, sharp proboscis holding a piece of wood, and two others dressed similar to the bearded man, like lumberjacks. The Man From Another Place is at a table with BOB and he talks of *garmonbozia* and Formica. We hear Jeffries say it was a dream they all live inside. The Man From Another Place tells BOB, "with this ring I thee wed," referring we assume to the green-stone gold ring with the Owl Cave symbol on it. Off-screen Jeffries moans, "the ring, the ring," and reveals the location of the room: "It was above a convenience store." We remember from the series that a room above a convenience store is where BOB and MIKE stayed at one point while they were killing together, so then we can infer that this room is an extension of The Black Lodge, or at least that all the inhabitants are. The bearded man – who is likely Margaret the Log Lady's husband who died in a fire the night of their wedding and who before that had brought her a jar of scorched engine oil which he described as a key to a gateway, namely to The Black Lodge – slaps his knee twice. Jeffries tells his colleagues he's been to one of these meetings of those people in that room, then gets even more excitable and says he "found something...and then there they were..." BOB and The Man From Another Place are seen walking through the red curtains of The Black Lodge and then Jeffries disappears from the office. When they call the front desk to see if he's left the building, they learn he was never there, and furthermore, Agent Chester Desmond is officially missing. Coop and Cole examine the security footage and Jeffries is on it, so then was in fact there.

Coop goes to Deer Meadow himself and meets with Carl at the trailer park. Carl shows him Deputy Cliff's trailer, which is the last place Carl saw Agent Desmond. Coop instead is interested in another lot, empty, where the dirty and derelict trailer used to be. Coop wants to know who last rented this spot. An old woman and her grandson, Chalfont was the last name, same as the people who rented the spot before them. Desmond's vehicle is discovered nearby. On the windshield in lipstick is written, "Let's Rock." Coop confides in Diane – on tape, alas – that this a confusing situation, even for one of Cole's blue rose cases, and the only thing he's certain of is that Teresa's killer will strike again. He just doesn't know when or where.

But we do.

33 minutes into the film, we at last cut to the town of Twin Peaks one year later, seven days before the murder of Laura Palmer, who we see alive and walking to school. She's joined by Donna (not Lara Flynn Boyle but Moira Kelly;

Boyle was otherwise committed) and ogled by Mike and Bobby. At school she sees James, her secret lover, and snorts cocaine in the bathroom.

During gym period Laura, wearing only a towel, meets with James in a back corridor. She wants to be kissed, but he wants more, he loves her, but she says she's already gone like a turkey in the corn. He pays more attention to the turkey part of this statement than the gone part. That'll haunt him. Laura is teary-eyed and shaking, but they make out and some of that towel falls away.

After school Bobby finds Laura. He's been looking for her all afternoon and their encounter is chilly and barbed. He's suspicious but she's manipulative and turns on her charm to calm him down.

At the Hayward's, Donna asks if Laura is going to see James that night. Laura is defensively private, calling nighttime her time. Laura says she might go see Bobby instead and Donna offers her opinion that Bobby is a goof and James is the one. The dreamy way she describes him indicates her true feelings. Laura's agreement doesn't convey the same depth or breadth of emotion, even though she's wearing the half-a-heart necklace he gave her. Velocity in a vacuum is discussed, and Laura makes it into a melancholy metaphor for the futility of existence, the insignificance of the individual, and the absence of higher power. Ah, to be a teenager.

Back at her own house, no one's home so Laura smokes a butt and writes in her secret diary, which she keeps behind her dresser. Everything's cool til she notices a few pages have been ripped out. This terrifies her and she leaves with her diary and drives to see Harold Smith, the agoraphobe on her Meals on Wheels route. He asks who could've torn the pages out? BOB, obviously. This confuses Harold because BOB isn't real. Laura disagrees: someone tore the pages out, that makes BOB real, along with the fact that he's been raping her since she was 12. She says he comes in through her window at night (which is on the second story) and is getting to know her now, he's started speaking to her. Harold, afraid and tearful, asks what he says? She says he either wants to be her, or kill her. Then she grabs Harold by his collar and hisses in his face "Fire walk with me." For a split second her face goes white, her lips black and her teeth yellow (similar to what happened to Windom Earle's appearance once or twice in the series once he started visiting The Black Lodge), and an instant later she collapses into his arms sobbing uncontrollably. She tells Harold he has to hide the diary, he's the one who made her write it all down, after all, and BOB doesn't know about him so he and it will be safe here. They kiss passionately and then she leaves, crying, and tells him she doesn't know when she can come back, maybe never, which is a declaration that leaves him despondent.

Back in Philly, Coop is confiding in Albert that he knows Teresa's killer will strike again, but he doesn't know enough to stop it. When the time comes, though, he says that Albert will help him catch the culprit. Coop is intuiting this, so Albert decides to put his intuition to the test with a series of questions: will the next victim be a man or a woman? A woman. Hair color? Blonde. Other things about her? She's a high school student, sexually active, a drug user, and she's crying out for help. Albert points out that this describes half of the teenage girls in America, so asks something more specific: what's she doing right now? Preparing a great abundance of food.

Sure enough, at that moment in Twin Peaks Laura is preparing to embark on her Meals on Wheels route. Diner waitress Heidi usually goes with her, but she's got a bloody nose today so Norma asks Shelly to take her place. Shelly's hesitant, on account of secretly banging Bobby, Laura's (public) boyfriend, but she agrees anyway. While loading the car, Laura is approached by Mrs. Tremond/Chalfont and her grandson, who is wearing a white plaster mask with a prolonged, sharp proboscis identical to the one we saw him put on in the room above the convenience store. The old woman gives Laura a painting of an empty room with an open door in the corner and says it would look nice on her wall. The grandson whispers, "The man with the mask is looking for the book with the pages torn out. He is going to the hiding place. He is under the fan now." Laura knows pretty much what this means and it freaks her out enough that she bails on Shelly.

At her house, Laura is standing under the fan. She creeps upstairs and into her room. There she sees BOB hiding behind her dresser. She runs terrified from the house and hides in nearby shrubbery, sobbing uncontrollably.

Everything gets worse when she sees her father, Leland, emerge from the house seconds later. This is the horrible, heart-wrenching moment in which Laura learns that BOB is inhabiting her own father.

Laura shows up an emotional wreck at the only place she feels safe, Donna's house, and demands to know of the other girl if she is her best friend. Donna doesn't know exactly what's going on, but she knows enough to answer, "Always" and comfort her friend.

That evening back at the Palmer's, Leland is waiting at the set dinner table when Laura comes home. He tells her to sit down, then chides her for sitting down without washing her hands. He goes over to inspect them and finds dirt under the nail of her left ring finger. Sarah enters with dinner. Leland starts to get a little weird by grabbing Laura's half-a-heart necklace and asking tauntingly if it's from a lover. Sarah tries to get him to back off, but to no avail. Leland knows the necklace isn't from Bobby, he knows there's someone new in his daughter's life. Sarah keeps trying to get him to back off but she starts to lose it a little. Laura is silently terrified, but Leland takes his seat and they try to have a normal dinner. That is, once Laura washes her hands. She leaves, crying, to do so. Even without the threat of BOB this is a horrifying look at domesticity. You really never know what's going on in people's homes.

Later the Palmers' are in their respective bedrooms. Leland breaks from BOB long enough to have a good cry. He goes to Laura weeping and tells her how much he loves her in a sweet, remorseful, fatherly way. He leaves her be, but this encounter has her more upset than ever. She asks a painting of angels if it's true, "it" being that her father is the abuser she knows as BOB. We don't hear an answer, but immediately after this she hangs up another painting, the one Mrs. Tremond/Chalfont gave her, and goes to bed. She dreams of the room in the painting. In it she goes through the door in the corner and there is Mrs. Tremond/Chalfont beckoning her through another door into another room where her grandson waits. He snaps and red curtains cover the screen, then she is moving across the chevron flooring of The Black Lodge to a pedestal on which Teresa's ring sits. Cooper enters this room. Somehow the Man From Another Place is already there. He asks if Coop knows who he is. Coop shakes his head. "I am the arm," the Man says, "and I sound like this:" he hoots. The Man then offers Laura, in whose perspective we are still viewing this scene, Teresa's ring. Coop implores her not to take it. This is when Laura wakes and finds herself in bed with Annie, bloodied in Caroline Earle's dress as we last saw her in the series' season two finale. Annie introduces herself and says she's been with Dale and Laura, and good Dale is in The Black Lodge and can't leave. She wants Laura to write this last bit in her diary. Laura then wakes again. She is alone in bed, but in her hand is Teresa's ring. Laura gets out of bed and opens her bedroom door to peer into the hallway. There's nothing there. But when she looks at the painting on her wall, she sees herself in it standing in the doorway as she is now. Behind her in the painting are the curtains of The Black Lodge. And then Laura's consciousness is in the painting, watching herself in bed asleep.

Then, at last, she wakes for real. It's morning. There's no ring. There's nothing different about the painting. Laura takes it down anyway. And she doesn't write anything in her diary.

At Leo and Shelly's, Leo is belligerently showing his wife how he likes his kitchen tile cleaned. She sasses him and he reels her in with some domestic abuse. The phone interrupts. It's Bobby calling for Leo and looking for coke, but Leo's not helping the kid out, Bobby already owes him 5k. So Bobby tries Jacques Renault at The Road House. Jacques can help him for 10k. That's a ton of blow in 1992. I assume. They set up a meet for midnight two days from now, "by the sound of sawing wood."

That evening at the Palmers' Laura is home alone and having a nice stiff drink when Donna drops by. She notices Laura is dressed to the nines in a tight miniskirt with her hair done up. Donna asks where she's going and Laura gives the coolest answer: "Nowhere fast and you're not coming."

Laura's first stop is The Road House, where runs into the Log Lady outside, who places a hand on her forehead like she's checking the girl's temperature and tells her "when this kind of fire starts, it is very hard to put out. The tender boughs of innocence burn first, and the wind rises, and then all goodness is in jeopardy." It is a touching, maternal moment and Laura feels the weight of it.

Inside Julee Cruise is singing with the band before a red curtain when Laura enters. The music draws out the girl's eternal sadness. She takes a table and starts to cry. That's when Donna comes in, having followed her friend. Donna sees her crying but goes to the bar instead. Laura pulls it together and nods at Jacques, who then taps a fella at the bar on the arm and directs him Laura's way. He and a buddy take their drinks over to join her. Apparently Laura is hooking tonight. Donna joins the table and says she wants to "boogie." The men eagerly wonder if she's a part of the deal. Laura says she isn't but Donna downs a shot to prove she's a big girl and Laura decides to test how big she's willing to go. The long and the short of it is, they're both willing to go pretty far. They end up at a strip club in Canada where basically a drug-fueled orgy transpires between the girls, the Johns, and Jacques, aka "The Great Went." Ronette Pulaski shows up halfway through this scene; seems she and Laura know each other from being "hospitality girls" at One Eyed Jacks. Jacques refers to she and Laura as his high school sandwich, and he looks hungry if you know what I mean. Then out of nowhere Ronette says she's been dead a year, Teresa Banks, she means. Ronette says she was going to get rich by blackmailing someone. Jacques remembers this, says Teresa called him before she died asking what their fathers looked like, Ronette and Laura's. This sets off Laura, but Jacques steers away from the touchy subject by suggesting the two of them come up to his cabin later that week, Thursday, maybe. From there the debauchery continues. At one point Laura notices Donna half naked and getting loved on by her John, and she flips the fuck out, screaming at Jacques to get Donna out of there, seemingly terrified for the other girl's mortal safety. She doesn't want this kind of life for Donna, and so they leave.

The next morning Leland comes to pick up Laura from Donna's. All Donna can remember from the night before is that Laura got mad at her for wearing something of hers. It's all good, they're still besties, Laura just doesn't want Donna to be like her, she's too good for that. Donna wants to know why Laura sells herself. That's when Leland walks in. Seeing the two girls jars a memory he has of Laura and Ronette sitting on a motel bed together, both barely dressed in lingerie. He snaps out of this, collects his daughter, and they go to meet Sarah for breakfast. On the drive, a reckless driver in a truck with a camper tailgates them anxiously. Laura asks if there's something wrong with their engine, it smells like it's burning. We remember, of course, that's the smell of scorched engine oil is indicative of spirits from The Black Lodge like BOB, as there is a puddle of it at The Black Lodge entrance in Glastonbury Grove. At a crosswalk the truck pulls up beside them. The driver is Philip Gerard, aka MIKE the one-armed man, and he accuses Leland of stealing the corn. The burning engine smell gets worse. Gerard mentions the room above the convenience store, the Formica table there, the "look on her face," and he uses Leland's name specifically when he tells him the thread will be torn. MIKE/Gerard then shows Laura his pinkie, where he's wearing the Owl Cave ring from her dream. "It's him," he screams at her, "It's your father!" Then he drives away. Laura and Leland are understandably freaked out. He retreats into memory, specifically of being in bed with Teresa Banks, telling her how much she looks like his Laura. Teresa is asking when he'll be back in town on business. Soon he says, and next time he wants to party with the girlfriends she talked about. He then covers her eyes with his hand and asks her, threateningly, who he is? She's smart enough to give him the right answer: she doesn't know. Laura's concerned shouts bring him back to the moment. She wants to know who that man was and why he looked familiar. Leland/BOB plays dumb as he's remembering seeing those girlfriends of Teresa's: it's the same scene he saw back at Donna's house, Laura and Ronette Pulaski waiting for him on the motel room bed. This understandably rattles him and he takes off before the girls can see him, paying Teresa for her trouble. As he flees, the Tremond/Chalfont grandson in his plaster mask frolics about the motel parking lot. In the present moment again Leland composes himself. Laura is emboldened enough by her fear to ask him if he came home during the day last week. She means the day she saw BOB in her room. He says no and screams at some nearby mechanics. She thought she saw him, she presses. Now that she mentions it, he thinks he did, on Friday, he had a headache and was in the area, so popped in for an aspirin. He asks if she was there then because he didn't see her. She says she saw him from down the street, which is only half a lie.

Later Laura is in her bedroom thinking about how the ring on Mike's pinkie was the same as the ring the Man From Another Place tried to give her and the man in the dark suit, who we know was Coop, told her not to take. It's also the ring Teresa wore, she remembers now. This revelation triggers a strobing blue light that would seem to indicate the coming of BOB. Brave in her anguish, Laura asks the light who it is, really. Downstairs Leland is pacing, recalling the memory of murdering Teresa in her trailer with a pipe.

The next day Laura is taping her safety deposit box key in a baggie into her diary after snorting the last of the cocaine from said baggie. At school, she tells Bobby she needs to score. He gives her a little to tide her over until that night, when he's supposed to meet Jacques' man for the big buy. They set up a rendezvous an hour before that. By midnight when they meet with Jacques' man – who we recognize as Deputy Cliff from the Deer Meadow prologue – Laura's wasted. Cliff tries to rob Bobby, but Bobby is armed and kills him. Bobby freaks but Laura's too far gone to care. They flee the scene.

James shows up at Laura's house the next day. She comes outside to see him. They had a date last night but she never showed. He knows it's because of drugs. He asks when he can see her, but Leland appears on the porch, so she has to go.

That night she's cutting lines in her bedroom. In their bedroom, Leland brings Sarah a drugged glass of milk. She takes it, almost knowingly. He makes sure she finishes it all, then turns on the fan in the stairwell. Sarah falls into a dazed, troubled state. She has a vision of a white horse, just as she did during the series in the episode when Leland/BOB killed Maddy. In both instances, it is the drugging that seems to bring on the vision. Upstairs in Laura's room a blue light starts to strobe. All coked up on the verge of delirium, Laura slides the comforter off her bed seductively, eyes on the window. BOB crawls through as she writhes erotically. He creeps to her bed. Onto it. Onto her. She trembles at his touch but doesn't recoil, in fact she seems to become increasingly aroused at his touch. As BOB begins to take her she demands to know who he is. That's when she sees her father's face, sees his form on her, in her, and she screams.

The next morning at breakfast every Palmer seems normal again except for Laura, who is still understandably traumatized. She breaks down and leaves the table. Leland follows. He tries to find out what's wrong but she's not pretending anymore, she knows the truth about what's been happening to her, and she tells him to stay away. This stoically angers him. All day Laura remains in a doleful daze, and oddly enough no one seems to notice the crying girl in the fourth row of homeroom. From here on out, astute viewers know the rough timeline of what's to come; this is, after all, the last day of Laura's life. That evening she's at Bobby's, he's trying to make out but she's trying to cop enough coke to get through the night without falling asleep. Bobby knows then she doesn't really love him and maybe she never has, she's just using him. Somehow this is okay with him – probably because he doesn't love her either, his heart is Shelly's – and he gives her a little coke for her to take home. She does it in her bedroom. Around 10:30 she gets a call from James and agrees to meet him. She stops to look at the painting of the angel on her wall. As she watches, just the image of the angel disappears. This would seem an obvious metaphor: not even Heaven can help her now. James picks her up and they ride off into the night. But a motorcycle is a loud thing, and Leland has seen them leave. The BOB in him is boiling over.

James and Laura go out to the woods. She's hopped up, talking all fatalistic. She can sense what's coming. She mocks James' earnest emotions and slaps him. He's more steadfast in his belief in their love in the face of her denial of it. They embrace. She does love him, she just can't allow herself to. They kiss, then she realizes BOB might try to kill James if he finds out about him. BOB is a jealous lover, not of her body but her heart, which is maybe why Bobby was never bothered by the spirit; BOB only wants to destroy her pure happiness. She tells James about Bobby killing Jacques' man in the woods, then offers to take him to the body. He doesn't believe her, and she lets it go, addled as her mind is in the moment. She proclaims how unknown she is, even by her closest friends, him included. It seems to give her a moment of sad lucidity and she tells him his Laura is gone, she disappeared, and what he sees is the girl who's left. Then like she's abandoning a puppy she withdraws all affection from him, turns cold and resistant to his advances. She tells him to take her home. But at the stoplight, fatefully, she hops off, embraces him, shouts her love for him to the wind, then runs away into the forest, crying. He lets her go. For his childish petulance, he will never see her alive again.

Laura meets up with Jacques, Leo and Ronette and they go to Jacques's cabin for some booze, drugs, and S&M. Waldo the mynah bird is there, and outside, Leland/BOB watches through the window. Jacques goes outside for some fresh, cool air after a strenuous round of roughing up Laura and Leland knocks him out by breaking a bottle over his head. Leo hears this ruckus and goes to investigate as Laura begs to be untied. Leo sees Jacques unconscious and bleeding on the ground, figures someone did it, so bolts, leaving Laura bound. Leland enters the cabin and apprehends the women then runs them through the dark woods. Gerard/MIKE is running through the woods as well, following the echoes of the girls' screams.

At the train car, horror unfurls. Leland ties the girls together. Rather, Leland is gone, and BOB is here now. Both girls know they are going to die. BOB toys with Laura while Ronette, ignored for the moment, prays. As the ferocity heightens, an angel briefly manifests in the train car. When it disappears, Ronette's ropes have been untied. Outside MIKE bangs on the train car door to be let in. Ronette opens the door and starts to escape but BOB grabs her, beats her unconscious, then tosses her out of the car anyway. MIKE tosses the ring inside the car as the door is closing. In a moment of anguishing catharsis, Laura accepts her fate and puts on the ring as Leland begs with BOB not to make him kill her. It doesn't work. BOB savagely murders Laura. He takes her necklace and leaves it on a mound of dirt, wraps her in plastic and carries her from the scene, leaving Ronette unconscious in the dust. He sets Laura adrift in the river then goes to the entrance of The Black Lodge in Glastonbury Grove, just down from the train car. He enters and finds himself in a red room with MIKE and the Man From Another Place. Leland is bleeding from his gut. Laura's body washes up on shore. In the Lodge, BOB stands next to Leland, who is floating above the floor. MIKE, using his arm the Man From Another Place as a conduit, tells BOB he wants all the *garmonbozia*, which means Leland's pain and sorrow. BOB puts his hand on Leland's wound and takes it away, throwing the blood on the floor where it disappears. Creamed corn – the visual reference for *garmonbozia* as seen in the Phillip Jeffries scene – is eaten by the Man From Another Place. A monkey shows its face. The sun breaks on Laura's beached body as the plastic is pulled from her face. And in The Lodge, Laura is with Cooper. An angel appears to them and this, if only for the moment in this timeless place, seems to bring Laura peace; delirious, demented, slightly demonic peace. The angel seems to claim Laura's spirit in a wash of white light.

Narratively, this delivers us right back where we started in the series, with Laura freshly killed and the mystery ready to unfurl. Two hours and fifteen minutes Lynch took just to advance the plot to its beginning. I get why people were pissed. The first few times I was too. However, as the coming of a third season has cleared my head a little, I've considered the idea that there was no way, given how the series ended, that we were going to get a satisfactory ending to TWIN PEAKS in a two, two-and-a-half, or even a three-hour movie. TWIN PEAKS was always a slow-boil with great hooks, that's ultimately what led to its downfall: it was too intriguing to move at the pace it wanted, people wanted answers sooner because the questions were too burning. To try and wrap everything up in a movie, even though that's what the majority of the fan base wanted him to do, would have ultimately cheapened the entire project. Lynch had to aim smaller than that, he had to expand the story without going too far, so he went back and he showed us the biggest missing puzzle piece: the last few days of Laura's life.

And of course there's the notion that it was Lynch and Frost's plan all along to revisit the series after 25 years; in the second season finale Laura says as much to Coop in The Black Lodge when she tells him "I'll see you again in 25 years." This came true. 25 years later, TWIN PEAKS season 3 was in production. To be fair, this notion was somewhat debunked by Frost recently when he was explaining how he and Lynch got back together: it was because of the "25 years" line, but only because Frost noticed it while re-reading the script and found it interesting, not because it was a part of a grander scheme. Or so they say...

Overall, while FIRE WALK WITH ME does a lot in terms of filling in the character of Laura, especially in regards to displaying the kind of torment she was under, there's a lot in the film that doesn't feel like the TWIN PEAKS we know, and that's because, oddly enough, David Lynch is responsible for most of the story. In terms of the series, outside of the overarcing plot, Lynch's name only appears on the scripts for the pilot and three out of 29 episodes. Especially in the second season when Lynch was busy with other projects, much of the series' narrative direction came from Frost, Harley Peyton and Engels. Now, Engels is the co-writer FIRE WALK WITH ME, but unlike the series, this isn't a partnership, this is a David Lynch film, so ultimately it answers to his artistic sensibilities. What's realized on the large screen might be more true to the director's vision and intentions for TWIN PEAKS, but that doesn't help it gel with the series, which tempered Lynch's excesses with Frost's measured storytelling. Without the co-creator on board scriptwise, this TWIN PEAKS doesn't feel quite the same. This can be seen as advantageous, though, because this isn't the same kind of story as was told in the series, which was about the real world reaching into this other realm to pull out secrets, this was about that realm reaching into ours to drag out victims; it's a stranger offshoot with metaphysical undercurrents in every frame, it is a nightmare brought to life and as such follows non-linear, at times nonsensical nightmare-logic.

At the time of its release, most people chose to look at FIRE WALK WITH ME as a failure, or as at best a letdown. It is neither of these things. It is different, of that there's no denying, but in the much larger context of the TWIN PEAKS universe, especially now that said universe is broadening to the scale of another 18 episodes, FIRE WALK WITH ME is more important than ever in regards to understanding everything that's come before, and preparing for what is yet to come.

PERSPECTIVES

"I don't know when I can come back. Maybe never."

Laura Palmer

THE PHILLIP JEFFRIES IMPLICATIONS

How one character in one scene of FIRE WALK WITH ME could hold clues to season three

About halfway through the "Deer Meadow" prologue that opens David Lynch's TWIN PEAKS prequel film FIRE WALK WITH ME, there is a scene that coincides with the first appearance of Special Agent Dale Cooper in which another Agent named Phillip Jeffries (played by David Bowie) comes into Gordon Cole's office in Philadelphia and starts screaming and relating a bizarre experience to Cole, Coop, and Albert Rosenfield that involves someone named Judy, a manifestation of The Black Lodge, and its inhabitants. It is a cryptic scene to say the least, one of the most discussed in a film full of much-discussed moments, and it would seem to have all sorts of implications that are never explored, let alone resolved. But it is also a scene imbued with great meaning and ultimately was the first shift towards a broader mythology behind TWIN PEAKS. By examining the components of the scene as it exists and as it was written in subsequent drafts of the script, as well as a key deleted scene, we can see how Phillip Jeffries and his story may in fact provide hints – ideological if not narrative – as to what we can expect from the series' third season, slated to begin next year on Showtime.

The scene as it exists: In Philadelphia at 10:10 am on February 16th, Special Agent Dale Cooper meets with Gordon Cole because he's worried about a dream he had pertaining to this exact day at this precise time. He then leaves the office to go and check if there is a time delay on the security camera in the hallway. He does this by standing in front of the camera for a few seconds then going to an adjacent room to check the camera's monitor. The first time he does this, he isn't on the monitor, so there's no delay. But he checks again anyway, and the second time he isn't on the monitor either, so there still is no delay. Down the hall, an elevator opens. The third time Coop checks, he sees himself on the monitor, so there is a delay. A man in a white suit and tropical shirt briskly exits the elevator. While Coop is watching himself onscreen, the man in the white suit walks past his image into Cole's office. Coop rushes in as though danger is afoot. Albert Rosenfield (Miguel Ferrer) is there now, too. The man in the white suit is Phillip Jeffries, a long-lost agent who opens a passionate diatribe (in a Southern accent) with the cryptic statement: "I'm not going to talk about Judy. In fact, we're not going to talk about Judy at all. We're going to keep her out of this." He then points angrily at Cooper and asks the room "Who do you think this is there?" Jeffries is obviously in a state of mental distress, and possibly insane. It seems he was sent out on a case two years ago and that was the last anyone here has seen or heard from him. Cole asks where he's been, and Jeffries says he wants to tell them everything, but he doesn't have a lot to go on. At this point the scene dissolves to a dingy, boarded over room that crackles with electricity. In the room are BOB, the Man From Another Place, a bearded man (Jurgen Prochnow), Mrs. Tremond and her Grandson Pierre from episode nine of the series ("Coma"), a man in a red suit and a white mask with a prolonged, sharp proboscis holding a piece of wood, and two others dressed similar to the bearded man, like lumberjacks. The Man From Another Place is at a table with BOB and he talks of *garmonbozia* and Formica. We hear Jeffries say it was a dream they all live inside. The Man From Another Place tells BOB, "with this ring I thee wed," referring to the green-stone gold ring with the Black Lodge insignia on it. Off-screen Jeffries moans, "the ring, the ring," and reveals the location of the room: "It was above a convenience store." We remember from the series that a room above a convenience store is where BOB and MIKE stayed at one point while they were killing together, so then we can infer that this room is an extension of the Black Lodge, as its occupants would certainly seem to signify. The bearded man slaps his knee twice. Jeffries tells his colleagues he's been to one of these meetings of those people in that room, then gets even more excitable and says he "found something...and then there they were..." BOB and The Man From Another Place are seen walking through the red curtains of the Black Lodge and then Jeffries disappears from the office. When they call the front desk to see if he left the building, they learn he was never there, and furthermore, Agent Chester Desmond (who the first part of the prologue features) has disappeared from Deer Meadow. Coop and Cole examine the security footage and Jeffries is on it, so then was in fact there.

The scene as written: There are a few notable lines of dialogue that were excised from various drafts of the script before shooting that help fill in some of the bigger blanks of the scene. After Jeffries tells them he doesn't have a lot to go on, there's another mention of Judy that was cut out: "But I'll tell you one thing: Judy is positive about this," followed by the even more-weighty and cryptic line, "Her sister's there, too. At least part of her." Then between saying he "found something," "and then there they were," the mysterious lady comes up again in the deleted phrase "in Seattle at Judy's."

And that key deleted scene I mentioned is actually a split scene of sorts, with the first part intended to open the larger scene and the second to close it. In both parts, Jeffries is in Buenos Aires. The first part sees him entering a lavish hotel and checking in. The clerk hands him a message left by "a young lady," which given the context of the rest of the scene we might assume is Judy. He then teleports into Philadelphia and things progress as filmed. At the end of the scene, after Jeffries vanishes, we see him reappear in the Argentinian hotel stairwell, scaring the crap out of a bellboy and scorching the wall behind him. Seems to be a pretty painful process, teleportation, if Jeffries' screams are to be believed. These screams are the only aspect of these deleted scenes that made it into the finished film, as overlay during his disappearance.

Laid out like this, the Jeffries scene can still seem convoluted, more so even, but all the pieces are there, it's just a matter of how you put them together. Let's start with the inhabitants of that room above the convenience store.

The Man From Another Place and BOB we definitely know, and Mrs. Tremond and her Grandson we've met before, but only briefly and it wasn't made explicit that they were of the same classification as BOB and the Man, though it was obvious that they had some connection to the otherworldly forces at play. They appear only four times in all of TWIN PEAKS, twice in the series – when Donna Hayward meets them, and again by mention when Donna takes Cooper to their house, only to find the Mrs. Tremond who lives there is much younger and doesn't know these other people – and twice in FIRE WALK WITH ME: in this scene, and later when they appear to Laura as she's loading up her Meals On Wheels orders and give her the painting of the open door. In the film's latter scene the pair go by the surname Chalfont. While their intentions and link to the Lodges are unclear, they are here revealed to be a pair of spirits in league somehow with others within The Black Lodge specifically. Likely they are bait of sorts, lesser agents used to help lure wanted souls like Laura's.

Of the remaining four inhabitants of the room above the convenience store, the man in the red suit and the white mask is credited as "The Jumping Man," and the other three men dressed like lumberjacks are "Woodsmen." In regards to The Jumping Man – so named because all we see him do is jump, never speak – there's not much to make of him but his connections to other inhabitants. His suit is similar to that of The Man From Another Place; his mask is similar to though more detailed than one Pierre Tremond dons towards the end of this scene, and that he wears in the later scene when confronting Laura; and the only time The Jumping Man acknowledges another character is when BOB signals to him, and he stops jumping. Could it be then, that as The Man From Another Place is a part of MIKE (the arm, specifically), and Pierre could presumably be a part or familiar of his Grandmother's, so too could The Jumping Man be an acolyte or some sort of subservient to BOB? Whoever he is, it's worth noting that he does not appear in any draft of the script, including the shooting draft; Lynch cooked him up on set.

As for the Woodsmen, only one of them is ever seen in detail, the bearded man, who is sometimes referred to as The Electrician for the way electricity crackles around him. The other two Woodsmen sit silent on either side of Mrs. Tremond/Chalfont and Pierre. The Electrician is in a chair of his own beside the couch, and popular opinion has it that he is the husband of Margaret Lanterman, a.k.a. The Log Lady. We remember from the series Margaret says her husband died in a fire the night of their wedding decades before Laura Palmer was killed. The other prominent mention of him comes in the final episode of season two when Margaret brings Cooper a jar of scorched engine oil her husband collected from Glastonbury Grove in Ghostwood Forest – where the entrance to the Lodges is located – that he told her was for "opening a gateway." The electricity that pops around him could be discerned as remnants of the fire that brought him into The Black Lodge.

From the introduction of these new inhabitants, some of whom we know, some of whom we do not, we are also introduced to the concept that what we know of The Black Lodge and its spirits from the series is only a small fraction of what and who it actually constitutes. This idea that the mythology is broader than expected or believed is expanded even further by the implications surrounding the Jeffries-scene's biggest question mark: Judy.

There are two dominant theories as to who exactly Judy was meant to be, but they both start in the same place: Judy was the subject of an investigation to which Jeffries was assigned and during which he disappeared. Given how he refers to her by first name, how he doesn't want to involve her in this unpleasantness, and the familiarity and implied trust between them some excised lines would connote – "Judy is positive about his" – we can infer some relationship developed between the two of them, at least on Jeffries' emotional end. From there the theory splits somewhat. The more obvious theory derived from the film as it exists is that Judy is another victim of BOB or The Black Lodge. After all, there is a pattern at play now thanks to the bit of prologue before Jeffries that involved Agent Chet Desmond: Desmond is sent to investigate the murder of Teresa Banks, Leland/BOB's first known victim, and he disappears; one year later Dale Cooper would be sent to investigate the murder of Laura Palmer, Leland/BOB's second known victim, and he too would disappear into the Lodge. And apparently years before both these instances, Phillip Jeffries might have been sent to investigate someone named Judy, who may or may not have been murdered by Leland/BOB or some other incarnation or spirit, and he definitely disappeared. Another excised line reveals Judy had a place in Seattle, which puts her well within range of both Leland/BOB and The Black Lodge, and that same line and others around it (both included in the filmed scene and cut out) indicate that at Judy's place in Seattle, Jeffries found something, possibly while investigating her disappearance or murder, that made the inhabitants of The Black Lodge appear to him, or more likely transported him to their realm. This "something" is the Lodge ring, which was worn by both Teresa Banks and Laura Palmer, and which Jeffries mutters about forlornly while telling his tale. If the ring was in Judy's possession, it can be assumed that she too wore it once, and counts among the ranks of victims. In the event she is dead, it certainly doesn't prevent her from communicating with Jeffries, especially if she is a victim of The Black Lodge. She could be the good division of herself running around the real world, she could be an evil doppelganger doing the same, or she could be reaching out through Jeffries' dreams, similar to how Cooper and Laura encountered each other after her death.

But if you incorporate the cut lines, the deleted scene, and a little knowledge of the story behind-the-scenes, there's another theory as to Judy's identity that's even more captivating: that she's the twin sister of Josie Packard. This theory stems off the deleted lines "Her sister's there, too. At least part of her." These were supposed to be spoken by Jeffries as he starts his explanation of the meeting he attended in the room above the convenience store. They would seem to indicate that this sister of Judy's was either in the Lodge or was close to it, like in Twin Peaks. The deleted scenes in the hotel suggest that Judy is now Argentina, and based on some personal motivation it was she who left the note with the desk clerk that propelled Jeffries to go – either of his own will or under enchantment – to Philadelphia and reveal to the investigating authorities, and Cooper specifically, what he knows about The Black Lodge. This could be because as someone touched by the Lodge, whether she's living or dead, Judy knows what has happened to Teresa and what will happen to Laura, and concerned for her sister's proximity to all this (perhaps even precognizant of Josie's eventual fate) she pleads with Jeffries to reveal himself. As for why we think Judy is related to Josie specifically, that actually comes directly from FIRE WALK WITH ME co-screenwriter Robert Engels, who said in an interview with the magazine *Wrapped in Plastic* (#58, April 2002):

"The thing with Judy has to do with where David Bowie came from...He was down there [Buenos Aires], and that's where Judy is, I think Joan Chen [Josie] is there, and I think Windom Earle is there. It's this idea that there are these portals around the world, and Phillip Jeffries had one hell of a trip to Buenos Aires and back! He really doesn't want to talk about Judy because that reminds him of whatever happened to him."

When the interviewer pressed and asked if Josie and Judy were sisters, Engels quite definitively stated:

"Yes. Yes, I think that is true."

The cut line about Judy's place in Seattle can also be seen as a kind of confirmation of this: during the series it was remarked that Josie often went to Seattle to shop and for recreation; given Josie's inherent secrecy, it is not hard to imagine she had a twin sister living there about whom she never said a word to anyone, perhaps to protect her from Thomas Eckhardt. Or it could be that portions of both theories are true, and Judy is indeed dead when TWIN PEAKS the series starts and in that timeline when Josie visits the Emerald City she stays in her dead sister's old apartment where Jeffries found the ring.

The only other mention of Judy in FIRE WALK WITH ME comes at the very end of the film when a monkey says her name. It's as weird to see as it is to read. There's a lot of confusion surrounding this, but I myself like the idea laid out by John Thorne, co-publisher of *Wrapped in Plastic* who in an essay in his indispensable book THE ESSENTIAL WRAPPED IN PLASTIC: PATHWAYS TO 'TWIN PEAKS' theorizes that the monkey is Jeffries, based on one little detail about the room above the convenience store that I left out. In one very quick shot, a monkey is seen peeking out from behind a mask. Blink and you miss it but it's there. And the only other entity known to be at that meeting besides the inhabitants above-described is Jeffries himself, lured into the Lodge by his obsession with Judy and perhaps transformed once there into a lesser lifeform (albeit one with human-like intelligence and thus some capacity for understanding).

And of course I'm sure you caught the mention of Windom Earle that Engels made. This ties the scene to The Black Lodge even more, as we know Earle has been obsessed with it since the 60's when he was on Project Blue Book looking for the entrance in Twin Peaks. The fact that he's in Buenos Aires with a known-missing fellow agent hints at collusion, Earle perhaps gathering information from Jeffries because the latter agent has been in the Lodge at this point and Earle has not. However Judy fits in with this group will likely be forever unknown, but she is obviously the linchpin (pardon the pun) to this intriguing subplot and were the story to have continued with a third season directly on the heels of the second, or sequel to the prequel film, she likely would have played a major role.

What does all this mean now that we're actually getting a third season? Though most of the above information was cut out for time and narrative considerations, it's apparent from this and also the end of season two and that Lynch and crew were intending to expand the mythology of The Black Lodge and those who dwell within it. New spirits might have been introduced, new hosts, new victims, as well as new environments with their own portals. Before season three was announced I often thought that a good way to continue the series without having to continue the actual events of the series would be to anthologize it, pick another location with a Lodge entrance and focus on how it effects the citizens there, with only tangential links to Twin Peaks the town; this way the Lodge is the focus and you could take the show anywhere and populate it with anyone. We already know TWIN PEAKS season three has filmed in Paris for certain and possibly in New Mexico. Could it be that we're going to see some of the other places that offer access The Black Lodge? Could it be that some of the literally hundreds of new cast members aren't residents of Twin Peaks at all but rather of somewhere entirely different? And could it be one of these places that BOB/Coop has moved onto?

All this is of course purely speculative, especially since neither Kenneth Welsh, who played Windom Earle, nor Joan Chen are listed as among the cast for the new season, and Chen has even spoken publically saying she was not asked to return. David Bowie, of course, sadly passed away earlier this year, but it was reported shortly after that he had been scheduled to appear in a cameo role but died before the role could be shot.

So now that we've gone all through this, ask yourself a question: why bring Jeffries back? Aside from sheer shock value or star power – neither of which are customary tactics for Lynch – we're talking about one character in one scene, not even of the series but the movie, which most people don't care for and even the ones who do don't completely understand, his scene in particular. It is arguably the most confusing footage in the entire TWIN PEAKS universe, so what about this scene could have relevance a quarter-century later?

The Black Lodge is a big place with many rooms and thus presumably many inhabitants. Lynch himself has said the place changes based on the person who enters it, meaning it is, like many afterlives, tailored to your personal fears and desires. It makes sense then that what you experience while being lured in and ensnared is not the same as what you experience when you become a more permanent resident. Could it be that once he was in the broader Lodge, wandering among the plethora of spirits, shadows selves and doppelgangers claimed by the Lodge over millennia, that Cooper and Jeffries somehow reunited? Helped each other escape? Or could it be that Jeffries was set to reappear so that he might lend his experience and expertise to locating or freeing Cooper? Again, all this is purely speculative on my part, but you can see how the implications of the Jeffries' scene tied to the knowledge that Lynch intended to reintroduce the character opens some very, very interesting possibilities for the third season, all of which hint at an even darker atmosphere than the original series or FIRE WALK WITH ME.

And of course, just because Welsh isn't on the cast list, or Chen is saying she wasn't asked to return, or Bowie is said to have passed away before filming his role, doesn't actually mean they won't appear. Lynch is adamant that we know less than nothing about what he has in store for the TWIN PEAKS revival, and that could absolutely involve a red herring or three. Or perhaps a monkey...

I THEE WED: THE RING OF 'FIRE WALK WITH ME'

A totem of evil or a ticket to salvation?

Of all the information and revelations that come out of FIRE WALK WITH ME – about Laura, about BOB, about Leland – perhaps the most confounding, and I think certainly the most important, is the introduction of the "Owl Cave ring," a gold band with the Owl Cave symbol (a squared diamond with twin peaks like wings coming off its upper half) etched in some sort of jade-like stone. This ring does not appear nor is it mentioned in TWIN PEAKS the series, however the symbol on it does factor into the final episodes of season two. It is the tiny petroglyph hidden on the end of a stone rod in the cave wall that's revealed when Andy accidentally strikes with a pickaxe another petroglyph of a flame. This same symbol will be discovered later by Windom Earle etched in the ceiling across the cave, only inverted. By turning the rod so its symbol matches this other in the ceiling, the great petroglyph map that will eventually lead everyone to The Black Lodge is revealed. In FIRE WALK WITH ME, the ring bearing this symbol is inferred to be a most powerful totem, one that can mean the difference not only between life and death, but also between eternal salvation or damnation. Clues to the ring's meaning and purpose are all in FIRE WALK WITH ME, but like much else about the movie, they are not always obvious or straightforward and must be interpreted as much as they must be discovered.

Obviously, the ring being left out of the series doesn't mean anything other than it wasn't thought of until after the series ended. The ring isn't some grand Easter egg, though there are some important references to rings in general in the series. The most obvious of these is Cooper's ring, which really isn't even a noticeable detail until it's gone. When Coop is lying gut-shot on the floor of his room at The Great Northern in the second season premiere, the Giant appears to him and takes his ring, saying it will be returned if and only when Coop correctly interprets the clues given to him. True to this, following the stormy séance at The Road House later that season during which Coop learns the true identity of BOB, he finds his ring – a simple golden band – at his feet.

Elsewhere in the series, the entrance to The Black Lodge at Glastonbury Grove is located within a ring of sycamore trees, particular attention is paid to a ceiling fan and a record player in the Palmer house, Josie has her soul trapped in a drawer knob, Laura's eye holds the clue to who shot a video of she and Donna, the round glow of a stoplight hints at horrible secrets, and the three biggest food references in the series – doughnuts, pies, and cups of coffee – are each circular or otherwise ring-like in a fashion. While there are copious ways to interpret the artistic intentions of rings, circles, spheres or general roundness, it seems to me in the case of TWIN PEAKS this ring-referencing is temporal, it refers to a perfect circle, or an ouroboros if you will, of time, and seeks to evoke a sense of how the past influences the present and the future and the same in reverse, how the end is the beginning, the way that FIRE WALK WITH ME makes the narrative of TWIN PEAKS a perfect circle by going back a week before the start of the series to show us the most important facet of this story we'd yet to see: Laura Palmer. The end of the movie is the beginning of the series, which of course came years earlier. With that as a perspective, TWIN PEAKS the series contains many character arcs or smaller storylines that circle back to themselves: Donna starts off a simpering sidekick of Laura's, becomes emboldened by Laura's death and James' love, then loses this love and the truth of her identity (or at least her paternity) and reverts to a spineless crybaby; Ed and Norma start the series as illicit lovers, fight for legitimacy and attain it the briefest and happiest of moments before being relegated to their former emotional imprisonment; Bobby and Shelly live in fear of Leo until Leo is rendered harmless, only to be later empowered again; Andy and Lucy are divided by an unplanned pregnancy of dubious paternity and eventually reunited because of the same; Cooper comes to town healing from the hurt of love, finds love again then is hurt even worse. All of these stories are circular and operate inside the larger circle of the TWIN PEAKS/FIRE WALK WITH ME narrative like cogs behind a clock face.

But onto the matter at hand. There's a lot here in a variety of places, so I figure the best way to tackle the ring is chronologically, as Lynch and co-screenwriter Robert Engels intended. The ring first appears in FIRE WALK WITH ME in what is known as The Deer Meadow Prologue, or the first half-hour of the film in which Agent Chet Desmond (Chris Isaak) is investigating the murder of Teresa Banks. This sequence takes place a year before the murder of Laura Palmer, and culminates when Desmond makes his second visit to the Fat Trout Trailer Park, where Teresa lived. Already at this point the existence and absence of the ring has been noted by Desmond thanks to a tan line on a finger of her corpse, and a picture of Teresa he saw in her trailer upon his first visit to the park. His second visit comes at dusk and its primary purpose is to locate the trailer of a Deer Meadow deputy he suspects of possible wrongdoing, but in the process a dirty, derelict trailer captures his attention and lures him over. After first peering through the lighted windows and seeing nothing of note, Desmond kneels and looks under the trailer where he sees a mound of dirt with the ring atop it, turned so that its symbol is inverted as in the Owl Cave ceiling. Desmond reaches out for the ring, and the scene fades to black.

At the conclusion of the next sequence, known as the Phillip Jeffries scene, we learn that Agent Desmond has been reported missing and was last seen at the trailer park. This introduces the idea of the ring as a some sort of device for trans- or teleportation. The support for this idea had been set up earlier in this very scene by Jeffries who, in explaining the status of the Judy case says the lines, "I found something…and then there they were." Between these lines that made it onscreen, "the ring, the ring" was written into the original script along with dialogue that further indicates Jeffries found the ring at Judy's place in Seattle, and when he touched it he was suddenly transported – either physically or psychically – to the room above the convenience store where the denizens of The Black Lodge were having a meeting. In conjunction with these spirits, the ring then, we understand, is not just a means of dimensional relocation, it is also a device for the collecting of human souls, as that's the business of BOB and his ilk. This would explain why the ring was found in the trailer park: Teresa Banks was the last to wear it, and her soul now claimed for The Black Lodge by BOB via Leland, it was free to lure its next victim, seemingly Chet Desmond.

Cooper himself visits the trailer park investigating Desmond's disappearance, but the derelict trailer and the mound of dirt beneath it are both gone. When he asks about who last rented the lot, he's told by park manager Carl (Harry Dean Stanton) that the last tenants had been an elderly woman and her grandson. Though the last names don't match up, the viewer is meant to infer the Tremonds, Harold Smith's neighbors, are the duo being described here as the Chalfonts, especially as we just saw them in the room above the convenience store in the Jeffries scene. Given who last wore it and how she died, we the audience have already attached the ring to BOB, but as yet there's no actual proof it's his. However the Tremonds/Chalfonts – who also disappear without a trace in TWIN PEAKS the series – now have a direct connection to the ring, and whether they are its protectors, its collectors, or its administrators on a permanent or temporary basis is too early to tell at this point in the film, but for now they seem to be in possession of it and as such will serve as the link to the ring's next appearance in FIRE WALK WITH ME.

While loading up her car for Meals on Wheels, the elderly woman and her grandson appear to Laura and gift her a framed painting of an empty room. The next night, Laura dreams she has entered the painting, and by walking through its open door (as coaxed by Mrs. Chalfont and her grandson) eventually she winds up in the waiting room of The Black Lodge. Across the room on a white column is the ring. Cooper enters the room to find the Man From Another Place standing by the column. After a brief and cryptic monologue, the Man picks up the ring and offers it to Laura. As on the cave ceiling, as found on the mound of dirt by Desmond, and as worn by Teresa Banks, the symbol is shown to us inverted. Cooper tells Laura, implores really, not to take the ring, and this is quite clearly because of its ability to capture souls for The Black Lodge. This is when Laura awakes and finds her left arm numb –

as Teresa's was shortly before her death, as described by Irene the waitress – and a bloody Annie Blackburn in bed next to her. Annie tells her she's been with Laura and Dale, and the good Dale is trapped in The Black Lodge. She tells Laura to write it in her diary, which Laura will forget to do. Annie disappears but in Laura's hand is the ring from her "dream." She gets out of bed and sees an image of herself in the painting given to her by the Chalfonts, and that's when she wakes for real. It is morning, the painting is normal, and there is no ring in her hand or anywhere, for that matter.

So then if the ring is a metaphysical teleportation device that delivers souls to The Black Lodge, then it has to be introduced on a metaphysical level, like in a dream or a vision. The emphasis in this dream seems to be on Laura making a decision: the Man From Another Place offers her the ring, he doesn't force it on her; and Coop doesn't try to swat the ring away, he tries to convince Laura to make a decision regarding it, namely not to put it on. Even the way it is presented, with the symbol inverted as it was on the ceiling of Owl Cave, hints at willfulness: the map to the Lodge entrance wasn't revealed until Earle *decided* to twist the rod so the symbols matched.

Furthermore, now we've seen three agents of The Black Lodge try to push the ring on Laura: the elderly woman, her grandson, and the Man From Another Place, which means it is not the possession of one particular spirit. The question at this point becomes how does BOB factor into any of this, and it's a question answered by his one-time killing pal and current-nemesis MIKE.

Technically, it's Phillip Gerard, MIKE's Earthly host who provides the insight, though his delivery could use a little work. After a night of drinking, drugging and screwing strangers in Canada, Laura is picked up by Leland at Donna's house. While driving to meet Sarah for breakfast, they are accosted by a reckless driver who corners them when stopped at a crosswalk. This is Gerard, and he starts screaming ferociously at Leland about stealing the corn, and throwing in mentions of the room above the convenience store. It isn't Leland Gerard is screaming at, though, it's BOB. We know this for certain by Laura twice mentioning the stench of burnt engine oil, which we recall is what constitutes the puddle at the entrance to The Black Lodge and signifies the presence of BOB. Gerard as MIKE knows what BOB is cultivating in the Palmer house, and he wants to stop it. Which is why he shifts his screaming to Laura: "It's him! It's your father!" Pretty blatant, this, but there is a more subtle element to the scene. Once Gerard starts screaming at Laura, he reveals he's wearing the ring on the pinkie of his right hand. He doesn't say anything about it, he doesn't warn her not to take it as Coop did, but the simple act of showing it to her in this alarmed context links the ring with BOB, making BOB the fifth (behind MIKE at #4) spirit of The Black Lodge now connected to the ring. Interesting to note that in this instance, the ring isn't shown with the symbol inverted, nor is it shown right-side up, rather Gerard presents it on its side, which can be seen as another indication of a decision to be made: does Laura accept the ring right side up, or upside down? And is there a difference in implication? Short answer: yes.

Later that evening Laura puts some pieces together and realizes that the ring Gerard showed her, the ring from her dream, and the ring worn by Teresa – who she knows tangentially from some hooking she and Ronette Pulaski did back in the day – are all one and the same, and in a sense it is following her, hunting her. This realization manifests a blue, sourceless light which Laura asks, "Who are you? Who are you really?" If this is the direct conversation with the incorporeal spirit of BOB or some other manifestation of The Black Lodge that it seems to be, then it signifies a shift in Laura's attitude towards what is happening: no longer is she blindly afraid of the power coming to claim her, instead she curious, resignedly so perhaps, but she is seeking to understand what is happening, not just stop it. This understanding will eventually lead to her salvation, albeit by a gruesome route.

There are a handful of theories as to the ultimate purpose of the ring, but based on the evidence outlined above, I choose to subscribe to the idea supported by several forums, sites, message boards and TWIN PEAKS books that goes basically like this: the ring is a binder that marks souls for collection; as such, it is a prize bandied about by the spirits of The Black Lodge, because whoever can get a soul to put on the ring has claim to that soul. This supposition is best supported by the meeting in the room above the convenience store shown in the Jeffries scene in which the Man From Another Place talks of *garmonbozia* – which is interpreted as the essence of souls consumed by spirts of The Black Lodge to increase their nefarious power – and says the line, "with this ring, I thee wed." This would certainly seem to be a roundabout declaration that he who has the ring accepted by another soul can claim that soul for eternity, much as a marriage binds souls in the eyes of God or some other such force. It would also explain to an extent why when Laura "woke" the first time from her dream of the ring, her left arm was numb; wedding rings, of course, are worn on the left hand.

When the ring at last makes its way to Laura in the real world, she is being tortured by BOB in the train car. Torturing her is all he can do, because at that moment the ring is not in his possession, so he can't claim her soul. The ring is where we saw it last – with MIKE. But MIKE, knowing that the ring isn't just a binder to The Black Lodge, but The White as well, tosses it in the train car and that's when Laura decides to put it on; as shown to the camera, the symbol is again inverted. She knows what is coming if she does, she knows by now the ring will doom her, but she also knows that there's more than one way to make this decision: taking the ring is one thing, but the intention behind the taking is another. Laura isn't taking the ring as BOB's victim, someone yielding to the will of another, she's taking it as a mark of defiance, she is embracing the only spirit of The Lodges who sought to save her, MIKE, and by placing the ring on her finger when it is under his control she is in fact causing her own death, but by that same course of action she is empowering her soul, she is saving it and sending it (part of it, at least) to The White Lodge. BOB realizes this, and left with no other course of action now that her soul, her *garmonbozia*, which he has spent years pursuing, has been claimed by another, he savagely kills Laura.

Later, after Leland has set Laura's body, wrapped in plastic, adrift in the lake, he enters The Black Lodge where BOB is separated from him and his *garmonbozia* is given to the rightful winner of this 40-year soul-struggle, MIKE and his arm, the Man From Another Place. As for the soul of Laura Palmer, it is in a separate but similarly-decorated room, all red curtains and chevron flooring, but none of these predatory spirits are with her, only Coop, and he is standing over her in a comforting manner as blue light begins to strobe. But instead of heralding BOB as usual, the light softens and pales and an angel hovers over the room. Laura cries with a deranged smile on her face, as if she either can't control her happiness, or her mind has finally wilted. The last we see her she is being overtaken by pure white light.

And in the "real" world, TWIN PEAKS the series is ready to start.

For all the ways FIRE WALK WITH ME altered the TWIN PEAKS mythology, the introduction of the Owl Cave ring in particular blew the idea of The Lodges wide open and set the stage for a much larger realm of nefarious possibilities. And if you take into consideration the first law of thermodynamics, that matter including energy can be neither created nor destroyed, then perhaps the Owl Cave ring if worn with the symbol oriented as found by Coop, not Earle, might return souls from The Black Lodge, or at least release them into The White.

Regardless, I'd wager dollars to doughnuts we see the Owl Cave ring in season three of TWIN PEAKS, maybe even on the hand of Dale Cooper, or – god forbid – in his possession.

HIS GAL FRIDAY: EXPLORING DIANE

Everything there is to know about Special Agent Dale Cooper's Personal Assistant

Of all the characters that populate and pass through TWIN PEAKS, one has done more with less than any other: Diane, Special Agent Dale Cooper's personal assistant who is spoken to a dozen or more times in the series, but is never seen or heard from in return. She is more of a presence than a person – we don't even know her last name – which has led some to speculate on the veracity of her existence, but regardless she is obviously someone (or something) with whom Coop entrusts his most personal of thoughts. Diane is more than a mere assistant, she is a confidant, a sounding board, and a silent counselor to the Special Agent, she is a way to process the madness Coop encounters in Twin Peaks and in fact in his own life, and as such she is indispensable to him, his investigations, and indeed the narrative of the series.

Though there isn't a lot to learn about Diane the character, there are tidbits to be gleaned from the series, as well as THE AUTOBIOGRAPHY OF F.B.I. SPECIAL AGENT DALE COOPER: MY LIFE, MY TAPES – a paperback tie-in to the series – DIANE: THE TWIN PEAKS TAPES OF AGENT COOPER – an audio book tie-in – and the prequel film TWIN PEAKS: FIRE WALK WITH ME. Add to this a detailed account of the theory some fans hold that Diane isn't actually real, and speculation as to her role (as well as who could be playing her) in the upcoming season 3, and this is pretty much all there is to know about the most mysterious character in television's most mysterious landscape.

The most important thing to know about Diane we learn from the series itself in terms of how Cooper talks to her. There are basically three routes their conversations take: professional, speculative, and personal. The first kind of conversation is the most prevalent and the most obvious. Diane is, after all, Coop's assistant and secretary, and while he is on the road on cases in this pre-internet era she is to transcribe the tapes he sends her into reports that can be submitted to Regional Bureau Chief Gordon Cole and perhaps other, unnamed higher-ups. The second kind of conversation in which they engage, speculative, refers to the non-sequitur tangents Cooper passes off to Diane, such as his theories on the Kennedy assassination, or his musings on the flora of the Pacific Northwest. These are not the sort of things a man says to his subordinate, but rather to a friend. While these speculative observations certainly say more about Coop than they do Diane, it does say something about her that Coop would choose to share them with her, they paint her as someone he views as an intellectual equal, someone who is able to appreciate the same idiosyncrasies as him, or at least someone who is able to appreciate his appreciation. In regards to the last kind of conversation, personal, this sort cements Diane as not just an associate but a friend, and a highly-trusted friend at that. It is Diane to whom Cooper addresses what he thinks could be his last words when lying gut-shot on his hotel room floor in the second season premiere, it is Diane to whom he expresses his innermost fears about Windom Earle and regrets about Caroline, and it is Diane to whom he confides his first emotions for Annie Blackburn. In this way, Diane is Coop's diary, as well, she is a place to store the more meaningful events of his life, a place to hear them said out loud in his own voice, thus making them that much more real.

In 1991 early during the run of season two, The Diane Tapes – as the audiobook is colloquially known – was released. It featured excerpts of Coop's conversations with Diane from the series to date, as well as some newly-recorded entries that didn't further the mythology of the show or its central mystery, nor did they delve deeper into the woman on the other end of the microcassette recorder, but they did serve to bolster all the things the series taught us about Diane: that she is someone Coop depends upon in more than a professional measure. The new entries for the audio book were written by Scott Frost, series co-creator Mark Frost's brother, and they were all performed by Kyle MacLachlan, who garnered a Grammy nomination for his work. Though not too rare, copies of the original tapes – which are only on cassette – can be expensive to procure. But if you, ahem, check the internet, YOU just might find a TUBE in which the recording exists.

Later in '91, Scott Frost furthered his exploration into Cooper's tapes through the AUTOBIOGRAPHY paperback, which did actually give a little more insight into Diane, albeit in a way that helped fuel the speculation of some that she might not be more than a figment of Dale's imagination. These tape transcripts reveal that Cooper didn't just work in Philadelphia, he was raised there and educated in local Quaker institutions like Germantown Friends School and Haverford College. These transcripts aren't work-related at all, Coop is sharing himself with Diane here, all of himself, he is using her as a vehicle to catalogue and examine his life right up to the very day he is assigned to the Laura Palmer case in Twin Peaks. He tells Diane embarrassing stories about his first experiences with love, heartbreaking stories that delve into the twisted triangle of he, Caroline and Windom, and hopeful stories about his determination to be the best Special Agent the Bureau has ever seen. He so likes the idea of Diane listening to these stories, of being his confidant, that at one point he says he will address all of his tapes to her *whether she will ever listen to them or not*. This is the point at which Diane becomes so trusted that she is elevated to the role of counselor, closest confidant, and someone through whom Coop can not only come to know himself, but come to understand himself, as well. But this also opens the door for the theorists who think that Diane is more of a coping mechanism than a real person.

The place to start with this theory is at its root: why would Coop need to invent Diane, or continue talking to her once their professional relationship ended and she was no longer assisting him, which could also be the case? The answer is another woman: Caroline Earle. In the aftermath of Coop's affair with Caroline, which resulted in her murder at the hands of her husband and Coop's partner, Windom Earle, the man was devastated personally and professionally. It was the single most traumatic experience of his life (until passing through a certain red curtain, that is), and it left him uncertain how to trust himself, how to be the man of principle he thought he was in the wake of the revelation that he was flawed, weak, and selfish. So Diane was either created or resurrected from memory, the theory would have us believe, as a coping mechanism and a route by which Coop could rediscover his strengths and virtues. The strongest piece of evidence that Diane isn't real is, of course, the fact that she is never seen nor heard from. Coop never talks to her on the phone, he never receives any tapes back from her – or if he does they are never shown or intimated – and no one else refers to her, not Cole, not Albert, both of whom work with Coop and would presumably be familiar with his assistant. Aside from that, there are two particular scenes from the series that advocates of this theory point to as definitive proof: the "ear plugs" scene, and the "drink with Annie" scene.

The "ear plugs" scene happens in episode 5 and involves Coop rising in the morning after a particularly troublesome night's sleep. The Icelandic investors of Ben Horne's Ghostwood Estates development had arrived the evening before and proceeded to spend the dark hours frolicking and cavorting at the top of their joyous lungs. Fearing this will be a recurring nuisance, Coop records a message for Diane asking her to overnight him a pair of top-grade ear plugs; at the end of this narrative day, however, Coop is seen with these ear plugs. This would seem to be impossible when you consider that in order to receive them Coop would have had to mail the tape to Diane in Philadelphia, she'd have to receive it, transcribe it, procure the ear plugs then mail them *back* to Twin Peaks, all in a roughly sixteen-hour timeframe. To theorists, this proves Diane is little more than a diary/datebook, a forum for Coop's thoughts as well as his personal to-do lists.

The other scene, the "drink with Annie" scene, is more subtle. It happens at the end of episode 25 when Coop is walking through the lounge of The Great Northern after returning from his first expedition to Owl Cave. He's excitedly regaling Diane of the night's adventures – not from a professional perspective, but more like he's sharing the news with a friend – when he sees Annie sitting alone at the bar. He stops mid-sentence and reflexively shuts off and puts away his microcassette recorder. If you subscribe to the theory that Diane is a cognitive device and

191

not an actual person (or an actual presence in Coop's present life, at least), than you could infer this reaction as being symbolic of Coop discovering in reality a person (Annie) who can provide him the same things for which he's created Diane: understanding, compassion, and acceptance. When Coop finds love again as he does with Annie, he no longer needs the support of Diane, who would have been created after the tragic destruction of his last love, Caroline Earle. While Coop does talk to Diane after this point in the series, these remaining messages become more proactive and also more distanced, personally; he is a man on two missions at that point – stop Windom Earle and keep his burgeoning love with Annie alive. Diane has been relegated to a confidant again, but no longer his counselor.

Aside from these two instances, there is one other Diane moment related to TWIN PEAKS, and it's one that both supports and refutes the theory as to Diane's unreality. In a deleted scene from FIRE WALK WITH ME, Coop is shown leaning into an office and talking to Diane. Diane, of course, is never seen or heard, but Coop in the scene is unusually buoyant, he's friendly and upbeat, almost manic, and even a little flirtatious. It's almost off-putting, how out-of-character Coop feels here, which is probably why the scene was excised from the final cut. But people point to it as proof Diane is real. However, if you're looking for this to support the theory that Diane isn't real, this'll do that, too. In addition to the woman herself remaining unseen, we're never even shown the room to which Coop is speaking, only the doorway, and with no nameplate on the door, for all we know Coop could be talking to a mop in a utility closet and calling it "Diane." And his behavior is so over-the-top it wouldn't be a leap to describe it as "delusional."

Whether she's real or not (she is), there's no denying the importance of Diane to Dale Cooper and thus to the story of TWIN PEAKS. Many fans are hoping the character will at last be given a more significant and seeable role in the upcoming third season, and some are even speculating that Laura Dern, who has been confirmed as being added to the cast in an unconfirmed role, could be assuming the guise of Coop's Gal Friday. If so, that would make a lovely reunion for Dern and MacLachlan, who starred together in David Lynch's BLUE VELVET, the film he made right before diving into TWIN PEAKS. Talk about full circle...

APPENDICES

WRAPPED IN PLASTIC: THE ORIGINAL 'TWIN PEAKS' FAN MAG

They did it first, they did it best

I am a TWIN PEAKS fanboy. It probably didn't need to be said, seeing as how I author a column called #TwinPeaksTuesday, post pics of the cast on my social media accounts more often than I do those of my actual family, and I have the Owl Cave logo tattooed upon my flesh. I have been a TWIN PEAKS fanboy from the first moment I finished the pilot more than 20 years ago, and with each subsequent viewing of the complete series I become even more of a fanboy. And I am not alone. For the quarter-century since it was released, TWIN PEAKS has been adding new fans every single year, and with the show set to be continued into a third season over at Showtime, guaranteed it's about to be embraced by even more viewers. In fact, my bet is it's going to be the hottest, smartest, greatest thing on television in 2017, but that's a point for another time. The point now is, since its debut, TWIN PEAKS has accumulated some of the fiercest, most die-hard, and most loyal fans of any television show in the history of television shows. Even popular as THE SOPRANOS was, there isn't an annual festival dedicated to celebrating the series; as much as everyone loved FIREFLY, no one booed and walked out of the theater when SERENITY turned out to be a complete reboot instead of a concluding continuation of the series; and not even FRIENDS, which many industry insiders consider the most successful and popular TV show of all-time, had a magazine dedicated exclusively to its content and creators. TWIN PEAKS, on the other hand...

The Twin Peaks Festival has been held every summer in Washington State since 1993, the year after FIRE WALK WITH ME was released; fans of the show were so pissed when FWWM was revealed to be a prequel when it premiered at Cannes that they booed and walked out of the screening, and this is after Lynch's previous feature, WILD AT HEART, had *won* the acclaimed festival; and beginning in 1992 Craig Miller started publishing a magazine called WRAPPED IN PLASTIC, after the state in which Laura Palmer's body is found, with his friend John Thorne, and over the course of the next 13 years the two men established themselves as the series' first and perhaps finest fanboys. They are my godfathers, as they are to anyone who writes a TWIN PEAKS site, blog, or column, and so I thought I'd take some time to acknowledge their pioneering accomplishment.

The first issue of WRAPPED IN PLASTIC was released in October 1992 and thereafter bimonthly by co-editors Miller and Thorne, who were based out of the Dallas area and would tap out the issues on their desktop computers before binding them and shipping them out to subscribers and too-cool-for-school record stores across the country. In addition to plot dissections, character profiles and assorted ephemera, WRAPPED IN PLASTIC also carried more erudite articles such as "TWIN PEAKS and the American Literary Tradition," "The Interconnectedness of TWIN PEAKS and BLUE VELVET," "TWIN PEAKS, Folklore, and the Nature of Reality," such miscellanea as an episode guide to "Invitation to Love," the soap-within-a-soap of TWIN PEAKS, and an interview with the great Joe Bob Briggs on David Lynch, as well as articles on all things Lynch, from his films to his art to the man himself. So much more than a mere fanzine, WRAPPED IN PLASTIC was an academic journal for Peakies, it was where TWIN PEAKS commentary and criticism were born, and where they flourished over the course of 75 issues until the magazine ended its run in 2005, *14 years* after TWIN PEAKS was taken off the air.

So then not only did WRAPPED IN PLASTIC foster the intellectual fanbase of Lynch and Frost's series, it kept it alive and thriving for 700% longer than the series actually aired.

195

I first came to know WRAPPED IN PLASTIC around 2000 when I was working for one of those record stores mentioned above, this one in New Orleans. We carried it in a catch-all subculture magazine rack that included Ann Rice fan fiction and skin mags aimed at dudes who dug tattoos. It had been a few years since I'd seen the show, and those idle days at the counter flipping through the pages not only refueled my interest and passion, but also gave me a deeper insight and thus an altered way of thinking about the show when I watched it next. Until WRAPPED IN PLASTIC, I was only a TWIN PEAKS fan; after WRAPPED IN PLASTIC, I was a TWIN PEAKS fanatic. It had that effect on a lot of us, I would imagine, and in some small – or large – way helped keep alive the enthusiasm for the series that made a third season seem viable to modern-day TV executives.

Craig Miller passed away in November of 2012 at the age of 53. John Thorne recently published an essay guide and collection of essays called THE ESSENTIAL WRAPPED IN PLASTIC: PATHWAYS TO TWIN PEAKS and still runs a TWIN PEAKS blog called Above the Convenience Store, named for the spot where BOB and MIKE lived and as seen interspersed with David Bowie's scene in FIRE WALK WITH ME. Both men will forever be fondly remembered by TWIN PEAKS' fans as our first moderators, our information superhighway before the internet was everywhere, and, for all intents and purposes, the first global community of TWIN PEAKS' fans. I'm looking for a fitting way to close this, but I think there's only one word left.

Thanks.

I DO NOT INTRODUCE THE LOG: THE LOG LADY INTRODUCTIONS

Remembering the character and the woman who brought her to life: Catherine Coulson

Shortly after TWIN PEAKS was cancelled, the syndicated rights for the show were sold to Bravo, which at the time was still showing fine art and film-related content, and not reality shows centered on various contingencies of rich, crazy women. To honor the new airings, David Lynch teamed up with his longtime friend and collaborator Catherine Coulson – better known to the world as Margaret Lanterman, the Log Lady of Twin Peaks – to create brand new introductions to all 29 individual episodes.

Each intro takes place with Catherine in character holding her beloved log and discussing the episode at hand, but not in any clear or direct fashion – these were written by Lynch after all – rather in rhapsodic, cryptic, seemingly random musings that last anywhere between 30 seconds and three minutes and hint more at the theme and tone of the episode than they do any plot progression. To that point, only three characters are referenced by name in all the intros: Margaret herself once, Laura Palmer once, and Norma Jennings, owner of the Double R Diner, once in relation to pie. If these intros are to be looked at as anything, perhaps they're best understood as post-mortem summations by Lynch himself, a sort of closing poem in 29 verses, or a eulogy of 29 chapters.

As for Coulson herself, she started her career with Lynch back in the early 1970's when she played the titular character in his fifth-ever short film, THE AMPUTEE. From there she progressed behind the camera, serving as the assistant director on Lynch's groundbreaking feature ERASERHEAD. Jack Nance, the film's star and known to TWIN PEAKS' fans as "Pete Martell," was Coulson's ex-husband.

That's right, Pete and the Log Lady were married as young folks.

Coulson stayed behind the camera for most of the 70's and 80's, working as second assistant camera on films like Albert Brooks' MODERN ROMANCE, then rising to the position of first assistant camera on STAR TREK II: THE WRATH OF KHAN (!!!) and Jim Jarmusch's NIGHT ON EARTH. But it was her return to the world of David Lynch that would mold her into the pop culture staple she is today. NORTHERN EXPOSURE, EERIE INDIANA, PSYCH and PORTLANDIA have all spoofed the character, the latter show using Coulson herself.

The idea of a woman who carried around a log from which she divined clairvoyant messages was the result of conversations Coulson and Lynch had way back in the ERASERHEAD days, and the character crawled around the director's consciousness for a decade until he found the right place to deploy her: the tiny town of Twin Peaks nestled in the heart of Pacific Northwest logging country. The character was further developed into a widow, her lumberjack husband having died in a fire of mysterious circumstances long before the show began. The speculation by the end of the series was that her husband was another victim of The Black Lodge, a theory that finds support in the sequence in FIRE WALK WITH ME in which David Bowe's character, AWOL Agent Phillip Jeffries, is trying to explain to Coop and Gordon Cole where he's been the last two years. In the sequence within this sequence, the fabled room above the convenience store is shown; in it are the Man From Another Place, BOB, Mrs. Tremond and her grandson, and four others, the Jumping Man in a death mask with a long, sharp proboscis, a black man billed as The Electrician, and two bearded Woodsmen, one of whom is played by Jurgen Prochnow (DAS BOOT) and around whom fire briefly flashes. This Woodsman is thought to be the Log Lady's husband.

Coulson, an Oregon native, was a natural to play the part, and portrayed her as a kind of Greek chorus for the show. Her appearances weren't intended to advance the plot as much as they were to thicken and enrichen it with elements of the supernatural. Her dialogue, like the intros below, were existential riddles delivered in a monotone deadpan that was simultaneously chilling, humorous, heartbreaking and endearing. She was the soul of a show haunted with them, and maybe the only voice of reason in the whole series. To think of TWIN PEAKS without the Log Lady is to think of THE DIVINE COMEDY without Beatrice, or the ODYSSEY without Penelope. Coulson was our guide through those dark and wicked woods, even if we rarely understood where she was taking us. Which makes her the perfect character – the only character, really – to introduce the series to a new round of fans.

In September of last year, Coulson died at the age of 71 shortly after production began on the third season of TWIN PEAKS. Though she had signed to return, it's unknown how much work she'd done, if any. On her passing, Lynch spoke of his old friend's greatest qualities:

"She was always there for her friends – she was filled with love for all people – for her family – for her work. She was a tireless worker. She had a great sense of humor – she loved to laugh and make people laugh. She was a spiritual person – a longtime TM [transcendental meditation] *meditator. She was the Log Lady."*

Whether she'll physically be a part of season 3, you can bet the spirit of both the Log Lady and Catherine Coulson will infuse the series. She was, after all, Lynch's oldest friend on the production, and perhaps his favorite character.

All of the Log Lady intros are available on both the Definitive Gold Box DVDs of the series and The Complete Mystery Blu-Ray set, on which they've been digitally remastered, as well as individually online. Do yourself a favor and watch them on their own in succession, it takes less than an hour: seen at once like this, they tell their own version of TWIN PEAKS, more singular and less bound by reason, but still just as enthralling.

CALIFORNIA DREAMING: IS 'MULHOLLAND DRIVE' A 'TWIN PEAKS' MOVIE?

In which the author hypothesizes David Lynch's 2001 film is a follow-up to his infamous TV series

It's always seemed to me like TWIN PEAKS was a turning point in the career of David Lynch, a point at which he developed the themes and ideas that would ripple through the rest of his work. TWIN PEAKS feels like LOST HIGHWAY feels like MULHOLLAND DRIVE feels like INLAND EMPIRE in ways his other work doesn't share. There are currents of duality, dream states, dubious identities, the symbiotic relationship between sex and violence, and betrayal in each of these films, but two in particular, I've come to believe, share more than thematic similarities. Brace yourselves: I think TWIN PEAKS, FIRE WALK WITH ME, and MULHOLLAND DRIVE all exist in the same universe, because I think MULHOLLAND DRIVE, like those other works, is ultimately about The Black Lodge.

Okay, before I get into this, it isn't a theory for the casual fan, you have to have at least a cursory knowledge of the plots to TWIN PEAKS the series, its movie prequel FIRE WALK WITH ME, and MULHOLLAND DRIVE. Furthermore, you need to accept that MULHOLLAND DRIVE has two parts: the dream part had by Diane Selwyn (Naomi Watts) in which she is Betty and her lover Camilla Rhodes (Laura Harring) is amnesiac Rita that constitutes the first 2/3rds of the film, and then the final third of the film in which Diane is returned to her actual reality, which is pretty much the opposite of her dream. If you know all that, then we're cool to proceed.

Here are the bulletpoints to my theory:

- Diane Selwyn, like Laura Palmer, is an intended victim of The Black Lodge
- Joe, the hitman she hires in the final third of the film, is either possessed by or is a more-human manifestation of the Hobo behind Winkie's Diner.
- Said Hobo is a lesser spirit of The Black Lodge who aids in acquiring victims for possessing spirits, much the way Mrs. Tremond and her grandson aided BOB's attempts at Laura.
- Diane's possessing spirits are the Elderly Couple.
- The blue key is Diane's Owl Cave ring, the totem that binds her to the possessing spirit.
- Camilla is the catalyst to Diane's readiness for possession.
- Club Silencio is the L.A. version of The Black Lodge's waiting room.

Got all that? By understanding these points and taking an in-depth look at the film's final sequence in particular, I think that you are going to finish this essay and believe what I do: MULHOLLAND DRIVE is a TWIN PEAKS story. Here we go.

It all starts with Diane/Betty, because both are the same: Betty is a combination of who Diane was when she came to Los Angeles to pursue her dream of acting, who she thought she could be, and who she really is at present. When we finally meet the real Diane, we see this combination in her appearance, body language, and attitude: she isn't just jaded, she's bitter, she hasn't been disillusioned by Hollywood, she's been broken. She can't get any good parts, her lover is falling for another – of the opposite sex, no less, replacing her in a way she can't counter – and everything she wanted from life is getting further out of her reach every day, while the sickly simple reality of her meager existence becomes clearer. She's not the special person she dreamed of being. She has gone from being a bright-eyed, naïve young woman upon arrival – the woman we see at the start of her dream – to the opposite, dour, desperate, and all-too aware of the harsh realities of her chosen profession and its environment. This sense of duality marks her as similar to Laura Palmer, who was simultaneously a charitable homecoming queen and a drug-abusing sex pot. Also like Laura, and for that matter like Teresa Banks and Annie Blackburn, Diane is young, pretty, and blond. It is the corruption of Diane's pure soul by failure and heartbreak that make her a viable target for The Black Lodge, I think, which taps into people's greatest fears in order to claim their souls. By the structure of MULHOLLAND DRIVE, it can be interpreted that Diane's dream happens after a fight with Camilla that resulted in the latter woman leaving in a way that threatened the relationship. After Diane wakes, we see them reconcile slightly, only to soon after see Camilla's advancing relationship with the director (Justin Theroux) of the film they're both working on, Camilla as a lead and Diane in a much smaller and less significant role. When this relationship between Camilla and the director culminates in an engagement announcement, cruelly done in front of Diane, it pushes Diane to the breaking point, priming her soul for seizure by the spirits of The Black Lodge.

This tipping point manifests itself in the scene at Winkie's Diner in which Diane is hiring Joe to kill Camilla. As the Devil would when offering a deal, Joe makes sure she knows exactly what she's doing in setting this up, warning her that once she agrees, it can't be undone. This is a binding agreement, in other words. Joe then produces a blue key, and tells her when the deed has been done, she will find it. She asks what it opens. Joe laughs, but says nothing. This key serves the same purpose as the Owl Cave ring in FIRE WALK WITH ME, it is the totem that binds or weds a soul to a possessing spirit of The Black Lodge, but only if accepted willingly. The key, as we already know at this point of the film, will open a corresponding blue box. What we don't yet know but are about to learn is what the box holds. But the fact that the key is given to Diane by Joe makes him, as mentioned, either possessed by the Hobo behind the diner, or the Hobo himself just differently manifested. Either way, by hiring a hitman, Diane is giving into her fears of rejection and loneliness, she is allowing these fears to guide her, and once the action these fears have set in motion is accomplished, once her soul has forever crossed that line, she will be ready to be taken by The Black Lodge. All that will be left to do is for her to willingly part the curtain.

For the rest of my argument, one simply needs to take a close look at the final sequence of the film, which begins just after the above scene in Winkie's. We start with another slow approach to the rear of the diner, where earlier in the film the crusty Hobo was revealed. It's nighttime now, in contrast to the previous scene between Diane and Joe, in which it was daylight. The Hobo is there again, this time holding the blue box. It is placed in a paper bag and set on the ground. Seconds later, a miniaturized elderly couple runs out of the bag, presumably out of the box. These are the possessing spirits of The Black Lodge, the same elderly couple we met at the beginning of Diane's dream. You'll recall from both TWIN PEAKS and FIRE WALK WITH ME that one of the first ways The Black Lodge tries to stake a claim on souls is by coming to them in weakened states of consciousness like dreams or delusions. In Diane's dream, the couple sees her off on her way towards the warping of reality and fiction that will eventually cause her fragile psyche to shatter, thus making her ripe for their consumption.

The next thing we see is the blue key in Diane's apartment. So the deed has been done. Camilla, Diane's lover and rival, is dead. And Diane has accepted this, she has taken the key as it were, and thus unknowingly, she has invited the spirits of The Black Lodge to come for her soul. It's important to note we don't see her discover the key, we come into the scene with her having already found it, sitting on the couch staring at it. The discovery and subsequent acceptance of the key – MULHOLLAND's version of putting on the Owl Cave ring – happened, like Camilla's murder, in the interim between the scenes in and behind Winkie's Diner. Diane's fate is all but sealed, the only thing left is the possessing.

Diane in this moment is the worst we've seen her yet, she's expressionless, emotionless, trembling and pale, a shell of a person with no love anywhere in her life, no prospect of love or happiness or contentedness or even basic goodness ever again, only fear and hate lie ahead of her. At this point it's hard to tell if Diane knows what's happening, but the way she stares at the key indicates she knows it is something to fear, something that could unlock something even more horrible than the life her fears have carved out for her. There's a knock at her door. The tiny elderly couple are seen to crawl under it. The knocking continues but Diane pays it no mind. The light in the room starts to strobe blue – just like it did in Laura's bedroom when BOB would come to her in FIRE WALK WITH ME, or in the train car when she was murdered, or when Coop was in the waiting room in his dream and in the final episode of season two – which is a clear sign that The Black Lodge and its denizens have taken over this reality. Screaming starts, and suddenly Diane is on the run from the spirits, full-sized now and aggressively pursuing her with extreme and ravenous prejudice. They are giddy this close to possession, to consumption of the "garmonbozia" that constitutes her soul.

Blue light. Screaming. Blue light. Screaming. All so horribly and frighteningly familiar. Diane is cornered by the spirits in her bedroom. Their moment is at hand. But at the last second, the very last second, Diane makes one final decision, and though violent, I believe it saves her soul from eternity in The Black Lodge: she shoots herself. The spirits vanish into smoke that fills the room and the blue light slows its strobe to a twitching glow. The Hobo is seen again, then Diane as Betty – her ideal version of herself – with the details of her face washed out by a blinding white light, just like the one Laura was washed in at the end of FIRE WALK WITH ME. I take this to mean Diane's soul was claimed by The White Lodge instead of The Black, as was Laura's when she rejected her possession by willing her own death; suicide by another, you could say. There in the white light of The White Lodge we see Diane/Betty reunited with Camilla as Rita – Diane's ideal version of her lover, with no memory of any other affection. It makes sense Camilla would be there too because if she was killed by Joe and Joe is a possession or some other manifestation of the Hobo, an agent of The Black Lodge, then The White Lodge would have a claim on her soul as she wasn't killed for possession, but to aid in the possession of another. Camilla/Rita is just a collateral victim, like Ronette Pulaski was intended to be.

All of the above is punctuated, I believe, by the very last scene of the film in which we are returned to Club Silencio where a thick red curtain hangs as a backdrop, the emcee wears a red suit similar to the Man From Another Place's, and there is always music in the air, even when no one is singing.

Any of that sound familiar?

That's because Club Silencio is the waiting room of The Black Lodge in Los Angeles. If you recall, it's Rita and Betty who visit the club, which means it happens in the dream. The first time Laura and Coop both see their waiting room is also in a dream (in FIRE WALK WITH ME and TWIN PEAKS, respectively). And what happens this last time in the club? We see the singer, but there's no music, no song, and all she says is, "Silencio." The silence is because there's also no fresh soul to torture, the jig is up, the game is over. The waiting room is silent because it is empty.

What I've given you above is speculation, informed speculation to be sure, obsessively so, but it's not like I have actual evidence to give my theory a little support or any–

Oh. Wait. Yeah I do. Check out the first visit Rita and Betty take to Club Silencio. As they round the top of the stairs and start down to their seats, on the right of the screen there are two women, a brunette and a blonde, already seated and watching the show with blank expressions. If you freeze the frame and check closer, you'll see that these two women are none other than Ronette Pulaski (Phoebe Augustine) and Laura Palmer (Sheryl Lee).

Why even put them there, what's the point if not to make an allusion to TWIN PEAKS? And not just any allusion, it's not Big Ed and Norma sitting there, it's BOB's victims. And yes, I know Ronette Pulaski wasn't killed by BOB, but her soul was certainly scarred by him and The Black Lodge, and we don't know what happened to her after season two, which would have been a decade before this. Trauma like what Ronette went through could lead to mental issues that could lead to suicide or accidental death, and it isn't improbable to think The Black Lodge has some claim on her soul given her experiences with it and its agents. And in case you think this isn't real and that's not really them, think again. Phoebe Augustine, who played Ronette, is listed in the credits on IMDB (but not in the film) as "Woman in Club Silencio." Sheryl Lee is not listed either place, but I wouldn't list her either if I was Lynch and trying to keep this connection on the down low: her name is synonymous with TWIN PEAKS.

Further furthermore, in an interview with The AV Club a few years ago, actress Sherilyn Fenn (Audrey Horne) said that MULHOLLAND was originally conceived at the time of TWIN PEAKS as a spinoff for her character that never came to be:

"The Audrey spin-off that would've come about, it really ended up being the original idea for Mulholland Drive. That was either in between the first and second season or after the second season, but they were like, 'What if we did a movie, and it's Audrey in California?' And they talked about an opening scene of her driving along Mulholland Drive, and how she's a little bit older. Whatever it was going to be, it never ended up happening for me. But I was young, and I thought it sounded weird, because no one ever really did that. I was, like, 'Okay, but do people do that? Go from TV to a movie as the same character?' Then all those years later, David made the other one, and I didn't have anything to do with it."

I mean – so even if everything I laid out above is utter and total bullshit, at the very, very least we know that MULHOLLAND DRIVE as originally conceived was linked to the series. Could the idea have gone that you can take the girl away from TWIN PEAKS but not TWIN PEAKS from the girl? You gotta admit, Rita/Camilla is a dead ringer for older Audrey, and the girlish naiveté of Betty is also similar to Audrey's disposition. As a writer, I can see how you'd get from one idea to the separate other. Add to that the inclusion of Laura and Ronette, and if MULHOLLAND DRIVE isn't a TWIN PEAKS story, I'll eat my copy of THE SECRET DIARY OF LAURA PALMER with a cup of coffee and a slice of cherry pie.

So if true, what does this mean for the third season of TWIN PEAKS? Well, keep in mind Naomi Watts, Sheryl Lee, and Phoebe Augustine are all in the cast, as is Robert Forster, who has a small role as a detective in MULHOLLAND DRIVE. The roles of Watts and Forster are yet unknown by name, but we do know Forster is playing a cop. We also know – and this is really tantalizing – that there was some filming for season three done in an exclusive Parisian club conceived and co-owned by David Lynch. Know what that club is called? Do I even have to tell you? It's called Silencio.

And then there's this thing I've kind of been ignoring until now. Diane. As in, like "Diane, I'm holding in my hand a small box of chocolate bunnies." What if, just what if Diane Selwyn before she moved to L.A. to follow her dreams took a more practical route of employment and worked as a secretary for the FBI? And what if following the disappearance or whatever happened to her trusted, beloved boss, Special Agent Dale Cooper, Diane just couldn't work for the Bureau anymore so took off west to start a new life for herself? It's a stretch, I already admitted that, but it would certainly explain in part why Diane was targeted by The Black Lodge – she would know almost everything Coop did about it via his reports.

In the end, there's no absolute interpretation of MULHOLLAND DRIVE, the film was never intended to be just one thing, that's pretty much the point of it. And I know that Mr. Lynch isn't fond of fan interpretations of his films, but if that's the case, he shouldn't make his films so damn obtusely-fascinating. This is mostly just an exercise in extrapolation, a hypothesis that got stuck in my mind and just wouldn't go away until I did something about it. But you have to admit, my theory isn't impossible. Nothing is when we're talking about the art of David Lynch.

BIBLIOGRAPHY

Books

Dukes, Brad. *Reflections: An Oral History of Twin Peaks*. 2014

Frost, Scott. *The Autobiography of FBI Special Agent Dale Cooper: My Life, My Tapes*. 1991

Frost, Scott. *Diane...The Twin Peaks Tapes of Agent Cooper* (audiobook). 1991

Lavery, David. *Full of Secrets: Critical Approaches to Twin Peaks*. 1995

Lynch, Jennifer. *The Secret Diary of Laura Palmer*. 1990

Rodley, Chris. *Lynch on Lynch*. 1997

Thorne, John. *The Essential Wrapped In Plastic: Pathways to Twin Peaks*. 2016

Links

thecityofabsurdity.com/projects.html

twinpeakswikia.com

ACKNOWLEDGEMENTS

Thanks to Geoff Todd, Founder and EIC of One Perfect Shot where the "Between Two Worlds" column originated, who always posted my ramblings no matter how long or esoteric they got, and thanks to Neil Miller, my new EIC at Film School Rejects who allowed me to transition the column to my new home.

Thanks to my wife, Cory, for indulging my obsession and its effect on our viewing habits over the last year.

Thanks to the sources in the bibliography for their insight and in some case their friendship, and thanks to my fellow TWIN PEAKS' fans I've met online whose passion is something to which I aspire.

And thanks lastly to the creators, cast, and crew of TWIN PEAKS for giving me something to obsess about these last 25 years and now, apparently, beyond.

H. Perry Horton received his Bachelor's degree in Film Studies from the University of North Carolina at Chapel Hill, and his MFA in creative writing from The Jack Kerouac School of Disembodied Poetics at Naropa University in Boulder, Colorado. In addition to BETWEEN TWO WORLDS, Horton is the author of three published novels and six produced screenplays. He is currently the Associate Video Editor of One Perfect Shot for Film School Rejects.

Born and raised in rural North Carolina, Horton now lives with his wife in a small, quaint, unassuming town in Washington State. This is not a coincidence.

Made in the USA
Las Vegas, NV
01 October 2022